学术支持单位

国际儒学联合会
北京外国语大学比较文明与人文交流高等研究院
北京外国语大学北京中外交流文化研究基地

本书为 2019 年度教育部人文社会科学研究青年基金项目
《约翰·洛克"中国笔记"手稿研究》
（项目批准号 19YJCZH046）研究成果

儒学与欧洲文明研究丛书　主编：张西平　罗莹

Locke and China:
A Critical Study of John Locke's
"Notes on China"

洛克与中国：
洛克"中国笔记"考辨

韩　凌 / 著

北京大学出版社
PEKING UNIVERSITY PRESS

图书在版编目（CIP）数据

洛克与中国：洛克"中国笔记"考辨 / 韩凌著 . —北京：北京大学出版社，2019.10
（儒学与欧洲文明研究丛书）
ISBN 978-7-301-30831-8

Ⅰ.①洛… Ⅱ.①韩… Ⅲ.①汉学—研究—英国 Ⅳ.① K207.8

中国版本图书馆 CIP 数据核字（2019）第 219305 号

书　　　名	洛克与中国：洛克"中国笔记"考辨 LUOKE YU ZHONGGUO: LUOKE "ZHONGGUO BIJI" KAOBIAN
著作责任者	韩　凌　著
责任编辑	严　悦
标准书号	ISBN 978-7-301-30831-8
出版发行	北京大学出版社
地　　　址	北京市海淀区成府路 205 号　100871
网　　　址	http://www.pup.cn　新浪微博：@ 北京大学出版社
电子信箱	pkupress_yan@qq.com
电　　　话	邮购部 010-62752015　发行部 010-62750672　编辑部 010-62754382
印 刷 者	三河市博文印刷有限公司
经 销 者	新华书店
	720 毫米 ×1020 毫米　16 开本　26 印张　插页 4　430 千字 2019 年 10 月第 1 版　2019 年 10 月第 1 次印刷
定　　　价	98.00 元

未经许可，不得以任何方式复制或抄袭本书之部分或全部内容。
版权所有，侵权必究
举报电话：010-62752024　电子信箱：fd@pup.pku.edu.cn
图书如有印装质量问题，请与出版部联系，电话：010-62756370

彩图 1　洛克的墓

彩图 2　MS. Locke. c.27. 档案外观

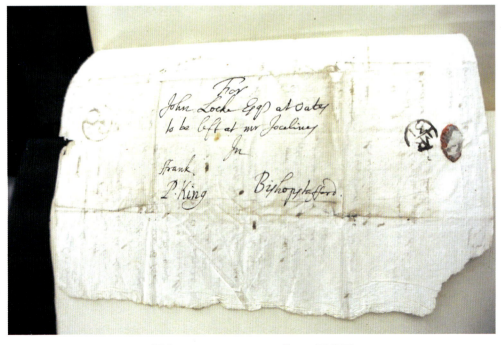

彩图 3　MS. Locke. c.27. 第 192 页背面

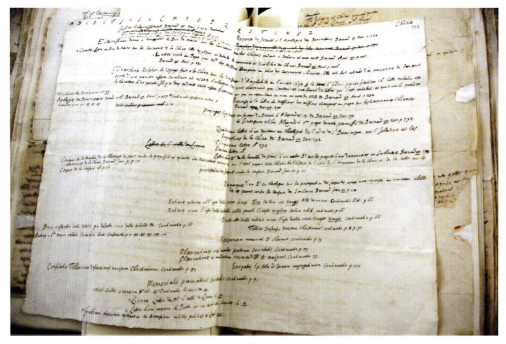

彩图 4　MS. Locke. c.27. 第 178 页

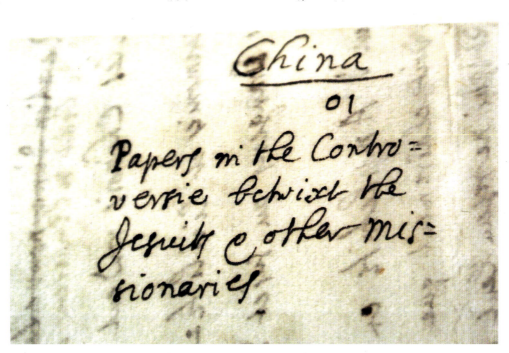

彩图 5　MS. Locke. c.27. 第 178 页背书

彩图 7　MS. Locke. c.27. 第 212 页背面

彩图 6　MS. Locke. c.27. 第 212 页正面

彩图 9 洛克藏《华人礼仪史》后环衬与勒口

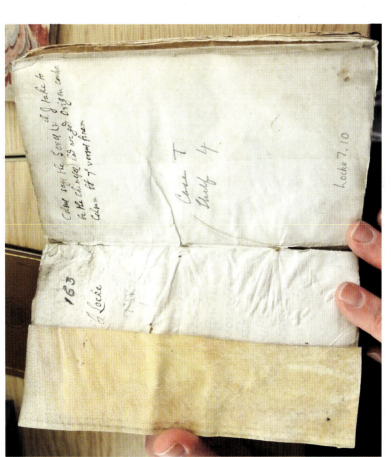

彩图 8 洛克藏《华人礼仪史》前环衬与勒口

a graduate, to speak after our manner,
of their university.

The eminently learned of the Literati
doe sometimes obtain by the edict of
the Emperor that that their tablet
of inscription shall be hung up in
the Temple of Confucius this they
look on as the greatest honour yt can
be done them. And to these also there
are ~~sacrifices~~ obtations made in the severall
citys & towns as often as there is any
sacrifice to Confucius

The account of Confucius & the
worship paid him read in the words of
Robordo the Jesuite Hist Cult
Sinensium p 253

Besides the solemn sacrifices
& other acts of devotion paid to
Confucius above mentioned there
is an other honour paid him
by the Literati who often in
his temple bow down to the ground
striking the earth with their
foreheads ag⁴ & ag⁴

Confucius
F 8 197

of their worship To them they address them selves after this manner Progenitors H 2
         Dear & most respected father never forget us or our
Funeral heirs grant to the men & women a child ren long life riches in
         abundance health & strength for yt we may enjoy a happy life to the extremity
when they are dead it is an inviolable of old age this is sd by the chief of the family
custome among the Chinesses to set erect a table we them making obeysances to the minister there
in the manner of an altar before the dead carps & then all the rest my their over
                                                  & place upon it his image or else table of
Temple   inscription, this altar being garnishd with
Those who are able build temples   flowers, perfumes & lighted lamps & tapors
& chappels to them In wch are kept All that come to condole kneel and prostrat
certain tables of chesnut wood   them selves thrice before this altar they sd
dedicated to them with   out offering some candles & odours
inscriptions in letters of a certain to the end that they may there be burnt
dimension   to this sense   upon the altar before the image or table
                                      of Inscription of the dead
The Throne or Seat of the
sould or spirit of N setting
down his name and dignity   vid Hist Cathay Semedum
                                     p 460 how the ceremonie
In the middle of the Temple   was performed in a Temple
there is a Altar with   wherein were six altars
other less   or altars upon
down about it upon wch these

tables of inscription   boy clad in the habit of the deceased
are placed. T'is said that at first a young was set upon the altar to represent him
                                      but this has been left off for many ages
In these temples two or three   & the table of Inscription is substituted in
times a year particularly in spring   the room of it. To this table the
& Autumn they with great solemnity   spirit of him whose name it bares is
sacrifice there to their dead Ancestors invited to come thither & rest upon it
H 2   & whatsoever is done during the ceremony
              as

彩图 12　Witsen's Map of Tartaria（威森的鞑靼地图），Amsterdam, 1705, 60cm x 51cm.

"儒学与欧洲文明研究丛书"编委会

学术顾问：滕文生

主　　编：张西平　罗　莹

编委会：（按姓氏拼音首字母排序）

杜维明	韩　凌
［日］井川义次	［日］堀池信夫
［德］郎宓榭（Michael Lackner）	李存山
［德］李文潮	李　颖
［法］梅谦立（Thierry Meynard）	孟　华
任大援	田辰山
［法］汪德迈（Leon Vandermeersch）	杨慧玲
张朝意	张隆溪

序言一

16世纪末以后中欧思想文化的交流互鉴及影响

中欧之间思想文化交流和互学互鉴的历史源远流长,对各自的发展都起到了取长补短、相得益彰之效。梳理和总结中欧思想文化交流和互学互鉴的历史,是一件有意义的事情。

从欧洲中世纪晚期以来,以儒学为主干的中国文明,就已通过来华的欧洲人和到欧洲留学的中国人,传入欧洲各国。意大利的耶稣会士利玛窦,是最早把中国历史文化介绍到欧洲的文化名人之一。他在中国生活了28年。1594年,利玛窦将儒学的经典著作"四书"即《大学》《中庸》《论语》《孟子》,翻译成拉丁文在欧洲传播,他认为孔子的儒家思想同基督教的教义如出一辙。在这之后的1626年,法国耶稣会士金尼阁又将"五经"即《诗经》《尚书》《周易》《礼记》《春秋》,译成拉丁文在欧洲传播。来华传教的耶稣会士们对中国儒学和其他历史文化典籍的介绍与提倡,在欧洲的思想文化界产生了很大影响。从16世纪末到18世纪将近二百年间,整个欧洲出现了"中国文化热"。一大批德国、法国、英国、意大利、俄罗斯等欧洲的著名学者,十分关注并不断研究中国的哲学、文学、历史和经济、政治、军事,发表了许多解读和推崇中国文明的卓识之见。

　　法国的启蒙思想家们，是最先研究中国儒学和中国历史文化并深受其影响的一批学者。1713年，孟德斯鸠曾同在法国皇家文库工作的中国福建人黄加略进行过长谈。他的《论法的精神》等著作，就受到儒学特别是宋明理学的影响。伏尔泰认为儒学的哲学思想没有迷信和谬说，没有曲解自然，是最合人类理性的哲学。狄德罗认为中国哲学的基本概念是"理性"，孔子的学说是以道德、理性治天下。霍尔巴赫认为"中国是世界上唯一的把政治和伦理道德相结合的国家"。以上这些学者都是法国百科全书派的领军人物。法国"重农学派"的创始人魁奈，也认为中国文明是欧洲政治经济应该学习的圭臬，他的重农主义思想就受到儒学"以农立国"的"自然之理"思想的影响。担任过法国财政部长的重农学派改革家杜尔哥，还提出过法国的发展需要借助中国文明的经验。

　　当中国的历史文化传入德国时，学者们的研究也是盛况空前。当时德国的不少学者不仅可以阅读到拉丁文本的中国先秦儒学典籍，而且可以阅读佛兰恺用德文翻译的董仲舒的《春秋繁露》。德国著名的思想家、哲学家、文学家，如莱布尼茨、康德、费尔巴哈、歌德、席勒等，都对中国历史文化进行过研究并发表了许多精辟的见解。莱布尼茨是欧洲第一位肯定中国文明对于欧洲文明十分有用的思想巨匠。在他倡导建立的柏林、维也纳、彼得堡的科学院中，探讨中国哲学与文化被列为重要的研究项目。他在1715年写的《论中国哲学》的长信中，表达了对中国先哲们的思想开放、独立思考、富于思辨、崇尚理性的尊崇和向往。他主张欧洲应该学习吸收中国的政治、伦理文化，中国则应该学习吸收欧洲的理论科学。莱布尼茨从《周易》中得到灵感而撰写的二进制学说，为德国哲学增加了辩证的思想因素。康德从儒家的哲学思想中受到启发而创建的用辩证的、联系的、发展的观点考察自然界的科学方法，开了德国古典哲学区别于英国经验主义和法国理性主义的先河。费尔巴哈认为孔子的"己所不欲，勿施于人"的思想，是"健全的、纯朴的、正直的道德体现"，是一种高尚的哲学伦理。被誉为德国文学史上最耀眼的"双子星座"的歌德与席勒，对中国文学怀有浓厚的兴趣，他们曾创作过《中德四季朝暮吟》《图兰朵》等关于中国的文学作品。

　　是不是可以这样说，中国儒家和道家、法家等诸子百家学说中的哲学伦理、政治思想、人文精神的精华，中国历史上的物质文明、精神文明、政治文明的精华,为欧洲的思想家、政治家所吸取和借鉴,对于冲破欧洲中世纪神学政治的禁锢,对于欧洲启蒙运动的兴起和欧洲近现代文明的发展,曾经提供过思想养料和政治动力,提供过四大发明为代表的物质技术条件,从而对欧洲文明的进步起到了积极的影响和作用。每忆及此,我们为中国文明能够对欧洲文明和世界文明作出重要贡献而感到光荣。

毫无疑义,思想文化的交流、传播及其影响,从来都是相互的。中国从欧洲的思想文化和经济、科学技术中,也学习、吸收、借鉴过不少进步思想、发展经验和先进技术。欧洲文明的精华,对中国文明的发展也起到过积极的影响和作用。对此中国人民是记忆犹新的。

就在利玛窦来华传教期间,中国明代的不少学者和官员,就向他学习过欧洲的思想文化和科学技术知识。其中最有名的是徐光启、李之藻。徐光启当过明朝礼部尚书,同时是一位杰出的农学家、科学家。1600年,他结识了利玛窦,抱着"一物不知、儒者之耻"的虚心态度向利玛窦请教西方科学。他同利玛窦合译了欧几里德的数学名著《几何原本》,并根据利玛窦的讲授撰写了介绍欧洲水利科学的著作《泰西水法》,还吸收欧洲的天文历法知识制定了《崇祯历书》。徐光启是明代末年中国学者中学习西方科学文化的领袖群伦的人物,是中西文化交流的先驱之一。李之藻精通天文、数学,也是明代杰出的科学家。他曾同利玛窦合作撰写和编译了《浑盖通宪图说》《同文算指》等介绍欧洲天文、数学等自然科学知识的著作,同葡萄牙人傅汎际合译了亚里士多德的名著《论天》和《辨证法概论》。这些欧洲的思想文化和科学技术知识在中国的传播,对于中国社会的发展和进步所起的促进作用是功不可没的。

近代以来,欧洲的各种思潮更是纷纷传到中国。欧洲各国的许多人文科学和自然科学的重要典籍,从哲学、历史、文学、艺术到经济、政治、法律、科技,先后在中国翻译出版发行。这些读物,其涉及领域之广、数量之多,可以用中国的一句成语来形容,叫作"山阴道上,应接不暇"。就德国而言,我想举出在文学艺术和哲学方面的几位大家及其作品,他们给中国人民留下了深刻印象与认识。歌德的《浮士德》《少年维特之烦恼》,席勒的《阴谋与爱情》《欢乐颂》,在中国几乎是耳熟能详的。王国维、梁启超、鲁迅、郭沫若等中国文化名家,对这些作品都曾给予高度评价。康德、费尔巴哈、黑格尔可以说是中国人了解最多也是对中国近现代哲学产生过重要影响的德国哲学家。在20世纪初，随着马克思、恩格斯的学说在中国广泛传播，作为其先驱思想来源之一的费尔巴哈、黑格尔的哲学思想在中国也传播开来，影响了中国的哲学界。中国的伟大领导者毛泽东的重要哲学著作《实践论》《矛盾论》，显然也是吸收了费尔巴哈、黑格尔的哲学思想中关于唯物论和辩证法思想的合理内核。马克思、恩格斯无疑是对中国现代文明的进步和现代历史的发展影响最大的德国人。在中国人民的心目中，马克思、恩格斯不仅是伟大的哲学家、思想家、经济学家，而且是为中国的革命和建设提供了科学指导思想的理论导师。1899年2月至5月《万国公报》第121—124期连载了英国传教士李提摩太翻译、上海人蔡尔康笔述的介绍英国社会学家本杰明·颉德的著作《社会进化》一书主要内容的文章，1899年5月这些文章结集出版，书名定为《大同学》。从这本书中，中国人最早知道了马克思、恩格斯的名字及马克思主义学说。其后，中国共产党的早期领导人李大钊、陈独秀、李达等人，成为马克思主义在中国的主要传播者。马克思主义学说一旦与中国实际相结合，包括与中国优秀传统文化相结合，就给近代以来积贫积弱的半殖民地半封建的中国，带来了翻天覆地的历史巨变。中国共产党领导中国人民经过长期奋斗和艰苦探索，终于成功地走上了建设中国特色社会主义的康庄大道。

历史发展到现在，世界已进入经济全球化时代，科学技术日新月异，各国的经济文化社会联系日益紧密，人类文明无论在物质还是精神方面都取得了巨大进步。但是经济全球化的发展和新自由主义的盛行，也带来了许多问题和弊端。诸如无限度地追逐高额利润、无休止地争夺和滥用资源、无节制地追求高消费的生活方式，以及脱离实体经济追逐金融投机等，由此造成资源破坏、环境污染和各种冲突不断，造成国家之间、地区之间、社会成员之间的贫富悬殊，造成物质至上而精神道德沦丧的现象，造成经济危机和社会危机。这些问题，是国际社会亟待解决的紧迫问题。解决这些问题的出路和办法在哪里，可以借鉴的历史经验和历史智慧在哪里？各国的政治家、有识之士和专家学者，都在思考和探索。要解决这些问题，当前最重要的是世界各国要加强平等协商，各种不同文明要加强对话和交流，要充分吸取不同国家、不同文明的思想文化精华。不论是经济还是社会的发展，都应实现同合理利用资源和保护环境相协调的可持续发展；不论是国家之间还是地区之间，都应消除政治军事冲突而实现持久和平；不论是发达国家还是发展中国家，都应实现互利互惠和共同繁荣。这是全世界人民所希望达到的目的。

在解决上述问题的过程中，儒学文化是可以而且能够发挥重要作用的。世界上一些有识之士已认识到了这一点。1988年，诺贝尔获奖者在巴黎举行主题为"面向二十一世纪"的集会。在会议的新闻发布会上，瑞典的汉内斯·阿尔文博士就指出：人类要生存下去，就必须去吸取孔子和儒家学说的智慧。美国著名学者约翰·奈斯比特在其著作《亚洲大趋势》中也指出：要重新重视孔子为代表的儒家思想，借以抵御日下的世风，防止职业道德破坏、享乐式消费、个人主义膨胀以及政治狂热。他们的这些看法，可以说在不少国家的政要和专家学者中已成为共识。

儒学作为一种具有世界影响的思想文化遗产，蕴含着丰富的思想财富。这些思想财富，无论是对解决当今国家与社会治理和经济文化发展中的问题，还是对处理当今国家与国家关系、各种经济社会关系以及人与自然关系等方面的问题，仍然具有自己的价值。比如，儒学中包含着关于安民、惠民、保民、"以民为本"的思想，关于敬德、明德、奉德、"惟德是辅"的思想，关于中和、泰和、和谐、"和而不同"的思想，关于仁者爱人、以己度人、以德为邻、"协和万邦"的思想，关于自强不息、厚德载物、俭约自守、"天人合一"的思想，关于安不忘危、存不忘亡、治不忘乱、"居安思危"的思想等。从这些思想中，是可以找到解决经济全球化和新自由主义带来的问题和弊端所需要的重要智慧、经验与历史借鉴的。我们国际儒学联合会的同仁，愿意同各国的思想家、政治家和专家学者们一道，共同为此作出努力。

国际儒学联合会会长　滕文生
2019年7月

序言二

在与西方思想的对话中展开儒学研究

一、全球史观下新的思考

在19世纪后由西方所主导的人文社会科学研究中,西方文化是人类思想的中心,它代表着人类的未来。其根据是现代化的社会发展模式和思想都是由西方人所确立的。西方所以取得现代化的显著成就,获得这样的地位,那是因为西方有一整套的思想文化传统。文化的优越导致了发展的优越,文化的先进导致了社会的先进。西方文化的这种地域性的经验就成为全球性的经验,放之四海而皆准;西方文化的自我表述就成为全球各类文化的统一表述。希腊,文艺复兴,地理大发现,启蒙运动……西方成为所有非西方国家的榜样,西方的道路应是全球各个国家的发展道路,西方的政治制度和文化观念应成为全球所有国家的制度和理念。于是就有了目前被人们广泛接受的"东西之分""现代与传统"之别的二元对峙的模式。东方是落后的,西方是先进的;西方代表着现代,东方或者非西方代表着传统。东方或者非西方国家如果希望走上现代之路,就一定要和传统决裂,就一定要学习西方。"化古今为中西",只有向西方学习,走西方之路,东方或非西方国家与民族才能复兴。

不可否认,西方文化中确有许多有价值的东西,也为人类的文明与文化提供了宝贵的经验和理念,有不少经验和理念也的确值得东方去学习。但中西对峙、现代与传统二分的模式显然有着它的弊端。仅就历史而言,这样的思路美化了西方的道路,把西方文化与精神发展史说成了一个自我成长的历史,把在漫长历史中阿拉伯文化、东方文化对其的影响与贡献完全省略掉了。特别是西方在启蒙时期的东西文化之间的交流与融合的历史完全被忽视了,当然同时,自大航海以后西方在全球的殖民历史以及对其他文化的灭绝与罪恶也统统都不见了。从全球史的观点来看,这是有问题的。

弗兰克和吉登斯认为:"当代世界体系有着至少一段5000年的历史。欧洲和西方在这一体系中升至主导地位只不过是不久前的——也许是短暂的——事件。因此,我们对欧洲中心论提出质疑,主张人类中心论。"①世界的历史是各个民族共同书写的历史,西方的强大只不过是近代以来的事情,而这种强大的原因之一就是西方不断地向东方学习。在希腊时期,"对俄耳甫斯(Orpheus)、狄俄尼索斯(Dionysus)、密特拉斯(Mithras)的崇拜充斥着整个希腊—罗马世界,这说明在耶稣之后的若干世纪里,基督教学说和信仰很有可能与印度宗教共享了一种遗产。这些问题都值得深思,关于孰先孰后的疑虑很难决断,但是有一点确凿无疑,即任何试图将西方剥离出东方传统的行为都是一种人为的划分"②。文艺复兴前的几百年中,世界文明的中心是阿拉伯文明,文艺复兴起始阶段就是意大利人学习阿拉伯文,从阿拉伯文中翻译回他们已失的经典。之后在佛罗伦萨的顶楼上发现了希腊文献的手稿,重点才回到意大利本土。③"就连像弗雷德里克·特加特这样的一些西方史学家,早在数代人之前业已批判过'以欧洲为中心的'历史著作,主张撰写单一的'欧亚地区'史。特加特1918年指出:'欧、亚

---

① 安德烈·冈德·弗兰克、巴里·K.吉尔斯主编,郝名玮译:《世界体系:500年还是5000年》,北京:社会科学文献出版社,2004年,第3页。
② [美]J.J.克拉克著,于闽梅、曾祥波译:《东方启蒙:东西方思想的遭遇》,上海:上海人民出版社,2011年,第55页。
③ 参见[英]约翰·霍布森著,孙建党译,于向东、王琛校:《西方文明的东方起源》,济南:山东画报出版社,2009年;[德]瓦尔特·伯克特著,刘智译:《东方化革命:古风时代前近东对古希腊文化的影响》,上海:上海三联书店,2010年。

两大地区是密不可分的。麦金德曾指出过：若视欧洲史附属于亚洲史，即可非常深刻地认识欧洲史。……史学家们的老祖宗（希罗多德）认为，欧洲史各时期均留有跨越将东西方隔开的假想线而交替运动的印记。'"① 有了这样一个长时段、大历史的全球化史观，有了对西方文化自我成圣的神秘化的破除，我再来讨论16—18世纪启蒙时期与中国古代文化的关系。②

二、关于18世纪欧洲中国热

关于西方思想和中国思想在启蒙时期的相遇，要从大航海时代开始，"任何试图弄清楚欧洲和亚洲思想会面问题的研究都必须在这一语境下展开"③。

从社会侧面来看，启蒙时期中国古代文化对欧洲的影响表现在18世纪的中国热。"启蒙时期正是中国清朝的早期和中期，这时中国在世界历史上的影响达到了巅峰。……中国在世界历史和世界地理上都引人注目，其哲学、花卉和重农思想受到密切的关注，其经验被视为典范。……世界历史上任何一个时期都没有像启蒙时期这样，使得中国的商业贸易相对而言如此重要，世界知识界对中国的兴趣如此之大，中国形象在整个世界上如此有影响。"④ 在社会生活层面，当时的欧洲上流社会将喝中国茶，穿中国丝绸的衣服，坐中国轿，建中国庭院，讲中国的故事，作为一种使命和风尚。Chinoiserie这个词汇的出现，反映了法国当时

---

① 安德烈·冈德·弗兰克、巴里·K.吉尔斯主编，郝名玮译：《世界体系：500年还是5000年》，北京：社会科学文献出版社，2004年，第15页。
② 近来学界亦开始出现试图摆脱西方中心主义的视角，分别从中国与西方两个角度，来分析明清之际中国社会的转变，并将其与西方国家同期发展进行对比的出色研究，例如：[美] 王国斌著，李伯重、连玲玲译：《转变的中国：历史变迁与欧洲经验的局限》（南京：江苏人民出版社，1998年）一书。
③ [美] J.J.克拉克著，于闽梅、曾祥波译：《东方启蒙：东西方思想的遭遇》，上海：上海人民出版社，2011年，第57页。
④ [英] S. A. M. 艾兹赫德著，姜智芹译：《世界历史中的中国》，上海：上海人民出版社，2009年，第275—276页。也参见：Berger, Willy R., *China-Bild und China-Mode in Europa der Aufklärung*, Cologne: Böhlau, 1990. Chen Shouyi, "The Chinese Garden in Eighteenth Century England," *T'ien Hsia Monthly 2*（1936）, pp. 321-339; repr. in Adrian Hsia（ed.）, *The Vision of China in the English Literature of the Seventeenth and Eighteenth Centuries,* Hongkong: The Chinese Univ. Press, 1998, pp. 339-357.

对中国的热情。这"突出地反映了这样一个事实：在一个相当长的时期中，各个阶层的欧洲人普遍关心和喜爱中国，关心发生在中国的事，喜爱来自中国的物"①。

正如我们在前面所研究的，来华耶稣会士的关于中国的著作在欧洲的不断出版，特别是柏应理的《中国哲学家孔子》的出版，在欧洲思想界产生了深刻的影响。来华耶稣会士的这些介绍儒家思想的著作，所翻译的儒家经典，引起了欧洲思想界的高度重视。

德国哲学家莱布尼茨是当时欧洲最关心中国的哲学家。他和来华传教士有着直接的接触和联系，他见过闵明我，他与白晋保持了长期的通信；他出版了德国历史上第一本关于中国的书《中国近事》；在礼仪之争中；他明确站在耶稣会一边，写了《论尊孔民俗》这一重要文献；晚年他写下了他哲学生涯中关于中国研究最重要的文献《中国自然神学论》。

从思想而言，中国思想的两个关键点是和莱布尼茨契合的。其一，他对宋明理学的理解基本是正确的，尽管他并没有很好地看到宋明理学中"理"这一观念的伦理和本体之间的复杂关系，但他看到理的本体性和自己的"单子论"的相似一面。其二，他从孔子的哲学中看到自己自然神论的东方版本。在西方宗教的发展中，斯宾诺莎的自然神论开启了解构基督教人格神的神学基础，传统神学将自然神论视为洪水猛兽。从此斯宾诺莎只能生活在阿姆斯特丹，靠磨眼镜片为生。莱布尼茨通过自然神论来调和孔子与基督教的思想，在这个意义上，"莱布尼兹是当时唯一重要的哲学家，认为中国人拥有一门唯理学说，在某些方面可与基督教教义并存"②。尽管，莱布尼茨的理解有其欧洲自身思想发展的内在逻辑，但

---

① 许明龙：《欧洲18世纪"中国热"》，太原：山西教育出版社，1999年，第121页。关于18世纪欧洲各国中国热的专题研究，亦可参阅严建强：《18世纪中国文化在西欧的传播反其反应》，杭州：中国美术学院出版社，2002年。
② ［法］艾田浦著，许钧、钱林森译：《中国之欧洲》（上），郑州：河南人民出版社，1992年，第427页。

他看到孔子学说中非人格神的崇拜是很明确的。①

如果说莱布尼茨从哲学和宗教上论证了孔子学说的合理性，那么伏尔泰则从历史和政治上论证了孔子学说的合理性。卫匡国的《中国上古史》《中国哲学家孔子》，在欧洲出版后引起了思想的轰动，这两本书中的中国纪年彻底动摇了中世纪的基督教纪年。②"《风俗论》是伏尔泰的一部重要著作，在这部著作中，伏尔泰第一次把整个人类文明史纳入世界文化史之中，从而不仅打破了以欧洲历史代替世界史的'欧洲中心主义'的史学观，……他说东方的民族早在西方民族形成之前就有了自己的历史，我们有什么理由不重视东方呢？'当你以哲学家身份去了解这个世界时，你首先把目光朝向东方，东方是一切艺术的摇篮，东方给了西方一切。'"③如果中国的历史纪年是真实的，基督教的纪年就是假的，梵蒂冈就在骗人，欧洲的历史也就是一部谎言的历史。借助中国，借助孔子，启蒙思想家们吹响了摧毁中世纪思想的号角。而伏尔泰这位18世纪启蒙的领袖是穿着孔子的外套出场的，他的书房叫"孔庙"，他的笔名是"孔庙大主持"。④

魁奈也是推动18世纪法国中国热的重要人物。魁奈对孔子充满了崇敬之情，他说："中国人把孔子看作是所有学者中最伟大的人物，是他们国家从其光辉的

---

① 参见［德］莱布尼茨著，［法］梅谦立、杨保筠译：《中国近事：为了照亮我们这个时代的历史》，郑州：大象出版社，2005年；李文潮编：《莱布尼茨与中国》，北京：科学出版社，2002年；桑靖宇：《莱布尼茨与现象学：莱布尼茨直觉理论研究》，北京：中国社会科学出版社，2009年；胡阳、李长铎：《莱布尼茨二进制与伏羲八卦图考》，上海：上海人民出版社，2006年；孙小礼：《莱布尼茨与中国》，北京：首都师范大学出版社，2006年；［美］方岚生著，曾小五译，王蓉蓉校：《互照：莱布尼茨与中国》，北京：北京大学出版社，2013年；张西平：《欧洲早期汉学史：中西文化交流与西方汉学的兴起》，北京：中华书局，2000年。Mungello, David E., *Leibniz and Conpcianism: The Search tor Accord*, Honolulu: Univ. of Hawaii Press, 1977, Mungello, David E., "Confucianism in the Enlightenment: Antagonism and Collaboration Between the Jesuits and the Philosophes", *in China and Europe* (1991), pp. 95-122. Gottfried W. Leibniz, *Discours sur la theologie naturelle des Chinois, à M. de Remont*. Translation of *Discours and Novissinw Sinica* in Daniel J. Cook & Henry Rosemont, *Gonfried Wilhelm Leibniz: Writings on China*, Chicago Open Court, 1994.

② 参见吴莉苇：《当诺亚方舟遭遇伏羲神农——启蒙时代欧洲的中国上古史论争》，北京：中国人民大学出版社，2005年。

③ 张西平：《中国与欧洲早期宗教和哲学交流史》，北京：东方出版社，2001年，第371页。

④ 参见孟华：《伏尔泰与孔子》，北京：中国书籍出版社，2015年；张国刚、吴莉苇：《启蒙时代欧洲的中国观：一个历史的巡礼与反思》，上海：上海古籍出版社，2006年；张西平：《中国与欧洲早期宗教和哲学交流史》，北京：东方出版社，2001年。

古代所留传下来的各种法律、道德和宗教的最伟大的革新者。"①他从孔子学说中找到自己经济学说的思想基础——自然法则。重农学派的自然秩序理论主要受益于中国古代思想，魁奈说："中华帝国不是由于遵守自然法则而得以年代绵长、疆土辽阔、繁荣不息吗？那些靠人的意志来统治并且靠武装力量来迫使人们服从于社会管辖的民族，难道不会被人口稠密的中华民族完全有根据地看作野蛮民族吗？这个服从自然秩序的广袤帝国，证明造成暂时的统治经常变化的原因，没有别的根据或规则，只是由于人们本身的反复无常，中华帝国不就是一个稳定、持久和不变的政府的范例吗？……由此可见，它的统治所以能够长久维持，绝不应当归因于特殊的环境条件，而应当归因于其内在的稳固秩序。"②这个内在固有的秩序就是"自然秩序"，这正是他的学说的核心思想。

魁奈重农学派与中国古代思想之间的渊源和联系，这是经过学者反复研究得到证明的问题。利奇温认为，魁奈的学说"特别得力于中国的文化传统"③，中国学者谈敏认为："重农学派创立自然秩序思想，其重要思想来源之一，是得自中国的文化传统；尤其是这一思想中那些在西方学者看来不同于欧洲主流思想的独特部分，几乎都能在中国古代学说中找到其范本。"④

---

① ［法］弗朗斯瓦·魁奈著，谈敏译：《中华帝国的专制制度》，北京：商务印书馆，1992年，第37—38页。
② L. A. 马弗利克：《中国：欧洲的模范》，转引自谈敏：《法国重农学派学说的中国渊源》，上海：上海人民出版社，1992年，第162页。
③ 参见［德］利奇温著，朱杰勤译：《十八世纪中国与欧洲文化的接触》，北京：商务印书馆，1962年，第93页。
④ 谈敏：《法国重农学派学说的中国渊源》，上海：上海人民出版社，1992年，第161页。有的学者从魁奈的书名《中华帝国的专制制度》（*Le despotism de la Chine*）就认为魁奈是批评中国专制主义，是法国中国热的一个转折点，正像看到孟德斯鸠对中国专制主义的批评一样。实际上即便在孟德斯鸠的批评中，他自己也感到把专制主义一词完全套用在中国是不完全合适的，在魁奈这里更是如此。这里并非为中国的制度辩护，只是在理解这些西方学者的思想时，要实事求是。把重农学派说成"回到封建的农业社会""从重农角度讲，他们是维护封建制度的""重农主义推崇中国重视农业"，亚当·斯密比重农学派更加重视经济的自由发展等，这些议论基本上没有读懂重农学派的基本理论，不了解这一学派在西方经济学说中的地位。马克思对于魁奈的《经济表》，给予很高评价。他说："重农学派最大的功劳，就在于他们在自己的《经济表》中，首次试图对通过流通表现出来的年生产的形式画出一幅图画。"（［德］马克思：《马克思恩格斯全集》第二十三卷，北京：人民出版社，1972年，第648页）他还指出"魁奈医生使政治经济学成为一门科学，他在自己的名著"经济表"中概括地叙述了这门科学"。（［德］马克思：《哲学的贫困》，《马克思恩格斯全集》第四卷，北京：人民出版社，1958年，第138页。）

在启蒙运动中始终有两种声音,从孟德斯鸠到卢梭,启蒙思想也在不断发生的演进与变化,这种变化最终在1793年孔多塞(Marie-Jean-Antoine-Nicolas de Caritat, Marquis de Condorcet, 1743—1794)的《人类精神进步史表纲要》中表达了出来,此时,以进步为核心的启蒙观念确定了下来。此时中国成为与进步对峙的"停滞的国家"。如他所说:"我们就必须暂时把目光转到中国,转到那个民族,他们似乎从不曾在科学上和技术上被别的民族所超出过,但他们却又只是看到自己被所有其他的民族一一相继地超赶过去。这个民族的火炮知识并没有使他们免于被那些野蛮国家所征服;科学在无数的学校里是向所有的公民都开放的,惟有它才导向一切的尊贵,然而却由于种种荒诞的偏见,科学竟致沦为一种永恒的卑微;在那里甚至于印刷术的发明,也全然无助于人类精神的进步。"①

这样我们看到启蒙运动从伏尔泰到孔多塞,它走过了一个完整的过程,对中国从赞扬变为批判。其实中国仍是中国,这种中国观的变化是欧洲自身思想变化的结果。"中国形象发生颠覆性的转变,归根结底是欧洲人看待中国时的坐标已经斗转星移,从尊敬古代变为肯定当今,从崇尚权威变为拥戴理性,从谨慎地借古讽今变为大胆地高扬时代精神。因此中国曾经被作为圣经知识体系的从属物而被尊敬,被作为古老文明的典范而被尊敬,但瞬间又因为同样的原因被轻视。借耶稣会士之手所传递的中国知识在17—18世纪的欧洲人眼里堆积起的中国形象其实没有太大变化,只是这个形象的价值随着欧洲人价值观的变化而改变了。"②

应该如何看待启蒙时代的这种变化的中国观呢?中国思想在启蒙时代的影响应该如何评断呢?

三、中国思想在启蒙运动中的价值

历史说明了文化之间的互动和交错,单一的文化中心论是不成立的,无论是西方文化中心还是中国文化中心主义,当我们指出中国文化对18世纪欧洲的影响

---

① [法]孔多塞著,何兆武、何冰译:《人类精神进步史表纲要》,北京:生活·读书·新知三联书店,1998年,第36—37页。
② 张国刚、吴莉苇:《启蒙时代欧洲的中国观:一个历史的巡礼与反思》,上海:上海古籍出版社,2006年,第324页。

时，并不是倡导一种"西学中源说"，历史早已证明那是把中国文化引向封闭的错误思潮。在如何看待中国思想在启蒙运动中的影响时，有两个问题需要特别注意。

第一，中国思想是否传播到了欧洲，启蒙思想家们是否读到了中国古代哲学儒家的作品，这是一个知识论的问题。在这个问题上有的学者将其分为两种立场："研究西方的中国观，有两种知识立场：一是现代的、经验的知识立场；二是后现代的、批判的知识立场。这两种立场的差别不仅表现在研究对象、方法上，还表现在理论前提上。现代的、经验的知识立场，假设西方的中国观是中国现实的反映，有理解与曲解，有真理与错误；后现代的、批判的知识立场，假设西方的中国观是西方文化的表述（Representation），自身构成或创造着意义，无所谓客观的知识，也无所谓真实或虚构。"①不可否认，从后现代主义的理论出发，可以揭示出西方中国形象的一些特点，但将现代经验的知识立场和后现代的批判知识立场对立起来本身就是有问题的，尽管从后现代主义的立场来看，这种对立是天经地义的事。知识的传播和知识的接受是两个密不可分的阶段。知识是否流动？知识流动的具体内容如何？接受者如何接受和理解知识？他们的文化身份对所接受知识的影响如何？这些理解和他们所在的时代思想关系如何？这是一个问题的两个方面。"启蒙思想家在关于中国讨论时，绝大多数情况下是建立在误读基础上的"，这样的判断只说明了问题的一个方面。不能因为接受者对知识的理解受到自身文化的影响而产生了对异文化的"误读"，就否认知识在传播中的真实性，同样，不能因传播者在传播知识时受其自身文化的影响，对其所传播的知识附上自身的色彩，就完全否认了所传播知识仍具有真实的一面。中国后现代主义的知识立场夸大了知识传播和接受主体的自身文化背景对知识传播和接受的影响，并且将文化之间的交流、知识在不同文化之间的流动完全龟缩为一个主体自身文化背景问题，将丰富的历史过程仅仅压缩为主体自己的文化理解问题。这样也就"无所谓客观的知识，也无所谓真实或虚构"。显然，这种理解是片面的。

---

① 周宁：《西方的中国形象》，周宁编：《世界之中国：域外中国形象研究》，南京：南京大学出版社，2007年，第4页。

这涉及启蒙时期欧洲知识界所了解到的关于中国知识,所接触到中国古代文化思想究竟是真实的,还是虚假的?或者启蒙时期所形成的中国观和中国有关还是根本和中国没有关系,中国仅仅是一个方法,一个参照系,在这些学者看来:"关于西方的中国观的客观认识与真实知识这一假设本身就值得商榷。我们分析不同时代西方的中国观的变异与极端化表现,并不是希望证明某一个时代西方的某一种中国观错了而另一种就对了,一种比另一种更客观或更真实,而是试图对其二元对立的两极转换方式进行分析,揭示西方的中国观的意义结构原则。"①西方对中国的认识自然有其自身的原因,但所接触和了解的外部因素的多少和真假当然对其内部因素的理解有着直接的影响。把外部因素作为一个虚幻的存在,其内部思想和文化转换的结构当然无法说清。

在笔者看来,尽管后现代主义的知识立场有一定的价值,但完全否认现代知识立场是有片面性的。中国知识和思想在启蒙运动中引起了巨大的思想震动,这本身是欧洲思想内部的原因所造成的,但正是在耶稣会士所介绍的儒家思想的观照下,儒家自然宗教的倾向,中国历史编年的真实性,中国政治制度在设计上比欧洲的更为合理,例如科举考试制度等,才会引起了欧洲思想的震动。如果中国思想文化不具备一定的特质,就不会引起启蒙思想家如此大的兴趣。就伏尔泰来说,毋庸讳言,伏尔泰论及中国、宣传孔子,在一定程度上是出于实际斗争的需要,即所谓的"托华改制"。这一点,尤其在"反无耻之战"中更显突出。但儒家本身的特点无疑是重要的,如孟华所说:"孔子思想的核心是'仁',它的基本含义是'爱人'。而伏尔泰终其一生不懈追求的,正是这种将人视为人,能够建立起人际间和谐关系的人本主义。"②就魁奈来说,中国的思想对他来说是真实的,是他经济思想的重要来源,如谈敏先生所说,他的研究就是"试图以确凿的事实和大量的资料,系统地论证法国重农学派经济学说甚至西方经济学的中国思想渊源,具体地勾勒出重农学派在创建他们的理论体系时从中国所获得的丰富滋养及其对后代经济学家的影响;展示中西文化交流对于18世纪经济科学发展的重要意义,驳斥那些无视东方经济思想对于世界经济思想的贡献与影响的荒谬言

---

① 周宁:《西方的中国形象》,周宁编:《世界之中国:域外中国形象研究》,南京:南京大学出版社,2007年,第6页。

② 孟华:《伏尔泰与孔子》,北京:新华出版社,1993年,第146页。

论，弘扬中国古代经济思想的光辉成就"①。

中国思想和文化在16—18世纪的传播是一个复杂的历史过程，欧洲启蒙时期对中国古代思想与文化的接受也是一个复杂的历史过程，中国思想和文化在16—18世纪产生如此大的影响，在欧洲形成了持续百年的中国热，这既是欧洲自身社会发展的一个自然过程，也是中国思想文化融入欧洲社会发展的一个过程，这既是欧洲思想变迁的内部需要的一个表现，也揭示了中国思想文化特点所具有的现代性内涵。我们不能仅仅将其看成欧洲精神的自我成圣，完全否认中国知识在启蒙运动中的作用，完全无视中国思想文化的现代性内涵对启蒙思想的影响，将此时的启蒙发展完全归结于欧洲思想自身发展的逻辑，这不仅违背了历史，也反映出了这种观点对欧洲思想自身成圣的神话的相信和迷恋。将欧洲的发展史神话，这正是欧洲逐步走向"欧洲中心主义"的重要一步。如果我们运用后现代的理论，来证明这一点，按照后现代主义思潮来说，这才恰恰是"自我殖民化"。

我们必须看到，这段历史不仅彰显出了中国古代文化的世界性意义，同时"这段历史又告诉我们：中国的传统并不是完全与近现代社会相冲突的，中国宗教和哲学思想并不是与现代思想根本对立的，在我们的传统中，在我们先哲的思想中有许多具有同希腊文明一样永恒的东西，有许多观念同基督教文明一样具有普世性。只要我们进行创造性的转化，中国传统哲学的精华定会成为中国现代文化的有机内容。东方在世界体系中也并非无足轻重，在西方走向世界时，东方无论在思想上还是在经济上都起着不可取代的作用"②。因此，1500—1800年间是中西文化的伟大相遇，这是人类文明史上少有的平等、和平交流的一段历史，是中国和西方文化交流史中最重要、最具有现代意义的一段历史，它是中国与西方共同的文化遗产，"未来的中西交流将更多地呈现出1500年到1800年间中西方的互动与互惠"③。

第二，对启蒙运动后期所确立的进步史观应进行解构。孔多塞最终所确立的以进步为核心的启蒙观是欧洲思想走向自我中心主义的开始。孔多塞写于1793

---

① 谈敏：《法国重农学派学说的中国渊源》，上海：上海人民出版社，1992年，第366页。
② 张西平：《中国与欧洲早期宗教和哲学交流史》，北京：东方出版社，2001年，第492页。
③ ［美］孟德卫著，江文君、姚霏译：《1500—1800：中西方的伟大相遇》，北京：新星出版社，2007年，第188页。

年的《人类精神进步史表纲要》,以进步史观为核心,将人类历史发展分为九个时期,由低到高,最终达到完美阶段。他把中国安排在人类历史发展的第三个时代,他对中国历史与文明的安排为以后黑格尔的《历史哲学》对中国思想的评价打下了基础。[①]正如学者所说:"启蒙主义者努力在知识与观念中'发现'并'建设'一个完整的、体现人类幸福价值观的世界秩序,该秩序的核心就是进步,进步的主体是西方,世界其他地区与民族只是对象,这其中既有一种知识关系——认识与被认识,又有一种权力关系,因为发现与被发现、征服与被征服往往是同时发生的。启蒙主义者都是欧洲中心的世界主义者。他们描述世界的目的是确定欧洲在世界中的位置,他们叙述历史是为了确立自由与进步的价值,并将欧洲文明作为世界历史主体。启蒙运动为西方现代文明构筑了一个完整的观念世界,或者说是观念中的世界秩序。它在空间中表现为不同民族、国家、风俗及其法律的多样的、从文明到野蛮的等级性结构;在时间中表现为朝向一个必然的、目标的、线性的、可以划分为不同阶段的进步。启蒙主义都是历史主义者,他们将世界的空间秩序并入时间中,在世界历史发展的过程中理解不同民族文明的意义和价值。其线性的、进步的历史观念已不仅是人类经验时间的方式,甚至是人类存在的方式。所有的民族、国家都必须先在历史中确认自己的位置,无论是停滞的或进步的,在历史之外或在历史之中,然后才在世界的共时格局——即文明、野蛮的等级秩序——中找到自己的位置。"[②]这个分析是正确的,指出了孔多塞所代表的后期启蒙思想家的问题所在——一种强烈的西方中心主义,说明了孔多塞的历史观的西方立场。

实际上当孔多塞这样来解释中国时,当时的中国并未停滞,不但没有停滞,当时的中国仍是一个强大的中国。1800年前的中国是世界上人口最多,经济规模最大、国民总产值第一的强盛大国,当时的中国正处在康乾盛世时期。弗兰克说得更为明确:"整个世界经济秩序当时名副其实地是以中国为中心的。哥伦布以及在他之后直到亚当·斯密的许多欧洲人都清楚这一点。只是到了19世纪,欧洲

---

① 参见张国刚:《18世纪晚期欧洲对于中国的认识——欧洲进步观念的确立与中国形象的逆转》,《天津社会科学》2005年第3期。
② 周宁:《西方的中国形象》,周宁编:《世界之中国:域外中国形象研究》,南京:南京大学出版社,2007年,第49—50页。

人才根据新的欧洲中心论观念名副其实地'改写'了这一历史。正如布罗代尔指出的，欧洲发明了历史学家，然后充分地利用了他们对各自利益的追求，而不是让他们追求准确或客观的历史。"①

所以，揭示出启蒙时期思想的实际发展过程，说明欧洲思想不是一个自我成圣的过程，仅仅回到希腊，西方思想家发展不出来近代的启蒙思想观念。但西方思想的当代叙述完全不再提到这段历史，他们改写西方思想文化的发展史，并设置一个二元对峙的思想和文化发展的模式，将其作为训导东方国家的思想文化模式。在这个意义上，这种做法不仅无耻，也反映出西方思想自启蒙后的堕落，尤其至今一些西方文化思想领袖希望按照这样的逻辑继续改造这个世界时，将其称为文化帝国主义是完全可以的。后殖民主义理论的意义在于揭示出启蒙以来西方思想发展形成的真实历史和逻辑，说明了东方的价值和西方的虚伪。但绝不是用后殖民主义理论去论证西方思想的合理性、开放性，西方思想自我调节、自我成圣，西方近代思想自我发展的逻辑的合理性。我们决不能从这段历史的叙述中，按照后现代主义的理论框架，强化西方在启蒙后所形成的思想文化特征的合理性。这样的论述将重点放在西方思想的自我成圣、自我逻辑的发展，强调西方思想自身发展的逻辑的合理性、自洽性，东方只是一个没有实际价值的他者，西方近代思想的形成全在西方自身的内因。这样的一种研究实际上仍只是研究西方，东方只是个陪衬，中国只是个背景，从而没有真正从全球化的角度考虑文化与思想的互动，没有揭示在这个历史过程中东方思想的价值，没有用这段真实的历史去揭示当代西方思想和文化主流叙述的虚伪性。因而，这样一种用后殖民主义理论来论证启蒙思想的内在形成逻辑的合理性的做法，恰恰违背了后殖民主义理论的初衷，这是用后殖民主义逻辑为西方辩护的一种自我殖民化。对于这种思想和认识应该给予足够的认识。

这说明，当启蒙思想家以进步史观设计历史时，在历史事实上就存在问题，即便当时中国相比于欧洲发展慢了一些，但并未停滞。在启蒙后期孔多塞、马戛尔尼把中国说成停滞的帝国肯定是不符合事实的。历史是一个长时段的发展，

---

① ［德］贡德·弗兰克著，刘北成译：《白银资本——重视经济全球化中的东方》，北京：中央编译出版社，2000年，第169页。

100年是一个短暂的瞬间，今天中国重新崛起，其道路和特点都和西方的道路与特点有很大的不同，历史已经对启蒙后期开始形成的欧洲中心主义和19世纪主导世界的西方中心主义做出了最好的回答。从今天的历史来看，启蒙后期的思想家的傲慢是多么的可笑。

四、启蒙精神与中国传统文化

历史充满了复杂性。启蒙时期中国古代文化在欧洲的影响也呈现出多元的色彩。学术界在理解启蒙与中国文化的关系时，大都不注意启蒙运动真实历史与中国文化之间的多元复杂关系，从而对启蒙思想和中国文化关系不能做出学理与历史的综合性分析与解释。

通过弘扬启蒙思想，来批判中国传统文化——这是一种看法。这种思维实际上已经接受了现代与传统、东方与西方二元对峙的思维方式，加之缺乏比较文化的立场和对全球史研究进展的关注，因而，完全不知中国文化在1500—1800年间与西方文化的基本关系和状态，不知当时中国在全球化初期的地位。所以，当弗兰克说出当时的中国是世界经济中心时，在中国学术界引起轩然大波，一些学者极为震惊。这种看法自然无法理解中国传统文化，尤其是儒家文化为何被启蒙思想所接受、所赞扬。在他们赞扬启蒙之时，内心已经将中国文化作为启蒙思想的对立面，而完全不知中国文化恰恰曾是启蒙思想家的思想源泉之一，也无法理解从这段历史可以看出中国传统文化，特别是儒家文化具有现代思想的内涵，只要经过创造性转换完全可以成为中国当代文化的重要资源。在这个意义上，这些学者并未真正理解启蒙运动。历史的吊诡在于，20世纪80年代的文化热中，对启蒙的崇拜和信仰有其合理性，就是到今天启蒙精神仍有其文化和思想价值，因为，启蒙运动所留给人类的"自由""民主""科学""理性"仍有其重要的价值。但将这些启蒙精神和中国传统思想完全对立起来是对启蒙思想形成历史的不了解。同时，对启蒙时期思想家们所提出的"科学""理性""进步"的一味赞扬，说明这样的看法不了解启蒙思想家在形成这些观念时的缺失，尤其启蒙思想后期所形成的"进步"观念背后的"欧洲中心主义"的立场，从而缺乏一种对启蒙的反思，特别是对西方近百年来在启蒙思想下所走过的实际历史过程的反思。①

通过批判启蒙思想，来弘扬中国文化——这是另一种。很长期时间以来，在西方思想文化上启蒙运动都是作为一场伟大的思想文化运动而载入史册的。正如著名的罗兰·N.斯特龙伯格所指出，18世纪为世界贡献了这样的观念："人类现在和将来都会'进步'，科学技术对推动人类进步起了最大作用，人类的目的就是享受世俗的幸福。虽然有越来越多的知识分子对这些说法表示怀疑，但大多数平民百姓可能还是信奉它们。与许多社会科学一样，现代自由主义和社会主义都是在18世纪孕育出来的。今天的公共政策的目标也是由启蒙运动确定的：物质福利、幸福。人们还会想到宗教宽容、人道主义、法律面前人人平等，言论自由以及民主和社会平等。所有这些都主要源于这个世纪。更深入地看，很显然，我们的基本思维习惯以及我们的语言方式，也主要受到启蒙运动的影响。"②

以批判当代西方社会思想为其特点的后现代思潮兴起后，启蒙运动的地位发生了变化，启蒙开始成为批判的对象。后现代主义是对启蒙的一种反思、质疑和批判。一些思想家"开始对现代性的总体观念提出批判，并提出'后现代'以同'现代'相对抗，这些思想家的思想被称为'后现代主义'。"③这样一种反叛倾向首先是从尼采开始的，在他看来现代社会不是一个健康的社会，它是由废物组成的病态胶合物。沿着这条思路，利奥塔、德里达、福柯、罗蒂等西方哲学家

---

① "'人本主义在上世纪（19世纪）末叶达到顶峰。帝国主义的欧洲统治全球，但文化的欧洲则相信这是对世界文明进步的贡献'；'一些欧洲人发觉他们的人本主义掩盖了和包庇了一场可怕的非人惨剧。他们还发觉自己所认为是惟一的文化其实只是世界文化之林中的一枝文化，而自己的这个文化曾居然认为有权蔑视其他文化并予以毁灭之。'"［法］莫兰著，康征、齐小曼译：《反思欧洲》，"文化批判与文化自觉——中文版序"，北京：生活·读书·新知三联书店，2005年，第7页；参见［英］汤林森著，冯建三译，郭英剑校订：《文化帝国主义》，上海：上海人民出版社，1999年。当下中国学术与思想界如何创造性的转化中国传统文化，如何在合理吸收西方近代思想文化精神合理内核的基础上清理"西方中心主义"，是一个根本性的问题。在中国即将成为一个世界性大国之时，思想的创造与独立、本土资源的发掘和百年西方中心主义的清理成为我们绕不过去的一个重大问题。20世纪80年代的启蒙已经瓦解，思想已经分野，那种思想方案更适合于崛起的中国，这要待历史回答。参见许纪霖、罗岗等：《启蒙的自我瓦解：1990年代以来中国思想文化界重大论争研究》，长春：吉林出版集团有限责任公司，2007年。
② ［美］罗兰·斯特龙伯格著，刘北成、赵国新译：《西方现代思想史》，北京：中央编译出版社，2005年，第196页。
③ 姚大志：《现代之后——20世纪晚期西方哲学》，北京：东方出版社，2000年，第229页。

各自展开了自己的论述,从而形成了后现代思潮,而另一些哲学家如哈贝马斯将继续沿着启蒙的方向完善这个理论。

西方这样的思考自然引起中国学者的注意,学者杜维明认为:"启蒙心态从18世纪以来,是人类文明史到现在为止最有影响力的一种心态。科学主义、物质主义、进步主义,我们现在熟悉的话语,都和启蒙有密切关系。社会主义和资本主义都是从启蒙发展出来的。市场经济、民主政治、市民社会,还有后面所代表的核心价值,比如说自由、理智、人权、法制、个人的尊严,这些价值也都从启蒙发展而来,而这个力量不仅是方兴未艾,而且在各个地方已经成为文化传统中间不可分割的部分。所以我进一步说,在文化中国的知识界,文化的传统之中,启蒙心态的影响远远要超出儒家的、道家的、法家的、佛教的、道教的、民间宗教带来的影响。"①启蒙的问题在于:第一,人类中心主义(anthropocentrism);第二,工具理性(instrumental rationality)以及宰制性的科学主义;第三,个人主义;第四,西方中心主义。由此,杜先生认为:"经过了西化,经过了现代化,儒家传统的人文精神,人文关怀,可以和启蒙所带来的最强势的人文主义进行深层的对话,现代西方启蒙所开发出来那么多的光辉灿烂的价值,特别是科学技术方面的价值,和人的个人的个性解放,人的精神的发展,儒家的人文精神和现代西方人文主义之间的对话和互动的空间有没有,有哪些课题需要讨论,这是我关注的问题。"②正如学者所概括的:"作为儒家的现代传人,如何在启蒙反思中发挥儒家思想的积极作用,是杜维明相关思考的理论兴奋点之一。"③对此,一些学者的基本主张是:"儒家天人合一的人文主义可以在自身、社群、自然和上天四层面为超越启蒙凡俗的人文主义提供思想资源。"④

启蒙思想还是中国传统思想?看起来似乎有些对立。但一旦我们进入实际的历史境遇,就会看到将启蒙与中国传统思想对立起来的认识是值得反思的。

从我们上面所介绍的启蒙思想家对中国文化的接受来看,儒家思想和启蒙思

---

① [美]杜维明:《"启蒙的反思"学术座谈》,《开放时代》2006年第3期,第6页。
② 同上文,第8页。
③ 李翔海:《杜维明"启蒙反思"论述评》,《中国社会科学院研究生院学报》2011年第5期,第33页。
④ 同上文,第29页。

想并不是对立的,儒家思想曾是滋润启蒙思想的重要外部资源,它与启蒙精神相连,而又有别于西方启蒙思想。因此,在重建中国文化传统的现代意义时,我们不能完全将儒家思想和启蒙思想对立起来,而是可以从启蒙思想家当年对中国文化的跨文化理解中,纠正其偏误,赋予儒家文化以符合现代生活的新意,开出启蒙思想之新意。

例如,启蒙思想家利用中国文化的理性精神来解构中世纪的宗教,这里说明儒家思想中的理性精神是有其合理的一面。但启蒙思想家在理解儒家的理性精神时,并不全面,启蒙思想所确立的理性最终演化成为工具理性主义。这样他们并未深刻理解儒家思想的理性精神和宗教精神的融合,儒家思想的半哲学和半宗教特点。儒家的理性主义和启蒙思想的工具理性之间有着契合与差别,这样如何在保持启蒙理性精神的同时,发挥儒家理性与神圣性合一的资源,人文理性主义的资源,克服启蒙以来的工具理性之不足。同时,如何学习启蒙精神,将儒家实用理性转化成为不同于工具理性的现代理性,这都给我们留下宽阔的学术空间。

又如,启蒙思想家通过耶稣会士所介绍的中国富足的世俗生活,赞扬了个人主义。因此,将中国传统文化说成是一个压制个人的专制文化史是说不过去的,即便在孟德斯鸠那里,他对中国的专制文化也做了特别的处理,而魁奈专制主义并非是在批评意义上使用,如克拉克所说:"必须记住,启蒙思想家口中的'专制'绝非批评之辞,在这里中国乃是被视为受开明统治者治理的国家典范,也就是说,这种类型的国家不会根据统治者的一时兴起而作出决定,它将视法律而定,它将以全体人民的幸福为目的,它将以社会一切方面的和谐运转作为统治者最关注的核心问题。魁奈自己和他的同时代人一样,把中国视为理想社会,它为欧洲提供了一个可供模仿的范本。"①

但中国文化中对个人的肯定又不同于启蒙所开启的物质主义的个人主义,或者说凡俗的个人主义,乃至人类中心主义。儒家的人文主义正如陈荣捷教授在《中国哲学文献选编》中指出的:"中国哲学史的特色,一言以蔽之,可以说是人文主义,但此种人文主义并不否认或忽视超越力量,而是主张天人可以合

---

① [美] J.J.克拉克著,于闽梅、曾祥波译:《东方启蒙:东西方思想的遭遇》,上海:上海人民出版社,2011年,第71页。

一。"①按照这样的理解,中国的天人合一的人文主义既不是启蒙思想家所倡导的世俗个人主义,也不是后来由此演化成为的人类中心主义。

自然,孔多塞等后期启蒙思想家所提出的"进步"观念也有其合理性,进步总是比落后要好。但这种进步不是一种以欧洲为中心的线性进步观,不是一种人类中心主义的无限索取自然的进步观,不是以西方文化取代其他多元文化的进步观。在这个意义上,中国传统的"天人合一"的自然观,"和而不同"的文化观,都可以作为修正孔多塞所代表的启蒙思想家进步观的重要思想资源。

目前关于启蒙思想与中国思想的讨论中大都是在纯粹理论范围内展开的,但思想是历史的思想,没有历史的思想史是永远无法高飞的。历史是智慧的源泉,只有在一个长时段的历史中,我们才会体悟到真理。通过对1500—1800年间中西文化交流史的研究,通过对中国传统文化在启蒙时期的传播和影响接受研究,我们可以从根源上对启蒙做更为全面的反思,可以走出启蒙思想与中国传统思想对立的思考模式,克服后现代主义对启蒙片面批判和固守在启蒙思想内部发展思想的两种倾向,从中国的历史和启蒙的历史做出新的解释,将历史重新激活,将中西思想重新融合。这是我们的祈盼,亦是我们编订此套丛书的初衷。②

因应目前学界关于儒学研究的最新学术动向,一并汇总极具代表性的重要研究成果,本套丛书既收录有视野恢弘、横跨明清两代中西哲学交流史的通论型研究著作,例如张西平《中国和欧洲早期思想交流史》和堀池信夫《中国哲学与欧洲的哲学家》的研究专著;亦有专门针对目前学术界未能给与充分重视、实则能充分体现儒家思想在启蒙现代性构建过程中的地位和作用的研究专题,例如杜维明和孟华主编的《儒家思想在启蒙时代的译介与接受》和井川义次的《宋学西渐——欧洲迈向近代启蒙之路》都侧重于考察18世纪儒学与启蒙运动之间的互动关系,探讨儒家以"仁"为核心的伦理道德观,以及"仁政德治"的政体主张,对欧洲启蒙思想家的启迪作用并为他们的宗教、社会、政体改革提供了精神养料和可资借鉴的模式。张西平和李颖主编的《启蒙的先声:中国文化与启蒙运动》则经由梳理"中学西传"的历史脉络,展现儒家思想与启蒙运动和西方汉学兴起

---

① 陈荣捷编著,杨儒宾等译:《中国哲学文献选编》,南京:江苏教育出版社,2006年,第1页。
② 参见许纪霖、罗岗等:《启蒙的自我瓦解:1990年代以来中国思想文化界重大论争研究》,长春:吉林出版集团有限公司,2007年。

的紧密关系。梅谦立《从邂逅到相识：孔子与亚里士多德相遇在明清》一书则反向探讨了明清来华耶稣会士用儒家术语翻译、书写的亚里士多德主义的汉语著作，经由这种经典的交织使亚里士多德思想在中国文化土壤上呈现出新的阐释可能和丰富内涵。此外，丛书亦关注目前国内年轻学者对"西文文献中的中国"的最新研究成果，例如韩凌《洛克与中国：洛克"中国笔记"考辨》一书借助英国经验主义哲学家洛克的"中国笔记"手稿，系统梳理洛克的"中国观"，进而弥补17世纪中西文化交流史研究链条中所缺失的重要一环，亦即洛克对中国的认识和评价；罗莹《康熙朝来华传教士拉丁文儒学译述整理研究》一书在对康熙朝来华三大天主教修会传教士拉丁语儒学译述进行文献编目整理的基础上，细致呈现出当时来华传教士内部围绕儒学宗教性问题，分裂为"支持中国文化适应政策""反对文化适应政策"及"文化调和激进派"等不同态度并试图分析其儒学观的根本性分歧所在。

我们期待借助不同文化本位和新老代际的研究者的多元研究视角，来呈现这一关注儒家思想的学术共同体，对其在不同历史阶段发展特点的审视及评论，从而反观中国人的哲学精神和宗教追求有别于西方的种种特点，经由文本上的旅行来实现横亘千古中西之间跨文化的对话，进而减弱自我认识的片面性，坦诚面对那个褒贬不一却始终具备丰沛生命力的儒家思想，及其在人类思想史进程中所蕴含的世界性意义。愿我们能以史为鉴，以更为广阔的胸怀迎接一个以文明交流超越文明隔阂、以文明互鉴超越文明冲突、以文明共存超越文明优越的伟大历史时代。

张西平　罗　莹
2019年7月

序　在文化互动中重新认识东西方文化

一、在东西文化互动的历史中认识西方文化的东方之源

近代以来，西方文化伴随着工业革命的成功成为一种强势文化，强大起来的西方将其成功归于其文化的支撑。在中国近代最流行的就是"现代与传统、东方与西方"的二元对峙。似乎东方若要走向现代化，只有走西方之路，只有批判自己的文化，学习西方文化。这样的一种西方文化优越论一直桎梏着我们对西方文化和自身文化的认识。这种认识掩盖了一个基本的历史事实，即东方文化不仅是西方文化之根，同时也长期是西方文化发展的重要动力和精神导师。只是到了19世纪西方取得了世界发展的领导权后，西方人开始掩盖这一切，将西方文化说成一个自我成圣的伟大文化，甚至将白人文化说成一种优于其他人种的文化。西方中心主义开始盛行。

我们看希腊文化与东方文化的关系。希腊是西方文化之根，西方哲学家们都将希腊称为欧洲文化的童年。实际上，希腊文化的形成主要是受到埃及文化、亚述文化等东方文化的影响。希腊历史学之父希罗多德在《历史》中说过："埃及人如何来到伯罗奔尼撒半岛，他们做了什么，使得自己成为希腊那一部分的国

王,别的作家已经记载过了;我因此不增加什么东西,而是接着提到几点别人没有讨论过的东西。"他还认为,希腊的纪念仪式、习俗都是从埃及搬来的。希腊人是从埃及人那里学会了"占卜术,并将他在埃及学到的许多东西几乎原封不动地带到了希腊,……希腊几乎所有神的名字都来自埃及"①。为何希腊和埃及有如此紧密的关系呢?这是因为埃及人曾经殖民过希腊。这些都有历史学的根据,在希腊悲剧中仍可找到大量埃及古代语言的残存。实际上,近东的亚述、苏美尔文化,即古代美索不达米亚的居民创造了世界上最早的辉煌文明。"这一文明对推动人类的进步发挥了巨大的作用。这一地区孕育了许多世界之最:诞生了世界上第一座城市;最早的议会制雏形;最早的国家行政学院;发明了世界上最早的灌溉农业,开展了人类最早的对外贸易,实践了最早的封建租佃制和资本主义生产方式;创造了人类最早的公司形式,最早的职业经理人,最早的股权激励形式;诞生了最早的文字,最早的学校,最早的图书馆;出现了第一次社会改革,第一部法典,第一起法律判例,第一部农人历书,第一部药典;产生了最早的宇宙观,最早的伦理观,最早的人本观,最早的科学知识;流传着最早的史诗与神话,最早的寓言,最早的谚语和格言,最早的爱情诗,最早的《圣经》故事原型;等等。"②

希腊正是从东方的两河流域文明和埃及文明中学习到了文字、文学、艺术、宗教,当然也包括科学技术才成长起来。希腊从巴比伦学到天文学和数学知识,学到巴比伦人发明的水钟、日冕和把一天分成十二部分的方法,学到巴比伦人观测到的黄道和黄道十二宫图,学到了埃及的几何学、日历和医学。西方一些严肃的学者完全承认这一点,为更为清晰地表达东方文化和西方文化的关系,学者们明确地说:巴比伦与亚述文明是西方的祖先,东方是西方文化之根,这才是真实的历史。

只是到了18—19世纪西方才开始将自己和东方文化分开,将埃及人说成和非洲人一样:快活,热爱享乐,孩子气地爱吹牛。他们编造出希腊文化本质上是欧洲的,以及哲学和文明发源自希腊,希腊文明是纯粹欧洲的,与腓尼基人和亚

---

① [美]马丁·贝尔纳著,郝田虎、程英译:《黑色雅典娜:古典文明的亚非之根》,长春:吉林出版集团有限责任公司,2011年,第83—84页。
② 于殿利:《巴比伦与亚述文明》,北京:北京师范大学出版社,2013年,第3页。

述、苏尔美文化没有任何关系。①

二、东方是欧洲近代思想形成的重要力量

由于近代以来西方逐步率先走向现代化,在他们强大起来以后,开始慢慢地修改历史,将自己的发展和成就说成是欧洲自身思想发展的结果,与其他文化没有关系。例如欧洲近代的进步起源于文艺复兴,但这和东方没有什么关系。"欧洲并没有从东方汲取什么创造现代科学所不可或缺的东西;另一方面,其借鉴的价值仅仅是因为它被融入到了欧洲的理性传统之中。当然,这些理性传统是在(古)希腊创建的。"②显然,这种说法并不符合历史的实际。希腊的典籍在中世纪后已经很难找到,希腊思想和文化的保存在于阿拉伯的百年翻译运动中,他们将绝大多数希腊的文献翻译成了阿拉伯文。文艺复兴就是将这些阿拉伯文的希腊文献重新翻译回意大利文等欧洲语言,从中发挥出新的思想。一些欧洲中心论者认为,阿拉伯人并没有多少新的思想,他们只不过是保存下来了希腊的文献。这种傲慢的态度违背了基本的历史事实。因为阿拉伯学者并不仅仅翻译了希腊的文献,他们也从波斯、印度(以及中国)吸收了大量的医学、数学、哲学、神学、文学和诗歌方面的成就。"然后,他们在犹太科学家和翻译家的帮助下,创造了一种新的知识体系,这不仅仅是对希腊知识的简单纂合,也是对希腊思想的批判继承,同时使它们在新的方向上得到进一步的发展。"③这个过程说明了这样的事实:巴格达处在全球经济的中心,它不仅接受了新的亚洲思想,而且对其重新改造,然后传播到伊斯兰教的安达卢西亚地区。这点,一些西方学者也是承认的,他们说:"西方人发现穆斯林所拥有的缜密思维和渊博学识,远远超过了从古罗马那里所获得的……在人类文明的历史上,可能没有人能够比他们(欧洲人)更安于窃用这些外族遗产了,除非是希腊人在公元前6世纪就汲取了这些东方(埃

---

① 在这个意义上德国哲学家雅斯贝尔斯提出的"轴心说"都是值得怀疑的。文明的起源是古埃及文明、两河流域的古巴比伦和亚述文明、古印度文明和古代中国文明,希腊文明是进入不了这个圈的。希腊文明是在巴比伦和亚述文明影响下发展起来的。
② [英]约翰·霍布森著,孙建党译,于向东、王琛校:《西方文明的东方起源》,济南:山东画报出版社,2009年,第156页。
③ 同上书,第157页。

及)文明。"①

　　文艺复兴和启蒙运动是欧洲走向现代化之路的两个重要环节，而西方这两个最重要的文化变革都和东方有着密切的关系。

　　当来华耶稣会士将中国经典陆续翻译成欧洲语言，在欧洲各国出版后，在欧洲逐步形成了18世纪的中国热。中国热表现出中国古代文化对欧洲的影响。同时，来华耶稣会士关于中国的著作在欧洲的不断出版，特别是柏应理的《中国哲学家孔子》的出版，在欧洲思想界产生了深刻的影响。来华耶稣会士这些介绍儒家思想的著作，所翻译的儒家经典引起了欧洲思想界的高度重视。莱布尼茨、伏尔泰、重农学派代表人物魁奈均受到中国古代思想的启发和影响。

　　如果说莱布尼茨和伏尔泰分别从哲学和宗教、历史和政治角度论证了孔子学说的合理性，那么洛克则是从经验论哲学出发，从儒家学说的特点看到其非宗教性。他说："儒教经典不承认纯粹精神，因此信仰儒教的中国人不相信人的灵魂不朽，然而他们也不认为灵魂一离开肉体就立即消失或完全寂灭。……'上帝'字面上的意思是指'最高的主宰'或'至高无上的王'。从古代的中国人和哲学家开始，直到今天，'上帝'指的都是'物质的天'。"②洛克这样解读儒教经典是为了说明欧洲人所信奉的上帝观念并没有普世性。正如韩凌在本书中所做的分析："本部分（手稿）最核心的观点为：中国哲学不可动摇的基础是'万物同一体'。自古希腊哲学以降，从伊壁鸠鲁、德谟克利特到17世纪的斯宾诺莎，'万物同一体'一直是欧洲唯物论的核心观念。因此对洛克来说，信仰'万物同一体'的中国哲学必然是无神论。"③洛克看似只是摘录并罗列了《中国礼仪史》等文献中对中国宗教和礼仪的描述，实际上却奇迹般地透过传教士们晦涩冗长并且时常自相矛盾的描述抓住了中国宗教的内核，最终得出"中国的统治阶级——士大夫们——都是纯粹的无神论者"的结论。可见，洛克从中国哲学中找到论证他的哲学的根据，他的《人类理解论》这部西方哲学名著包含了中国的智慧。

---

① [英]约翰·霍布森著，孙建党译，于向东、王琛校：《西方文明的东方起源》，济南：山东画报出版社，2009年，第157页。
② 见本书，第53、59页。
③ 见本书，第165页。

通过历史说明西方文化和东方文化的历史渊源，破除19世纪以来将西方文化说成自我成圣神话，解除掉西方文化所披覆的神圣光环，将其还原成一个地域性文化，化解那种将西方文化等同于现代化文化的神话。这是我们走向文化自信的第一步。当然，这个过程不是走向东方中心主义，不是否认西方文化对世界文化的贡献，并不是停止我们学习优秀西方文化的步伐，而是以一种平等的态度、实事求是的态度，在与西方文化的交流互鉴中发展中国自己的文化。

三、新的文明观——文明互鉴

1969年，英国广播公司（BBC）出品的十三集电视片《文明》向观众展示了人类文明，但事实上，那只是一个灿烂辉煌的西方文明，那是卢瓦尔河城堡，是佛罗伦萨的宫殿，是西斯廷教堂，是凡尔赛宫，是香榭丽舍大街。编导者的言外之意很明显：基督教文明之前的时代以及东方都是不开化的。这显然是对人类历史的片面解释。

英国历史学家汤因比突破西方中心主义的历史观，在其著名的《历史研究》中构建了一种文明形态史论，以文明为历史研究的单元，对世界多样文明同等地研究，探究世界文明演化的法则与规律。他认为人类文明的产生和演化是多元的；在6000年人类历史上，世界上有过26种文明，分别为西方基督教文明、东正教文明（它可分为拜占庭文明和俄罗斯文明）、伊朗文明、阿拉伯文明（它与伊朗文明可合为伊斯兰文明）、印度文明、远东文明（它可分为中国文明和朝鲜文明、日本文明）、古代希腊文明、古叙利亚文明、古代印度文明、古代中国文明、木诺斯文明、苏美尔文明、赫梯文明、巴比伦文明、古代埃及文明、安第斯文明、古代墨西哥文明、育加丹文明、玛雅文明，以及5个停滞的文明，即波利尼西亚文明、爱斯基摩文明、游牧文明、斯巴达文明和奥斯曼文明。

不论汤因比所列举的文明是否周全，但文明的多样性是历史发展的基本形态，这一点得到了绝大多数的学者的肯定。汤因比的多样文明论是对西方中心主义的超越。1998年联合国大会正式通过决议，确认世界上存在着不同的文明，并把2001年定为"文明对话年"，提出要展开不同文明的对话与交流，保持文化的多元性。2001年联合国科教文组织大会通过《世界文化多样性宣言》，把文化的多样性提升到"人类共同的遗产"的高度来认识，认为这是保证人类生存的必需条件。这两个重要的决议不仅反映了当前世界文明的实际状况和发展趋势，而且表达了世界各族人民要求发展和保持自己文明的热切期盼，为正确处理不同文明之间的关系提供了坚实的基础。

人类社会的各个文明乃至国家的发展除其内部原因外，与外部文明或文化的交流与互动是其发展和变化的重要原因。梁启超当年在谈到中国历史的研究时曾说过，根据中国的历史的发展，研究中国的历史可以划分为："中国的中国""亚洲的中国"以及"世界的中国"三个阶段。所谓"中国的中国"的研究阶段是指中国的先秦史，自黄帝时代直至秦统一，这是"中国民族自发达自竞争自团结之时代"；所谓"亚洲之中国"的研究阶段是中世史，从秦统一后至清代乾隆末年，这是中华民族与亚洲各民族相互交流并不断融合的时代；所谓"世界之中国"的研究阶段为近世史，自乾隆末年至当时，这是中华民族与亚洲各民族开始和西方民族交流并产生激烈竞争之时代，由此开始，中国成为世界的一部分。

其实，梁任公这样的历时性划分未必合理，但他提出的在世界研究中国的观点是正确的。实际上中国和世界之间的关系是一直存在着的，尽管中国的地缘有一定的封闭性，但中国文化从一开始就不是一个封闭的文化。中国和世界的关系，并不是从乾隆年间才开始。梁任公自己为了说明这一点就提出过两个在当时令人匪夷所思的问题：第一，"刘项之争，与中亚细亚及印度诸国之兴亡有关系，而影响及于希腊人之东陆领土"；第二，"汉攘匈奴，与西罗马之灭亡，及欧洲现代诸国家之建设有关"。他试图通过以这两个在常人看来完全风马牛不相及的历史事实来说明中国史从来不是在一个封闭的圈子里展开的，世界各国的历史是相互关联的。因而，梁任公的真正目的在于说明：要将中国史放在世界史中加以考察。

梁启超这样立论他的中国历史研究时有两个目的：其一，对西方主导的世界史不满意，因为在西方主导的世界史中，中国对人类史的贡献是看不到的。1901年，在《中国史叙论》中他说："今世之著世界史者，必以泰西各国为中心点，虽日本俄罗斯之史家（凡著世界史者，日本俄罗斯皆摈不录），亦无异议焉。盖以过去现在之间，能推衍文明之力以左右世界者，实惟泰西民族，而他族莫能与争也。"①在这里，他对"西方中心论"的不满已经十分清楚。其二，从世界史的角度重新看待中国文化的地位和贡献。他指出中国史主要应"说明中国民族所产文化，以何为基本，其与世界他部分文化相互之影响何如？说明中国民族在人类全体上之位置及其特性，与其将来对于全人类所应负之责任"②。虽然当时中国积贫积弱，但他认为："中国文明力未必不可以左右世界，即中国史在世界史中，当占一强有力之位置也。"③

梁启超提出新史学已百年，此后的历史学家在这方面已经取得了很大的进步。雷海宗先生曾指出世界史研究中应注意两点：第一要注意中国与世界其他地区的联系，和彼此间的相互影响；第二要注意中国对世界人类文明发展的贡献。这两条说明了研究明清之际中西文化交流史的世界史意义。这个时期是西方所谓的大发现时期，而这个时期对西方真正产生影响的是中国文化，这证明了中国文化的全球意义。吴于廑教授相互关联的四篇论文：《游牧世界与游牧民族》（《云南社会科学》1983年第1期）、《世界历史上的农本与重商》（《历史研究》1984年第1期）、《历史上的农耕世界对工业世界的孕育》（《世界历史》1987年第2期）、《亚欧大陆传统农耕世界不同国家在新兴工业世界冲击下的反应》（《世界历史》1993年第1期）也说明了这一点。这样，对中国文化的研究在世界范围展开，就有了一种全球化的观点，而且直接走出了欧洲中心主义。

目前的世界史研究和中国史研究是分离的，这导致我们无法从全球史角度展开。后现代史学反对19世纪以来的宏大叙事，批评那种以西方为主，非西方为副的历史叙述，他们主张力图从不同文化间的互动（interaction），而不是一种文化对另一种文化的影响（effect）着眼，重绘人类历史画卷。历史就是世界各族互动的结果。人类的历史就是不同社会、不同地区、不同民族、不同国家之间的"跨文化互动"。文化交流史就是文化的互动。

文明因在不同的历史境遇中形成和发展，每一种文明都有着自己的特质，多种多样的文明构成了这个丰富多彩的世界。但在人类历史上，如何对待不同文明却有着惨痛教训，这就是在地理大发现后，西方殖民者对非洲文明、印度文明、

---

① 梁启超：《中国史叙论》，《饮冰室合集》文集之六，北京：中华书局，1989年，第2页。
② 梁启超：《中国历史研究法》，《饮冰室合集》专集之七十三，北京：中华书局，1989年，第7页。
③ 梁启超：《中国史叙论》，《饮冰室合集》文集之六，北京：中华书局，1989年，第2页。

印第安文明、印加文明的掠夺、摧残和灭绝。

西方人用刀和火耕作了这个世界，地理大发现既是人类对世界的伟大发现，同时也是西方文明对其他文明的一次摧毁。马克思说："美洲金银产地的发现，土著居民被剿灭，被奴隶化，被埋于矿坑，正在开始的东印度的征服与劫掠，非洲被转化为商业性黑人猎夺场所，都表示了资本主义产生时代的曙光。这些牧歌式的过程，是原始积累的主要要素。"①西方的资本在这个历史过程中虽然成为"历史的不自觉的工具"②，但对人类文明的多样性却是一种历史性的灾难。这就是历史的二律背反。

如果说在人类历史进程中，文明与进步的二律背反使一些文明消亡，那么从20世纪初期的世界民族国家独立运动，迫使殖民主义完成了它的历史使命，非西方国家开始登上世界历史舞台。西方文明独占鳌头的局面逐渐被非西方文明的国家发展和进步所打破。这样，西方文明与世界其他非西方文明的关系再度成为一个世界性的问题，这包括西方文明同伊斯兰文明的关系，同拉美文明的关系，同亚洲各国文明的关系，其中同中华文明的关系日益成为一个核心性问题。

那么，我们该如何理解中华文明的重新崛起呢？中华文明将如何与西方文明以及其他文明和谐相处？正是在这样的背景下，习近平主席提出了"文明互鉴"的新文明观。2014年3月27日，习近平主席访问联合国教科文组织总部并发表演讲，他说："文明因交流而多彩，文明因互鉴而丰富。文明交流互鉴，是推动人类文明进步和世界和平发展的重要动力。"③这一论述，深刻揭示了文明交流互鉴的意义和文明发展规律，及文明在世界和平发展中的重要作用。不可否认，人类文明的交流的确充斥着暴力、战争、征服等激烈的碰撞方式，但同时，人类历史上也存在着文明之间和平的交流。亨廷顿认为人类文明之间实现和平交流是极其困难甚至是不可能的，在当下世界"文明冲突"将主宰全球。习近平主席关于文明互鉴与文明和谐的思想，有力地反驳了以亨廷顿为代表的"文明冲突论"者的意见，明确指出"文明冲突"完全可以避免，并提出解决文明差异的具体办法，说明了文明差异的必然性与合理性。这就说明任何文明都是具有特殊性的文

---

① [德]马克思：《马克思恩格斯论殖民主义》，北京：人民出版社，1962年，第297页。
② 同上书，第31页。
③ xinhuanet.com/world/2014-03/28/c_119982831_2.htm. 访问时间：2019年7月20日。

明,从来没有一种人类普遍存在的文明形态,人类共同认知的文明特点和形态只有存在于不同的特殊文明形态之中。无论哪一种文明,其最根本的价值都不在于其是普遍的,而在于其是特殊的,在于其发展的历史和成果是独特的,在于其对整个人类文明的贡献是独一无二的。

总之,韩凌博士《洛克与中国:洛克"中国笔记"考辨》一书的出版意义重大。本书在世界范围率先开启了"洛克与中国"研究,不仅推进了中西文化交流史和比较哲学研究,更以具体翔实的个案研究使我们得以重新认识东方与西方的关系,重新确立一种新的文明观。

张西平
2019年7月25日写于游心书屋

目 录

导 论 ··· 1

第一章 "中国笔记"的时代背景 ·· 10
    第一节 启蒙早期的欧洲大陆与英国 ·· 10
    第二节 17—18世纪欧洲"中国热" ·· 12
    第三节 中西初识与"礼仪之争" ·· 15

第二章 "中国笔记"的历史与现状 ·· 23
    第一节 "拉夫雷斯档案"简介 ··· 24
    第二节 洛克"中国笔记"文献概述 ·· 34

第三章 "中国笔记"的文本与要点 ·· 39
    第一节 转写与翻译说明 ·· 39
    第二节 英文转写与中文译稿 ·· 42
    第三节 "中国笔记"要点总结与分析 ·· 162

第四章 "中国笔记"的基础：洛克书信与中国 ·· **171**
    第一节 洛克现存书信简介 ·· 173

　　　　第二节　洛克书信中关于中国的部分 …………………… **173**
　　　　第三节　小结 …………………………………………… **186**

第五章　"中国笔记"的核心：洛克著作与中国 ………………… **190**
　　　　第一节　洛克早期未刊作品与中国 …………………… **190**
　　　　第二节　《人类理解论》与中国 ……………………… **197**
　　　　第三节　小结 …………………………………………… **210**

第六章　"中国笔记"的知识来源：洛克藏书与中国 …………… **211**
　　　　第一节　洛克藏书概述 ………………………………… **211**
　　　　第二节　洛克的中国藏书 ……………………………… **218**
　　　　第三节　小结 …………………………………………… **233**

第七章　"中国笔记"的直接知识来源：《华人礼仪史》 ……… **236**
　　　　第一节　洛克"中国笔记"直接知识来源的认定 …… **236**
　　　　第二节　《华人礼仪史》是一本什么样的书？ ……… **238**
　　　　第三节　小结 …………………………………………… **244**

结　论 ……………………………………………………………… **247**

主要参考文献 ……………………………………………………… **250**

附录1　《游记与旅行丛书》（*Collection of Voyages and Travels*）…… **260**

附录2　约翰发自厦门的信（全文）…………………………… **262**

附录3　"中国笔记"索引所列《华人礼仪史》相关章节拉丁文原文 …… **266**

附录4　"中国笔记"索引所列《华人礼仪史》相关章节的英文译稿 …… **330**

后　记 ……………………………………………………………… **377**

导 论

17—18世纪是中欧文化交流的蜜月期，以来华耶稣会士为主要媒介，中国与西欧的文化互证互识达到前所未有的高度，而无论从规模还是从影响上说，"中学西传"均远远超过"西学东渐"，成为该时期文化交流的主流。中国文化经由利玛窦（Matteo Ricci）、龙华民（Nicolò Longobardoo Longobardi）、卫匡国（Martino Martini）、闵明我（Domingo Fernández Navarrete）等来华传教士之手译介到欧洲，再经过基歇尔（Athanasius Kircher）、杜赫德（Jean Baptiste du Halde）等欧洲知识分子进一步的编织渲染，对欧洲思想，尤其是启蒙运动，产生了深刻的影响。

相较于马勒伯朗士（Nicolas de Malebranche）的《对话》[①]和莱布尼茨（Gottfried Wilhelm Leibniz）的《中国近事：为了照亮我们这个时代的历史》[②]

[①] 全名为《一个基督教哲学家和一个中国哲学家的对话——论上帝的存在和本性》（*Entretien d'un Philosophe chrétien et d'un Philosophe chinoise sur l'existence et la nature de Dieu*），1708年出版。中译本见［法］马勒伯朗士著，庞景仁译：《一个基督教哲学家和一个中国哲学家的对话》，载《中国哲学史研究》1982年第3期。

[②] 拉丁文原名*Novissima Sinica: Historiam nostril temporis illustratura*，1697年出版。中译本见［德］莱布尼茨著，［法］梅谦立、杨保筠译：《中国近事：为了照亮我们这个时代的历史》，郑州：大象出版社，2005年。

《论中国人的自然神学》①等作品②，洛克（John Locke）在公开出版的著作中仅两次明确提到中国③。在17—18世纪欧洲思想家对中国的巨大热情映衬下，洛克一直被认为对中国不感兴趣。美国学者方岚生（Franklin Perkins）就曾质疑："莱布尼茨着迷于中国这一现象让人吃惊并且值得我们关注的理由正在于它与同时代的同行对中国的索然无趣形成了鲜明的对比。……作为'经验论者'的洛克，怎么会对非欧洲世界的经验如此无动于衷？"④

事实上，洛克对所有"非欧洲世界的经验"都兴致盎然、孜孜以求，并且在作品中大量引用关于这些"经验"的游记文学。就中国而言，洛克收藏了大量关于中国的书籍，通过书信多方打听关于中国的资讯，并在《人类理解论》（第四版）中明确表述了对中国人信仰的判断。1702年前后，洛克在悬挂着中国地图的书房中再次回到中国问题，写下了以中国哲学与宗教为核心的专题笔记——"中国笔记"。1704年洛克去世后，包括"中国笔记"在内的洛克手稿先作为私人收藏在金家族世代传承，后于1947年被牛津大学收购并命名"拉夫雷斯档案"。洛克手稿无疑是洛克生平与思想研究的宝藏，一直受到广泛关注。然而"中国笔记"藏于西方，讲述中国，属于中国人看不到、西方人看不懂的文献，因此近三百年来从未引起研究者的注意。

---

① 原名为《致德雷蒙先生的信——论中国的自然神教》（*Lettre à M. de Rémond sur la théologie naturelle des Chinois*），写于1716年。中译本见庞景仁的译文，载《中国哲学史》1981年第3、4期和1982年第1期；又见秦家懿编译：《德国哲学家论中国》，北京：生活·读书·新知三联书店，1993年，第67—134页。
② 莱布尼茨论中国的其他作品参见Daniel J. Cook and Henry Rosemont Jr., *Gottfried Wilhelm Leibniz: Writings on China*. Chicago La Salle: Open Court, 1994。
③ 其一是《人类理解论》第一卷第四章第八节："驻华的传教士们，甚至于耶稣教派的人们，一面虽然十分赞美中国，一面亦异口同声地告我们说：中国底统治阶级——士大夫们——都固守中国的旧教，都是纯粹的无神论者。"（［英］洛克著，关文运译：《人类理解论》（上册），北京：商务印书馆，1959年，第50页）；其二是《政府论》上篇第141节："我恐怕很伟大和文明的民族中国人，以及东西南北四方其他几个民族，他们自己不大会关心这个问题吧。"（［英］洛克著，瞿菊农、叶启芳译：《政府论》（上篇），北京：商务印书馆，1982年，第117页）。
④ ［美］方岚生著，曾小五译，王蓉蓉校：《互照：莱布尼茨与中国》，"前言"，北京：北京大学出版社，2013年，第5页。

在西方思想史领域，洛克研究是非常重要的课题，大家频出，硕果累累，①然而洛克的"中国观"从来不为人知。在中西文化交流史领域，"启蒙时代"欧洲大陆"唯理论"与中国文化的关系备受关注，"莱布尼茨与中国"一直是研究热点，②而由于一手资料的匮乏，同时期英国"经验论"被认为与中国文化没有

---

① 洛克研究的权威著作多出自西方学者尤其是英国学者之手，如洛克传记：Richard I. Aaron, *John Locke*, Oxford: Oxford University Press, 1971; Maurice Cranston, *John Locke: A Biography*, Oxford: Oxford University Press, 1985等。洛克手稿研究：John Locke, Benjamin Rand (ed.), *An Essay Concerning the Understanding, Knowledge, Opinion, and Assent*, Cambridge: Harvard University Press, 1931; John Locke, Richard I. Aaron and Jocelyn Gibb (ed.), *An Early Draft of Locke's Essay Together with Excerpts from His Journals*, Oxford: Clarendon Press, 1936; John Locke, Dr. Wolfgang von Leyden (ed.), *Essays on the Law of Nature*, Oxford: Clarendon Press, 1954。洛克藏书研究：John Harrison and Peter Laslett, *The Library of John Locke*, Oxford: Oxford University Press, 1965。洛克书信研究：John Locke, E. S. de Beer (ed.), *The Correspondence of John Locke* (in eight volumes), Oxford: Clarendon Press, 1976—1989。《人类理解论》版本校勘：John Locke, *An Essay Concerning Human Understanding*, edited with a foreword by Peter H. Nidditch. Oxford: Clarendon Press; New York: Oxford University Press, 1979。洛克思想研究：John W. Yolton (ed.), *John Locke: Problems and Perspectives*, London: Cambridge University Press, 1969; John W. Yolton, *Thinking Matter: materialism in eighteenth-century Britain*, Oxford: Basil Blackwell, 1984; John Locke, *Two Treatises of Government*, edited with an introduction and notes by Peter Laslett, New York: Cambridge University Press, 1988; Leo Strauss, J.A. Colen and Svetozar Minkov (ed.), *Toward Natural Right and History: Lectures and Essays by Leo Strauss, 1937—1946*, Chicago: The University of Chicago Press, 2018; C. B. Macpherson, *The Political Theory of Possessive Individualism: Hobbes to Locke*, Oxford: Oxford University Press, 1962; John Dunn, *The Political Thought of John Locke*, Cambridge University Press, 1969; James Tully, *A Discourse on Property: John Locke and His Adversaries*, Cambridge University Press, 1980等。中国学者的洛克研究虽数量不多，但各个时期也不乏佳作，如吕大吉：《洛克物性理论研究》，北京：中国社会科学出版社，1982年；王楠：《劳动与财产：约翰·洛克思想研究》，上海：上海三联书店，2014年；李季璇：《从权利到权力：洛克自然法思想研究》，南京：江苏人民出版社，2017年；[英]约翰·洛克著，胡景钊译：《论人类的认识》，上海：上海人民出版社，2017年；吴飞主编：《洛克与自由社会》，上海：上海三联书店，2012年等。迄今为止，国内外的洛克研究作品从未提及洛克对中国的理解和认识。

② 在中西文化交流史框架下，洛克"中国观"研究属启蒙时代"中学西传"研究中的"影响史"研究范畴，即17—18世纪中国对欧洲的影响。首先关注这一主题的20世纪20—30年代，陈受颐、方重、钱锺书、范存忠等学者在欧美大学撰写的学位论文以及回国后发表的系列文章，如陈受颐：《十八世纪英国文化中的中国影响》（芝加哥大学博士学位论文，1928年），《十八世纪欧洲文学里的〈赵氏孤儿〉》（《岭南学报》1卷1期，1929年12月），《鲁滨孙的中国文化观》（《岭南学报》1卷3期，1930年9月），《〈好逑传〉之最早的欧译》（《岭南学报》1卷4期，1930年9月），《十八世纪欧洲之中国园林》（《岭南学报》2卷1期，1931年7月）等；方重：《十八世纪英国文学中的中国》（斯坦福大学博士论文，1931年），中文本发表在武汉大学的《文哲季刊》2卷1—2期，（转下页）

（接上页）并收入作者的《英国诗文研究集》（商务印书馆，1939年）；钱锺书：《十七、十八世纪英国文学中的中国》（牛津大学学士论文，1937年），后发表于《中国文献目录学季刊》（*Quarterly Bulletin of Chinese Bibliography*）1940年第1卷和1941年第2卷；范存忠：《中国文化在英国：从威廉·坦普尔到奥列佛·哥尔斯密斯》（哈佛大学哲学博士论文，1931年），后出版为遗作《中国文化在启蒙时期的英国》（上海外语教育出版社，1991），还发表《约翰生，高尔斯密与中国文化》（《金陵学报》1卷2期，1931年），《十七八世纪英国流行的中国戏》（《青年中国季刊》2卷2期，1940年），《十七八世纪英国流行的中国思想》上下篇（《中央大学文史哲季刊》1卷第1—2期，1941年），《〈赵氏孤儿〉杂剧在启蒙时期的英国》（《文学研究》1957年第3期）、《中国的思想文物与哥尔斯密斯的〈世界公民〉》（《南京大学学报》1964年第1期）等文章。（以上文献信息详见葛桂录：《雾外的远音：英国作家与中国文化》，"自序"，福州：福建教育出版社，2015年，第9—11页。）此外，梅光迪、张沅长、周钰良也写过相关的文章；20世纪40年代初，萧乾曾主编涉及中国题材的英文作品集《千弦之琴》（*A Thousand Strings*）。20世纪80年代起，明末清初中西文化交流史的研究在中国再度活跃，呈现蓬勃发展的局面，取得了一大批研究成果。黄一农的《明末清初天主教传华史研究的回顾与展望》（载《新史学》1996年第7卷第1期）、徐松海的《耶稣会士与中西文化交流论著目录》（载黄时鉴主编：《东西交流论谭》第二集，上海文艺出版社，2001年）、许明龙的《中国学界近年来明末清初中西文化交流史研究之管见》（见许明龙：《东传西渐：中西文化交流史散论》，北京：中国社会科学出版社，2015年）分别从译文译著、论文论著、系列丛书、教研队伍的壮大和研究深度的推进等方面对20世纪80年代以来的研究成果进行了文献综述。就"17—18世纪中国对欧洲影响"这一主题，主要成果包括：忻剑飞：《世界的中国观：近二千年来世界对中国的认识史纲》，上海：学林出版社，1991年；忻剑飞：《醒客的中国观：近百多年世界思想大师的中国观感概述》，上海：学林出版社，2013年；许明龙：《孟德斯鸠与中国》，北京：国际文化出版公司，1989年；许明龙：《黄嘉略与早期法国汉学》，北京：中华书局，2004年；许明龙：《欧洲十八世纪中国热》，北京：外语教学与研究出版社，2007年；许明龙：《东传西渐：中西文化交流史散论》，北京：中国社会科学出版社，2015年；李天纲：《中国礼仪之争——历史·文献和意义》，上海：上海古籍出版社，1998年；李天纲：《跨文化的诠释：经学与神学的相遇》，北京：新星出版社，2007年；张西平：《中国与欧洲早期宗教和哲学交流史》，北京：东方出版社，2001年；张西平：《欧洲早期汉学史——中西文化交流与西方汉学的兴起》，北京：中华书局，2009年；张西平主编：《莱布尼茨思想中的中国元素》，郑州：大象出版社，2010年；张西平：《儒学西传欧洲研究导论：16—18世纪中学西传的轨迹与影响》，北京：北京大学出版社，2016年；张西平：《20世纪中国古代文化经典在域外的传播与影响研究导论》，郑州：大象出版社，2018年；张国刚等著：《明清传教士与欧洲汉学》，北京：中国社会科学出版社，2001年；张国刚：《从中西初识到礼仪之争——明清传教士与中西文化交流》，北京：人民出版社，2003年；张国刚、吴莉苇：《启蒙时代欧洲的中国观：一个历史的巡礼与反思》，上海：上海古籍出版社，2006年；吴莉苇：《当诺亚方舟遭遇伏羲神农——启蒙时代欧洲的中国上古史论争》，北京：中国人民大学出版社，2005年；吴莉苇：《中国礼仪之争：文明的张力与权力的较量》，上海：上海古籍出版社，2007年；吴莉苇：《近代早期欧洲人的中国地理观，1500—1800》（博士后报告），历史学：北京大学，2005年；王尔敏编：《中国文献西译书目》，台北：台湾商务印书馆，1975年；朱谦之：《中国哲学对于欧洲的影响》，福州：（转下页）

（接上页）福建人民出版社，1985年；谈敏：《法国重农学派学说的中国渊源》，上海：上海人民出版社，1992年；秦家懿编译：《德国哲学家论中国》，北京：生活·读书·新知三联书店，1993年；孟华：《伏尔泰与孔子》，北京：新华出版社，1993年；韩琦：《中国科学技术的西传及其影响》，石家庄：河北人民出版社，1999年；李文潮、H.波塞尔编，李文潮等译：《莱布尼茨与中国：〈中国近事〉发表300周年国际学术讨论会论文集》，北京：科学出版社，2002年；计翔翔：《十七世纪中期汉学著作研究——以曾德昭〈大中国志〉和安文思〈中国新志〉为中心》，上海：上海古籍出版社，2002年；严建强：《18世纪中国文化在西欧的传播及其反应》，杭州：中国美术学院出版社，2002年；阎宗临：《传教士与法国早期汉学》，郑州：大象出版社，2003年；秦家懿：《秦家懿自选集》，济南：山东教育出版社，2005年；庞景仁著，冯俊译、陈修斋校：《马勒伯朗士的"神"的观念和朱熹的"理"的观念》，北京：商务印书馆，2005年；吴旻、韩琦编校：《欧洲所藏雍正乾隆朝天主教文献汇编》，上海：上海人民出版社，2008年。承接20世纪30年代中英文学关系史路向的包括：张弘：《中国文学在英国》，广州：花城出版社，1992年；葛桂录：《雾外的远音：英国作家与中国文化》，银川：宁夏人民出版社，2002年。英国汉学史路向的包括：熊文华：《英国汉学史》，北京：学苑出版社，2007年；胡优静：《英国19世纪的汉学史研究》，北京：学苑出版社，2009年。文献汇编类的包括：张允熠、陶武、张弛编著：《中国：欧洲的样板——启蒙时期儒学西传欧洲》，合肥：黄山书社，2010年；何兆武、柳卸林主编：《中国印象——外国名人论中国文化》，北京：中国人民大学出版社，2011年等。研究类译著包括：〔德〕利奇温著，朱杰勤译：《十八世纪中国与欧洲文化的接触》，北京：商务印书馆，1962年；〔法〕艾田蒲著，许钧、钱林森译：《中国之欧洲》，郑州：河南人民出版社，1992年；〔英〕G.F.赫德逊著，王遵仲、李申、张毅译，何兆武校：《欧洲与中国》，北京：中华书局，1995年；〔德〕夏瑞春编，陈爱政等译：《德国思想家论中国》，南京：江苏人民出版社，1995年；〔法〕安田朴著，耿昇译：《中国文化西传欧洲史》，北京：商务印书馆，2000年；〔法〕维吉尔·毕诺著，耿昇译：《中国对法国哲学思想形成的影响》，北京：商务印书馆，2000年；〔美〕邓恩著，余三乐、石蓉译：《从利玛窦到汤若望：晚明的耶稣会传教士》，上海：上海古籍出版社，2003年；〔美〕魏若望著，吴莉苇译：《耶稣会士傅圣泽神甫传：索隐派思想在中国及欧洲》，郑州：大象出版社，2006年；〔德〕柯兰霓著，李岩译：《耶稣会士白晋的生平与著作》，郑州：大象出版社，2009年；〔美〕J.J.克拉克著，于闽梅、曾祥波译：《东方启蒙：东西方思想的遭遇》，上海：上海人民出版社，2011年；〔法〕谢和耐、戴密微等著，耿昇译：《明清间耶稣会士入华与中西汇通》，北京：东方出版社，2011年；〔美〕方岚生著，曾小五译、王蓉蓉校：《互照：莱布尼茨与中国》，北京：北京大学出版社，2013年；〔法〕谢和耐著，耿昇译：《中国与基督教：中西文化的首次撞击》，北京：商务印书馆，2013年；〔美〕唐纳德·F.拉赫著，刘绯等译：《欧洲形成中的亚洲第二卷·奇迹的世纪》，北京：人民出版社，2013年；〔美〕唐纳德·F.拉赫、〔美〕埃德温·J.范·克雷著，许玉军译：《欧洲形成中的亚洲第三卷·发展的世纪》，北京：人民出版社，2013年；〔法〕蓝莉著，许明龙译：《请中国作证：杜赫德的〈中华帝国全志〉》，北京：商务印书馆，2015年；〔美〕孟德卫著，张学智译：《莱布尼兹和儒学》，南京：江苏人民出版社，1998年；〔美〕孟德卫著，江文君、姚霏译：《1500—1800：中西方的伟大相遇》，北京：新星出版社，2007年；〔美〕孟德卫著，潘琳译：《灵与肉：山东的天主教，1650—1785》，郑州：大象出版社，2009年；〔美〕孟德卫著，陈怡译：《奇异的国度：耶稣会适应政策及汉学的起源》，郑州：大象出版社，（转下页）

关系。

2010年，英国学者安·泰尔博特（Ann Talbot）女士[①]出版《"知识之汪洋"：游记文学对约翰·洛克著作的影响》[②]，系统梳理了洛克著作中对游记文学的使用，并尝试分析游记文学对洛克思想发展的影响。洛克收藏的游记文学内容涉及世界各地，而洛克著作中提到的游记文学大部分是关于非洲和美洲新大陆的，中国游记所占比例很小，因而中国并非该书的重点。该书共15章，其中第10章名为"'一个伟大而文明的民族'：洛克、中国和唯物论"（"A Great and Civilized People": Locke, China and Materialism），主要讨论《人类理解论》中论及的"无神论社会"与远东游记之间的关系，重点介绍了三本暹罗游记和两本关于中国的书，即《中华帝国历史、政治、伦理及宗教概述》（*Tratados historicos, politicos, ethicos y religiosos de la monarchia de China*, 1676）和《华人

（接上页）2010年等。原始文献类译著包括：［意］利玛窦、［比］金尼阁著，何高济、王遵仲、李申译，何兆武校：《利玛窦中国札记》，北京：中华书局，1983年；［法］戈岱司编，耿昇译：《希腊拉丁作家远东古文献辑录》，北京：中华书局，1987年；［法］尼古拉·马勒伯朗士等著，陈乐民试译并序：《有关神的存在和性质的对话》，北京：生活·读书·新知三联书店，1998年；［葡］曾德昭著，何高济译：《大中国志》，上海：上海古籍出版社，1998年；［法］李明著，郭强、龙云、李伟译：《中国近事报道（1687—1692）》，郑州：大象出版社，2004年；［美］苏尔、诺尔编，沈保义、顾卫民、朱静译，《中国礼仪之争西文文献一百篇（1645—1941）》，上海：上海古籍出版社，2001年；［捷克］严嘉乐著，丛林、李梅译：《中国来信（1716—1735）》，郑州：大象出版社，2002年；［法］杜赫德编，郑德弟、朱静等译：《耶稣会士中国书简集：中国回忆录》，郑州：大象出版社，2001—2005年；［德］莱布尼茨著，［法］梅谦立、杨保筠译：《中国近事：为了照亮我们这个时代的历史》，郑州：大象出版社，2005年；［葡］安文思著，何高济、李申译：《中国新史》，郑州：大象出版社，2016年；［比］高华士著，赵殿红译：《清初耶稣会士鲁日满常熟账本及灵修笔记研究》，郑州：大象出版社，2007年；［西］帕莱福、［比］鲁日满、［意］卫匡国著，何高济译：《鞑靼征服中国史·鞑靼中国史·鞑靼战纪》，北京：中华书局，2008年；［西］闵明我著，何高济、吴翊楣译，《上帝许给的土地：闵明我行记和礼仪之争》，郑州：大象出版社，2009年；［德］阿塔纳修斯·基歇尔著，张西平、杨慧玲、孟宪谟译：《中国图说》，郑州：大象出版社，2010年；［西］门多萨撰，何高济译：《中华大帝国史》，北京：中华书局，2013年等。到目前为止，国内外中西文化交流史的成果中均未提及洛克的"中国观"。

[①] 安·泰尔博特，英国学者。1978年毕业于英国曼彻斯特大学，2008年获得英国波尔顿大学（University of Bolton）授予的哲学博士学位，主要从事启蒙时代欧洲哲学和拉丁文、法文和英文等古代手稿研究。

[②] Ann Talbot, *"The Great Ocean of Knowledge": The Influence of Travel Literature on the Work of John Locke*, Leiden: Brill, 2010.

礼仪史》（*Historia Cultus Sinensium*）。

由于"中国"并非该书的研究重点，加上该书成文时作者刚刚发现"中国笔记"，对其内容并不熟悉，因而该书对"中国笔记"的介绍异常简略。同时，由于作者对于中国材料不熟悉，论及洛克与中国的关系时虽面面俱到，但总是匆匆带过，并未深入展开。具体来说，该书对"中国笔记"的文献情况介绍仅用了约230字的一小节，与博得礼图书馆菲利普·郎（Philip Long）所编的《拉夫雷斯档案总目》①相比，这段介绍只是增加了"中国笔记"的小标题。而对于"中国笔记"的知识来源，作者当时还无法确定："我们并不清楚洛克的（中国）笔记源自何处，有可能是《华人礼仪史》这本书，因为洛克在这本书里用铅笔列出了一个页码表。"②另外，作者原计划将"中国笔记"的转写稿作为附录出版，但由于笔迹辨认的困难，加上作者对笔记中所涉中国内容不熟悉，到该书出版时，作者只粗略转写了洛克"中国笔记"的部分内容，达不到出版要求，只得放弃转写，转而在第10章正文中对手稿内容作了少量引用。

《"知识之汪洋"：游记文学对约翰·洛克著作的影响》对本研究的价值主要体现在两个方面：（1）首次指出洛克"中国笔记"的存在并对其进行了简要介绍和初步分析；（2）除"中国笔记"之外，还指出了洛克与中国关系的很多有益线索，比如洛克曾在书信中提及中国、洛克收藏的两本关于中国的书籍、洛克"中国观"的背景和特点等。本研究开始之初就是循着该书中提到的各种线索逐步展开的。

本书以洛克"中国笔记"手稿为核心内容，试图追问与解答两个根本问题：（1）洛克"中国笔记"是什么？（2）洛克"中国笔记"从哪里来？为回答第一个问题，本书遵循西方"语文学"传统梳理文献来源与现状，并对手稿进行辩读、转写、翻译、注释和整理，完整、准确地呈现"中国笔记"这一全新史料。为回答第二个问题，本书对"中国笔记"追本溯源，一方面梳理其时代背景，一方面整理其认识基础和知识来源，力图将"中国笔记"放在中西文化交流史的历史文化语境中，系统梳理洛克的"中国观"。

---

① P. Long, *A Summary Catalogue of the Lovelace Collection of the Papers of John Locke in the Bodleian Library*, Oxford University Press, 1959.

② 原文：It is not clear where Locke took these notes from; it was possibly the Historia Cultus Sinensium in which he penciled a list of page numbers. 见Ann Talbot, *"The Great Ocean of Knowledge": The Influence of Travel Literature on the Work of John Locke*, Leiden: Brill, 2010, p. 190。

本书分为七章、四大部分：**第一部分**是洛克"中国笔记"的时代背景研究，从"启蒙时代"、欧洲"中国热"和"礼仪之争"三个角度介绍洛克"中国观"产生的历史文化语境（第一章）；**第二部分**是洛克"中国笔记"的手稿研究，分别从文献来历、档案现状、手稿转写和翻译、文本要点总结与分析几个角度对"中国笔记"这一全新史料进行全面系统的呈现（第二、三章），是全书的重点；**第三部分**是"中国笔记"的认识基础研究，分别从洛克书信和洛克著作两个方面梳理洛克在写"中国笔记"以前对中国的认识与理解（第四、五章）；**第四部分**是"中国笔记"的知识来源研究，其中洛克藏书（第六章）是洛克"中国观"的主要知识来源，《华人礼仪史》（第七章）是洛克"中国笔记"的直接知识来源。

严格来讲，本研究属于交叉学科的综合性研究。首先，在文献学层面，"中国笔记"是启蒙早期英国思想家洛克亲笔手书的读书笔记，因此本研究属于"西方文献学"中"语文学"路向的稿本研究。[①]本研究的首要任务是对这份洛克书写于17—18世纪之交的手稿进行整理、辩读、转写、翻译、注释，分别整理出完整的英文转写稿和中文翻译稿，将这份古代手稿的文本全貌呈现在世界面前。其次，在中西文化交流史层面，"中国笔记"是"中学西传"过程中，英国早期启蒙思想家接受中国文化的典型个案。本研究遵循比较文学"影响研究"的路数，在洛克的著作和书信中反复梳扒，逐步摸清洛克与中国的事实联系，即洛克关于中国的知识是从哪里来的。最后，在西方思想史层面，"中国笔记"是中国文化影响启蒙思想的力证，也是洛克思想发展的特殊一环。本研究将"中国笔记"放在启蒙思想和洛克思想发展的时代背景中，追溯与挖掘"中国笔记"与《人类理解论》（第四版）以及洛克与伍斯特主教论战的关系，客观评价中国对洛克思想的影响。总之，本书以洛克"中国笔记"的稿本为核心，以欧洲思想史为背景，

---

① 《中国大百科全书》对"文献学"的定义为："以文献和文献发展规律为研究对象的一门学科。"套用这一定义，我们将西方类似的研究称为"西方文献学"。鉴于中西不同的学术传统和学科分类，"西方文献学"的研究内容与研究方法与中国的文献学有较大的差别，主要的研究路向包括古文书学（diplomatics）、语文学（philology）、书籍学（bibliography）、当代文献整理（documentation）等。而手稿研究（codicology）又分为稿本（autograph，作者亲笔书写的手稿）和抄本（manuscript，他人传抄的手稿）两类。参见何朝晖、李萍：《西方文献学的概念和理论体系及其启示》，载《大学图书馆学报》2012年03期；张强：《西方古典文献学的名与实》，载《史学史研究》，2012年第2期。

以17—18世纪中西文化交流中的"中学西传"为主线,力图将洛克"中国笔记"放在欧洲的时代背景和知识变迁之中进行研究,兼顾历史性和哲学性。

　　需要说明的是,洛克"中国笔记"研究属从无到有的开创性研究,需要逐步从大量的外文文献中挖掘和提取相关的材料,同时这些外文文献大都没有中文译本,需要逐条翻译整理,很难凭一人之力在短时间内完成。另外,我的主要学科背景为英语语言文学,在海外汉学研究领域实属新人,对本课题中涉及的很多问题还在逐渐学习和加深理解的过程当中。受时间和能力所限,我在成文的过程中对研究范围和研究深度都进行了限定。首先,本书以洛克"中国笔记"的文本研究为核心内容,"启蒙时代"、欧洲"中国热"、"礼仪之争"等中西文化交流史和欧洲思想史当中的重大问题只作为时代背景出现,不展开讨论。其次,本书的主题为洛克"中国观"研究,主要围绕"中国笔记"手稿、著作和书信梳理洛克"中国观"形成和发展的过程,暂不深入讨论与洛克哲学的关系。即便如此,本研究与中西文化交流史和欧洲思想史的数个大题目紧密联系,横跨几个学科,又涉及众多全新材料和专门知识,这使得我在研究的过程中一直惴惴不安,唯恐贻笑大方。迫于时日,只得倾尽全力,放手一搏,惟愿以翔实的一手资料和扎实的个案研究全面呈现洛克的"中国观",补充和修正现有的研究结论,推动洛克思想研究和17—18世纪中西文化交流史研究的发展。

第一章 "中国笔记"的时代背景

中西文化交流史可分为"西学东渐"和"东学西传"两个方向,同时每个方向又分为"传播史"和"影响史"两个研究路向,而后者从学科分类上讲已经进入对象国思想史的范畴,洛克"中国观"研究即是如此。洛克在构建自己的哲学体系时使用了来自中国的材料,并依据"礼仪之争"的文献亲笔写下关于中国宗教的读书摘要——"中国笔记",因而从中西文化交流史的角度讲,洛克"中国观"是17—18世纪"礼仪之争"背景下启蒙思想家对中国文化接受史的一部分;而从欧洲思想史的角度讲,洛克"中国观"又是17世纪后半叶英国早期启蒙思想的一部分。因而,本章主要从"启蒙时代"、欧洲"中国热"和"礼仪之争"三个方面简要介绍洛克"中国观"的时代背景。

第一节 启蒙早期的欧洲大陆与英国

与其他"时代""主义""学派"一样,"启蒙时代"也是后人对欧洲思想史中一段特定时期的概括命名。《劳特利奇哲学史》第五卷《英国哲学和启蒙时代》说:"启蒙时期通常指17世纪后期至18世纪的大部分时期。'启蒙'这一术语直到19世纪才开始流行，之后关于启蒙运动，诞生了大量文献。"① 我们通常将欧洲思想史17世纪中期到18世纪末期的这段时间称为"启蒙时代"，而教权衰落和理性兴起是这个时代最明显的特征。

"启蒙时代"早期，一方面全欧洲陷入宗教紧张：15—16世纪的宗教改革造成教派林立的局面；到了17世纪，教派分裂带来的教派差异和神学上的正统之争格外突出，前者导致教派间纷争迫害不断，后者则导致神学问题的绝对主导地位；1648年，"三十年战争"结束，留下一个惨遭破坏的德意志诸侯国，信奉天主教的法国成为欧洲大陆的主要力量，似乎准备入侵新教国家荷兰。另一方面欧洲知识界正在发生变化：1632年伽利略发表关于地心说的评论；1637年笛卡尔发表了《方法论》；中世纪的经院哲学正被牛顿、波义耳等发起的新科学所取代。

英国的启蒙运动发生于切尔伯里的赫伯特②（Herbert of Cherbury）和剑桥柏拉图主义者③之前，有时也将1688年光荣革命作为它的起点。光荣革命之前，高教会派④一直处于统治地位，书刊审查制度盛行，宗教没有多样性。光荣革命之后，自由派的影响加强了，在洛克的积极推动下，1695年英国废除了审查法，并且从未复辟，这确保了完全的出版自由。"自然神论""物质论"等思潮率先在英国兴盛就部分得益于英国的出版自由，这是英国在启蒙运动早期所做的突出贡献之一。1689年英国出台《容忍法案》，规定除了天主教徒和神格惟一论派

---

① 书中列出有代表性的关于启蒙时代的作品有：诺曼·汉森（Norman Hanson）的 *The Enlightenment* (London: Penguin, 1968)、彼得·盖伊（Peter Gay）的 *The Enlightenment: An Interpretation*, 2 vols (New York: Knopt, 1966,1969)、约翰·W. 约尔顿（John W. Yolton）等编的 *The Blackwell Companion to the Enlightenment* (Oxford: Blackwell, 1991)等。参见［英］斯图亚特·布朗（Stuart Brown）主编，高新民等译，《英国哲学和启蒙时代》，"导言"，北京：中国人民大学出版社，2009年，第2—21页。
② 切尔伯里的赫伯特（1582—1648）著有《论真理》(*De veritate*, 1624)和《论世俗宗教》(*De religione laici*, 1645)，他提出宗教的共有信念主要有：存在着神，神应予崇拜，美德和仁慈是崇拜的主要组成部分，我们应该忏悔自己的罪孽，末世将受惩罚或报偿。
③ 指17世纪上半叶在剑桥大学接受教育，在神学上有自由倾向的一群哲学神学家。
④ 17世纪英国的三大基督教派别为天主教、英格兰国教（即圣公会，Church of England）和清教（加尔文教），其中圣公会的保守派被称为"高教会派"（High Church），在教义、崇拜礼仪和教会的规章制度等方面强调保持天主教的传统和维护教会的权威；开明派被称为"低教会派"（Low Church），强调信仰《圣经》、个人的悔改得救和道德修行，主张简化崇拜仪式，着重新教体制，贬低天主教的传统和教会的权威。

（Monarchians）的信徒外，所有基督教徒都享有宗教自由，这等于以法律的形式确立了宽容精神的地位，这是英国为启蒙运动所做的另一个突出贡献。正是由于这两点，英国被认为是"启蒙运动"的发源地。作为"光荣革命"圣徒的洛克则以"经验论"和"宗教宽容说"正式拉开了"启蒙时代"的大幕。

第二节 17—18世纪欧洲"中国热"

与"启蒙时代"一样，"中国热"的高潮一般被认为发生在18世纪的法国。许明龙先生在《欧洲十八世纪中国热》中说："18世纪欧洲'中国热'的主要内容是中国文化西传和欧洲人对于中国文化的接受，我们不妨称之为东学西传。"[①] 许先生所说的欧洲"中国热"既包括东学西传的传播史，又包括东学西传的接受史，但实际研究中，受篇幅和学力所限，我们通常在"礼仪之争"的题目下更关注传播史，在欧洲"中国热"的题目下更关注接受史，两者共同构成17、18世纪东学西传的完整图景。许先生还将欧洲"中国热"分为"俗"和"雅"两个层次："所谓俗，是指下至市井细民、上至王公贵族对中国所表现的狂热，这种狂热或为好奇心所驱使，或出于对异国情调的追逐，较多表现为购买中国商品，收藏中国器物，了解有关中国的奇闻趣事，模仿中国人的建筑、园林、装饰和衣着等等。一般地说，俗层次对中国的兴趣偏重物态文化，……并未给欧洲留下多少深刻的印记，……所谓雅，是指学者、思想家等知识分子对中国所表现的巨大兴趣、关注和研究。雅层次的'中国热'主要表现为对中国文化的理性思考，除了对中国本身作比较深刻的分析研究之外，还将中国作为参照物探讨欧洲的诸多问题，从而显现了中国文化对于欧洲思想的影响。不过，俗与雅两个层次的'中国热'虽然有区别，却并不各自独立，应该说它们是同一大潮中的两股支流，前者引发了后者，后者深化了前者。"[②] 当然，同一个人也可能表现出"俗"与"雅"两方面的"中国热"。以洛克为例，洛克早期作品如《两篇政府短论》和《自然法论文集》中对中国的关注可以归为"了解有关中国的奇闻趣事"的"俗"的层次；而思想成熟时的《人类理解论》（第四版）中对中国的关

---

① 许明龙：《欧洲十八世纪中国热》，"前言"，北京：外语教学与研究出版社，2007年，第2页。
② 同上。

注和晚年的"中国笔记"则表现了对中国宗教的理性思考,属于"雅"的层次。

在"雅"的层次,17、18世纪的启蒙思想家们将中国文化与抗拒宗教愚昧和皇权专制结合起来,从而形成了一股欧洲知识界的"中国热"。①如前文所述,"礼仪之争"为欧洲思想界提供了关于中国的大量素材,中国在启蒙时代的欧洲成了不可不谈的时髦话题,启蒙思想家们积极地了解和评说中国文化,有的甚至直接参与到"礼仪之争"当中(如莱布尼茨和马勒伯朗士)。从对中国文化的态度来看,启蒙思想家对中国文化的态度基本分为三类:(1)通过比较认同中国文化,以培尔、莱布尼茨、伏尔泰为代表;(2)通过比较批评中国文化,以马勒伯朗士、休谟、维科、孟德斯鸠为代表;(3)综合上述两种态度理性批判和评估中国文化,以狄德罗、魁奈为代表。②从研究主题来看,当时欧洲学界关于中国的讨论主要围绕三个热点问题:(1)天赋观念问题——中国人是不是无神论者?(2)原初语言问题——中国文字是不是原初语言?(3)人类早期历史纪年问题——中国上古史记载是否可信?③

基于论题,我更加关注17—18世纪英国的"中国热"及其特殊性。相较于其他欧洲国家,17世纪的英国是一个早熟的文明,完成了宗教改革后不久,又成功地进行了社会革命,率先走上资本主义道路。在中西文化交流史领域,英国知识界的"中国热"主要集中于17世纪,到18世纪已提前降温,呈现了与整个欧洲"中国热"相区别的独特面貌。正如钱锺书先生在《十七、十八世纪英国文学中

---

① 关于启蒙时代欧洲"中国热"的具体情况参见[德]利奇温著,朱杰勤译:《十八世纪中国与欧洲文化的接触》,北京:商务印书馆,1962年;忻剑飞:《世界的中国观:近二千年来世界对中国的认识史纲》,上海:学林出版社,1991年;[法]维吉尔·毕诺著,耿昇译:《中国对法国哲学思想形成的影响》,北京:商务印书馆,2000年;朱谦之:《中国哲学对欧洲的影响》,上海:上海人民出版社,2006年;张国刚、吴莉苇:《启蒙时代欧洲的中国观:一个历史的巡礼与反思》,上海:上海古籍出版社,2006年;许明龙:《欧洲十八世纪中国热》,北京:外语教学与研究出版社,2007年;[法]艾田蒲著,许钧、钱林森译:《中国之欧洲》,桂林:广西师范大学出版社,2008年;忻剑飞:《醒客的中国观:近百多年世界思想大师的中国观感概述》,上海:学林出版社,2013年。
② 参见薛其林:《17—18世纪欧洲学者的中国文化观》,《湘潭师范学院学报》第21卷第五期,2000年9月。
③ 关于这三个问题的讨论参见张国刚、吴莉苇:《启蒙时代欧洲的中国观:一个历史的巡礼与反思》,上海:上海古籍出版社,2006年,第13—177页。

的中国》中所说："人们常说18世纪的英国存在'中国热'。但如果我们的研究正确的话，真正对中国表现出高度热情的是17世纪的英国。在我们接下来要谈的18世纪英国文学中，中国完全失去了所有荣光。中国形象也许依然'神秘'，但绝对不再'辉煌'。曾在17世纪为儒家赢得赞誉的自由形式'极精微的思想'，在18世纪被批评为形而上学和神学的浅薄。甚至是曾如此吸引17世纪作家的中国文化的古老，在18世纪作家的眼中也贬值了。而17世纪'原初语言'的追寻者曾如此钟爱的中国历史与语言的稳定性，在18世纪的哲学家眼中也成了停滞不前的象征。"① 值得注意的是，钱先生所说的"中国热"指的是对中国文化的"热情"或"崇拜"，侧重的是异质文化对中国文化的评价。而我们在中西文化交流史中所说的"中国热"通常包括"呈现"和"评价"两个部分："呈现"侧重传播，即传播大量关于中国文化的信息以呈现某种中国形象；"评价"侧重接受或影响，即异质文明对中国文化的认知和态度。从这个意义上说，17世纪英国对中国文化的呈现和评价大都是积极的。而到了18世纪，呈现依然是丰富而积极的，但评价逐渐降低，英国学者对中国文化的态度从"推崇痴迷"转为"批评嘲讽"，因而说英国的"中国热"主要集中于17世纪，到了18世纪就提前降温了。

钱先生接着又指出英国"中国热"提前降温的两个矛盾之处：其一，"18世纪英国文学中流露的对中国的态度与生活中正相反。矛盾的是，英国生活中

---

① 原文：It has often been said that England in the eighteenth century was Sinomaniac. But if our survey is correct, it is England in the seventeenth century which showed high admiration for the Chinese. In eighteenth century English literature, as we shall have occasion to show, China is virtually stripped of all her glories. She may be still *ignota* [Latin: unknown] but she is certainly no longer *pro magnificâ*. The very freedom form "oversubtle thoughts" which had won praise for Confucianism in the seventeenth century was in the eighteenth criticized as mere shallowness in metaphysics and theology. Even the antiquity of Chinese civilization which had so attracted seventeenth century writers was discredited by eighteenth century ones. The absence of changes in Chinese history and language which had so endeared China to seventeenth century hunters of the "primitive tongue" was singled out by eighteenth century philosophers for condemnation as a sign of unprogressiveness. 见钱锺书：《钱锺书英文文集》，北京：外语教学与研究出版社，2005年，第129—130页。

中国热正在升温的同时，英国文学中的中国热已经降温"①。这里钱先生说的是"雅"与"俗"的矛盾，18世纪"中国热"在"俗"的层次依然在升温，而在"雅"的层次已经降温了。其二，"在东方学研究方面，英国人一直落后于法国人。……但（法国人）对中华文明的熟悉并没有产生不屑；正相反，法国对中国的推崇在18世纪达到高潮"②。这里钱先生讲的是英国与法国对中国文化态度的矛盾，相比之下，法国人对中国文化更为了解，不仅没有因为了解而鄙视，反而愈加推崇；英国人对中国文化的了解不及法国人，却先于法国人批评中国文化。

究其原因，钱先生认为："这样的矛盾情况只是审美趣味转变之吊诡的有一个例子，同时也是概括时代精神时不可避免的个例。"③换言之，钱先生将英国"中国热"的提前降温归结为偶然和个例。事实上，任何偶然和个例也都有其必然性和规律，英国"中国热"的提前降温与英国特殊的地理位置、民族特性以及当时的政治经济环境都有关系。总的说来，17世纪资产阶级政治革命率先在英国发生，专制制度的废除和生产力的发展使得启蒙时期的英国对自身文化的自信心更强，虽然热衷于利用中国来批判本国的政治，但对中国文化本身更加挑剔，加上英国人孤立、现实的民族特性，英国的"中国热"比欧洲大陆更早降温就不让人惊讶了。关于英国"中国热"的特殊性值得专文研究，此处不进一步展开。

第三节　中西初识与"礼仪之争"

欧洲关于中国的历史记忆主要有两个线索：其一是希罗多德的《历史》及希

---

① 原文：As a matter of fact, the eighteenth-century English attitude towards China as revealed in literature is the reverse of that as revealed in life. Paradoxically enough, sinophilism seems to have waned in English literature as it waxed in English life。见钱锺书：《钱锺书英文文集》，北京：外语教学与研究出版社，2005年，第142页。

② 原文：In oriental studies the English have always lagged behind the French. ... But this familiarity with Chinese civilization did not breed any contempt among the French at all; on the contrary, their admiration for China became excessive in the eighteenth century。见钱锺书：《钱锺书英文文集》，北京：外语教学与研究出版社，2005年，第142—143页。

③ 原文：This discrepancy is only another example of that inscrutability of the whirligig of taste, and the inevitable loose-jointedness in generalizations about the spirit of the age。见钱锺书：《钱锺书英文文集》，北京：外语教学与研究出版社，2005年，第143页。

腊罗马时代的诗文对希伯波里安人的记载；其二是拉普林尼的《自然史》等作品对丝国（Seres）和赛里斯人的介绍。然而12世纪以前的中西交往主要是中国与亚洲其他国家间的交往，受交通所限，欧洲与中国的直接往来非常罕见。尽管如此，从中世纪开始，受为上帝服务和寻求黄金的驱动，欧洲人一直怀着一个"中国梦"，努力寻求前往东方的途径。随着蒙古人西征，13—14世纪的欧洲的旅行家、商人、使节、传教士开始通过西亚的陆路来到中国，并留下了一批关于蒙古和中国的旅行报告，如柏朗嘉宾（Jean de Plan Carpin）的《蒙古史》（*Histoire des Mongols*）、《鲁布鲁克东行记》（*The Journey of William of Rubruk to the Eastern Parts, 1253—1255*）、《海屯行记》（*The Journey of Het'nm I, King of Little Armenia, Central Asiatic Journal*）、孟高维诺（Giovanni da Montecorvino）等来华传教士的书信、《鄂多立克东游记》（*The Eastern Parts of the World*）、《马黎诺里游记》（*Der Reisebericht des Johannes Marignolla*）以及影响最大的《马可波罗游记》等。① 这些旅行报告虽然对欧洲民众影响不大，但却给知识阶层留下了深刻的印象。然而随着蒙古大帝国的瓦解，通往中国的陆路中断，欧洲人的"中国梦"再次破灭。随着大航海时代的到来，欧洲人实现"中国梦"的脚步大大加快了。16世纪，越来越多的欧洲人通过海路来到中国，中西文化交流史进入相对长期而稳定的"启蒙时期"。这个时期，欧洲人"中国梦"的动力依然是传教和经商，然而以耶稣会士为代表的天主教传教士是这一时期中西文化交流的主角，是欧洲中国知识的最主要来源。

15—16世纪的欧洲，与地理大发现并举的是宗教改革。1545—1563年特兰托会议的重要举措之一就是鼓励成立新修会。中世纪的隐修会以脱离尘世为目标，新修会则倾向于在俗世中旅行宗教义务。在这些新修会中，耶稣会无疑是最显眼的。正式成立于1540年的耶稣会在欧洲教育事业中占据半壁江山，在海外传教事业中则一度独领风骚。耶稣会的宗旨和方针在很多方面与传统修会有显著不同，然而对其海外传教事业帮助最大的是其创始人罗耀拉（Ignatius Loyola, 1491—1556）制定的两大原则：（1）走上层路线，即与主流社会保持良好的关系；

---

① 详见张西平：《欧洲早期汉学史——中西文化交流与西方汉学的兴起》，北京：中华书局，2009年，第8—32页。

（2）实行以学习传教地区的语言和风俗为必要条件的灵活传教方法。利玛窦的"适应政策"就是这两大原则的深化和具体化。

利玛窦的"适应政策"（又称"利玛窦规矩"）是秉承耶稣会的传统，同时结合中国文化的实际，以利玛窦为代表的在华耶稣会士所指定的创造性的传教路线，其目标是将基督教与中国文化相融合而建立一种"中国—基督教"式的综合体，实施的策略是"合儒易佛"和"是古非今"。基于对中国政治形势和文化内涵的判断，利玛窦选择了中国文化中的儒学作为与基督教融合的要素，同时批评佛教（以及道教），即所谓的"合儒易佛"；利玛窦又将儒学人为地分为"古儒"和"近儒"，声称从古代儒家经典中找到了"上帝"的论述，从而认为中国远古文化和基督教文化有相近性，同时将程朱理学作为无神论加以批判，认为当时盛行的理学是对古代儒学的背叛和歪曲，即所谓的"是古非今"。利玛窦主要通过四个方面的适应来贯彻这样的"适应政策"：（1）生活方面，儒服乘轿；（2）术语方面，用中国古籍中的"上帝"和"天"指代"God"；（3）伦理方面，以儒家的道德概念解释基督教伦理；（4）礼仪方面，将祭祖祭孔解释为政治性和社会性行为而允许执行。这四个方面使得耶稣会士成功地实现了"本土化"，然而实行起来，争议最少的是第一点，争议最多的是第四点，而最关键和最难处理的是第二点。① "适应政策"在中国发展得空前精致和有规模，也使得在华传教事业获得空前的成功，成为在华耶稣会的标志，然而围绕术语和礼仪问题的"礼仪之争"又最终导致耶稣会被解散。可以说，在华耶稣会兴于"适应政策"也败于"适应政策"。

以今天的眼光来看，"适应政策"成于对中国文化的尊重态度和灵活实用的传教策略；败于文化适应与文化本位主义之间的对立。利玛窦力图构筑的"中国—基督教"文明理想是以对基督教的潜移默化性的充分信任为依据的，是一个相当漫长的渐变过程。然而其他修会和罗马教廷显然没有利玛窦的耐心，因为他们已经意识到"适应政策"对于基督教教义的危险性。正如张国刚先生所说："他（利玛窦）的思维已经从有限度的文化适应跃迁到文化创造的程度，这对文

---

① 参见张国刚：《从中西初识到礼仪之争——明清传教士与中西文化交流》，北京：人民出版社，2003年，第363页。

明的发展与丰富而言自然是有益的，但对基督教本身来说却是危险的。这种'本土化'一步步开展到最后如果真的产生一种'中国—基督教'式的综合体，那它所代表的是基督教归化中国，还是中国归化基督教？"① 利玛窦试图在中国这样一个遥远而强大的东方国家创造一种全新的文明"共同体"，这已经突破了罗马教廷所能容忍的文化适应的限度，甚至颇有些自立为王的倾向，势必不为教廷所容。

耶稣会士对此并非毫无察觉，相反，在华耶稣会士抓紧一切机会向罗马教廷和欧洲公众宣传自己的传教成绩并为"适应政策"辩护。耶稣会士自16世纪末进入中国以来，经过多年的渗透经营，从17世纪开始，尤其是17世纪中叶以后，耶稣会士翻译中国经典，著书立说介绍中国文化，向欧洲输入了大量传教报告和介绍中国文化的公开出版物，苦心孤诣地向欧洲公众灌输一个"国强民富、道德高尚、实行开明君主制、国民信奉一种接近自然神论的宗教"的中国形象。② 17世纪比较典型的作品有庞迪我（Diego de Pantoja）的《一些耶稣会士进入中国的纪实》（1605）、金尼阁（Nicolas Trigault）编辑出版的利玛窦遗著《基督教远征中国史》（1615）、曾德昭（Alvaro Semedo）的《大中国志》（1642）、安文思（Gabriel de Magalhāes）的《中国新志》（1688）；卫匡国（Martino Martini）的《鞑靼战纪》（1654）、《中国新地图集》（1655）、《中国上古史》（1658）；柏应理（Philippe Couplet）的《中国帝王年表》（1686）和《中国哲学家孔子》（1687）、李明（Louis le Comte）的《中国现势新志》（1696）、白晋（Joachim Bouvet）的《中国皇帝历史画像》（1697）以及郭弼恩（Père Le Gobien）编辑出版的《耶稣会士通信集》（1702—1776）③等。④ 这

---

① 张国刚：《从中西初识到礼仪之争——明清传教士与中西文化交流》，北京：人民出版社，2003年，第361页。
② 吴莉苇：《当诺亚方舟遭遇伏羲神农——启蒙时代欧洲的中国上古史论争》，北京：中国人民大学出版社，2005年，第72页。
③ 巴黎耶稣会总会长郭弼恩创办的《通信集》是欧洲旅居中国和东印度传教士们的书信和报告集，1702至1776年共刊出34卷，其中16—26卷收载来自中国寄来的信。1843年在巴黎恢复出版，名为《耶稣会士中国通信集1689—1781年》。
④ 参见吴莉苇：《当诺亚方舟遭遇伏羲神农——启蒙时代欧洲的中国上古史论争》，北京：中国人民大学出版社，2005年，第73—75页。

些作品的首要目的就是引起人们对传教工作的兴趣并博得支持和同情，而它们也的确引起了公众的巨大兴趣。这些书大部分是当时欧洲的畅销书，社会影响力很大，同时也是当时主流学者的案头之作，我们在洛克藏书中就能看到它们的身影。

随着其他修会进入中国并积极地向欧洲输送关于中国的知识，耶稣会士对欧洲中国知识的垄断地位逐渐被打破。而耶稣会创立之初就定下的信检制度使得耶稣会读物具有高度一致性，这与17—18世纪之交"礼仪之争"的巨大纷争形成强烈反差，最初的朴实真挚如今成了矫揉造作，耶稣会士出版物的可信度开始受到质疑。

正如张国刚先生所说："礼仪之争是这时期中西文化交流的巨大背景墙，……是理解这一段中西文化交流史的核心所在，……它影响了耶稣会士叙述中国时的态度，也影响了耶稣会士向欧洲介绍中国文献时的选择，进而又影响了欧洲本土对中国文化的认识。"① 接下来，要回顾一下"礼仪之争"的内容、过程和性质。

"礼仪之争"（Chinese Rites Controversy）是中西文化交流史和天主教中国传教史上的重大事件，特指17世纪中叶到18世纪中叶天主教关于"天主"译名和中国礼仪习俗的一场争论。争论的焦点主要在于：（1）能否用中国典籍中的"天"和"上帝"来称呼天主教的"天主"；（2）能否允许中国天主教徒参加祭祖祭孔仪式。争论最先开始于天主教传教士内部，后扩展到罗马教廷与在华传教士之间，最终导致罗马教廷与中国皇帝之间的冲突和决裂。

以罗马教廷的政策转向作为划分依据，可以把礼仪之争分为四个阶段②：

---

① 张国刚：《从中西初识到礼仪之争——明清传教士与中西文化交流》，北京：人民出版社，2003年，第344页。
② 阶段划分和内容总结主要依据吴莉苇：《当诺亚方舟遭遇伏羲神农——启蒙时代欧洲的中国上古史论争》，北京：中国人民大学出版社，2005年，第65—66页、第79—80页。

表 1-1 "礼仪之争"的阶段和内容

阶段	时间	天主教内部的论争	罗马教廷的裁决	在欧洲的公众影响
第一阶段（初起）	1611—1656	1610 年利玛窦去世，礼仪问题初见端倪。1643 年多明我会士黎玉范（Jean-Baptiste Morales）到罗马质疑"适应政策"，耶稣会士随即派卫匡国（Martino Martini）赴罗马反诉。	罗马于 1645 年发布支持黎玉范意见的敕谕，又于 1656 年发布倾向耶稣会士的敕谕。	基本属于天主教内部的神学讨论，知者不多，论者寥寥。
第二阶段（停顿）	1656—1697	罗马对礼仪问题的讨论基本停顿，中国传教区实际上是在 1656 年敕谕的指导下平稳发展。	1645 年和 1656 年两道相互矛盾的敕谕同时有效。	发展为詹森派（Jansenist）神学家阿尔诺（Antoine Arnauld）和耶稣会士勒泰利埃（Michel Le Tellier）在索邦神学院的争论，但公众影响力不大。
第三阶段（高潮）	1697—1710	1697 年福建宗座代牧阎当（Charles Maigrot）发布禁止祭祖祭孔的训令并提交教廷审议。使者夏尔莫（Nicolas Charmot）在等待罗马开庭审议阎当训令期间，将此训令带到巴黎宗教界大加鼓动，导致索邦神学院先罗马而裁定中国礼仪不合法，并以公开谴责两位耶稣会士的著作①作为对此裁决的宣示。	1697 年教廷开始重新讨论礼仪问题，1704 年发布敕谕全面禁止基督徒参与祭祖祭孔，但未正式公开。1710 年正式公布，并发布新敕谕强调 1704 敕谕，并禁止讨论礼仪问题和出版相关文本。	巴黎宗教界哗然，继而礼仪问题从巴黎扩散到欧洲各地，欧洲一时间被关于礼仪之争的论文、书籍和宣传册淹没。上至莱布尼茨这样的名流，下至普通妇人都参与进来，礼仪之争从宗教论争扩大为 17、18 世纪之交的公众热点事件。
第四阶段（淡化）	1711 年以后	耶稣会士试图继续与教廷讨论但被拒。1773 年耶稣会被解散。	1715 年敕谕不再允许耶稣会士上诉，1742 年《自上主圣意》敕谕从法律上彻底禁断礼仪之争。1939 年教廷决议实际上肯定了"适应政策"。	欧洲人对礼仪之争的兴趣逐渐淡化。

---

① 指李明的《中国现势新志》和郭弼恩的《中国皇帝敕令史》。

如前文所述，以利玛窦为首的耶稣会士为适应中国文化，在术语问题上用中国文献中的"天"和"上帝"来指代基督教的"神"；在礼仪问题上将祭祖祭孔礼仪解释为世俗性、政治性活动而允许中国基督徒参加。然而，在术语选择上，耶稣会士内部就有不同意见；在礼仪问题上，其他修会大多反对耶稣会士的做法，认为这样的妥协已经损害了基督教的纯洁性。利玛窦去世后，争论先从中国传教区开始，后请罗马教廷裁决，甚至蔓延整个欧洲，酿成这场持续百年又草草收尾的混战。因此，"礼仪之争"是耶稣会士执行"适应政策"的必然结果。

"礼仪之争"从本质上说是天主教内部关于在华传教路线的论争，然而由于论争的内容涉及中国宗教和哲学的根本问题，耶稣会士和反对者不得不引经据典、著书立说，试图以西方思想框架来裁切和阐释中国文化。虽然以耶稣会士为代表的传教士们的聪颖和勤奋不容否认，然而，中国文化自身的复杂性和与西方文化的巨大差异使得他们走上的必然是一条不归路。他们所争论的是西方思想视角下中国宗教哲学的根本问题，如"中国人是不是偶像崇拜者？"，"中国人是不是无神论者？"今天的中国学者自己尚无法准确全面地回答这样的问题，遑论17世纪刚刚学会中文、对中国典籍一知半解的外国传教士呢？因此，"礼仪之争"中以耶稣会士为代表的传教士们所提供的中国知识必然是对中国文化的"雾里看花"式的文化误读。而这些"雾中花"被启蒙思想家进一步渲染雾化成为他们所需要的启蒙思想武器。正因为如此，"礼仪之争"的影响和意义不在中国，而在欧洲。

"礼仪之争"的双方为了辩护本方立场都创作了大量作品向欧洲人灌输他们对中国文化的认识，这成了欧洲人认识中国的起点，同时也引发了欧洲人对中国文化的强烈兴趣。"出版社源源不断地流出各种支持或反对耶稣会士的书和小册子，欧洲一时间几乎被关于'礼仪之争'的论文、书籍和宣传册淹没。……耶稣会士有关礼仪问题的作品刊与未刊的有50多份，而'礼仪之争'期间欧洲出版的同类作品近300部，仿佛礼仪问题对欧洲人比在中国的传教士更重要似的。"[①]
"礼仪之争期间，欧洲人撰写了数量惊人的有关中国的作品，几乎都是以耶稣会

[①] 张国刚：《从中西初识到礼仪之争——明清传教士与中西文化交流》，北京：人民出版社，2003年，第519页。

士那些耳熟能详的作品为依据，或汇编转述耶稣会士的言论，或根据他们自己的思想、学术、宗教观点的需要来摘抄利用中国知识，一时间中国成为他们指摘时弊、阐发思想、验证观点的时髦凭据。"[①] 洛克的"中国笔记"就是欧洲思想界对中国知识的重要回响之一。

综上所述，"启蒙运动""中国热"和"礼仪之争"是17—18世纪欧洲的三大主题。经济社会的巨大变革必然导致思想革命，新思想的发展迫切需要新的思想武器；"礼仪之争"和"东学西传"适时地为启蒙思想家提供了新武器，从而催生了欧洲知识界的"中国热"。而17—18世纪之交不仅是"礼仪之争"的最高潮，也是"启蒙运动"和"中国热"在英国的最高潮。作为英国"启蒙思想"的重镇，洛克在此时写下了"中国笔记"。

---

① 吴莉苇：《当诺亚方舟遭遇伏羲神农——启蒙时代欧洲的中国上古史论争》，北京：中国人民大学出版社，2005年，第78—79页。

第二章 "中国笔记"的历史与现状

1704年10月28日洛克逝世后,亲友按照其遗嘱对洛克的财产进行了分配,其中最重要的部分就是洛克的藏书和手稿。不同于十几年后莱布尼茨去世时,布伦瑞克家族对其文字资料的官方管理①,洛克的文字资料在其逝世后的近300年里一直属于私人收藏。随着时局的变化、收藏人境遇的改变和脾性的差异,洛克的藏书和手稿也有不同的遭遇,如今散落世界各地。幸运的是,洛克的几乎全部手稿和部分藏书完好地保存了下来,现藏于英国牛津大学的博得礼图书馆(Bodleian Library,简称B.L.)的珍稀档案室(Rare Books Room),名为"拉夫雷斯档案"(The Lovelace Collection of the Papers of John Locke),其中就包括洛克"中国笔记"手稿,档案编号B.L., MS. Locke c.27, ff. 178—212。本章首先简要介绍"拉夫雷斯档案"的来历、分类、编目和研究成果,而后介绍"中国笔记"手稿的文献现状和结构要点,以期全面呈现"中国笔记"的历史与现状。

---

① 为了撰写布伦瑞克家族的历史与家谱,莱布尼茨收集了不少鲜为人知的档案资料。1716年11月14日莱布尼茨逝世后,布伦瑞克家族按照当时的习惯做法,更出于担心对皇家不利的有关资料外流,即刻派人查封没收了莱布尼茨的所有文字资料。莱布尼茨的手稿现藏于德国汉诺威的莱布尼茨档案馆。参见李文潮:《莱布尼茨〈中国近事〉的历史与意义》;[德]莱布尼茨著,[法]梅谦立、杨保筠译,《中国近事:为了照亮我们这个时代的历史》,郑州:大象出版社,2005年,第102页。

第一节 "拉夫雷斯档案"简介

一、来历与归属

从1691年初开始，洛克定居在距离伦敦20英里的埃塞克斯郡（Essex）奥茨（Oates）的弗朗西斯·玛莎姆先生（Sir Francis Masham）和夫人玛莎姆女士（Dame Damaris Masham）①的乡间别墅（见图2-1）。玛莎姆一家给洛克带来了稳定的生活和家庭的温暖，玛莎姆夫妇的小儿子弗朗西斯·卡德沃思·玛莎姆（Francis Cudworth Masham，昵称Totty）在洛克刚刚到来时只有四岁，他为哲学家的晚年生活增添了无穷的快乐，因此后来成为洛克遗嘱的主要受益人之一。1704年10月28日，洛克在书房亲手合上自己的双眼，与世长辞，后被安葬于埃塞克斯郡东部的High Laver小镇的一个教堂墓区（见彩图1）。

图2-1　18世纪改建后的玛莎姆别墅

（洛克当时居住的是左侧有人形山墙的部分，右侧的方形建筑大约是1770年代扩建的。②）

---

① 玛莎姆女士（1659—1708）是剑桥大学基督学院院长、剑桥柏拉图学派领袖拉尔夫·卡德沃思（Ralph Cudworth）之女，幼年成长于剑桥柏拉图学派的学术圈子，长大后成为英国最早的女性哲学家和神学家之一，并与当时的很多著名学者保持通信，其中包括洛克与莱布尼茨。1691年洛克搬到奥茨以前，她已经与洛克通信十年。她与洛克通信时署名Philoclea，通信内容除了学术外，还有情诗。因此，他们的关系受到一些后世学者的诟病，例如洛克的诋毁者约翰·爱德华（John Edward）公开嘲讽他们为"奥茨的后宫"（the seraglio at Oates）。

② John Harrison & Peter Laslett, *The Library of John Locke*, Second Edition, Oxford University Press, 1965, p. 7.

洛克去世前曾于1704年4月11日签署遗嘱，后又于同年9月15日签署遗嘱修改附件，这两份文件现藏于牛津大学博得礼图书馆，档案编号B.L., MS. Locke. b. 5., item no. 14，其中涉及藏书和手稿归属的内容如下：

> *Item* I give to **Dame Damaris Masham** any four folios eight quartos and twenty books of less volume which she shall choose out of books in my library not otherwise disposed of by name; *Item* I give to **Mr. Anthony Collins** of the Middle Temple my *Plautus* in folio of Lambin's edition, *Gesneri Bibliotheca aucta per Simlerum, Kerchringii Spicilegium anatomicum, Catalogus librorum Bibliothecae Raphaelis Trichett du Fresne, Bibliotheca Thuana, Bibliotheca Heinsiana* and *Wisten's Map of Tartary* that hangs up in my study; *Item* I give to my cosen **Peter King** of the Inner Temple my *Harmonia Evangeliorum Toinardi, Poli Synopsis Criticorum, Les memoires de Monsieur Deagent, Marci Antonii de Dominis Epistola de pace Religionis ad Josephum Hallum*, all my manuscripts, and all my books that are interleaved, and the one moiety of all the rest of my books, not herein otherwise disposed of, together with the boxes they stand in; the other moiety of my said books, together with the boxes they stand in I give and bequeath to the said **Francis Cudworth Masham** aforesaid when he shall attain to the age of one and twenty years.①

根据洛克的遗嘱，洛克将自己的全部手稿留给了彼得·金（Peter King）②；除特别说明的少数几本外，洛克藏书被分为两半，分别留给彼得·金和弗朗西斯·卡德沃思·玛莎姆。据约翰·哈里森（John Harrison）和彼得·拉斯莱特（Peter Laslett）统计，洛克最终藏书目录中所列的藏书共有3641种、4042册，而

---

① 洛克遗嘱原件见B.L., MS. Locke b.5, item no. 14，本书引用转写稿见John Locke, E.S. De Beer (ed.), *The Correspondence of John Locke*, V8, Oxford: Clarendon Press, 1989, pp. 419–427，又见John Harrison & Peter Laslett, *The Library of John Locke*, Oxford University Press, 1965, p. 8。

② 彼得·金，洛克的外甥，其母安妮·金（Anne King）是洛克的叔叔彼得·洛克（Peter Locke, 1607—1686）的女儿。洛克终生未娶，亦无子女，彼得是他最亲近和信任的后辈。在洛克晚年定居奥茨期间，彼得常常前来探望和陪伴左右。就在洛克去世前不久，彼得还曾携新婚妻子到奥茨接受洛克的祝福。洛克临终前将半数藏书和所有手稿、书信赠予彼得，并指定他为遗嘱执行人。

1704年洛克去世时按照遗嘱分给彼得·金的一半藏书共1104种、1337册,分给弗朗西斯·玛莎姆的一半藏书共1093种、1282册,总计2197种、2619册,可见当时作为遗产分配的图书数量少于洛克的总藏书量[①]。(见图2-2)

Statistics of Locke's Library and its Division in 1704

Titles		Volumes
From all sources Comprising:	3,641	4,042 of which 662 were pamphlets.
Titles from Hyde	2,956	3,305 of which 610 were pamphlets.
Titles from other sources	685	737 of which 52 were pamphlets.
King Moiety:	1,104	1,337 and a 'Collection of Pamphlets' in addition.
Masham Moiety:	1,093	1,282 and 'Pamphlets', 'Nine bundles of pamphlets' in addition.
Total recorded as divided in 1704	2,197	2,619[1]

图2-2 1704年洛克藏书及分配情况[②]

如上文所述,洛克遗嘱中将自己的一半藏书留给了玛莎姆家的小儿子——当时只有17岁的弗朗西斯,并说明弗朗西斯21岁前由其母玛莎姆女士代为保管,如果弗朗西斯在21岁前去世,则将这一半藏书也交由彼得·金管理。弗朗西斯安然继承了这一半藏书,然而不幸的是,1776年6月14日第二代玛莎姆爵士(Samuel Masham)去世后,玛莎姆家族就不复存在了,洛克的藏书于是分崩离析,散落于世界各地,现在已知的基督学院(Christ Church)有几本,牛津的赫特福德学院(Hertford College)有一本,三一学院(Trinity College)有三本,剑桥的国王学院(King's College)有几本,还有的散落在马萨诸塞州剑桥的Athens,肯塔基州的New Haven,以及Brinkley, Sir Geoffrey Keynes住宅附近的Newmarket等地。这被认为是世界藏书史上的一大悲剧。[③]

根据遗嘱,洛克的另一半藏书和全部手稿都留给了彼得·金。彼得后来做了英格兰大法官(Lord Chancellor, 1725—1733在职),并获英王乔治一世授予

---

① 关于洛克藏书的具体情况见本书第六章第一节"洛克藏书概述"。
② 见John Harrison & Peter Laslett, *The Library of John Locke*, Oxford University Press, 1965, p. 56 Table 7。
③ 详见John Harrison & Peter Laslett, *The Library of John Locke*, Oxford University Press, 1965, pp. 57-61。

的男爵头衔。1835年，第八代金男爵（William King）与诗人拜伦的独生女奥古斯塔·埃达·拜伦（Augusta Ada Byron）①结婚，新娘的母亲是曾经的拉夫雷斯（Lovelace）男爵家族的后代。1838年，第八代金男爵被授予拉夫雷斯伯爵头衔，这就是"拉夫雷斯档案"（The Lovelace Collection of the Papers of John Locke）名称的由来。

洛克去世后的近300年中，他的手稿和一半藏书一直是金家族的私人收藏，并随着金家族四处搬迁。1932年为庆祝洛克诞辰300周年，金家族展出了部分藏书，这次展览对洛克藏书造成了前所未有的破坏。参展后，这部分藏书被按照尺寸分类，准备出售，但未曾售出。1951年12月，人们在第一代拉夫雷斯伯爵修建的位于Ben Damph Forest的狩猎屋的枪室里发现了它们。当时，这些书杂乱无章地放在临时架子上，有些书的封皮上散布着装潢时落下的白灰，有些书明显有老鼠咬过的痕迹。即便如此，洛克留给彼得·金的一半图书中有62%，即835本保存了下来，其中绝大部分保存得相当完好。②

1942年，当时的拉夫雷斯伯爵将洛克的大部分手稿和一部分藏书寄存在博得礼图书馆躲避战火。在随后的数年中，牛津大学克拉伦登出版社聘请英国杜伦大学的哲学讲师W. 冯·莱登（Wolfgang von Leyden）博士对这部分藏书和手稿的内容和重要性进行了详细考察，莱登博士于1946年向牛津大学学术委员会（Oxford University committee）提交了考察报告③。基于该报告，1947年博得礼图书馆正式以5000英镑的价格从拉夫雷斯伯爵手中购得洛克的几乎全部手稿④和

---

① 奥古斯塔·埃达·拜伦（Augusta Ada Byron, 1815—1852）是英国诗人拜伦与妻子安妮·伊莎贝拉·米尔班奇唯一的合法子嗣。1835年，埃达嫁给威廉·金（后来晋封为第一代拉夫雷斯伯爵），后获得头衔"奥古斯塔·埃达——拉夫雷斯伯爵夫人阁下"（The Right Honourable Augusta Ada, Countess of Lovelace）。这次联姻使得金家族在很长的一段时间里同时拥有洛克和拜伦的大量私人文稿。
② 关于洛克藏书的传承、保存和发现情况详见 John Harrison & Peter Laslett, *The Library of John Locke*, Oxford University Press, 1965, pp. 57-58。
③ 据W. 冯·莱登的记述，在他的报告之前，拉夫雷斯收藏的内容曾于1919年被报告给皇家历史档案局，但报告内容并不详细。W. 冯·莱登还详细记录了当时组成牛津大学学术委员会（Oxford University Committe）的专家。详见 John Locke, W. von Leyden (ed.), *Essays on the Law of Nature*, Oxford: Clarendon Press, 1954, p. 1, note 1 & 2。
④ 根据购买协议，当时的拉夫雷斯伯爵保留了1661年的摘录簿（commonplace book），后来该摘录簿被 Arthur Houghton先生购得，现藏于哈佛大学图书馆。

部分藏书，并命名为"拉夫雷斯档案"。1953年，博得礼图书馆又购得洛克写给彼得·金的165封信，一并收入"拉夫雷斯档案"。1960年Paul Mellon购得金家族收藏的大部分洛克藏书，并将其保存在位于弗吉尼亚州Uppervill, Oak Spring的私人图书馆，1964年约翰·哈里森和彼得·拉斯莱特根据洛克的藏书目录推测，这部分藏书约有840册。① 在之后的数年中，这部分藏书也陆续来到博得礼图书馆，并入"拉夫雷斯档案"。我重点关注的是"拉夫雷斯档案"中洛克手稿部分。

二、书信与手稿

"拉夫雷斯档案"中洛克手稿主要分为书信和手稿两大类：

（一）书信近3000封，其中除了洛克收到的书信外，还有约150封洛克所写回信的草稿。这些信件大多是英文的，也有几百封是拉丁文或法文的；通信对象既有当时的知名人士，也有无名小卒；信件的内容既有日常事务，也有严肃话题。除了家长里短、金钱往来等，通信内容主要涉及新书出版、科学研究、货币政策和殖民地事务。②

（二）各类手稿1000多件。数量最多的是洛克的账目，其次是书单、图书目录和神学、医学论文，再次是关于货币、经济、殖民地和政治史的文章，数量最少的是哲学手稿。洛克共有38本日记和笔记本现存于世，时间跨度长达50年，"拉夫雷斯档案"收藏了其中的大部分。③

---

① John Harrison & Peter Laslett, *The Library of John Locke*, Oxford University Press, 1965, p. 37.
② 关于洛克书信的具体情况见本书第四章第一节"洛克现存书信简介"，详见John Locke, W. von Leyden (ed.), *Essays on the the Law of Nature*, Oxford: Clarendon Press, 1954, pp. 1-2, 及E.S. De Beer (ed.), *The Correspondence of John Locke*, V1, Oxford: Clarendon Press, 1976, pp. XV-lxxix.
③ 关于洛克的笔记本和日记在博得礼图书馆"拉夫雷斯档案"之外的藏点详见John Locke, W. von Leyden (ed.), *Essays on the Law of Nature*, Oxford: Clarendon Press, 1954, p. 2, note 2。

三、编目与分类[①]

博得礼图书馆购得"拉夫雷斯档案"后,立即对其中的图书和手稿进行了分类、装订和编码。博得礼图书馆对"拉夫雷斯档案"的编码由三个部分构成:(1)名称(MS. Locke);(2)按照文稿尺寸编排的小写字母;(3)每个尺寸下面的序号。其中,文稿尺寸以装订后文稿的高度为准[②],15—20英寸编号为b(大于对开本);12—15英寸编号为c(对开本以内);9—12英寸编号为d(四开本以内);7—9英寸编号为e(八开本以内);5—7英寸编号为f(12开本至32开本)。以"中国笔记"为例,所在档案编号为B.L., MS. Locke.c.27., ff. 178—212,表示藏于博得礼图书馆洛克手稿c类(大对开)第27本档案第178—212页。

从手稿尺寸来看,b类(MS. Locke. b.)共6本,c类(MS. Locke. c.)共40本,d类(MS. Locke. d.)共8本,e类(MS. Locke. e.)共11本,f类(MS. Locke. f.)共34本。

从手稿内容来看,可分为以下几类。

(一)日记和私人文件

MSS. Locke. f. 1-10.为1675—1704年洛克的日记;

MS. Locke. c.25.为1625—1704年洛克的各种私人文件,按照时间排序;

MS. Locke. b.5.为洛克的正式文件,如MS. Locke. b.5.f.10.为1675年洛克获得的牛津大学颁发的行医执照、MS. Locke. b.5.f.14.为1704年4月11日洛克签署的遗嘱以及1704年9月15日的遗嘱修改附件。

(二)来往书信

MSS. Locke. c.3-23.为1651—1704年洛克收到的来信,按照写信人姓名的字母顺序排列,装订为21本;

[①] 本部分内容主要依据博得礼图书馆"拉夫雷斯档案"总目整理,也参考了洛克的手稿和传记。详见 P. Long, *A Summary Catalogue of the Lovelace Collection of the Papers of John Locke in the Bodleian Library*, Oxford University Press, 1959。

[②] 由于手稿多为大小不一的散片,实际编码时只能以装订后的文件夹尺寸为准。

MS. Locke. c.24. 为1652—1704年洛克写的信件或信件的草稿，按照收信人姓名的字母顺序排列；

MS. Locke. c.40. 为1698—1704年洛克写给彼得·金的信件。

（三）财产账目

MS. Locke. f.11-13. 为1649—1774年洛克的账簿；

MS. Locke. c.26. 为1611—1705年关于洛克财产的文件；

MS. Locke. b.1. 为1660—1704年洛克收支账目；

MSS. Locke. c.1-2. 为1671—1704年洛克的两本总账；

MS. Locke. f.34. 为三本小账本。

（四）书籍

MS. Locke. b.2. 为1675—1704年洛克的各种藏书目录；

MS. Locke. c.33. 为洛克写的读书备忘录，日期为1676—1679年、1683—1684年、1687—1688年和1690年；

MSS. Locke. f.15,18,29. 为洛克的三本笔记，主要是书单，也包括部分述评和备忘录；

MSS. Locke. f.16,17; e.3. 为洛克的藏书目录；

MS. Locke. c.35. 为洛克遗产赠予的文件。

（五）哲学和神学

MS. Locke. c.27. 为洛克关于神学和宗教的手稿；

MS. Locke. c.28. 为洛克关于哲学和宗教的手稿；

MS. Locke. e.7. 为洛克的论文 "Quest: whether the Civil Magistrate may lawfully impose and determine ye use of indifferent things in reference to Religious Worship"；

MS. Locke. f.26. 为洛克《人类理解论》的初稿；

MS. Locke. e.1.《人类理解论》（第四版，1700）增补内容的草稿；

MS. Locke. e.6. 洛克记录 "Lemmata" 条目的笔记本；

MS. Locke. f.31. 一本包含九篇拉丁文论法的本质的论文的笔记本；

MS. Locke. f.30. 一个羊皮纸箱，装着洛克关于圣经新约的笔记和关于法的本质的文章；

MS. Locke. f.32. 一个羊皮纸箱，装着洛克关于圣经的笔记；

MS. Locke. d.3. S. Brownover誊写的洛克的两本著作；

MS. Locke. e.2. 洛克几部作品的终稿；

MS. Locke. c.34. 詹姆斯·泰瑞尔（James Tyrrell）和洛克批判后来的伍斯特主教爱德华·斯蒂林弗利特（Edward Stillingfleet）著作的笔记；

MS. Locke. d.4.《关于宽容的第四封信》的部分手稿；

MS. Locke. e.10. Thomas Greaves誊写的关于圣经旧约和Apocrypha的文章；

MS. Locke. e.11. 丹尼尔·惠特比（Daniel Whitby）的"The Preface to the first Epistle to the Corinthians"的部分手稿；

MS. Locke. d.6. 威廉·金（William King）的《对罗马人的布道》（A sermon on Romans）。

（六）货币；（七）医学；（八）自然科学；（九）贸易与殖民地；（十）其他；（十一）附录，因第六——十一类与本书关系不大，故具体内容从略。

四、公开与研究

博得礼图书馆将"拉夫雷斯档案"向公众公开以后，洛克手稿研究领域陆续出现了很多优秀成果。本部分重点关注洛克手稿的公布过程和作为本研究基础的经典研究成果，因而将洛克手稿研究分为私人收藏和公众收藏两个阶段。

（一）金家族收藏阶段

1829年，第七代金男爵出版了洛克的第一本传记《约翰·洛克的一生》（The Life of John Locke）[①]。从洛克研究的角度，这位金男爵所写的传记称不上好作品。金男爵对洛克手稿的转写并不准确，编排顺序也很随意，还常常从不同的手稿或信件中抽出几段组成一篇新的手稿或信件，因而可信度较低。另外，本

---

① Peter King (7th Baron), *The Life and Letters of John Locke, with extracts from his journals and common-place books*. New ed. 1858.

书既没有目录,也没有索引,更没有注释,基本属于随笔漫谈性质,参考价值不高。但作为"拉夫雷斯档案"的所有人,这位金男爵几乎是当时唯一能接近洛克手稿的人,他所写的这本传记的主要价值在于首次公开了洛克手稿的部分内容。

1914年,哈佛大学的本杰明·兰德(Benjamin Rand)博士在《约翰·洛克与爱德华·克拉克书信集》(*The Correspondence of John Locke and Edward Clarke*)一书中发表了部分洛克书信;1931年,兰德博士又出版《理解、知识、观念与认同论》(*An Essay Concerning the Understanding, Knowledge, Opinion, and Assent*)①,发表了在拉夫雷斯伯爵收藏的洛克手稿中发现的《人类理解论》的初稿,兰德博士称之为"原稿"(the original draft)。

1935年乔斯林·吉布(Jocelyn Gibb)和阿伦(R. A. Aaron)教授又在拉夫雷斯伯爵收藏的洛克写于1661年的摘录簿中发现了另外一份《人类理解论》的初稿,并证实其写作时间早于兰德博士发现的版本,因此将写作时间在前的命名为"A稿"(Draft A),写作时间在后的命名为"B稿"(Draft B),并于次年出版了《洛克〈人类理解论〉的早期手稿》(*An Early Draft of Locke's Essay Concerning Human Understanding*)②。

(二)牛津大学收藏阶段

上文提到的莱登博士在1946年向牛津大学学术委员会提交了关于"拉夫雷斯档案"的调查报告后,又于1954年将洛克手稿中的9篇牛津时期的作品结集出版,定名为《自然法论文集》(*Essays on the Law of Nature*)③,副标题为 *The Latin Text with a Translation, Introduction and Notes, together with Transcripts*

---

① John Locke, Benjamin Rand (ed.), *An Essay concerning the Understanding, Knowledge, Opinion, and Assent*, Cambridge: Harvard University Press, 1931.
② John Locke, R. I. Aaron and Jocelyn Gibb (ed.), *An Early Draft of Locke's Essays together with Excerpts from his Journals*, Oxford: Clarendon Press, 1936.
③ John Locke, Dr. Wolfgang von Leyden (ed.), *Essays on the Law of Nature*, Oxford: Clarendon Press, 1954. 该书现有两个中译本,分别为[英]洛克著,李季璇译,《自然法论文集》,北京:商务印书馆,2014年(该译本翻译了该书的第二、第三两个部分,却将非常宝贵的第一部分——长篇前言略去,令人遗憾)和[英]洛克著,刘时工译,《自然法论文集》,上海:上海三联书店,2012年(该译本我尚未得见)。

of Locke's Shorthand in His Journal for 1676。该书以拉丁文与英文对照的形式发表了洛克约写于1660年的8篇拉丁文论文以及1664年作为基督学院道德哲学学监的告别演讲,并在"前言"中对"拉夫雷斯档案"和洛克的早期作品进行了详细的介绍,是本书的重要参考文献之一。另外,洛克的部分手稿是用速记(Shorthand)写成的,曾经被认为难以破译,后逐渐明确洛克主要使用的是杰瑞米·瑞奇(Jeremiah Rich)的速记系统。在该书第三部分①,莱登博士最终将"拉夫雷斯档案"中所有以速记写成的哲学日记破译发表,这是该书的另一大贡献。

1976—1983年,德比尔(E. S. de Beer)将八卷本的《洛克书信集》(*The Correspondence of John Locke*)②整理出版,该书收录的洛克书信大大超过了博得礼图书馆所藏"拉夫雷斯档案"的范围,搜集整理了3650封洛克的来往书信,至今依然是洛克研究最重要、最权威的资料之一,也是本书第四章"洛克书信与中国"最主要的材料基础。

1985年,莫里斯·克兰斯顿(Maurice Cranston)出版洛克的传记(*John Locke: A Biography*)③,大量使用了洛克手稿,尤其是洛克的书信,到目前为止,是洛克最经典的传记之一。我对洛克生平的认识多半得益于该书。

总之,"拉夫雷斯档案"的来历、分类和编目知识是展开洛克手稿研究的先决条件,也是国内学界非常陌生的领域,因而我花了比较多的笔墨进行介绍。同时,西方前辈学者对于洛克手稿的研究成果是本书对洛克"中国观"研究的重要基础,因此我将本书大量引用的一些极重要文献(如书信、早期论文等)先行列出。限于主题和篇幅,这里介绍的只是"拉夫雷斯档案"的冰山一角,旨在提供洛克"中国观"的文献背景。

---

① John Locke, Dr. Wolfgang von Leyden (ed.), *Essays on the the Law of Nature*, Oxford: Clarendon Press, 1954, pp. 246-281.

② John Locke, E. S. De Beer (ed.), *The Correspondence of John Locke* (in eight volumes), Oxford: Clarendon Press, 1976-1989.

③ Maurice Cranston, *John Locke: A Biography*, Oxford New York: Oxford University Press, 1985.

第二节　洛克"中国笔记"文献概述

一、档案现状

洛克"中国笔记"手稿现藏于牛津大学博得礼图书馆的珍稀档案室，归入神学和宗教类，档案编号B.L., MS. Locke. c.27.。该档案为大对开本，封面和封底为砖红色布面硬纸板，书脊为深红色软牛皮。书脊上方印有金色的"Theology and Religion"（神学与宗教）字样，书脊下方则印有金色的"MS. Locke. c.27."字样（见彩图2）。该档案边角磨损较为严重，应为经常翻阅所致，但手稿内容保存状态良好。档案内共有285页手稿，由数本笔记和众多散页装订而成，故纸张尺寸不一。

"中国笔记"手稿位于MS. Locke. c.27.档案的第178—212页，以黑色墨水书写于白色毛边纸上，页长约19厘米，页宽约16厘米。每页均以竖向中线为界，分为左右两个部分，左侧用于书写正文，右侧用于标注和增补。每页的右上角均用拉丁文标明主题，并用大写英文字母标明该主题在文末索引中对应的类别，该标识还同时出现在大部分手稿页面的左下角。此外，右上角的小标题附近还用铅笔标注了阿拉伯数字的页码，应为装订档案时标注，非出自洛克之手。

二、基本结构

"中国笔记"手稿由书目、正文和索引三大部分组成：

第一部分，MS. Locke. c.27.档案第178页，书目。该书目写在一张对折的八开白纸上，洛克先在白纸上用铅笔仔细打好了格子，而后用黑色墨水书写了书目（见彩图4）。该页背书："China 01 Papers in the Controversie betwixt the Jesuits & other missionaries"（中国01关于耶稣会士与其他传教士之间争论的文献）（见彩图5）。

该书目的格式是洛克习惯的"摘录簿"(commonplace book)①写法。书目右上角写着"China 178"②，页面最上方从左到右按"A—Z"的顺序列出23个大写的英文字母（按照洛克的习惯，索引中不出现"I、U、W"三个字母③），然后按作者首字母顺序将"作者、书名、出版地、出版时间、页码"列在对应的条目下，如上数第一个书目："Gobien, *Eclairissement Bernard 00 Mar p. 352"，指"郭弼恩，《澄清》④，Bernard出版，1700年3月，第352页"，列在条目G下。有些书作者不详，则按照书名首字母的顺序将相关信息列在对应的条目下。有些书未注具体的页码，应为全本参考。

经笔者初步辨认，该书目共列出约37本书，其中大部分是"礼仪之争"中耶稣会士和其他修会传教士所写的论争性文献。大部分书名为拉丁文，少数几本为法文和意大利文。洛克在一些书名的前面加了"×"号标记，应为着重号。此外，洛克在书名中出现的"Tien"（天）、"Xangti"⑤（上帝）、"Kingtien"（敬天）这三个中国哲学的关键概念下方加了下划线，以示强调。

第二部分，MS. Locke. c.27. 档案的第179—211页，正文。"中国笔记"正文

---

① "摘录簿"(commonplace book)最早是由文艺复兴时期的大学者（如Erasmus, Agricola, Melanchthon）所倡导的学习和记笔记的模式，是学者们在阅读重要的经典文本（如古罗马的经典作品）时摘抄经典段落以方便记忆的私人笔记，当时的文法学校有专门讲如何写"摘录簿"的课程。"摘录簿"的典型主题包括经典类的"荣誉、美德、友谊"等和宗教类的"上帝、创世记、信仰、希望"等。"摘录簿"并非简单的摘抄，而是作者对经典文本的选择、润色和发挥。到了现代早期，"摘录簿"已经是为所有学者熟知的学术传统了。1686年，洛克在《世界文库》(*Bibliothèque Universelle*)杂志上发表了一篇题为《摘录簿的新方法》(*Méthode Nouvelle de dresser des Recueils*)的论文，详细阐述了洛克对"摘录簿"传统的继承与修正。这是洛克公开发表的第一篇论文，1706年被译为英文出版。
② 其中"China"为洛克手写的小标题，"178"为后加的档案页码，非洛克所写。
③ 按照洛克时代的英文手写体，"I"与"J"、"U"与"V"非常相似，难以区分，故洛克在编书目或索引时均不用"I、U、W"。
④ 在毕诺的书后列出的参考文献里，我们可以找到"(1696)郭弼恩(Le Gobien)神父：《中国皇帝支持基督教圣旨的历史》，附有关于中国人对孔子及祖先崇拜礼仪的某些澄清，巴黎"（参见[法]维吉尔·毕诺著，耿昇译：《中国对法国哲学思想形成的影响》，北京：商务印书馆，2000年，第711页），此处洛克指的很可能是类似的文献。
⑤ 洛克"中国笔记"手稿书目中出现的"上帝"一词拼写为"Xangti"；手稿正文中拼写为"Xanti"；《华人礼仪史》拉丁文原文中拼写为"Xangti"。特此说明。

共33页，其中第180、182、184、189、198、206页为预留的空白页，而第187页背面书写了正面右侧补充内容的未完部分，因此洛克书写的"中国笔记"正文部分共28页，每页内容多少不一，共分为13个主题讨论中国的宗教和礼仪，具体见下表：

表2-1 "中国笔记"的结构与主题

序号	页码	索引号	主题	备注
1	第179—180页	—	中国的宗教（Sinensium Religio）	第180页为预留空白页
2	第181—182页	A	中国的神学（Sinensium Theologia），理（Li），太极（Taikie）	第182页为预留空白页
3	第183—184页	B	精神和人类灵魂（Spirite et Anima humana）	第184页为预留空白页
4	第185页	C	游魂和离魂（yue hoen & ly kuei）	
5	第186—187页	D1—2	上帝（Xanti, Rex altus）	
6	第188—189页	E	天（Tien）	第189页为预留空白页
7	第190—198页	F1—8	孔子（Confucius）	第198页为预留空白页
8	第199页	G	地球（Terra）、星体（Planetarum）、山川（Montium）、河流（Flumine）的守护神（Genÿ sive Spiritus）	
9	第200—206页	H1—6	祖先（Progenitores）	第206页为预留空白页
10	第207页	J	儒教（Literati）	
11	第208页	J2	偶像崇拜者（Idolatrae）、佛教（Bonzÿ）	
12	第209页	K	道教（Magi）	
13	第210—211页	L1—2	伊斯兰教（Mahometans）	

第三部分，MS. Locke. c.27.档案的第212页正反两面，索引。该页正面是主题索引，编号A—L（见彩图6）；反面是页码索引（见彩图7）。

三、专题笔记

从内容来看,洛克在"中国笔记"中共讨论了关于中国宗教的13个主题。其中,"中国的宗教""中国的神学、理、太极""精神和人类灵魂""游魂和离魂""上帝""天"这六个主题从不同角度分析了儒教的基本性质,并用西方哲学术语对儒教的关键概念——"天""上帝""理""太极"——进行了阐释。"孔子""地球、星体、山川、河流的守护神""祖先"这三个主题则详细记述了中国人"祭祖""祭孔"及其他祭祀(如"祭山神""祭河神""祭城隍")的礼俗。"儒教""偶像崇拜者、佛教""道教"和"伊斯兰教"这四个主题则讨论了中国的儒教、佛教、道教及伊斯兰教的历史、基本信仰及其信徒在中国社会的地位。可见,"中国笔记"从西方基督教哲学的视角关注中国宗教的性质、概念、礼仪、派别等方面,系统而全面。

从结构来看,"中国笔记"前有参考书目,后有索引,正文分13个小标题,每个小标题至少占一页。其中,"宗教""神学""精神和人类灵魂""天""孔子""祖先"这六个主题后还分别预留了空白页。显然,洛克认为对这几个主题的研究还不够充分,应该还计划了后续的工作。另外,考虑到"中国笔记"原本就是由旧信纸装订而成,添加新页、重新装订是比较容易的,预留空白页似乎不是非常必要。因此,洛克很可能计划近期就对这六个主题的内容进行补充。

由此可见,在博得礼图书馆将之与其他手稿装订在一起以前,"中国笔记"就是以"摘录簿"(commonplace book)的格式写成的较为系统的专题笔记,而非随手涂写的随笔散页。洛克在"中国笔记"中系统研究了中国人的信仰问题,并且预留了后续研究的空间。中国很可能是洛克更大学术计划[①]的一部分。

四、写作时间

"中国笔记"属未刊手稿,写作时间不明。我推测"中国笔记"写于1702年前后,主要依据为该手稿的参考书目和所用的纸张。

"中国笔记"的参考书目中列出约37本书。这些书的出版时间非常集中,

---

① 种种迹象表明,洛克晚年一直准备写一部关于"道德"的专著,并为此搜集了大量资料。

除少数几本出版于1688、1689和1701年1月外，绝大部分均出版于1700年①。因此，"中国笔记"的写作时间应该在1700—1704年之间。如果想获得更加准确的写作时间，我们可以从手稿所用的纸张中找到进一步的线索。

仔细观察"中国笔记"手稿，我们会发现这些手稿所用的纸张均有不同程度的折痕、污迹或破损，部分纸张的背面还有信件或便签的全文或部分内容，有的纸张上还有清晰的邮戳或红色蜂蜡（见彩图3）。显然，洛克将当时所收信件的信封和信纸的空白处裁成相似大小（约相当于今天的B5尺寸），用于书写笔记②。"中国笔记"手稿几乎全都写在这些旧信封或信纸的背面。我们可以从这些信封和信纸的发信时间推测出"中国笔记"更加准确的写作时间。

我找到的几处线索为：（1）"中国笔记"手稿第181页和第185页都写在信封的背面，两页所用信封的邮戳时间分别为1696年4月28日和同年12月24日；（2）手稿第207页和第211页均写在信纸背面，前者背面为1702年爱德华·克拉克（Edward Clark）写给洛克的信，后者背面为1702年洛克写的信件草稿。

那么，结合从参考书目中推测出的写作时间，我们有理由相信"中国笔记"的写作时间为1702年前后。

---

① 书目中约15本书明确标注出版时间为1700年，还有很多未标出版日期的事实上也是1700年出版的。
② 这是洛克时代通行的做法。17世纪后半叶，西欧和中欧国家的邮政服务已经比较成熟，速度较快而且比较可靠，书信成为人们交流的主要渠道之一。当时的人们常将信写在信纸的一面，而后将信纸折叠，直接将信纸背面的空白页作为信封；如果该信件还有其他附件，则另用一张纸将信与附件包住，充作信封。不论是折叠信纸还是另用信封，人们都会用红色蜂蜡将信固定住，通常还会加盖印鉴，最后写上地址。人们在收到信后还会在信纸上背书发信人、收信时间等信息。因当时纸张颇为昂贵，收信人通常不会丢弃信件，而是将信封或信纸的空白处再次使用。而人们在打升蜂蜡的时候有时会不小心损坏信件，这就是为什么我们在这个时期的手稿中常常看到红色的蜂蜡、损坏的纸张、清晰的地址和背书等。显然，细心又节俭的洛克也有这样的习惯。不仅如此，从1667年开始，洛克会在自己收到的信件背面注明写信人的姓名和写信的日期；1686年底开始，洛克还会加注自己回信的日期。详见 John Locke, E.S. De Beer (ed.), *The Correspondence of John Locke*, V1 "Introduction", Oxford: Clarendon Press, 1976, p. lvi.

第三章 "中国笔记"的文本与要点

第一节 转写与翻译说明

一、转写说明

我在转写洛克"中国笔记"手稿时,转写原则和方法主要参考了R. I. Aaron 和Jocelyn Gibb对《人类理解论》"A稿"的转写[1],W. von Leyden对《自然法论文集》手稿的转写[2],以及德比尔对洛克书信的转写[3]。正如R. I. Aaron和Jocelyn Gibb在 *An Early Draft of Locke's Essay* 一书的"前言"中所说:"这种类型尤其是这种年代的手稿,引人入胜的不只其内容,还有其拼写和标点。"[4]因此,我在

---

[1] 参见John Locke, R. I. Aaron and Jocelyn Gibb (ed.), *An Early Draft of Locke's Essays Together with Excerpts from His Journals*, Oxford: Clarendon Press, 1936。
[2] 参见John Locke, Dr. Wolfgang von Leyden (ed.), *Essays on the Law of Nature*, Oxford: Clarendon Press, 1954。
[3] 参见John Locke, E. S. De Beer (ed.), *The Correspondence of John Locke* (in eight volumes), Oxford: Clarendon Press, 1976–1989。
[4] 原文:... a manuscript of this sort, and particularly of this date, is of interest not merely on account of its content, but also for its spelling and for its punctuation. 见John Locke, R. I. Aaron and Jocelyn Gibb (ed.), *An Early Draft of Locke's Essays Together with Excerpts from His Journals*, Oxford: Clarendon Press, 1936, p. xxviii。

转写的过程中，从页面布局、段落分行、前后顺序、标点拼写到错误修改，都力图保持洛克手稿的原貌；同时，为适应中国读者的阅读习惯，又做了适当的调整，具体做法如下：

1. 保持手稿的段落分行，使转写稿与原稿的页、段、行一一对应；

2. 尽量保持了手稿的页面布局。因为洛克手稿的大部分内容均写在页面的左侧，有部分注释性内容和后加入的内容写在手稿的右侧，所以我只在手稿内容出现在页面右侧或手稿顺序发生比较大的改变时进行了说明。如无特殊说明，则该部分内容书写于页面左侧，并按正常顺序排列。

3. 洛克习惯于在一页纸的左侧书写，右侧则用来做补充说明或注释，但由于反复补充和订正，洛克手稿中有部分内容顺序比较杂乱，给阅读造成极大障碍，因此我在转写时进行了必要的调整。按照上下文的意思将手稿页面右侧的内容放在该页左侧正文最合适的位置，以利阅读，并在方括号中对原稿的位置和顺序予以详细说明。

4. 洛克的多数手稿页面的右上方或左下方均有大写英文字母标识，对应手稿最后一页的索引。为了保持一致，我在转写时将每页的标识统一放在该页右上角小标题下方。

5. 与当时很多手稿一样，如果某个主题在一页中未结束，洛克手稿习惯于在每页手稿的末尾和下页手稿的开头重复同一个词或一个词的某一部分，以示连接，我在转写时保持了这些起连接作用、有时并不完整的词。

6. 洛克时代的英语还没有完全固定，拼写、大小写和标点相较于现代英语都比较随意，例如，"mandarin"这个词，洛克有时将之拼写为"mandarine"，有时拼写为"mandarin"；又如，"cry"这个词的第三人称单数，洛克有时将之拼写为"cryes"，有时拼写为"cries"。此外，手稿中还有大量当时的习惯拼法，如noe (no), noething (nothing), doe(do), soe (so)等，并且全文的标点数量很少，且使用非常随意。按照西方手稿转写的习惯，转写人应保持这些体现时代特色和作者风格的不规则拼写，然而这样做虽然学术性强，却会给阅读带来极大的障碍。考虑到中国读者的阅读习惯，我在转写时采用了现代英语的拼写，并按照现代英语的习惯添加了标点，同时修改了明显的语法和拼写错误。不过，除标点外，凡涉及修改之处，我均在脚注中进行了详细说明。

7. 洛克在手稿中常常使用缩写，有些是时代性的，有些是个人性的。据 R. I. Aaron 和 Jocelyn Gibb 统计，洛克在早期手稿中常使用的缩写有：" yt, ym, ys, wch, wt, wth, sd (said), yu (you), yr (your), agt, nāal (natural), māal (material), agreemt, phia (philosophia), ye (the)"①。据我的统计，洛克在"中国笔记"中使用的缩写包括：Tis (It is), yt (that), wch (which), agn (again), agt (against), ye (the) 等。为方便阅读，我在转写时将这些缩写还原为完整的拼写。

8. 由于手稿破损、污渍、涂写等原因造成的手稿无法辨认的地方，我在转写时用［？］标记，并在脚注中说明了无法辨认的原因，以及我按照上下文意思所做的猜测，供读者参考。

二、翻译说明

1. 为方便与手稿原文及转写稿对照，我在翻译时尽量保持了与原稿及转写稿一致的页、段、行，页面位置等标识也与转写稿一一对应。

2. 翻译时尽量采取直译，力图呈现手稿原义。有些概念根据上下文的需要做了不同的处理，如"Literati"一词，有时我译为"文人"或"读书人"；有时译为"儒生"；当与"道教""佛教"并列时，我将之译为"儒教"。

3. 翻译稿的注释均为研究性注释，除了介绍基本史实和概念外，大部分注释是我对"中国笔记"中的概念与观点的阐释与评论。

4. 为方便读者阅读和比对，本书将的英文转写稿和中文译稿以英汉对照的方式进行排列，以期更好地呈现"中国笔记"的全貌。

---

① John Locke, R. I. Aaron and Jocelyn Gibb (ed.), *An Early Draft of Locke's Essays Together with Excerpts from His Journals*, Oxford: Clarendon Press, 1936, p. xxviii.

第二节　英文转写与中文译稿

Aqz001

179
Sinensium①
Religion

The Religion of China, properly speaking, is that② of the <u>Literati</u>, which though now it be the name of one of the three sects③ into which all the heathen inhabitants of that large empire are divided. Yet the two other are but new amongst them & the religions they have introduced are foreign④ & borrowed from other countries. So⑤ that he that⑥

[To the right-hand side of the page]
joyne with the Literati in opinion &

[Back to the left-hand side of the page]
worship⑦ may be truely
said to⑧ tread in the steps of his ancestors

---

① It's Latin, meaning "Chinese".
② After "that", "which" was crossed out in Locke's ms.
③ After "sects", "which" was crossed out in Locke's ms.
④ Locke put it as "foraigne".
⑤ Locke put it as "Soe".
⑥ After "that", "follows & keeps to" was crossed out in Locke's ms.
⑦ Before "worship", "that" was crossed out; After "worship", "of the Literati" was crossed out in Locke's ms.
⑧ After "said to", "keep" was crossed out in Locke's ms.

Aqz001

179
中国的宗教

严格来说，
<u>儒教</u>是中国的国教，
即便如今儒教
只是这个大帝国居民
所信奉的三大宗教之一。
另两大宗教都是
后来的、
源自其他国家的
外来宗教①。
因此，只有那些

［页面右侧］
相信儒家思想，并且

［回到页面左侧］
信仰儒教的人
才算是真正跟随了祖先的脚步，

---

① 纵观洛克的"中国笔记"，洛克对于中国的佛教和道教了解不多，尤其是对道教，可以说是知之甚少。因此洛克在这里将中国的本土宗教——道教——与佛教一样归为外来宗教，并认为相较于儒教，道教是后来的，这显然是不符合事实的。

& to keep to the ancient religion of
China.

The sect of the Idolaters or Bonzÿ as it is called
had its original from
India & was introduced by Foe
into China about 65 year after the birth of
our Saviour as is believed.①

The Literati have no other Deitÿ but the
material heaven.

The Chineses in their philosophy② acknowledge
no③ spiritual substance distinct from body.
Anciently indeed, they acknowledged an unconceivable
subtle④ being which some understand to be pure
space & they acknowledged to be that first
principle from whence all other things had their
being & that they worshiped under the name
of Tien <u>heaven</u> or Xanti the supreme Lord

[To the right-hand side of the page]
but that long since degenerating into grosser & more

---

① Locke put this sentence as "The sect of the ~~Magi as they are~~ called[sic] Idolaters or Bonzÿ as it is called had its original from ~~original from one Foe~~ India & was introduced by Foe into China about 65 year after the birth of our Saviour as is believed."

② Locke put it as "philosophie".

③ Locke put it as "noe".

④ Locke put it as "subtile".

遵从了中国的古老
宗教。

佛教源于印度,
据说佛于
我们的救世主
诞生后65年
将其介绍到中国。

儒教唯一的神就是
"物质的天"。

中国人的哲学不承认
独立于物质实体的精神存在。
事实上,古代中国人承认
一种不可思议的微妙存在,
有人称之为"纯粹空间",
中国人将之视为"第一律"①,
即万物存在之源,
也就是中国人信仰的
"天"或"上帝"。

[页面右侧注]
然而很久以前,这一存在逐渐降低为

---

① 此处洛克是借用古希腊罗马哲学(如柏拉图哲学)中的"第一律"来指称世界万物的本源和根本动力。基督教哲学中的"第一律"是上帝,而中国古代经典用"天"或"上帝"指万物的本源,接下来洛克将探讨中国的"天"或"上帝"与基督教的"上帝"是不是一回事。

corporeal conception they signify① nothing

other by those words now but the material②

heavens which ever since is③

the worship.④

Aqz002

181
Sinensium
Theologia⑤
Li
Taikie⑥
A

The Sect of the Literati who are

distinct from the two others, viz the Magi

& the Bonzÿ, hold the heaven to be the

principle of all things,⑦

whither⑧ by the name of heaven they understand

a very subtle matter, which they call <u>Li</u> or

<u>Taikie</u>,

---

① Locke put it as "signifie".
② Page torn. There is "vis" after "material" in with Locke's ms. It could be "visible".
③ Page torn. Nothing remains after "is".
④ Page torn. There is "w" after worship. It could be "whereafter".
⑤ It's Latin, meaning "theology".
⑥ After "Taikie", "Tian" was crossed out.
⑦ After "things", "by which they now" was crossed out.
⑧ Locke should have got it wrong. Instead of "whither", "whether" makes more sense here.

更具体、更物质的概念。自此，
中国人提到"天"或"上帝"的时候，
他们指的只是"物质的天"；
人们祭祀的也是"物质的天"①。

Aqz002

181
中国的神学

理
太极
A

不同于道教和佛教，
儒教将"天"视为
世界万物的规律。
儒教的"天"是
一种非常微妙的物质，
名曰"<u>理</u>"或
"<u>太极</u>"。

---

① 此处手稿部分损毁，参见转写稿。

[To the right-hand side of the page]

Taikie was anciently god,

the cause of all things. Now

it is nothing[①] but māā prima[②].

[Back to the left-hand side of the page]

divided & formed with the various

figures & shapes of things, which is what is to be

found in the ancient classic[③]

writings of the Sect of the Literati

& still retained by[④] almost all of that

sect. Or whither[⑤] by the name of Heaven, they

mean something more excellent ie. an intel-

ligent active principle or nature th*at* creates

& governs all things. Attributed by

some to the founders of this sect &

pretended to be opinion of the present

emperor[⑥], & of[⑦]

many[⑧] of the Literati in his

court.

---

① Locke put it as "noe thing".
② It's Latin, meaning "material prime matter".
③ Locke put it as "classick".
④ After "by", "the greatest part" was crossed out.
⑤ Again, Locke should have got it wrong. Instead of "whither", "whether" makes more sense here.
⑥ After "emperor", "emperor" was crossed out.
⑦ After "of", "several of the" was crossed out.
⑧ Before "many", "Sect of the Literati" was crossed out.

［页面右侧注］
古时候，"太极"是神
和万物之源；如今，
"太极"只是物质第一性。

［回到页面左侧］
（接上文"理"或"太极"——译者）
由万物的各种不同形态
分离聚合而成，
儒教经典如是说，
今天绝大多数儒教徒
依然这样认为。
儒教也将"天"理解为
某种更完美的存在，
即一种创造并统摄万物的
智慧的、能动的规律或本质①。
有些人②认为
这是儒教创始人的观点，
并声称当今皇帝和
很多在朝为官的士大夫
同样持此观点。

---

① 此处洛克讨论了儒家的"天"和"上帝"的两种可能的理解。前者是称为"理"或"太极"的模糊存在，这在洛克看来是物质的；后者是智慧的和能动的，这就非常接近于全能、全知、全善的基督教上帝了，那么就是精神的。
② 应指以利玛窦为代表的耶稣会士。

It is① acknowledg[ed]② on all hands that what
ever may have been the opinion of the
ancient Chineses, the whole Sect of the
Literati for these four or 500 years
backwards have acknowledged no③ other④
first principle or original or cause of all things
but the material heaven, which therefore they
have worshiped under the name of
<u>Xanti</u> or <u>Tien</u> as their Supreme Deity⑤.

Aqz003

183
Spiritus et Anima humana⑥
B⑦

The⑧ Sect of the Literati⑨
admit⑩ no⑪ true⑫

---

① Locke put it as "Tis".
② Locke put it as "acknowledg".
③ Locke put it as "noe".
④ After "other", "deity" was crossed out.
⑤ Locke put it as "deitie".
⑥ It's Latin, meaning "spirit and human soul".
⑦ "B" is put at the left bottom of the page in Locke's ms. On the right-hand side of the page, Locke wrote "Chin hoan, Genÿ" as a subtitle. It's actually more relevant with the content of Aqz005.
⑧ After "The", "principles" was crossed out.
⑨ After "Literati", "believe heaven" was crossed out.
⑩ Before "admit", "to be the pri aknowledge" was crossed out.
⑪ Locke put it as "noe".
⑫ After "true", "spirits" was crossed out. It seems Locke was not happy with this paragraph, so he ended with starting all over.

这说明从各方面来讲，

不管古代中国人的观点如何，

最近四五百年来，

整个儒教一直将"物质的天"

视为唯一的第一律、源或因，

因而儒教以"<u>上帝</u>"

或"<u>天</u>"之名，

将"物质的天"

视为"至高无上的神"。

Aqz003

183
精神和人类灵魂
B

儒教不承认

纯粹精神①

---

① 洛克在手稿中将"精神"（spirit）划去，并在下一行重写。

The principles of the Sect of the
Literati admit no① true spirits & so②
the Chineses③ of that sect④ acknowledge⑤
not⑥ the⑦ souls of men
be immortal. Never the less they
do⑧ not think that they are extinguished
perfectly⑨ perish as soon as they
are separated from the body.

[To the right-hand side of the page]
They⑩ do⑪ not believe
that the souls of men
have a permanent duration but after
40 days are reduced to their first principle.

[Back to the left-hand side of the page]
They
imagine them to be a part of that subtle
matter which they call <u>Li</u> or <u>Taikie</u>,

---

① Locke put it as "noe".
② Locke put it as "soe".
③ After "Chineses", "ack" was crossed out.
④ After "sect", "ack" was crossed out.
⑤ Locke put it as "acknowlede".
⑥ "not" is indistinct in Locke's ms.
⑦ After "the", "immortality of the" was crossed out.
⑧ Locke put it as "doe".
⑨ After "perfectly", "vanish" was crossed out.
⑩ Locke put it as "The".
⑪ Locke put it as "doe".

儒教经典不承认
纯粹精神，
因此信仰儒教的中国人
不相信人的灵魂不朽，
然而他们也不认为
灵魂一离开肉体
就立即消失或
完全寂灭。

［页面右侧注］
（对灵魂离开肉体存在的时间做明确的说明——译者）
中国人认为人的灵魂
不能永远存在，
而是在（肉体死亡——译者）
40天后归于第一律。

［回到页面左侧］
他们
将灵魂想象为他们称之为
"理"或"太极"的微妙物质的一部分，

which being separated from the body by death
is spread in the air & joins① itself again to other parts of②
that prime genial exceeding subtle matter
called <u>Li</u> or <u>Taikie</u> which is everywhere.
Hence they find③ no④ difficulty to imagine
that some part of that subtle matter which comprises
the souls of the deceased is prevailed with
by their sacrifice & oblations to come to
& rest upon the tablet which bears the name
of the party.

[To the right-hand side of the page, vertical center]
Chin hoan
Genÿ

---

① Locke put it as "joynes".
② After "parts of", "<u>Li</u> or <u>Taikie</u>" was crossed out.
③ Locke put it as "finde".
④ Locke put it as "noe".

一旦人死后灵魂脱离肉体,
便散布于空气中,
并再度融合于无所不在的
名为"理"或"太极"的
终极微妙物质。因而,
他们很容易想象构成死者灵魂的
微妙物质的某些部分
(在人死后——译者)依然存在,
并且当他们祭祀和祈祷时,
还能降临并停留在
写有死者姓名的牌位上。

[页面右侧,垂直居中]
城隍
守护神①

---

① "城隍"和"守护神"写在本页手稿右侧垂直居中位置,看起来像书签式标记,提示此页主题"精神和人类灵魂"与第199页主题"城隍、守护神"有关联。

Aqz004

$$\left.\begin{array}{l}\text{Yeu Hoen}\\ \text{Ly Kuei}\end{array}\right\}$$ ①

Spiritus et
Anima errant②

C③

They have also solemn ceremonies④ at times appointed
to those they call the wandering souls
or spirits which have no⑤ settled abode
or fixed place. These are the souls⑥
of those who died without heirs. To
those⑦ they offer edible things
for their use, to this end that they would
do⑧ no⑨ hurt to men, would remove
their infirmity & do⑩ them other
good turns.

[to the right-hand side of the page]
Anima
humana

---

① These two words are Chinese, meaning "离魂" and "游魂".
② It's Latin, meaning "spirit and wandering soul".
③ On the right-hand side of the page, Locke wrote "Anima humana" which means "human soul" as a subtitle.
④ After "solemn", Locke first crossed out "sacrifices" and changed it to "ceremonies". Then "ceremonies" was also crossed out. Locke should have got it wrong. So the transcriber kept "ceremonies".
⑤ Locke put it as "noe".
⑥ Locke put it as "soules".
⑦ After "to those", Locke put "to those" again. He should have got it wrong.
⑧ Locke put it as "doe".
⑨ Locke put it as "noe".
⑩ Locke put it as "doe".

Aqz004

185
{游魂
离魂
精神和游魂
C

有时中国人也举行隆重的仪式来
纪念那些居无定所的灵魂或精神，
他们称之为"游魂"。
游魂是那些
没有后嗣的死者的灵魂。
中国人向游魂奉献吃的东西
供其享用，这样
游魂不但不会害人，
还为人们去除疾病，
并赐予人们其他福报。

［页面右侧，垂直居中］
灵魂
人类①

---

① "灵魂"和"人类"写在本页手稿右侧垂直居中位置，类似书签式标记，提示此页主题"游魂与离魂"与第183页主题"精神和人类灵魂"有关联。

Aqz005

186
Xanti①
Rex Altus②
D1

Xanti literally③ signifies <u>the high King</u> or supreme Emperor.
By④ this name, the⑤ ancient Chineses & philosophers
from⑥ all antiquity backward
quite⑦ down to this time mean⑧ nothing⑨
but the material heaven

[Inserted, to the right-hand side of the page]
or what in the stars or heavenly bodies is most refined
& excellent, an inherent virtue in the māāl⑩
heaven, which influences & governs things here
below & therefore they call it the high or supreme
Emperor. To which though they refer
the changes & events of things. Yet
they allow no understanding nor knowledge

---

① It's Chinese, meaning "上帝".
② It's Latin, meaning "high king".
③ Locke put it as "literali".
④ Before "by", "high" was crossed out.
⑤ After "the", "Chineses" was crossed out.
⑥ After "from", one word was crossed out. It's unrecognizable.
⑦ Before "quite", "ages past" was crossed out.
⑧ Locke put it as "meane".
⑨ Locke put it as "noe thing".
⑩ Material

Aqz005

186
上帝

D1

"上帝"字面上的意思是指
"最高的主宰"或"至高无上的王"。
从古代的中国人和哲学家开始,
直到今天,"上帝"指的都是
"物质的天",

[页面右侧注]
或者说是星体或天体中
最纯净完美的部分,
即"物质的天"里影响和统摄
天下万物的某种内在德行,
因而中国人称之为"上""帝"。
中国人用"上帝"指称事物的变化和发展,
但是中国人不认为"上帝"理解或知晓这一切。

in it & those ways of speaking are
like those in this part of the world:
"So[①] it pleased the Fates" or "Fate
would have it so[②]" though they allowed
no[③] knowledge in fate at all.

[Back to the left-hand side of the page]
or a most subtle
matter or quintessence which they call <u>Li</u> or
<u>Taikie</u>, which dispersed through the parts
of the universe,
[Inserted]
mixing itself with all heavenly & earthly bodies,
remaining in greatest plenty
in those things which had the greatest excellency
of nature. From which it appears that they never
acknowledge[④] any pure spirits wholly void of matter.
It being the[⑤] settled & unmovable[⑥] foundation
of all their philosophy[⑦], "<u>That all things are One</u>".[⑧]

It is impossible to bring into use in China
any European name to express god by both because

---

① Locke put it as "soe".
② Locke put it as "soe".
③ Locke put it as "noe".
④ Locke put it as "acknowledg".
⑤ After "the", "sacred" was crossed out.
⑥ Locke put it as "unmoveable".
⑦ Locke put it as "philosoph".
⑧ Locke underlines this twice.

中国也有与世界这一端（指西方——译者）

类似的说法，比如

"命中注定"

"命该如此"，

但"命"是盲目的。①

［回到页面左侧］

（"上帝"——译者）还指中国人称为

"理"或"太极"的某种

最微妙的物质或精髓，

遍布宇宙各处，

［插入］

融于天地万物，

尤聚于造化神秀所钟之物。

由此可见，中国人不承认

完全独立于物质的纯粹精神。

中国哲学既定的、

不可动摇的基础是

<u>"万物同一体"</u>②。

在中国，用任何欧洲名称来指称

"God"都是不可能的，原因有二：

---

① 此处洛克讨论的是中国的"上帝"与基督教的"God"的不同。洛克认为从某种程度来说，中国的"上帝"类似于西方的"命运"，指事物的发展和变化，但本身是无知无觉的、盲目的，这与基督教"全能、全知、全善"的"God"截然不同。

② 手稿中将"万物同一体"（That all things are one）用两道下划线标注出来，说明洛克认为这是中国哲学最重要的原则，也是最能说明问题的地方。古希腊哲学以降，从古时的伊壁鸠鲁、德谟克利特，到17世纪的斯宾诺莎，"万物同一体"一直是欧洲唯物论的核心观念。洛克全力强调中国人相信"万物同一体"就是将中国哲学与唯物论联系起来，而对于洛克时代的知识分子来说，这种联系就等于认定中国哲学是一种唯物论哲学。

they have no character to write it in, and because[①]
our names of god would not be able to excite in their minds[②] the idea of the thing signified. Therefore the first missionaries that came amongst them made choice of <u>Tien Chu, Lord of heaven</u> to signify[③] god[④] as fit by its signification amongst them to excite in their minds[⑤] an Excellent Being, Master[⑥] & Sovereign[⑦] over heaven[⑧] which is the substance to which the Chinese[⑨] ascribe[⑩] superiority of nature above any other thing. Some are of a mind[⑪] that <u>Xanti</u> from[⑫] the first founding the Chinese Empire & the Sect of the Literati 3000 years since signified

---

① After "because", "they have noe idea in their minde" was crossed out.
② Locke put it as "mindes". After "minds", "any" was crossed out.
③ Locke put it as "signifie".
④ After "god", "w" was crossed out.
⑤ Locke put it as "mindes".
⑥ Before "master", "superior" was crossed out. From the context, Locke should have crossed it out. He might want to underline it or have crossed it out by mistake.
⑦ Locke put it as "Soveraigne". Locke crossed a word out and changed it into "Soveraigne". The word crossed out is unrecognizable.
⑧ After "heaven", "which is the thing in the opinion of the Chinese" was crossed out.
⑨ Locke put it as "Chines".
⑩ After "ascribe", "ascribe" was crossed out.
⑪ Locke put it as "minde".
⑫ Between "Xanti" and "from", a mark looking like "Q" was inserted.

其一,没有中国字来书写"God",

其二,我们用来指称"God"的名称

无法使中国人的头脑中产生它所指代的概念。

因此,那些最早融入中国人当中的传教士[①]

选择了"天主"这个词来指称"God"。

他们认为这是个合适的词,

原因是"天主"这个词的意思

能够使中国人的头脑里

产生一种完美存在,

即"天主"和"天帝",

中国人认为

这种完美的存在

从本质上超越任何其他事物。

有些人[②]认为从三千年前

中华帝国以及儒教的建立之初开始,

[①] 指利玛窦等耶稣会士。利玛窦刚进入中国时最早使用"天主"一词来指称"God"。据说利玛窦早在1583年就使用过这一术语,而在他之前,罗明坚在肇庆教化的一位青年也使用了"天主"一词。参见张国刚:《从中西初识到礼仪之争——明清传教士与中西文化交流》,北京:人民出版社,2003年,第391页注释1。

[②] 指以利玛窦为代表的耶稣会士。

Aqz006

187
Xanti
D2

signified the true god for
the space of above 2000
years together. Others with strong
reasons oppose this & contend that
it always signified the material heaven

[To the right-hand side of the page]
& is an honourable name which they give to that

[Back to the left-hand side of the page]
or some energetical power of it which
they call Li & Taikie. They
who speak most in favour of the
Chineses as the worshipers of the true god

[To the right-hand side of the page]
pretend that Xanti signified the true
immaterial god from the beginning of the
empire till about the sixtieth year
of Christ. But that then the[①] Literati

[①] The word before "literati" is blurred in Locke's ms. It looks like "the".

Aqz006

187
上帝
D2

在之后的两千多年时间里，
"上帝"这个词指的都是"真正的上帝"①。
另一些人②则强烈反对这一观点，
他们认为"上帝"这个词一直指的都是
"物质的天"，

［页面右侧］
中国人用"上帝"这个词尊称"物质的天"，

［回到页面左侧］
或者"物质的天"的某种"气"，
他们称之为"<u>理</u>"或"<u>太极</u>"。
而主张中国人信仰"真正的上帝"
的那些人③

［页面右侧］
声称从中华帝国建立之初到
公元六十年左右，
"<u>上帝</u>"指的都是
"真正的非物质的上帝"，

---

① 指基督教的"神"（God）。
② 指利玛窦"适应政策"的反对者，如龙华民、闵明我等。
③ 指的是以白晋为代表的索隐派，他们比利玛窦走得更远，认为在中国古代经典中可以找到上帝的影子。

the better to oppose the growing sects of
the Idolators & magi left of the
notion of any immaterial being &①

[Locke wrote the following paragraph on the next page (Aqz007) which is the front side of a letter cover. Locke indicated the sequence with two arrow marks. Thus the next page is not numbered in Locke's MS.]

Aqz007

187v

&② consequently made their chief③ god
which was <u>Xanti</u> to be nothing but
the material heaven & its influence. It so④ degenerated from their
former⑤ doctrine concer-
ning god & the immortality
of the soul⑥, so⑦ that ever since
that or at least for about 500 years
backwards, <u>Xanti signifies nothing
but the material heaven</u>. The
Literati nay all the whole

---

① There is an arrow mark after "&".
② There is an arrow mark before "&".
③ Locke put it as "cheif".
④ Locke put it as "soe".
⑤ After "former", "ancient" was crossed out.
⑥ Locke put it as "soule".
⑦ Locke put it as "soe".

第三章 "中国笔记"的文本与要点 67

只是后来为了更好地对付
日益壮大的佛教和道教，
儒教不再提起任何非物质存在①，

［洛克将此处之后的部分内容写在该页的背面，即信封正面的空白处，并使用相对应的两个箭头来标识。这部分内容在洛克手稿中没有编号，本书将之编为Aqz007 (f.187v)。］

Aqz007

［187背面］

这使得中国人的主神"上帝"
仅指"物质的天"及其力量。
因此，"上帝"从古代经典中
与"God"和灵魂不朽相关的概念
下降了。从此以后，
最起码在今天之前的
约五百年②中，
"上帝"仅指"物质的天"。
（如今——译者）儒家
以及全体中国人
都将"上帝"理解为

---

① 指的是儒教为了更好地与佛教和道教相区别而避免提及非物质存在的概念。
② 此处手稿数字不清楚，可能是500，也可能是900。

body of the Chinese nation① understand
nothing by Xanti but the material
heaven or its influence & effective
power.

[Back to the left-hand side of Aqz 006]
The Emperor himself is②, [as]
it③ were, the high priest of
his whole country for he alone offers sacrifice
twice a year to Xanti in the name
& for the whole people as their representative

[To the right-hand side of the page]
or as chief④ & head of the sect of the
Literati, for he is not only supreme magistrate
but the high priest of his people.

[Back to the left-hand side of the page]
To this purpose, there are⑤ two magnificent temples in the two imperial palaces⑥ at
Nankin & Pekin, the usual residence
of the Emperor and no⑦ where else.

---

① It means "not only the Literati, but also the whole Chinese nation".
② After "is", "the only" is crossed out.
③ Before "it", "priest of" is crossed out.
④ Locke put it as "cheif".
⑤ Locke crossed out "Xanti has" and change it to "there are".
⑥ After "palaces", "only" was crossed out.
⑦ Locke put it as "noe".

"物质的天"
及其影响和作用力。

［回到手稿第187页（Aqz006）的左侧］
皇帝本人同时也是
整个国家的最高神职人员。
皇帝每年以全国百姓之名，
代表全国百姓
祭祀"上帝"两次。

［手稿第187页（Aqz006）页面右侧］
（祭祀"上帝"时——译者）
皇帝也以儒教领袖或首脑的身份出现，
这是因为皇帝不仅是最高的世俗统治者，
也是其子民的最高神职人员。

［回到手稿第187页（Aqz006）页面左侧］
为此①，只在南京和北京
作为皇帝日常居所的
两座皇宫里，
建有两座恢弘的寺庙，

---

① 指为了皇帝祭祀"上帝"，也就是祭天。

When[①]

[To the right-hand side of the page]
he is hindered from officiating, he substitutes some of his chief[②] ministers to perform the solemnities wherein they sacrifice great numbers of sheep & oxen with[③] the addition of many rites.

[Back to the left-hand side of the page]
And more of the time[④] when he is present, he sacrifices twice a year to the material heaven or its energy[⑤] assisted by some of his great mandarins or the chiefest[⑥] of the Literati in that performance.[⑦] It is a settled rite amongst them for the Emperor every year to sacrifice to the Heaven & the Earth in the acknowledgement of the benefits received of them.

---

① After "when", "by his affairs of state" was crossed out.
② Locke put it as "cheif".
③ After "which", "it" was crossed out.
④ The word after "the" is smudged in Locke's ms. It could be "time" in the context.
⑤ Locke put it as "energie".
⑥ Locke put it as "cheifest".
⑦ After this sentence, "The emperor sacrifices every year to the heaven & also to the earth." was crossed out.

其他地方都没有。

［页面右侧］
当皇帝忙于国事，分身乏术时，
他会在首辅大臣中挑几个
代替自己祭祀。在这些祭祀中，
除了履行很多礼仪外，
中国人会奉献大量的牛羊。

［回到页面左侧］
多数时候，
皇帝会亲自主持祭祀。
皇帝每年亲自祭祀"物质的天"
或其"精气神"两次，
一些重要官员和儒教领袖会辅助皇帝祭祀。
皇帝每年祭祀天地，
并宣布从天地获得的福祉，
这是中国人的传统礼仪。

Aqz008

188
Tien
E

<u>Tien</u> properly signifies the heavens in general, ie the stars & planets, the most noble & excellent part of the visible world

[Inserted, to the right-hand side of the page]
beyond which they do not acknowledge any more excellent substance

[Back to the left-hand side of the page]
which therefore the Chineses thought worthy of divine honours & count the worship paid them one of the most laudable customs of their country.

Aqz008

188
天
E

"天"可以指
天的统称、星体和星球,
它们是可见世界中
最高贵、最完美的部分,

［页面右侧］
中国人认为再没有比它们更完美的物质了,

［回到页面左侧］
因而中国人觉得
它们应当受到神圣的礼遇,
同时将对它们的祭祀
视为中国最值得称道的
风俗之一。

The Tartars who in the last age
overran Tartary① have taken to the religion of the Literati of China
&② follow their Idolatrous
worship in everything especially that
which is paid to the heavenly bodies &
their motions whereunto they
ascribe great power & virtue.

Confucius & their other ancient
philosophers acknowledged no③ other
original of all things but the material
heavens & that is worshiped.

The Chineses of the Sect of the
Literati hold the heaven to be the most excellent
of all things that exist & to be the most beneficial
to all the rest &④ for that reason to be
chiefly⑤ worshiped.

---

① Locke put it as "Tartarie".
② Before "&", "of the Chineses" was crossed out.
③ Locke put it as "noe".
④ After "&", "therefore" was crossed out.
⑤ Locke put it as "cheifly".

在过去的几十年里
横扫中国①的鞑靼人②
皈依了中国的儒教,
也开始对万物进行偶像崇拜。
他们尤其崇拜天体及其运动,
并将其视为伟大的力量与德行之源。

孔子和儒家其他古代哲学家
认为只有"物质的天"
才是万物之源,
因此儒教崇拜"物质的天"。

信仰儒教的中国人
认为"天"是万物中
最完美的存在,
并有益万物,
因而将其作为主要崇拜对象。

---

① 鞑靼地区(Tartary)指13和14世纪蒙古人控制的亚洲北部和欧洲东部的广大地区。而《马可波罗行纪》中将鞑靼地区分为东鞑靼和西鞑靼,东鞑靼指由旭烈兀及其后代统治的伊利汗国,它以帖必力思为都会,东滨阿姆河,西临地中海,北界里海、黑海、高加索,南至波斯湾;西鞑靼指由术赤的儿子拔都、别儿哥及其后代统治的金帐汗国,即钦察汗国,它东起额尔齐斯河,西到斡罗思,南起巴尔喀什湖、里海、黑海,北到北极圈附近,并对东欧各公国享有宗主权。而此处洛克是用中国北部的鞑靼地区来泛指中国。

② 鞑靼人(Tartars)是古时汉族对北方各游牧民族的统称,自唐迄元先后有达怛、达靼、塔坦、鞑靼、达打、达达诸译,其指称范围随时代不同而有异。欧洲人按照马可·波罗的习惯,把中国北方的少数民族通称为鞑靼,明清之际入华的传教士也沿用这个称呼,称满族为鞑靼,如帕莱福的《鞑靼征服中国史》、鲁日满的《鞑靼中国史》、卫匡国的《鞑靼战纪》等。

Aqz009

190
Confucius
F1

Confucius has a temple or chapel① in every city built near the school in which his tablet is placed with this inscription in golden letters "The throne or seat of the soul② of the most holy & super excellent chief③ master Confucius. On this tablet they

[To the right-hand side of the page]
suppose the spirit of Confucius to be present and rest there on during their oblation & other ceremonies performed to him. In the front of this Temple, there is this inscription, "<u>The Temple of Learning</u>④" or "<u>the Temple of the Dead Master</u>".

[Back to the left-hand side of the page]
In this Chapel⑤ or temple, all the men of letters of the place assemble

---

① Locke put it as "chappol".
② Locke put it as "soule".
③ Locke put it as "cheif".
④ Locke put it as "learneing".
⑤ Locke put it as "chappel".

Aqz009

190
孔子
F1

每个城市里
靠近学校的地方
都有孔庙,
里面供奉孔子的牌位,
上书金漆大字:
"大成至圣先师孔子神位"。

[页面右侧注]
中国人相信
在他们祭孔或举行其他仪式的时候,
孔子的魂魄就栖于这个牌位之上。
孔庙正前方刻着
"<u>文庙</u>"或"<u>先师庙</u>"。

[回到页面左侧]
每年春分和秋分,
地方上的所有文人

every vernal and autumnal equinox

that they may there worship Confucius

as the① founder & common father

of the Chinese philosophy② & learning.

The Governor or chief③ mandarin④

of the place performs⑤ the office of priest,

taking⑥ to him others of the learned Literati

as ministers in the ceremony⑦,

by⑧ whom

all⑨ things are performed both preparatory to

& in the solemnity after the same manner

as in their oblations to their ancestors,

only with these differences that the time

of beginning their solemnity is

always the night before the equinox.

The

---

① After "the", "common" was crossed out.
② Locke put it as "philosophie".
③ Locke put it as "cheif".
④ Locke put it as "mandarine".
⑤ Locke put it as "performes".
⑥ Locke put it as "takeing".
⑦ After "ceremony", "as after the" was crossed out.
⑧ Before "by", "several ministers as in the when" was crossed out.
⑨ Locke put it as "al".

都会聚集在孔庙祭孔，
他们视孔子为
中国哲学的奠基人
和中国学术之父。

地方行政长官或主要官员
担任主祭官，
另一些儒生担任参祭官①。
祭孔仪式从准备到实施
都与祭祖仪式如出一辙，
唯一的区别是
开始祭孔的时间
一直是春分或秋分的前夜。

---

① 祭孔仪式的参祭人员一般由主祭官、陪祀官、分献官、通赞、引赞、鸣赞、读祝生、乐舞生组成，洛克所说的ministers应该是泛指主祭官之外的其他参祭人员，本书中统一译为参祭官。

Aqz010

191

Confucius

F2

The day before the equinox

the chief[①] mandarin[②] as priest for the

time, with his other select ministers

as officers for that time, prepare in the hall of their college[③] the

rice, pulse & other fruits of the

earth which are to be offered. & the Mandarin

in the court of the temple, where

on stand lighted tapers, burns[④]

frankincense & other perfumes[⑤] on

coals[⑥] placed there to that purpose. After

which he ties the beasts to be sacrificed as

before, & when the hog is approved of,

he with great respect bows to it

& salutes it before it is killed[⑦], & then

it being killed[⑧] by the butchers. The

Mandarin[⑨] who officiates as

---

① Locke put it as "cheif".
② Locke put it as "mandarine".
③ Locke put it as "colledg".
④ Before "burns", "burning" is crossed out.
⑤ Locke put it as "parfumes".
⑥ Locke put it as "coles".
⑦ Locke put it as "kild".
⑧ Locke put it as "kild".
⑨ Locke put it as "Mandarine". Before "Mandarine", "pri" was crossed out.

Aqz010

191
孔子
F2

春分或秋分的前一天，
担任主祭官的官员
和其他被推选出来的参祭官
在学院的大殿中
准备好献祭所用的
米、谷物和其他农作物①，
然后来到孔庙的院子里，
主祭官在香案上点燃香烛，
并在专门用来焚香的炭火上
焚烧乳香②和其他香料。
然后主祭官把祭祀用的牲畜
按照原样捆好。
祭祀用的猪被认可之后、
被宰杀之前，
主祭官会非常恭敬地
向它鞠躬致敬。

---

① 中国祭孔时，祭品有猪、牛、羊三牲，还有盐、猫血、苋米、菱角等。
② 乳香是一种气息芬芳的树胶脂，源自某种鲍达乳香树，原产于阿拉伯、印度和埃塞俄比亚。乳香的英文"frankincense"源于古法语"franc encens"，指高级、贵重的香料。西方的宗教仪式常用乳香，如古埃及和古罗马的祭司曾大量使用乳香在神庙中制造异香缭绕的神秘气氛。乳香也是犹太教圣殿中所燃的香料之一，旧约全书前五卷中经常提到乳香。《马太福音》第二章第11节记载，来自东方的贤士带了黄金、乳香和没药去伯利恒朝圣，将其奉献给降诞于人间的耶稣。

priest pays his reverence again to
the hog after the same manner &
then the hair being shaved①
are kept with the guts & the blood
till the next day.

The next morning the mandarin
with his ministers chosen for this solemnity &
the whole body of the Literati assemble
in Confucius's temple before②
cock crowing. The tapers
being

Aqz011

192
Confucius
F3

being lighted, they burn incense
& perfumes③ on the altar. And the
Master of the Ceremonies giving④ the
sign⑤, the music⑥ strikes up.

---

① After "shaved", "of &" was crossed out.
② Before "before", three words were crossed out. It's illegible.
③ Locke put it as "parfumes".
④ Locke put it as "giveing".
⑤ Locke put it as "signe".
⑥ Locke put it as "musick".

而后屠夫杀猪时,
担任主祭官的官员
要再次以同样的方式
向献祭的猪致敬。
之后会剃掉猪毛,并
与内脏和猪血一起
留待第二天使用。

第二天早上,
主祭官和参祭官们
以及全体儒生
于鸡鸣前
在孔庙集合。

Aqz011

192
孔子
F3

他们点燃香烛,
并在香案上焚香。
通赞示意后
便开始奏乐。

After this, the Mandarin① lifts② up the hair and blood of the sacrifice in a dish before the inscribed tablet. The master of the ceremonies crying out at the same time, "The hair & blood are offering." which done they③ all in a long train go out into the court of the temple where they bury the blood & hair & then return in the same order into the temple every one into his place & then the master of the ceremonies cries④ out, "The spirit of Confucius descends." which is no sooner said but the priest or mandarin⑤ takes a bowl⑥ full of wine & pours it upon a man of Straw & then they take the tablet⑦ inscribed with Confucius's name out of the cabinet in which it is kept and place it on the altar, reciting a prayer where is contained⑧ exceeding great praises of Confucius.

---

① Locke put it as "mandarine". After "mandarine", "the" was crossed out.
② Before "lifts", "master of" was crossed out.
③ Before "they", "upon which" was crossed out.
④ Locke put it as "crys".
⑤ Locke put it as "mandarine".
⑥ Locke put it as "bowle".
⑦ After "tablet", "inscribed with of inscription which Confucius's tablet" was crossed out.
⑧ Locke put it as "conteind".

主祭官将盘中盛放的毛血
高举至孔子牌位前,
同时通赞唱:
"毛血为供奉"。
而后所有人
排长队走出孔庙,
来到院子里,
并将毛血埋在那里,
然后再按同样的顺序
回到孔庙内。
所有人就位后,
通赞唱:
"孔圣人神降",
与此同时,
主祭官端起满满一碗酒
倒在一个稻草人上。
随后,
他们将刻有孔子名字的牌位
从神龛中取出,
并放置在香案上,
同时唱诵盛赞孔子的祭文。
这样祭孔仪式就进入第二部分。

[To the right-hand side of the page]

Every[①] city

[Inserted] by order of law has a magnificent

Temple[②] to Confucius.

& in these Temples, there are tables made

altarwise & all the other furniture of

a temple which is in many other of their temples.

This temple is placed near the schools

where they perform[③] their exercises

for their degrees & adjoining[④] to these

is the palace of the Mandarin[⑤]

who[⑥] is president & has the

inspection over those who have attained[⑦]

the highest degree in their literature.

In these temples is[⑧] the statue of

Confucius or his tablet of inscription

[Inserted] very finely wrought

in[⑨] golden letters a cubitaliis[⑩] & by him

---

① At the top of the right-hand side of the page, "all this" was crossed out. Then " Every city has a Temple to Confucius. The" was crossed out.

② Before "Temple", "has" was crossed out. There is an "a" in Locke's ms, however, this "a" should be crossed out.

③ Locke put it as "performe".

④ Locke put it as "adjoyning".

⑤ Locke put it as "Mandarine".

⑥ After "who", "has" was crossed out.

⑦ Locke put it as "atteind".

⑧ Locke crossed out "are" and changed it to "is" in his ms.

⑨ Locke crossed out "with" and changed it to "in".

⑩ It's Latin, meaning "lying down".

[页面右侧,关于孔庙的详细介绍]
依照律法规定,
每座城市
都有一座宏伟的孔庙,
庙内设有香案
和其他一些
中国寺庙中常见的设施。
孔庙都建在
中国人举行科举考试的学校附近,
地方行政长官的府邸也在附近。
地方长官在孔庙接见那些
文学成绩最好的应试者。

孔庙里供奉着
孔子的塑像或牌位,
牌位上以金漆
自上而下

stand the images of some of the most
eminent of his scholars who are
by the Chinese① made② saints but of
a lower degree.

His writings have the same authority
there as the Gospel with us.

They invite the Spirit of Confucius
to come & remain upon the tablet of
inscription & partake of the things
offered to③ him.

[Back to the left-hand side of the page]
This being in this manner
Performed, they come to the se-
cond

---

① Locke put it as "Chines".
② Before "made", there is "are" which should be a mistake.
③ After "to", "them" was crossed out.

精书孔子之名。
孔子塑像或牌位旁边
则供奉着一些
儒教最杰出学者的塑像，
中国人将他们视为
比孔子低一级的圣人。

孔子著作之于中国人的权威
相当于四福音书之于我们。

中国人请孔子的魂魄
降临并栖于牌位之上，
以享用祭品。

［回到页面左侧］
如此，
进入祭祀仪式的
第二部分。

Aqz012

193
Confucius
F4

cond[①] part of the sacrifice. The
Master of the Ceremonies cries[②] out,
"Down upon your knees." & then they all
kneel. Then he cries[③], "Rise." & presently
they all stand up.

[Inserted, to the right-hand side of the page]
And if any one present should
neglect to obey his orders, he would
be looked on as a contempter of Confucius
(or his progenitors[④], when it is to their
progenitors that the ceremonies are
performing) & would be evil indeed.

[Back to the left-hand side of the page]
Then the Mandarin
or priest washes his hands & then one
of the ministers brings him a piece[⑤]

---

① It should be "second". Locke repeated the second half of the last word "second" in last page thus ended with "cond".

② Locke put it as "cryes".

③ Locke put it as "cryes".

④ It's Latin, meaning "ancestors".

⑤ Locke put it as "peice".

Aqz012

193
孔子
F4

祭孔仪式第二部分。
通赞唱"跪",
在场的所有人跪下。
通赞唱"兴",
在场的所有人再站起来。

［页面右侧］
如果在场有人
不听从通赞的指令,
这个人就会被视作
对孔子（或祖先,
如果当时是在祭祖的话）
不敬,罪大恶极。

［回到页面左侧］
然后地方行政长官
或主祭官浴手,
一个参祭官为他捧来

of silk & another a bowl① of wine. When he has these, the Master of the Ceremonies cries out, "Let the priest approach the throne of Confucius." Then the music② playing, he first offers the silk & then the wine to Confucius, lifting it up on high, upon which the master of the ceremonies crying four times, "Let us kneel." & "Rise." All③ that are present prostrate themselves and stand up as often. The④ piece⑤ of silk is burnt & a collect⑥ in praise of Confucius is repeated. In like manner, after many⑦ kneelings and & risings, the wine is offered with a prayer wherein [Inserted] he addresses himself to the spirit of Confucius as present. One of the Collects⑧ used in these sacrifices to the honour of Confucius was composed by one of their Emperors.

---

① Locke put it as "bowle".
② Locke put it as "musick".
③ Before "all", "the prostration & standing up are as often performed by th" was crossed out.
④ After "the", there is another "the" in Locke's ms. It should be a mistake.
⑤ Locke put it as "peice".
⑥ After "collect", "to the" was crossed out.
⑦ After "many", "rising" was crossed out.
⑧ After "Collects", "repe" was crossed out.

一块帛和一碗酒①。

通赞唱

"主祭官近孔子神位",

然后奏乐,

主祭官向

置于高处的孔子牌位

先献帛,再献酒。

而后通赞唱四次

"叩,兴"②,

在场的所有人叩拜四次。

然后举柴焚祝帛,

并再次奏乐颂扬孔子。

献酒的时候

同样要叩拜多次,

同时一个祭官

会宣读一段祭文,

口气如同孔子魂魄在场一般。

所有的这些祭孔的仪式中

有一段乐

出自一位中国的皇帝所做。③

---

① 中国国学网对于祭孔仪式的该部分的记载:"捧帛生以帛跪进,承祭官接帛拱举立献案上,执爵生以爵跪进,承祭官接爵拱举。"参见http://www.confucianism.com.cn/html/A00030019/4109658.html,《祭孔程序及礼仪》。访问时间:2019年6月1日。
② 明代礼,久别见尊者要四拜示敬;对先师四拜,以达久敬之思。
③ 宋太祖建隆元年(960年),亲谒孔子庙,诏增修祠宇,绘先圣先贤先儒像,释奠用永安之乐。此处可能是指永安乐。

Aqz013

194
Confucius
F5

Then they come to the third① part of the
sacrifice. The Master of the Ceremonies
cries, "<u>Drink the wine of prosperity
& happiness.</u>" Then as before, he cries②, "<u>Let us
Kneel.</u>" And speaking to the priest,
he says, "<u>Drink the wine of hap-
pines.</u>" And then he drinks it off,
which done the Master of the Ceremonies
crying, "<u>Take the flesh of the sacrifice.</u>"
A minister brings it to the priest
& he with both his hands lifting it up
on high offers it, accompanying it with
two collects, the later of which concludes,
"Thus what we have offered to thee is clean &
of a sweet savour. These ceremonies being
performed, we mortals rest in peace.
But the spirit is rejoiced. The consequence of these sacrifices shall be
the obtaining of wealth & happiness.

Last of all,③

---

① Locke put it as "3ᵈˢ".
② Locke put it as "cryes".
③ After "After it all", "they accompany the" was crossed out.

Aqz013

194
孔子
F5

接下来是祭孔仪式的第三部分。
通赞唱：
"<u>饮福酒</u>"，
而后同前，
通赞唱"<u>跪</u>"。
通赞对主祭官唱：
"<u>饮福酒</u>"，
主祭官将酒饮尽。
通赞唱："<u>受胙</u>"。
参祭官将祭品交予主祭官，
主祭官双手举起献祭，
这一过程伴着两段乐，
其中第二段的结尾是
"我们所奉献的祭品是
洁净而美味的。
举行了这样的仪式，
肉体安息而精神愉悦。
祭祀会带来财富和幸福。"①

最后，他们将孔子

---

① 现行各地文庙使用的乐曲和歌词基本上是沿用北宋大成府所编撰的，共有十四首，传到明、清时期保留了六首，其中清代祭孔典礼撰馔所用的《咸和之曲》："牺象在前。豆笾在列。以享以荐。既芬既洁。礼成乐备。人和神悦。祭则受福。率遵无越。"本段内容与此类似。

they① carry back the
tablet of inscription to its place & all
the② assistants accompany his spirit
which they believe or pretend descended
& rested on that tablet③
during④ all the ceremony and take
their leave of him with a solemn prayer.

[To the right-hand side of the page]
Amongst other things contained in
their prayers, they say thus, " All strive
to offer sacrifices to thee. Whatever
we offer thee is pure, therefore let thy
spirit come to illuminate us and be
present with us." They⑤ conclude,
"We have with all reverence sacrificed
to thee. We have beseeched thee to be
present & receive our oblations of a
sweet savour. Now we accompany thy
spirit which is returning to his place. The
sacrifice is ended & we receive by it all
manner of good fortune."

---

① Before "they", "spirit of Confucius" was crossed out.
② After "the", "company" was crossed out.
③ After "tablet", "at the time of" were crossed out.
④ Before "during", "the" was crossed out.
⑤ After "they", there is another "they" in Locke's ms. It should be a mistake.

及其他圣人的牌位搬回原位，
所有参与祭祀的人
陪伴着孔子的魂魄，
中国人相信
在祭孔的过程中，
孔子的魂魄
降临于牌位上。
然后他们用庄重的祈祷
恭送孔圣离开。

［页面右侧注，对祈祷文内容的补充说明］
中国人在祈祷文中
还提到如下内容：
"所有人都争相向您献祭，
我们奉献给您的都是清洁的，
因此，请您的魂魄降临照亮我们
并与我们同在。"
祈祷文的结尾是这样的：
"我们怀着敬意向您献了祭，
我们知道您就在这里，
接受我们味道甜美的贡品。
现在我们陪伴您的灵魂归位。
祭祀结束了，
我们通过祭祀获得各种福报。"①

---

① 清代祭孔典礼送神所用的《咸和之曲》："有严学宫。四方来宗。恪恭祀事。威仪雝雝。歆兹唯馨。神驭还复。明烟斯毕。咸膺百福。"本段内容与此类似。

Aqz014

195
Confucius
F6

prayer. The flesh of the Sacrifice
is divided amongst the Assistants

[To the right-hand side of the page]
which they eat then or carry home
with them.

[Back to the left-hand side of the page]
And those who eat of them persuade① themselves that they shall receive by Confucius
blessings & happiness.

[To the right-hand side of the page]
The Master of the Ceremonies②, before
they break up, predicts & promises to them,
for the honour they have done Confucius,
all manner of prosperity of probity, wit
& parts & whatever else appertains to
the acquiring of knowledge③ & the attaining
of honour.

---

① Locke put it as "perswade".
② Locke put it as "Ceremonys".
③ Locke put it as "knowledg".

Aqz014

195
孔子
F6

祭祀用的肉
分给祭官们，

［页面右侧注］
他们当场分食
或带回家去，

［回到页面左侧］
他们认为
这样会得到孔子的
保佑和祝福。

［页面右侧注］
在参祭的人们散去之前，
通赞会向人们预言并许诺说，
因为祭祀了孔子，
他们将得到各种财富、
智慧、机敏、才能，
以及与获得知识、
获取功名相关的一切。

[Back to the left-hand side of the page]
Besides these two anniversary
sacrifices

[Inserted, to the right-hand side of the page]
made by the governor of every
city attended by all the other officers and literati

[Back to the left-hand side of the page]
in Spring and
Autumn, Confucius has other less
solemn devotions paid him all
the year round by the men of letters

[To the right-hand side of the page]
by genuflections, prostrations & incense & lighting
tapers before his image or <u>tablet of inscription</u>.

[Back to the left-hand side of the page]
For[①] first, the graduates in
their universities[②], as soon as they
have got their degrees, march from
the school to Confucius's Chapel[③].
& there before his tablet of inscription,
tapers burning on the Altar where it

---

① Before "For", "For first, the Doctors, Masters & Batchelors at the taking of their degrees as soon as they have got their degrees." was crossed out.
② Locke put it as "universitys".
③ Locke put it as "Chappol".

［回到页面左侧］
除了这两次

［页面右侧注］
由每个城市的行政长官举办、
城里所有官员和儒生参加的

［回到页面左侧］
春祭和秋祭外，
孔子整年都享受着
读书人非正式的祭祀，

［页面右侧注］
他们在孔子的塑像
或牌位前跪拜、烧香。

［回到页面左侧］
首先，孔子的牌位前所设的
供桌上一直燃着香，
大学的毕业生
一旦获取功名
就会从学校步行至孔庙，
向孔子奉献香烛，

is placed, they①

by② offering incense & odour

[To the right-hand side of the page]
which they themselves buy & pay for

[Back to the left-hand side of the page]
& prostrating③ themselves four times before him④,
pay their veneration to him as to their common Father & Master.

Aqz015

196
Confucius
F7

Besides this, the mandarins⑤ or gove-nors of towns & other magistrates⑥, before⑦ they enter upon their offices, repair to Confucius's⑧ temple and there express their veneration of him

---

① After "they", "pay their veneration unto" was crossed out.
② Before "by", "him" was crossed out.
③ Locke put it as "prostrateing".
④ After "him", "as is above mentioned" was crossed out.
⑤ Locke put it as "mandarines".
⑥ After "magistrate", "For" was crossed out.
⑦ Before "before", "in China" was crossed out.
⑧ After "Confucius's", "his" was crossed out.

［页面右侧注］
这些香烛由毕业生自己出资购买，①

［回到页面左侧］
并在孔子的牌位前
叩拜四次，
尊孔子为
他们共同的先祖和老师。

Aqz015

196
孔子
F7

其次，地方行政长官
和其他官员在上任之前
通常会拜谒孔庙，
并举行上述祭孔仪式
来致敬孔子。

---

① 在当时的牛津大学，学生毕业时需要自己支付相关的费用，因此洛克对中国的毕业生自己支付祭孔的花费这件事特别关注了一下。

in the foregoing ceremonies.

Thirdly, the mandarin or chief[①] magistrate of every city, twice every month, viz at new & full moon, before he goes to the bench for the hearing of causes, being attended with all the other officers & men of letters, repairs to the same temple of Confucius & there in like manner, tapers being lighted on the altar, he burns incense & odours

[To the right-hand side of the page]
at which solemnity, all the[②] graduate Literati are bound by the imperial law to assist,

[Back to the left-hand side of the page]
& makes his several prostrations, as above said, before the tablet of inscription. All those oblations & ceremonies in honour of Confucius are[③] so[④] firmly established[⑤] by the imperial law & by constant usage that whosoever omits them

---

① Locke put it as "cheif".
② After "the", one word was crossed out. It's illegible.
③ After "are", "estab" was crossed out. Locke must have intended to write "establish".
④ Locke put it as "soe".
⑤ Locke put it as "establish". It should be a mistake.

其三，每个城市的行政长官
每月朔望升堂审案之前，
也会在其他官员和文人陪同
拜谒孔庙，
同样在供桌上点燃香烛，
并由行政长官
焚烧各种香料，

［页面右侧注］
帝国的法律规定
所有从学校毕业的儒生
都必须从旁协助，

［回到页面左侧］
并如上文所述，
要在孔子的牌位前多次叩拜。
帝国的法律和一贯的践行
使得这些尊孔的礼仪和仪式根深蒂固，
任何无视它的人都很可能
受到丢官、夺爵，甚至丧命的处罚。

does it upon penalty of loss of his
place & degree & sometimes of life itself.

It is to be observed for the better understanding of this that no① man in China
is preferred to any place of civil dignity or②
trust, except he be a scholar &③
a

Aqz016

197
Confucius
F8

a graduate, to speak after out manner,
of their universities④.

The eminently learned of the Literati
do⑤ sometimes obtain by the edict of
the Emperor that⑥ their tablets
of inscription shall be hung up in
the Temple of Confucius. This they

---

① Locke put it as "noe".
② After "or", "honour" was crossed out.
③ After "&", "has taken" was crossed out.
④ Locke put it as "universitys".
⑤ Locke put it as "doe".
⑥ After "that", there is another "that" in Locke's ms. It should be a mistake.

为了更好地理解这一点,
我们应该知道,
在中国有机会担任行政职务的
只有学者和

Aqz016

197
孔子
F8

我们所说的大学毕业生。①

有时,皇帝会钦命
将一些大儒的牌位供于孔庙,
这被读书人视为最高荣誉。
在一些地方,
当举行祭孔典礼时,
人们会同时祭拜这些大儒。

---

① 在当时的欧洲,担任公职不需要学位,而需要学位的职务通常是宗教职务,因而对洛克来说,在中国只有获得学位的人或学者才能做官的情况与欧洲是非常不同的。

look on as the greatest honour that can be done them. And to those also, there are oblations[①] in the several cities[②] & towns as often as there is any sacrifice to Confucius.

The account of Confucius & that worship paid him read in the words of Roberedo[③], the Jesuits, Hist Cult Sinensium[④], P. 453.

Besides the solemn sacrifices & other acts of devotion paid to Confucius above mentioned, there is another honour paid him by the Literati, who often in his temple bow down to the ground, striking[⑤] the earth with their foreheads again & again.

---

① Locke crossed out "sacrifices" and changed it to "oblations" in his ms.
② Locke put it as "citys".
③ Bartolomé Roboredo. Roboredo was president of the Macao Jesuit college and had written a reply to Morales' criticisms of Jesuit accommodationism. See J.S. Cummins, *The Travels and Controversies of Friar Domingo Navarrete 1618-1686*, 1962, p. lxiii.
④ *Historia Cultus Sinensium SEU VARIA SCRIPTA De Culibus Sinarum, inter Vicarios Apostolicos Gallos aliosque Missionarios, & Patres Societatis Jesu controversis ie. The History of the Chinese Rites or various writings about the Chinese rites debated among the French Apostolic Vicars and other missionaries and the Fathers of the Society of Jesus.*
⑤ Locke put it as "strikeing".

于孔子的记述和祭孔仪式
参见耶稣会士罗博雷托①
在《华人礼仪史》
第453页②的记述。

除了上述祭孔的正式仪式
和祭祀活动外,
儒生还通过另一种方式
向孔子致敬,
即在孔庙中反复向孔子叩首。

---

① 全名巴尔托洛梅·罗博雷托（Bartolomé Roboredo）,马尼拉的西班牙耶稣会士,曾任日本和中国传教区司库及中国澳门耶稣会学院院长。1635年,利安当（Antonio de Santa Maria Caballero）、黎玉范（Juan Baptista de Morales）和另两位传教士Francisco Dias、Francisco de la Madre de Dios编写了两份《通告》（Informaciones）,正式挑战中国耶稣会士的适应政策。这两份文件被送往马尼拉,马尼拉总主教和宿务（Cebu）主教以此为依据正式谴责耶稣会士在中国的"惯例",并给罗马去信指控。1638年12月26日,罗博雷托为其中国传教区同僚发表了一份辩护词。而后马尼拉总主教和宿务主教再次给罗马写信撤回指控。然而,罗博雷托只在澳门住过几个月,从未去过中国。他用"偶像"、"祭坛"和"献祭"这样的词来谈论中国人,这其实承认了托钵修士论点的本质,即允许中国基督徒参加的礼仪实为迷信,也等于断言中国人是多神论者。但他力图为这些东西在礼仪中的角色和基督徒参加礼仪的举动开释,他说祭坛上放着一枚十字架,以助归化者指向他的信念与目的,基督徒心怀纯洁的目的。罗博雷托宣称他的观点以日本和中国视察员神父李马诺提交总会长的材料为基础,而非常了解中国传教区的视察员显然比澳门或马尼拉的任何人都更清楚耶稣会士在中国的行为和习惯。罗博雷托的辩护词在礼仪之争中恰恰被托钵修士所利用,反证耶稣会士适应政策的不合理,起到了反作用。参见张国刚:《从中西初识到礼仪之争——明清传教士与中西文化交流》,北京:人民出版社,2003年,第416—417页。又参见 J. S. Cummins, *The Travels and Controversies of Friar Domingo Navarrete 1618-1686*, 1962, p. lxiii.
② 因原稿涂改,看不清此处页码为第453还是第753页。根据上下文,初步认定为第453页。

Aqz017

199
Terra①
Planeta②
Montium③
Flumine④
Spirit sive Genÿ⑤
G
240

The Sect of the Literati⑥

according to the principles of their philosophy⑦

[To the right-hand side of the page]

worship also the principal

parts of the world and

[Back to the right-hand side of the page]

sacrifice⑧ also to the tutelar spirits of

the stars, earth, mountains & rivers and to the Idol

"Chin hoan", ie The Tutelar Genius

---

① It's Latin, meaning "earth".
② It's Latin, meaning "planet".
③ It's Latin, meaning "mountain".
④ It's Latin, meaning "river".
⑤ It's Latin, meaning "spirit or god of a place". Locke crossed out "Chin hoan" and changed it to "Spirit sive Genÿ" in his ms.
⑥ After "Literati", "have also other" was crossed out.
⑦ Locke put it as "philosophie".
⑧ Before "sacrifice", "sephi" was crossed out.

Aqz017

  199
  地星体 山河 精神或守护神
  G
  240①

根据教义，儒教

［页面右侧注］
也崇拜世界的各主要部分，

［回到页面右侧］
除了祭天以外，
他们也祭祀星辰、大地、山川、河流之神，
以及"<u>城隍</u>"

---

① 指《华人礼仪史》第240页。

of each city① as well as to the heaven.
Indeed② they acknowledge③ no④ true
spirits, but they call by this name a subtle
matter which they suppose to abound & to be most
active in the Heavens, in the Earth & in men.

To these they offer the same sacrifices
& use the same rites that they do⑤
in the worship of their ancestors.

"Chin hoan" or the tutelary Genius of each
city⑥ is worshiped with same ceremony that
their ancestors are and has Temples.

Aqz0018

200
Progenitores⑦
H1

The politie & government of
the Chineses seems principally
to be founded in a great veneration

---

① Locke put it as "citty".
② Locke put it as "Indee". Before "Indeed", "& earth" was crossed out.
③ Locke put it as "acknowledg".
④ Locke put it as "noe".
⑤ Locke put it as "doe".
⑥ Locke put it as "citty".
⑦ It's Latin, meaning "ancestors".

即每个城市的守护神。
事实上,
中国人并不承认真正的精神①,
他们所说的精神指的是
充盈于天、地、人之间的
某种微妙物质。

中国人祭祀这些神灵的
仪式和礼仪
一如祭祖。

<u>城隍</u>,即每个城市的守护神,
也享受与祭祖相同的祭祀典礼,
人们也会为其建庙。

Aqz018

200
祖先
H1

中国人的政体和统治
似乎主要建立于子女
对于父母的极大尊重

---

① 指非物质的精神(immaterial spirit)。

& absolute obedience of children to their parents, settled[①] all manner of ways in the minds of offspring[②]. To fix this deep & root it thoroughly in their minds, they have brought it into the religion of their country & have only[③] accustomed all that are borne in their country by a constant practice & universal fashion of their country to pay the whole deference[④] to their parents[⑤] whilst they are here, but have taught them[⑥] to depend on them for their happiness[⑦] when they are

[To the right-hand side of the page]
gone[⑧]. So[⑨] that is the[⑩] common & settled[⑪] opinion of the Chineses that the

---

① Locke put it as "setled".
② Locke put it as "ofspring".
③ After "only", "taught thei" was crossed out.
④ After "deference", "upon" was crossed out.
⑤ After "parents", "here" was crossed out.
⑥ After "them", "by" was crossed out.
⑦ Locke put it as "happyness".
⑧ Locke put it as "gon".
⑨ Locke put it as "soe". There is another "soe" in Locke's ms. It should be a mistake.
⑩ After "the", a word was crossed out.
⑪ Locke put it as "setled".

和绝对服从的基础之上，
这种古老的行为方式①
在华夏子孙的心目中根深蒂固。
为了将这种行为方式
深植于中国人的观念当中，
中国人将之融入了国教。
所有在中国出生的人
都被潜移默化地统一教化：
父母在世时，
要对父母绝对服从；
父母去世后，
则会得到父母的保佑。

［页面右侧注］
因此，中国人普遍深信
家族的繁荣依赖于
祖先的荫庇。

---

① 指"孝"。

fortune of their families① depends upon
their dead progenitors

[Back to the left-hand side of the page]
&② made it the most general
part of the religion of their
country to③ pay divine
honours to their deceased ancestors④
when they are gone⑤ & to make their
deceased ancestors the chief⑥ object
of

Aqz019

201
Progenitores
H2

of their worship.

[Inserted, to the right-hand side of the page]
To them they address themselves after this manner,
"Dear and wise respected father, never forget us or our
house. Grant to the men, the⑦

---

① Locke put it as "familys".
② Before "&", "gon" was crossed out.
③ After "to", "pray & sacrifice" was crossed out.
④ In Locke's ms, "deceased ancestors" was crossed out. It should be a mistake.
⑤ Locke put it as "gon".
⑥ Locke put it as "cheif".
⑦ Locke abbreviated it as "yᵉ".

[回到页面左侧]
这使得崇敬祖先
成为中国宗教中
最主要的部分,
因而祖先成了
中国人的主要信仰对象。

Aqz019

201
祖先
H2

[页面右侧]
中国人以这样的方式向祖先祷告：
"亲爱的、明智的、尊敬的父亲,
不要忘记我们和我们的家①。

---

① 此处手稿无法辨认。

women & children long life, riches in
abundance①, health & strength, so②
th*at* we may enjoy a happy life to the
extremity of old age." This is said by
the chief③ of the family who then makes
his obeisance to the inscribed tablet &
then all the rest in their order.

[Back to the left-hand side of the page]
Funeral *[Heading]*
When they are dead, it is an inviolable
custom among the Chineses to④ erect a table
in the manner of an altar before the dead corpse

[To the right-hand side of the page]
& to place upon it his image or else tablet of
inscription, this altar being garnished with
flowers, perfumes⑤ & lighted lamps and tapers.
All that come to condole kneel and prostrate
themselves thrice before this altar thus set
out offering some candles & odours⑥
to⑦ the end that they may there be burnt

---

① Locke put it as "aboundance".
② Locke put it as "soe".
③ Locke put it as "cheif".
④ After "to", "set" was crossed out.
⑤ Locke put it as "parfumes".
⑥ After "odours", "to which" was crossed out.
⑦ Before "to", "are" was crossed out.

请您赐予男人、女人和孩子长寿、富足、
健康和力量,
保佑我们一世幸福。"
家主如是祷告之后,
向牌位叩拜,
而后家族里的其他人依次叩拜。

［回到页面左侧］
葬礼
按照中国人的风俗,
人一过世,
就要在死者的遗体前摆一张桌子
作为供桌,

［页面右侧］
桌上安放死者的画像或牌,
供桌以鲜花、香料
以及点燃的灯和香烛装饰。
所有前来吊唁的人
都在供桌前叩拜三次,
奉上蜡烛和香料,
并将之焚于死者画像

upon the altar before the image or tablet

of inscription of the dead.

[Back to the left-hand side of the page]

Temples *[Heading]*

Those who are able build temples

& chapels[①] to them, in which are kept

certain tablets of chestnut wood dedicated to them with

inscriptions in[②] letters of a culiil[③]

dimension[④] to this sense,

"The Throne or Seat of the

soul[⑤] or spirit of N" setting[⑥]

down his name[⑦] and dignity.

In the middle of the Temple

there is a[⑧] altar with

other lesser[⑨] altars upon

down about it, upon which these

tablets[⑩] of inscription

are placed.

---

① Locke put it as "chappols".
② After "in", "in" was crossed out.
③ It could be an abbreviation of the Latin word "cubitalibus", meaning "lying down".
④ After "dimension", "The" was crossed out.
⑤ Locke put it as "soule".
⑥ Locke put it as "seting".
⑦ After "name", "with" was crossed out.
⑧ After "a", "table or" was crossed out.
⑨ After "lesser", "tables or" was crossed out.
⑩ Before "tablets", "his tablets" was crossed out. After "tablets", "tablets" was crossed out.

或牌位前的供桌上。

[回到页面左侧]
祖庙[①]
那些有能力为祖先
建祖庙或祠堂的人
会在祖庙内供奉
用栗木制成的祖先牌位，
上面竖向书写：
"某某之神位"，
并注明先人的姓名和尊称。

祖庙的正中
设一个供桌，
周围还有其他
小一些的供桌，
祖先牌位就供奉在
这些供桌上。

---

① 这里指的是世家大族的宗祠，俗称"家庙"或"祠堂"。为保持与英文名称的相对一致，在关于祖先祭祀一节译者将Temple统一译为"祖庙"。

[As a reference, to the right-hand side of the page]

Vid[①] *Hist Cultus Sinensium*

P 460 how the ceremony[②]

was performed in a Temple

wherein were six altars.

[Back to the left-hand side of the page]

It is[③] said that at first a[④]

[To the right-hand side of the page]

boy clad in the habit of the deceased

was set upon the altar to represent him,

but this has been left off for many ages

& the <u>tablet of Inscription</u> is substituted in

the room of it. To this tablet, the

spirit of him whose name it bares is

invited to come thither & rest upon it

& whatsoever is done during the ceremony

is

[To the right-hand side of the next page]

is[⑤] addressed all

to[⑥] the tablet as the

seat whither the spirit of the dead

---

① It's Latin, meaning "see".
② Locke put it as "ceremonie".
③ Locke put "It is" as "Tis".
④ After "a", "lad young" was crossed out.
⑤ Before "is", there is "all" in Locke's ms. It is out of sequence so it's omitted in the transcription.
⑥ Before "to", there is "offered" in Locke's ms. It is out of sequence so it's omitted in the transcription. Relating to last line, "All offered" may be a separate comment.

第三章 "中国笔记"的文本与要点 123

［页面右侧注］
参见《华人礼仪史》
第460页，在一座
内设六个供桌的家庙
举行的祭祖仪式。

［页面右侧下方，说明祭祖牌位的情况］
据说最开始
人们会把一个穿着死者衣服的男孩
放在供桌上来代表死者，
但这样的风俗已被废止多年。
人们现在用牌位替代，
先人的魂魄会回到
各自的牌位上。

［本页右下方写不下，下接手稿第202页（Aqz020）右侧上方，继续说明祭祖牌位的情况］
祭祖典礼上所供奉的一切都献给牌位。
人们相信在祭祀过程中，
死者的灵魂会被请回到牌位上，

person① is invited to
reside there during the ceremony
& to accept of the sacrifice & offerings made to it. The wine is offered
to draw the spirit thither & much good
is promised to the head of the family to
himself & the rest of the family,
for having performed those ceremonies.

Besides those tablets of Inscription,
they have sometimes the images of
their Ancestors which they set upon their
altars before the tablets.

[Back to the left-hand side of the page]
In these temples two or three
times a year, particularly in spring
& autumn, they with great solemnity
sacrifice there to their dead Ancestors
as

---

① After "person", "resides" was crossed out.

享用祭祀和供奉。
人们以酒招魂。
他们相信
这些祭祀仪式会给家主
及整个家族带来福报。

除了<u>牌位</u>，
中国人有时也在
牌位前的供桌上
供奉祖先的画像。

［回到本页（Aqz019）页面左侧下方］
通常每年的春秋两季，
中国人会在祖庙中
举行非常隆重的祭祖仪式，
祭祀四世祖先。

Aqz020

202
Progenitores
H3

as far back as to the 4ᵗʰ generation.

Officers *[Heading] [Inserted]*
Some days before[①]
the[②] oblation, the first borne or
head[③] of the family,
with three or 4 others of the chief[④]
of the family are chosen, who as priests, deacons,
clarks, to officiate & perform[⑤] their
several parts in this ceremony[⑥].
These[⑦] set apart a day for this purpose
by lot and prepare themselves for it
by fasting and abstaining from their
wives three days before. The
day before the solemnity, they choose a
goat[⑧] or hog or other beast for the sacrifice

---

① After "before", "that appointed" was crossed out.
② Before "the", "for" was crossed out.
③ Before "head", "cheif of the" was crossed out.
④ Locke put it as "cheif".
⑤ Locke put it as "performe".
⑥ Locke put it as "ceremonie".
⑦ After "these", "designe" was crossed out.
⑧ Locke put it as "gote".

Aqz020

202
祖先
H3

祭官

祭祀前几天,
人们会推选家族中的长子或家主,
以及另外四个家族中的重要成员,
分别担任主祭、从祭和执事,
主持祭祀并履行典礼中的不同职责。①
为此,这些人要专门斋戒一天,
并在祭祀开始前的三天中
不与妻子同房。
祭祀前一天,
他们选择一只羊或猪
或其他牲畜作为祭品,

---

① 此处洛克用英国国教的各级神职人员(priests, deacons, clarks)来指称中国祭祖典礼上的各级祭祀人员,而通常中国民间的祭祖仪式上有司仪一名、执事两名、诵祭一名、主祭官一名、从祭一人,因此译者做了简单的对应。

[To the right-hand side of the page]
as ox or cocks & hens, but that which is preferred① before all other is the head of an hog.

[Back to the left-hand side of the page]
Their way of choosing it is this: They pour hot wine into the ears of the hog or goat. & if the beast thereupon shake its head, they judge② him fit for the sacrifice; If not, they reject it as unfit. The beast they tried and approved of is presently slain in their presence. That very night before cock crowing, all the kindred repair to that chapel③ or tomb where all things being set in a readiness, the

[Inserted, to the right-hand side of the page]
Those who are not able to erect temples have a room in their houses consecrated & dedicated to their dead fathers'④ spirits, in which they hang up their tablets with [?]⑤ of a [?][?]⑥.

---

① Locke put it as "prefered".
② Locke put it as "judg".
③ Locke put it as "chapol".
④ Locke crossed out "Ancestors" and changed it to "fathers".
⑤ After "with", there's an illegible word in Locke's ms.
⑥ There are two words, looking like "polum deep" in Locke's ms. However, it doesn't make sense.

[页面右侧注]
如去势公牛、公鸡或母鸡，
但猪头最佳。

[回到页面左侧]
中国人选择祭品的方式如下：
将热酒灌入猪或羊的耳朵，
晃头的牲畜就是合适的祭品，
不晃的就不合适。
经过检验合格的牲畜
当着在场人的面被立即宰杀。
当天晚上，
鸡鸣以前，
所有族人赶往祠堂或祖坟，
将祭祀用的东西准备就绪。

[页面右侧注]
那些建不起祖庙的人
会在家里设一个房间
专门供奉祖先的魂魄，
他们会在这个房间里
挂上祖先的牌位①。

---

① 此处手稿无法辨认。

Aqz021

203
Progenitores
H4

the tapers lighted & set upon that altar
covered with roses and other flowers,
with incense and perfumes[①]
smoking. The master of the ceremonies[②]
cries with a loud voice, "<u>Down upon your knees.</u>"
Whereupon they all presently kneel down
before the inscription three or four times,
bowing themselves till they touch the
ground with their foreheads. One of
those who officiate reciting in the mean-
time some set forms[③] of prayers. This
done, the master of the ceremonies[④] crying,
"<u>Rise</u>", they all stand up upon their legs.
Then the chief[⑤] of those who officiate,
who performed the part of the priest, standing close to the Altar takes in both his
hands a cup of wine, lifts it up on high
above his head & offers it.

---

① Locke put it as "parfumes".
② Locke put it as "ceremonys".
③ Locke put it as "formes".
④ Locke put it as "ceremonys".
⑤ Locke put it as "cheif".

Aqz021

203
祖先
H4

供桌上摆放着点燃的香烛，
覆盖着玫瑰和其他鲜花，
香烟缭绕。
司仪大声喊
"<u>跪</u>"，
人们立即在牌位前跪下，
行叩拜礼三到四次。
与此同时，
一个主持祭祀的人①
会诵读一些现成的祈祷文。
司仪大喊：
"<u>起</u>"，
人们都站起身来。
而后站在供桌附近的主祭官
双手端起一杯酒，
高举过头顶敬祖先。
司仪大声喊：
"<u>敬酒</u>"，

---

① 指诵祭。

The① master of

the ceremonies crying② aloud, "The wine is offering." Whereof the priest drinks a

part③ & the rest he pours out

upon an image of a man made of straw

which is places there. After this, he pulls④ off the hair of

the beasts. These with the horn,⑤ with their blood being first lift up & offered

are buried in the court. But the heads dressed up with flowers &

flesh he⑥ lifts up & offers before the tablet.

of inscription. The master of

the

[Inserted as a footnote, to the right-hand side of the page]

They think the souls⑦ come & partake

of the meat & drink that is offered them.

Aqz022

204

Progenitores

H5

the ceremonies crying out at the

---

① Before "The", "a goblet full of wine" was crossed out.

② Locke put it as "crieing".

③ Before "part", "little &" was crossed out.

④ Locke put it as "puls".

⑤ Locke crossed out "is pulled of which" and changed it to "These with the horn".

⑥ Locke crossed out "are" and change it to "he".

⑦ Locke put it as "soules".

主祭官将杯中酒喝掉一部分,
并把剩余的酒倒在
一个事先放在那里的稻草人上。
然后主祭官将祭牲的毛拔下来,
将之与事先准备好献祭的血
一起埋在院子里,
再举起装饰着鲜花的(祭牲的——译者)
头和肉敬献于牌位面前。

［页面右侧注］
中国人认为魂魄会归来
享用献给它们的酒肉。

Aqz022

204
祖先
H5

与此同时,司仪大喊:

same time, "A goat or hog① is offering."

[As a foot note, to the right-hand side of the page]
The beast most used in those
offerings are hogs, goats & neets②.
But the hog is most esteemed. Of birds, the most used
are cocks & hens. Of fishes, what
they please.

[Back to the left-hand side of the page]
After the same manner, flowers, fruit,
pulses,③ silk stuffs also & paper
money④ is offered, which he burns in a fire
made before the temple door. At every
of which actions, there are several prayers
recited by one of those who officiate.
When this is all performed, the master
of the ceremonies

[Inserted, to the right-hand side of the page]
thanks them in the name
of the dead for the honours done them
&⑤ bids them expect for it plentiful harvests,

---

① Locke put it as "hogg".
② It means "cattle".
③ After "pulse", "Also" was crossed out.
④ Locke put it as "mony".
⑤ There is a mysterious mark similar to "VC" below "&" in Locke's ms. It could be an abbreviation of the first word "declares" of the next line. It could also mean something else.

"献牲"。

［页面右侧注］
祭祀中用的最多的牲畜是
猪、羊和牛，
但猪被认为是最好的。
其他常用的祭品还有
公鸡、母鸡和鱼，
依祭祀者的喜好而定。

［回到页面左侧］
主祭官还以同样方式献上
鲜花、水果、谷物和丝织品，
敬献的钱帛则在祖庙门前
生火焚烧。
每行一种敬礼，
就会有一个主持祭祀的人①
诵读几段祈祷文。
这一切都完成后，主祭官

［页面右侧］
以先人之名
感谢众人的祭祀，
并预言未来的丰收，

---

① 指诵祭。

[Back to the left-hand side of the page]

declares to them

that for this worship performed[①] to their

predecessors, they may[②]

expect[③] all manner

of prosperity, viz fruitful[④] harvests,

a numerous issue,[⑤] honours, health &

a long life. For they phansy the[⑥] soul[⑦]

[To the right-hand side of the page]

of him to whom they thus pay their devotion

is there present all the while and receives

their oblations, enjoying the perfumes[⑧] & edibles

that are there presented to them.

[Back to the left-hand side of the page]

Besides these solemn[⑨] oblations

every spring & autumn, they frequently

repair to these temples, particularly every

full & new moon, & there with[⑩] kneeling

---

① Locke crossed out "paid" and changed it to "performed".
② After "may", "go away" was crossed out.
③ Before "expect", "confident of b" was crossed out.
④ Locke put it as "fruitfull".
⑤ It means "a great number of children".
⑥ After "the", there's another "the" in Locke's ms. It should be a mistake.
⑦ Locke put it as "soule".
⑧ Locke put it as "parfumes".
⑨ Locke put it as "solemne".
⑩ After "kneeling", "respected" was crossed out.

[回到页面左侧]
同时向众人宣布,
祭祀祖先之后,
他们将得到各种福报,
比如丰收、多子、功名、健康和长寿。
中国人相信

[页面右侧]
在祭祀的过程中,
祖先的灵魂一直在场,
接受了他们的供奉,
并正在享用他们奉献的
香火和食物。

[回到页面左侧]
除了上述隆重的祭祀仪式外,
每年春秋两季,
尤其是朔望两日,
中国人也常常前往祖庙,

& bowing themselves to the ground three or four times before these tablets, wherein the names of their ancestors are written. They pay their devotion, lighting taper, & burning incense & perfumes[①], & offer flowers, fruits & nuts with other meats

Aqz023

205
Progenitores
H6

meats to them.

[To the right-hand side of the page, at the top]
These honours and respects they pay to their parents when dead, who treated them very ill whilst they were alive. This being the common opinion that those who are constant in these devotions & reverences to them shall be happy in this world & be blessed with riches, honours, health & a long life.

---

① Locke put it as "parfumes".

在祖先的牌位前
行叩拜礼三到四次,
并点燃香烛,
焚烧香料,
献上鲜花、水果、坚果和其他肉食
以祭拜祖先。

Aqz023

205
祖先
H6

［页面右侧上方］
即使父母在世的时候
对子女非常不好,
父母去世后,
子女还是给予他们
同样的荣誉和尊重。
中国人普遍相信
不断祭祀和尊敬祖先的人
能够获得现世的
财富、荣誉、健康和长寿等福报。

[Inserted, to the right-hand side of the page, in the middle]
Those who have temples have rooms
to dedicate in their houses where they have
the tablets of inscription before which they set meat
& fruits & flowers & offer incense & perfumes① &
burn② tapers.

These domestic③ tablets of their ancestors
which everyone has in his home chapel④, they salute
several times every day by genuflections,
prostrations, incense, perfumes⑤ &
prayers.

These prayers to them are for many
things of this life, but they ask⑥ for nothing⑦
of them relating to the other life.

[Back to the left-hand side of the page]
But the poorer sort⑧ who are of so⑨ mean
condition as not to have⑩

---

① Locke put it as "parfumes".
② Locke put it as "burne".
③ Locke put it as "domestick".
④ Locke put it as "chappol".
⑤ Locke put it as "parfumes".
⑥ Locke put it as "aske".
⑦ Locke put it as "noething".
⑧ Locke crossed out "they" and changed it to "the poor sort".
⑨ Locke put it as "soe".
⑩ Locke crossed out "be able to build" and change it to "have".

［页面右侧居中］
那些有祖庙的人
也会在家里专门设一些房间
来供奉祖宗牌位。
他们会在牌位前供奉
肉、果品和鲜花，并且燃烛焚香。

这些在家里供奉的祖宗牌位
与普通人在家祠供奉的牌位一样，
每天数次受到家人的参拜。
他们鞠躬叩头，
并焚香祷告。

他们向祖先祈求
很多现世的福报，
但这些祈求从不涉及来世。①

［回到页面左侧］
那些生活境遇不好、
修不起祠堂的穷人

---

① 这是与欧洲非常不同的地方。欧洲的一些基督徒也为自己死去的长辈祷告，但祈求的是死去的长辈在来世的安宁，而不是自己在现世的福报。

Chapels① dedicated to their deceased progenitors
make② the same offerings
with the same solemnities either③
at their tombs which are
always out of the towns or in their
private houses with less pomp &
solemnity. For there is scarce any
one to be found amongst the④ common people
who has not in his house a kind⑤ of
oratory where those tablets of his
ancestors are kept & where he
frequently pays his devotions to them
with kneelings, incense, perfumes⑥
& oblations of fruits & other
viands, praying to them for riches
& prosperity.

The Chinese⑦ keep also at home in their houses
<u>tablets of Inscription</u> of their ancestors.
Those they everyday salute more than once
with the humble posture before mentioned,
lighting up tapers to them, burning incense
& offering flowers, fruits & other edibles,

---

① Locke put it as "chappols".
② Before "make", "perform" was crossed out.
③ There are two "either"s in Locke's ms. It should be a mistake.
④ After "the", "mob" (meaning common people) was crossed out.
⑤ Locke put it as "kinde".
⑥ Locke put it as "parfumes".
⑦ Locke put it as "Chines".

也同样郑重地祭祖。
他们或者在城外的墓地,
或者在自己家里
进行不那么隆重庄严的祭祖仪式。
绝大部分普通人家里都有一个房间
供奉着祖先牌位,
人们时常在那里跪拜祖先,
奉上香烛、香、果品及其他食物,
同时向祖先祈求财富和繁荣。

中国人在家里
也供奉祖先牌位,
每日多次如上文提到的那样
恭谨参拜,
燃烛焚香,
供奉鲜花、果品和其他食物,

[Inserted, to the right-hand side of the page, at the bottom]
viand[①] mixing prayers & thanksgiving
with their offerings. For they believe
that thereupon their diseases, misfortunes
& sorrows are put to an end. They pray for
the perpetual prosperity of the empire, for
happiness[②], for a plentiful[③] harvest.
Their prayers to their ancestors have no[④]
regard to another life or to their souls[⑤] in
a future state. They expect no[⑥] such thing of
them, but they desire their help in this life
that they may have good luck as they had
before them & be able to imitate them
in their sayings & deeds. And they believe
they shall be so[⑦] much the more fortunate & happy
by how much the more they are sedulous & punctual
in these performances.

---

① It should be "viands", because "viand" is seldom used in singular form.
② Locke put it as "happyness".
③ Locke put it as "plentifull".
④ Locke put it as "noe".
⑤ Locke put it as "soules".
⑥ Locke put it as "noe".
⑦ Locke put it as "soe".

［页面右侧下方］
同时祷告并感谢祖先的恩赐。
中国人相信这样做
可以祛病消灾、排忧解难。
他们祈求整个帝国的长久繁荣,
也祈求幸福和丰收。
他们对于祖先的祈求
并不涉及来世或未来的灵魂,
他们并不考虑这些。
他们想要的是
祖先对他们现世的帮助,
他们希望能够延续祖先的好运,
并能够效法祖先的言行。
中国人相信祭祀时越是周到谨慎,
他们就会得到越多的福报。

Aqz024

                                                207
                                         Literati
                                                   J1

The Sect of the Literati is the most considerable of the three. All the officers of State & magistrates are of this sect & the Emperor himself is protector & chief[①] of it.

Aqz025

                                              208
                                        Idolatrae[②]
                                            Bonzÿ[③]
                                                 Foe
                                                   J2

The sect of the Idolaters had its original from India & was introduced into China by Foe about the 65 year of our Lord.

---

① Locke put it as "cheif".
② It's Latin, meaning "Idolaters".
③ It's Latin, meaning "Buddists".

Aqz024

207
儒教
J1

儒教是三大宗教之首。
所有中央官员和各级行政官员
都出身儒教，
皇帝本人就是儒教的保护人和领袖。

Aqz025

208
偶像崇拜者
佛教徒
佛
J2

佛教起源于印度，
约公元65年前后
由佛引入中国①。

---

① 相传东汉永平七年（64年），汉明帝刘庄（刘秀之子）夜宿南宫，梦见一个身高六丈、头顶放光的金人自西方而来，在殿庭飞绕。次日晨，汉明帝将此梦告诉给大臣们，博士傅毅启奏说："西方有神，称为佛，就像您梦到的那样。"汉明帝听罢大喜，派大臣蔡愔、秦景等十余人出使西域，拜求佛经、佛法。永平八年（65年），蔡、秦等人告别帝都，踏上"西天取经"的万里征途。在大月氏国（今阿富汗境至中亚一带），遇到印度高僧摄摩腾、竺法兰，见到了佛经和释迦牟尼佛白毡像，并恳请二位高僧东赴中国弘法布教。

They have very many monstrous
& filthy images on their pagodas
or Temples which they worship.
This sect is mightily disesteemed by
the Literati & counted infamous.①

Aqz026

209

Magi②

K

The sect of the Magi have

images as well as the Idolaters.

They both hold the immortality of the

soul③ & rewards & punishment in another

life.

Aqz027

210

Mahometans

L

Some Mahometans about 6 hundred since came

---

① The next paragraph goes as "The sect of the Magi do noe less abound in monstrous idols." It was crossed out altogether.

② It's Latin, meaning "magician", "wise men from the east".

③ Locke put it as "soule".

佛教的佛塔和寺庙中
供奉着很多
面目狰狞且污秽的塑像。
儒教非常蔑视佛教，
认为佛教声名狼藉。

Aqz026

209
道教
K

与佛教一样，
道教也有塑像。

道教和佛教
都相信
灵魂不朽和来世奖惩。

Aqz027

210
伊斯兰教[①]
L

六百多年前，

---

① "Mahometans" 一词为旧时西方对穆斯林的称谓，也可指代伊斯兰教。该词旧译为"回教徒"或"回教"，本书采用今译"穆斯林"或"伊斯兰教"。

into China out of some of the neighbouring countries. They
intermarried there with the Chinese women & have since mightily
increased, so that now there are① counted a million
of them there. It is a good while since that
they have a full liberty there &② are not
distinguished from the other Chineses but
only in religion. They have mosques,
[Inserted] by the king's permission,
in the principal cities③ & there④
worship⑤ god after their way,

[To the right-hand side of the page]
but are not very exact observers of their law.

[Back to the left-hand side of the page]
They⑥ are of all trades & callings, nay
they study,⑦ some of them, the Chinese learning & take⑧
degrees⑨ in it and come to be
officers⑩ in their

---

① After "are", "at le" was crossed out. Locke might have intended to write "at least".
② After "&", "live" was crossed out.
③ Locke put it as "Cittys".
④ After "there", "perform the" was crossed out.
⑤ Before "worship", "rites of that religion" was crossed out.
⑥ Before "They", "way." was crossed out.
⑦ It means "They not only are of all trades and callings, but also study…".
⑧ After "take", there is "degrees" in Locke's ms. There's another "degrees" at the beginning of the next line, so it's omitted in this transcription.
⑨ Before "degrees", "& are admitted to" was crossed out.
⑩ Before "officers", "mandarins of the lower order" was crossed out.

一些穆斯林徒从周边国家来到中国①。
他们与中国妇女通婚后，
人口激增，
如今中国有一百万穆斯林。
之后的很长一段时间，
他们在中国享有完全的自由，
除了宗教外
并不被区别对待。
国王允许他们
在各大城市修建清真寺，
并以自己的方式崇拜真主，

［页面右侧］
但他们并不严格遵守戒律。

［回到页面左侧］
他们从事各行各业，
有些人还学习中国的学问
并且获取功名，
成为司法官员或下级官吏。

---

① 此处指的应为唐宋时期侨居中国的穆斯林"蕃客"。唐宋时期，西亚的阿拉伯人以伊斯兰教为旗帜，曾建立了西濒大西洋、东至中国西部边陲的阿拉伯帝国。中国与阿拉伯帝国一东一西，横贯东、西的陆上"丝绸之路"和南中国海至波斯湾的海上"香料之路"，使两国在政治、经济和文化等方面保持着频繁的往来。据《旧唐书·西域传》等史籍记载，唐高宗永徽二年（651年）大食国第三任哈里发奥斯曼（644—656在位）首次遣使来华。中、阿两国正式缔交后，阿拉伯使节和"贡使"来中国不断，有时一年一次，有时一年两次。见于我国史书记载，仅唐代阿拉伯使臣来华次数就达37次之多，不被记载的民间商贸活动估计更为频繁。

courts of justice & mandarins[①] of the lower order. But those who are promoted to degree or to be mandarins[②] are looked upon by the rest as Apostates.

They preserve themselves by housing together. They take Chinese women for their wives, but never give their daughters[③] in marriage to the Chineses. Because in China the wife follows the husband, goes to her father-in-laws' house & there remains & follows his laws. & so[④] coming[⑤] a heathen, into a house of a mohametan becomes a mohametan, but going a mohametan into the house of a Chinese would infallibly turn[⑥] heathen.

Aqz028

211
Mohametans
L2

They have been in China about 700 years.

---

① Locke put it as "mandarines".
② Locke put it as "mandarines".
③ Locke crossed out "wives" and changed it to "daughters".
④ Locke put it as "soe".
⑤ Locke put it as "comeing".
⑥ Locke put it as "turne".

然而那些获取功名
或成为官吏的人
被其他穆斯林徒视为叛教者。

他们通过聚居来保护自己。
他们娶中国妇女为妻,
但从不允许自己的女儿嫁给中国人。
原因是在中国,
妻从夫,
而倒插门的女婿
则要服从岳父家的规矩。
因此,不信教的人进入穆斯林的家中
就变成了穆斯林,
而穆斯林进入中国人的家中
就一定变成不信教的人了。

Aqz028

211
伊斯兰教
L2

他们在中国已经生活了约700年。

They were called in by one of their Emperors out of Turquestan, who was engaged in civil broils at home. They did him such service that those that would were permitted to stay with the privilege[①] of naturalization, when they have since increased to the number. Since that, they vigorously assisted the Emperor Humru against the Tartars so that he remaining victorious. They grew into more esteem & were admitted into places of trust & influence in the government[②].

---

① Locke put it as "privileg".
② Locke put it as "governm".

中国的一位皇帝在内战时
将他们从土库曼斯坦召入中国。
因他们立下汗马功劳，
这位皇帝允许想留下的人留在中国，
并特许他们入籍①。
此后经年，
逐渐达到了今天的人数。
后来，
他们在抗击鞑靼人的战争中
有利地支持了洪武帝②，

---

① 根据时间推测，此处应指唐至德二年（757年）九月，唐廷曾借用大食等国及地区的军队，协助镇压安禄山的反叛一事。据两《唐书》及《资治通鉴》记载，至德二年九月，天下兵马元帅、广平王李俶（后来的唐代宗），率领汉蕃联军十五万，号二十万（《旧唐书·肃宗纪》《新唐书·郭子仪传》《册府元龟》说是十五万），发凤翔，东进讨贼。参加这支联军的，除朔方、安西等唐军外，尚有回纥、南蛮、大食、拔汗那等国及地区的军队（见两《唐书》肃宗、代宗纪，《资治通鉴》卷二一九）。

② 原稿中写的是"the Emperor Humru"，按照时间和史实推测，应指明太祖洪武帝朱元璋。据史料载，虽然穆斯林在元朝属于色目人，地位高于"南人"，但蒙古人强制穆斯林改变民族习惯的做法引起穆斯林的不满，很多穆斯林加入了汉族反抗元朝统治的斗争当中。明朝开国皇帝朱元璋手下有十大穆斯林名将，分别是徐达、胡大海、冯国用、冯胜、李文忠、邓愈、华云龙、丁德兴、蓝玉、沐英。明朝初年分封诸王时，除朱姓者外，异姓封王的只有徐达、常遇春、汤和、邓愈、李文忠、郭子兴和沐英七人，而这七人全是回族。在土耳其的皇宫档案馆中发现的波斯旅行家阿克巴尔于1516年在君士坦丁堡写的《中国纪行》一书，记述了作者在1500年来华游历的见闻。全书共二十一章，介绍了明代中国伊斯兰教的情况，记述了明王室与伊斯兰教的关系，皇帝到清真寺礼拜的情况，以及穆斯林文武大臣在明朝开国中的贡献与王室对他们的倚重，书中说："朝廷的七大重臣，始终均是由伊斯兰信士所任。又宫内的伊斯兰重臣，其地位也远较非穆斯林重臣的地位高。"另外，明洪武元年，明太祖敕建清真寺于金陵（南京），赐名"净觉寺"，该寺至今仍是南京有名的清真寺。在该寺落成后明太祖朱元璋常去该寺礼拜，并亲自撰写了《至圣百字赞》。《天方典礼》载："明洪武初，敕修清真寺于西、南两京及滇南、闽、粤，御书《百字赞》褒扬圣德。"《百字赞》全文如下："乾坤初始，天籍注名，传教大圣，降生西域，受授天经，三十部册，普化众生，信兆君师，万圣领袖，协助天运，保庇国民，五时祈佑，默祝太平，存信真主，加济穷民，拯救患难，洞彻幽冥，超拔灵魂，脱离罪业，仁覆天下，道贯古今，降邪归一，教名清真，穆罕默德，至贵圣人。"由此可见，穆斯林在明太祖抗击蒙古人统治的斗争中立下了汗马功劳，因此受到明太祖的礼遇，这与洛克手稿中的描述相符。

The Chineses despise them as foreigners[①] & they despise the Chineses as Idolators.

[①] Locke put it as "forainers". Locke crossed out "stran" and changed it to "forainers". Locke might have intended to write "strangers".

助其大获全胜,
因此赢得更大的尊重,
并获准担任政府中有影响力的重要职位。

中国人鄙视他们为外国人,
他们鄙视中国人为偶像崇拜者。

Aqz029

212

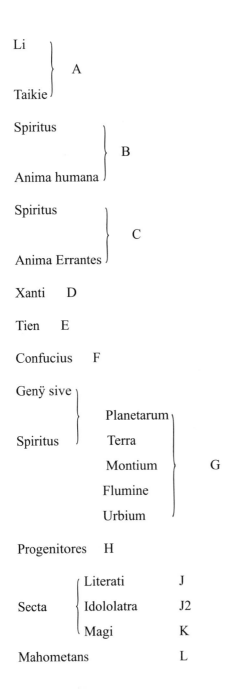

Aqz029

212

理 ⎫
　　⎬ A
太极 ⎭

精神 ⎫
　　⎬ B
人类灵魂 ⎭

精神 ⎫
　　⎬ C
游魂 ⎭

上帝　D

天　　E

孔子　F

守护神 ⎫　星体 ⎫
或　　 ⎬　地　 ⎪
精神　 ⎭　山　 ⎬ G
　　　　　河　 ⎪
　　　　　城　 ⎭

祖先　H

教派 ⎧ 儒教　J
　　 ⎨ 佛教　J2
　　 ⎩ 道教　K

伊斯兰教　L

Aqz030

212v

Progenitores   3-6. 43. 111-115. 117-118 219 221 229 H

- Spiritus   B

- Anima humana   87 B

- Confucius 7-11 152 186.190. 207 F

$\left.\begin{array}{l}\text{Terra   236. 238. 240}\\\text{Planeta   237}\\\text{Montibus   240}\\\text{Fluminibus   240}\end{array}\right\}$ G

- ~~Chin hoan~~ Genÿ   182 241 ~~A B~~ F①

$\left.\begin{array}{l}\text{- Ly Kuei}\\\\\text{- Yeu Hoen}\end{array}\right\}$ Spiritus et anima errantes   220 C

$\left.\begin{array}{l}\text{- Li}\\\\\text{- }\sout{\text{Taikie}}\end{array}\right\}$ 85. 86. 87. 122 126. 242 A

$\left.\begin{array}{l}\text{- Xanti}\\\\\text{Rex Altus}\end{array}\right\}$ 122. 123 126 127-144. 151. 242. 243 D

- Tien   136. 138. 139 141.236. 238. 244 E

Foe Idolotrae Bonzÿ   131-134 182 J2

Magi   137 K

Literati   J1

---

① [sic] It should be "G".

Aqz030

[第212页背面]

祖先　3-6. 43. 11-115. 117-118 219 221 229 H

- 精神　B

- 人类灵魂　87 B

- 孔子　7-11 152 186.190. 207 F

$\left.\begin{array}{ll}地 & 236.238.240\\ 星体 & 237\\ 山 & 240\\ 河 & 240\end{array}\right\}$ G

- 城隍 守护神　182. 241 A B F①

$\left.\begin{array}{l}- 离魂\\ - 游魂\end{array}\right\}$ 精神和游魂　220 C

$\left.\begin{array}{l}- 理\\ - 太极\end{array}\right\}$ 85. 86. 87. 122 126. 242 A

$\left.\begin{array}{l}- 上帝\\ 天主\end{array}\right\}$ 122. 123 126 127-144. 151. 242. 243 D

- 天　136. 138. 139 141. 236. 238. 244 E

佛教　131-134 182 J2

道教　137 K

儒教　J1

---

① 此处手稿有误，应为G。

第三节 "中国笔记"要点总结与分析

如上文所述[①],洛克"中国笔记"共分为13个主题讨论中国的宗教。现拟从中国的宗教派别、中国哲学的基础和儒教的关键概念、精神灵魂和守护神、孔子与祭孔仪式、祖先与祭祖仪式五个方面对"中国笔记"的要点进行总结与分析,以期提炼出"中国笔记"中洛克对中国宗教的认识要点,并分析洛克对中国理解的基本逻辑。至于中国哲学和宗教的基本概念——如"天""理""太极"等——的具体来源和内涵不在本书讨论范围之内。

一、中国的宗教派别

所涉章节:

B.L., MS. Locke. c.27., f.179. 中国的宗教

B.L., MS. Locke. c.27., f.207. 儒教(J1)

B.L., MS. Locke. c.27., f.208. 佛教(J2)

B.L., MS. Locke. c.27., f.209. 道教(K)

B.L., MS. Locke. c.27., ff.210-1. 伊斯兰教(L1-2)

要点:

洛克在上述章节中主要讲述了:

1. 中国有三大宗教,分别为儒教、佛教和道教。

2. 儒教是三教之首,是三教中最古老的本土宗教,也是中国的国教;佛教和道教都是后来的,并且是外来宗教。佛教源于印度,约公元65年传入中国。

3. 儒教唯一的神是"物质的天"。

4. 佛教和道教都有塑像,都相信灵魂不朽和来世奖惩。

此外,"中国笔记"的最后还比较详细地介绍了伊斯兰教在中国的发展史和风俗,并专门指出他们将中国人视为偶像崇拜者。

分析:

洛克关于中国宗教的知识主要来源于以耶稣会士为代表的来华传教士。利

---

① 参见本书表2-1。

玛窦"适应政策"的一个主要内容是"合儒易佛",因此明清来华传教士关于中国宗教的绝大部分作品都是关于儒家思想的,也有部分是批判佛教的,关于道教的内容少之又少。我们从洛克的"中国笔记"中不难看出这种知识来源上的不均衡。洛克对佛教了解不多,但知道佛教的来源以及传入中国的准确时间;对道教知之甚少,因此犯了将道教当作外来宗教的常识性错误。

事实上,中国的宗教派别和发展历史并非洛克关注的重点,洛克最关心的始终是"中国人是否为无神论者"这一主题。通过阅读天主教来华传教士的作品,洛克发现中国的三大宗教中,佛教和道教都相信灵魂不朽和来世奖惩,因此它们都相信绝对精神,是有神论;同时它们都有塑像,因此它们的信徒都是偶像崇拜者;而儒教只信仰"物质的天",因此儒教是无神论。而儒教为三教之首,代表了中国的宗教传统和信仰主流,因此研究中国人的哲学和信仰主要就是考察儒教(儒家思想)。

二、中国哲学的基础和儒教的关键概念

所涉章节:

B.L., MS. Locke. c.27., f.179. 中国的宗教

B.L., MS. Locke. c.27., f.181. "理"与"太极"(A)

B.L., MS. Locke. c.27., ff.186-7. "上帝"(D1-2)

B.L., MS. Locke. c.27., f.188. "天"(E)

要点:

1. 中国哲学的基础:

中国哲学不承认独立于物质的纯粹精神。中国哲学既定的、不可动摇的基础是"万物同一体"。

2. "天"与祭天仪式:

(1)"天"是可见世界中最高贵、最完美的部分,是万物之源,是儒教的主要崇拜对象。儒教认为"天"是世界万物的规律,是一种非常微妙的物质,又称"理"或"太极"。

(2)作为最高世俗统治者和最高神职人员(儒教领袖),皇帝每年两次举行祭天仪式。

3."上帝"：

（1）"上帝"是星体或天体中最纯净完美的部分，是统摄天下万物的内在德行；也是中国人称为"理"或"太极"的微妙物质，遍布宇宙各处，融于天地万物，尤聚于造化神秀所钟之物。

（2）派别之争与古今之辨：有些人认为儒教建立后的两千多年里，"上帝"这个词指的都是"真正的上帝"。也就是说，从中华帝国建立之初到公元六十年左右，"上帝"指的都是"真正的非物质的上帝"；只是后来为了更好地对付日益壮大的佛教和道教，儒教不再提起任何非物质存在，这使得中国人的主神"上帝"仅指"物质的天"及其力量。自此，"上帝"从古代经典中与"God"和灵魂不朽相关的概念下降为"物质的天"。另一些人强烈反对这一观点，他们认为从古至今，"上帝"这个词指的一直都是"物质的天"或者"物质的天"的某种"气"，即"理"或"太极"。

（3）中西之辨：中国人用"上帝"指称事物的变化和发展，但是中国人不认为"上帝"理解或知晓这一切。因此，中国人的"上帝"与西方的"命运"相似，都是盲目的。

（4）译名之辨：在中国，用任何欧洲名称来指称"God"都是不可能的，原因有二：其一，没有中国字来书写"God"，其二，我们用来指称"God"的名称无法使中国人的头脑中产生它所指代的概念。因此，那些最早融入中国人当中的传教士选择"天主"这个词来指称"God"，原因是"天主"这个词的意思能够使中国人的头脑里产生一种完美的存在。

4."理"与"太极"：

（1）儒教的"理"或"太极"是一种微妙物质，由万物的不同形态分离聚合而成，又称"天"或"上帝"。

（2）古今之辨与派别之争：儒教经典认为"天""理"或"太极"由万物的各种不同形态分离聚合而成，并将之理解为某种更完美的存在，某种创造并统摄万物的、<u>智慧的</u>、<u>能动的</u>规律或本质。有些人认为古今皆如此，另一些人不同意。然而，不管古代中国人的观点如何，最近四五百年来，儒教一直将"物质的天"视为"第一律"和"至高无上的神"。

分析：

本部分最核心的观点为：中国哲学不可动摇的基础是"万物同一体"。自古希腊哲学以降，从伊壁鸠鲁、德谟克利特到17世纪的斯宾诺莎，"万物同一体"一直是欧洲唯物论的核心观念。因此对洛克来说，信仰"万物同一体"的中国哲学必然是无神论。

儒教的关键概念，如"天""上帝""理""太极"基本是同一种微妙物质的不同名称，由万物的不同形态分离聚合而成，并统摄万物。围绕着这些关键概念，洛克论及了"礼仪之争"的几个关键问题，如"派别之争""译名之争""古今之辨""中西之辨"，叙述简要，态度明确。

"礼仪之争"是天主教内部的"派别之争"，一方为坚持利玛窦"适应政策"的耶稣会士，另一方为反对"适应政策"的传教士。双方争论的焦点为"译名之争"和"礼仪之争"。关于"译名之争"，洛克倾向于反对用欧洲名称指称"God"，支持早期来华传教士选用的"天主"一词。同时，虽然洛克对祭天、祭祖、祭孔的礼仪表现出了巨大的热情，但他更关注具体的仪式和风俗，并未讨论其性质。可见，洛克对天主教内部的"礼仪之争"并不感兴趣。（详见下文）

"古今之辨"是利玛窦的"适应政策"的重要理论基础，即将儒家分为"古儒"（古代儒家经典）和"近儒"（程朱理学）。以利玛窦为代表的耶稣会士一方面认为"古儒"与基督教有相似性，试图构筑一种中国—基督教文明；另一方面将佛教以及"近儒"作为批评对象。他们认为中国古代儒家典籍中的"天"和"上帝"被中国人用来指一个灵魂及人类的统治之主，其性质与基督教的"神"一样，是一切力量与法律权威的源泉，是伦理道德的至高约束者和捍卫者，全知全能，奖善罚恶。利玛窦在《天主实义》中用了几页来阐述"天"和"上帝"就是指基督教的"神"这一观点。1600年，范礼安同意了利玛窦以"上帝"指称基督教"神"的术语选择。不过这一决议从一开始就遭遇阻力，耶稣会内部对此也有不同看法，如龙华民（Nicolas Longobardi）从1597年到达中国以来就对这些术语的合法性表示怀疑。[①]洛克在论述儒教的关键概念时，多次提到"古今之

---

① 参见张国刚：《从中西初识到礼仪之争——明清传教士与中西文化交流》，北京：人民出版社，2003年，第391—392页。

辨"。概括来说，古代儒家经典将"天""上帝""理"或"太极"视为某种创造并统摄万物的、智慧的、能动的规律或本质；而近四五百年来，"天"只是"物质的天"。"中国笔记"中提到"古今之辨"不下五次，这说明洛克对这种区分非常感兴趣。毕竟，"创造并统摄万物的、智慧的、能动的规律或本质"是基督教上帝的特质。如果认可这样的"古今之辨"，就等于认可古代中国人信仰基督教的"上帝"。纵观"中国笔记"，洛克对"古今之辨"持回避加保留的态度。洛克在"中国笔记"中多次提到"不论古代中国人如何，如今'天'只是'物质的天'"。这一方面说明洛克无意卷入天主教内部的"礼仪之争"，另一方面说明对于不能直接阅读中文的洛克而言，没有足够的证据评判古代儒家经典。但在"中国笔记"手稿的第188页，洛克说："孔子和儒家其他古代哲学家认为只有'物质的天'才是万物之源，因此儒教崇拜'物质的天'。"这说明洛克对于"古今之辨"持保留态度。

相比于"古今之辨"，洛克似乎更倾向于中国的"上帝"与西方的"命运"之间的类比。中国和西方都有"命中注定""命该如此"之类的说法。在欧洲人的观念中，"命运"是盲目的、不自觉的；而全知全能的"God"是有目的的、自觉的。中国的"上帝"更像西方的"命运"，而不是基督教的"God"。这很类似龙华民《论中国宗教的某些要点》（巴黎，1701年）中对"理"的解释。龙华民认为"理"既无灵智，又无思维，仅仅是根据秉性之倾向的一种天命而行事；虽然某些人可能因为中国人给这种"理"或"太极"赋予一些仅适用于God的品质而认为它就是基督教的God，但最根本的区别是它不具备智力，不以思辨能力而仅以一种癖性倾向和自然理进行活动，所以"理"并非真正的上帝，而只是基督教所说的第一性物质。[①]

三、精神、灵魂和守护神

所涉章节：

B.L., MS. Locke. c.27., f.183. 精神和人类灵魂（B）

[①] 参见张国刚：《从中西初识到礼仪之争——明清传教士与中西文化交流》，北京：人民出版社，2003年，第513—514页。

B.L., MS. Locke. c.27., f.185. 游魂（C）
B.L., MS. Locke. c.27., f.199. 地球、星体、山川、河流的守护神（G）

要点：

1. 精神和人类灵魂：

（1）儒教不承认纯粹精神，因此不相信灵魂不朽。

（2）儒教认为灵魂是"理"或"太极"的一部分，人死后40天灵魂再度融合于"理"或"太极"。

（3）由于"理"或"太极"无所不在，因此人死后，灵魂的某些部分依然存在，能够回到牌位上接受祭祀。

2. 游魂：

没有后代的人死后，灵魂成为游魂。中国人祭祀游魂，以便游魂不会害人，而且还会带来其他福报。

3. 各种守护神：

儒教除了祭天以外，还崇拜和祭祀星辰、大地、山川、河流以及城市的守护神。中国人不相信纯粹精神，中国人所说的精神或守护神是充盈于天、地、人之间的某种微妙物质。

分析：

洛克在"中国笔记"一开篇就说过"儒教唯一的神就是'物质的天'"，这里又说儒教除了祭天之外，也崇拜和祭祀其他神，似乎是矛盾的。另外，如果儒教相信"万物有灵"并崇拜祭祀各种守护神的话，那么儒教就有泛神论的特征，而不是洛克在前文所说的无神论。但洛克认为中国人所说的"神"并不是基督教意义上的"神"，即纯粹精神，而是充盈于万物的某种微妙物质，因而中国人不相信纯粹精神，中国哲学是唯物论，儒教是无神论。这与上文讨论"天""理""太极""上帝"的逻辑是一致的。

四、孔子与祭孔仪式

所涉章节：

B. L., MS. Locke. c.27., ff. 190-7. 孔子（F1-8）

要点：

1. 孔子被中国人奉为"大成至圣先师"——中国哲学的奠基人和中国学术之父。孔子著作之于中国人的权威相当于四福音书之于欧洲人。

2. 每年春分和秋分都举行大规模的正式祭孔仪式，仪式分三个部分。

3. 除了每年两次的祭孔大典，读书人随时祭祀孔子。首先，读书人获取功名后，要祭孔；其次，官员上任前要祭孔；最后，地方官员每月朔望升堂审案前也要祭孔。

4. 所有祭孔的礼仪和仪式都受帝国法律保护，因而不断强化。

5. 在中国，只有学者或获取功名的读书人才有机会担任行政职务。

6. 有时皇帝钦命将一些大儒的牌位供于孔庙，与孔子共享祭祀，这被读书人视为最高荣誉。

分析：

洛克对于孔子及其著作在中国的权威地位的定义是准确的，对于祭孔仪式的描述非常具体也比较准确。本部分也涉及中国的政治制度与科举制度，指出只有获得功名的读书人才能做官，同时读书人获取功名后、官员上任前、官员审案前都要祭孔，加之皇帝本人就是儒教的领袖和保护人，因此祭孔受国家法律保护。总之，洛克对祭孔礼仪的描述和理解具体而准确，但对其性质——即祭孔礼仪是宗教性的还是世俗性的——未置一词，由此可见，洛克对祭孔礼仪本身以及中国的政治和科举制度很有兴趣，对"礼仪之争"本身没有兴趣。

五、祖先与祭祖仪式

所涉章节：

B. L., MS. Locke. c.27., ff.200-5. 祖先（H1-6）

要点：

1. 中国人的政体和统治都建立在"孝"的基础上，因而祖先是中国人的主要信仰对象。

2. 每年春秋两季，中国人会在祖庙举行隆重的祭祖仪式，祭祀四世祖先。建不起祖庙的穷人在家里祭祖。

3. 除了每年两次的正式祭祀，每月朔望两日，中国人也常常到祖庙祭拜祖先。

4. 中国人向祖先祈求很多现世的福报，如财富、荣誉、长寿、多子等，但这些祈求从不涉及来世。

分析：

与上文所述的"祭孔"一样，洛克对"祭祖"的具体礼仪及其与中国政治制度的密切关系的认识具体而准确，对其性质则闭口不提。洛克关注的焦点依然在中国宗教的性质以及与基督教的区别上面。他强调中国人向祖先祈求很多现世的福报，但这些祈求从不涉及来世，可见中国人不信来世和灵魂不朽。这与基督徒为死去的人祷告是截然不同的，基督徒的祷告是祈求死者的来世安宁，而中国人祭祖是祈求自己和家族的现世福报。联系上文对中国人对"精神""灵魂"的分析，人的"精神"或"灵魂"源于"理"或"太极"，人死后，"精神"和"灵魂"又归于"理"或"太极"，充盈于天地万物，无所不在。因此"灵魂"能够在祭祀的时候回到牌位上，并能够赐予祭祀的人现世福报，这并不是因为灵魂不朽，而是因为灵魂归于本源。从本质上说，中国人祭天、祭各种守护神、祭祖、祭孔都是在祭万物之源，即中国人说的"天""理""太极""上帝"这些名异而实同的最高存在。这样的理解在逻辑上是可行的，也基本符合中国哲学的思想内涵。

此外，洛克在"中国笔记"中还时常将中国与英国相对应，以便理解和描述对他来说十分陌生的中国文化。比如：

（1）在描述中国的祭孔、祭祖礼仪时与英国国教礼仪相对应，最典型的就是各种祭官的名称。

（2）将中国与英国的教育机构和考试制度相对应，将中国的学校称为"college"（对应于英国大学的各个学院），将中国获取功名的读书人称为"graduate"（对应英国的大学毕业生），并且注意到中国的科举考试采取笔试（英国的大学当时还主要是答辩类的考试），还特意提到大学生毕业时自己出钱购买香烛祭祀孔子（也是与英国大学毕业生的花费相对应）。

（3）中国政治制度与英国政治制度的对比，如在中国只有学者才能做官，而在英国担任公职不需要学位，需要学位的职务通常是宗教性职务；在中国，所有国家级官员和各级行政官员都出身儒教，皇帝本人就是儒教的保护人和领袖，这倒是与英国国教基本一致。

六、小结

洛克"中国笔记"表面上是一本读书摘要，对中国的宗教和礼仪"述而不作"。但事实上，洛克只是对天主教内部"礼仪之争"的两大焦点——"译名之争"和"礼仪之争"——"存而不论"，对中国宗教的关键概念和根本性质却观点鲜明，理解深刻。洛克看似只是摘录并罗列了《中国礼仪史》等文献中对中国宗教和礼仪的描述，实际上却奇迹般地透过传教士们晦涩冗长并且时常自相矛盾的描述抓住了中国宗教的内核，最终得出"中国的统治阶级——士大夫们——都是纯粹的无神论者"的结论。

这不由得让人想到与洛克同时代的莱布尼茨。在参考了龙华民和闵明我的作品后，莱布尼茨在《论尊孔》中得出了与参考文献完全相反的结论，即中国的祭孔礼仪是政治性和世俗性的，而不是宗教性的，因此可以被基督徒所接受。

在对中国思想的理解上，洛克和莱布尼茨都体现了一流思想家的敏锐洞察力，他们都透过纷繁复杂的文献材料，抓住了中国思想的部分本质。由于关注重点的不同，更重要的是由于本身哲学立场的不同，洛克与莱布尼茨对于中国哲学与宗教得出了不同的结论。我们不能对他们的结论作出价值判断或比较，只能说他们都从自己的哲学立场出发，从古老而复杂的中国思想中剪裁出了自己需要的材料，并为自己所用。他们对中国文化的理解必然有误读的成分，但他们的理解是基于欧洲思想背景和逻辑传统作出的合理判断，从这个角度讲，并不存在对中国文化的歪曲。直到今天，他们所论及的很多中国思想的基本问题连中国学者自己也很难说得明白，足见中国思想的复杂性。以洛克、莱布尼茨为代表的启蒙思想家以纯西方视角对这些问题的解读无疑是值得我们借鉴的"他山之石"。

第四章　"中国笔记"的基础：洛克书信与中国

洛克在"中国笔记"中对中国的关注和理解并不是孤立的、突然的。洛克一生钟爱游记文学，他所收藏的游记文学中有相当一部分是关于中国的①；洛克晚年一直将威森（Nicolaas Witsen）②的鞑靼地图（*Map of Tartary*）③挂在书房的墙上，并且在遗嘱中专门注明这幅地图的归属④；洛克还提议丘吉尔兄弟（A & J Churchill）⑤编辑出版了《游记与旅行丛书》（*Collection of Voyages and*

---

① 详见本书第六章。
② 威森（Nicolaas Witsen，1641—1717），阿姆斯特丹市长和外交家，鞑靼地理专家。其名在当时有"Nicolaes Witsen""Nicolaas Witsen"等多种拼写方式，本书采用现代荷兰语的拼法"Nicolaas Witsen"。特此说明。
③ 参见本书彩图12。
④ 洛克遗嘱中规定："Item I give to Mr. Anthony Collins of the Middle Temple my ... and Wisten's Map of Tartary that hangs up in my study."详见本书第二章第一节第一点。
⑤ 丘吉尔兄弟指Awnsham Churchill和John Churchill，辉格党人，伦敦出版商，与洛克多有合作，曾于1689年将《政府论》和《论宽容》匿名出版。

Travels）①，即便该书的长篇序言并非真的出自洛克之手，洛克至少为该书提供了指导意见和资料支持。此外，洛克在与亲友的私人书信中密切关注中国，在其已刊和未刊著作中也曾提及中国，这些都是洛克"中国观"的重要组成部分。由于"中国笔记"在写作时间上晚于提到中国的书信和著作，我姑且将这些书信和著作称为"中国笔记"的"前理解"。我所说的"前理解"并非严格意义上的解释学概念，而是表示在"中国笔记"成文之前洛克对中国的关注和理解。本书将在本章和第五章分别梳理"洛克书信中的中国"和"洛克著作中的中国"，试图归纳分析洛克"中国观"的形成时间、基本要点以及与"中国笔记"的内在联系。

17世纪后半叶，西欧和中欧国家的邮政服务已经比较成熟，速度较快而且比较可靠，书信成为人们交流的主要渠道之一。②与当时的大多数思想家一样，洛克与为数众多的各色人等保持着频繁的通信，因而洛克书信是研究洛克生平与思想的重要依据。如果忽视了洛克书信中对中国的关注，那么洛克的"中国观"注定是不完整的。本章旨在搜集整理洛克关注中国的书信，并整理书信中对中国关注的要点，初步分析洛克的"中国观"。（本章整理的书信均以德比尔编辑的八卷本《洛克书信集》③为底本。同时为便于读者查找，标注了每封信在《洛克书信集》中的卷册、编号、关键注释，以及通信双方姓名、日期及档案编号。特此说明。）

---

① 丘吉尔兄弟的《游记与旅行丛书》四卷本的初版于1704年正式发行，但在此之前，洛克已经收藏了该书的未刊版本；1732年再版时又增加了两卷；1744—1746年第三版；1752年第四版。该书在当时的影响力很大，该书的第一卷第一篇就是闵明我（Domingo Fernández Navarrete）的巨著《中华帝国历史、政治、伦理及宗教概述》（*Tratados historicos, politicos, ethicosy religious de la monarchia de China*）的英译本。参见本书附录1。

② 当时，英国与欧洲大陆之间的通信受天气影响，以阿姆斯特丹到伦敦为例，如果顺利，信件发出后的第三天就可以抵达，如果天气不好，则需要两到三周。当时邮政服务的主要问题是费用过高（关于洛克时代英国的邮政服务及收费标准，参见John Locke, E.S. De Beer (ed.), *The Correspondence of John Locke*, V1, Introduction, Oxford: Clarendon Press, 1976, pp. li-lii，和 pp. lxxvii-lxxix）。不过议员享有在英国国内免费寄信的特权，Edward Clarke和John Freke显然常常使用这一特权寄信给洛克。

③ John Locke, E.S. De Beer (ed.), *The Correspondence of John Locke* (in eight volumes), Oxford: Clarendon Press, 1976-1989.

第一节　洛克现存书信简介

洛克书信主要包括洛克写给他人的信和他人写给洛克的信，也包括少量与洛克相关的第三方之间的通信。1704年洛克去世之后不久，洛克书信就以各种形式屡次出版，比如丘吉尔兄弟于1708年出版的《洛克与几位朋友的通信》（Some Familiar Letters between Mr. Locke, and Several of His Friends），这是洛克书信首次公开出版。之后又有多种的版本，有的不够完整，有的不够准确。到目前为止，洛克书信集最好、最完整版本是德比尔编辑的八卷本《洛克书信集》。该书第一卷"前言"中对此前出版的洛克书信集做了详细的描述和点评。①

《洛克书信集》收集了现存的洛克书信共3650件。其中洛克写给他人的信共1023件，约880件为正式寄出的信，约100件是信件的草稿，还有一些残片和散片。其他为他人写给洛克的书信，还有少部分是第三方之间的通信。约350人曾与洛克通信。来往信件的日期则从1652年开始一直到1704年，而1687年以后，来往信件的数量相对增加。大部分信件来自英格兰，几百封来自法国和荷兰，还有一些来自美国、东印度等地。书信多为英文书写，但有几百封是法文或拉丁文或这两种语言的混合，还有几封是荷兰文，一封是希腊文。

第二节　洛克书信中关于中国的部分

洛克书信中数次提到中国，主要是关于与中国的贸易、在英国的中国人、最新出版的关于中国的书籍等内容。有些信件中虽然提到中国，其实内容与中国并没有直接关系，比如，有的信件中提到含有奎宁（quinine）、可用于退烧的金鸡纳树皮及类似的药用植物，信中称之为cinchona、china、china china、china root或peruvian bark。这些药材有的产自南美，有的产自中国。这些信件的内容多与洛克作为医生的活动有关，并不与中国直接相关。再比如，洛克时常托朋友在伦敦帮忙购买橘子，信中称China oranges，这些信件也与中国无关。

洛克现存书信中真正与中国相关的信件共15封，分布在《洛克书信集》第

---

① 详见 E.S. De Beer (ed.), The Correspondence of John Locke, V1, Introduction, Oxford: Clarendon Press, 1976, pp. xli–l。

五卷（1封）、第六卷（7封）、第七卷（6封）和第八卷（1封）。具体内容如下：

1. 第五卷　编号2028[①]

发信人：Dr. Pieter Guenellon

收信人：Locke

日期：6/16 March 1696

档案：B.L., MS. Locke c.11, f.71

主要内容：

这是一封法文信。Pieter Guenellon医生在信中告诉洛克一种新的手术方法取得了成功，并感谢洛克为自己的儿子所做的很好的规划。此外，他告诉洛克："威森用弗拉芒语写成的关于鞑靼的书已经印刷了，但要到夏天才会正式发行。Avril神父于1693年用法语写成的关于鞑靼的书对于理解威森的书很有帮助。"

信中提到的威森关于鞑靼的书名为《北东鞑靼》（Noord en Oost Tartarye）。该书集合了此前已刊和未刊的关于今西伯利亚不同地区的描述。该书1692年出版，然而直到1698年威森才公开发行此书。[②]

2. 第六卷　编号2219[③]

发信人：Locke

收信人：Dr. (later Sir) Hans Sloane

日期：15 March 1697

档案：B.M., Sloane MS. 4036, ff.290-I.

---

① 参见John Locke, E.S. De Beer (ed.), *The Correspondence of John Locke*, V5, Oxford: Clarendon Press, 1979, pp. 556-557。

② 详见Ibid., p. 556注释1。

③ 参见John Locke, E.S. De Beer (ed.), *The Correspondence of John Locke*, V6, Oxford: Clarendon Press, 1981, pp. 35-36。

主要内容：

洛克在给汉斯·斯隆的信中提到自己于1678年在巴黎发现的一个罕见病例——一个长着极长指甲的年轻人，并随信寄去洛克取得的指甲的部分样品。接着，洛克说："最近在奥茨附近出现了一个日本人。我得知此事的时候，他已经离开，不然我必找机会与他会谈，我听说他懂一些英文。我们与日本的贸易往来很少，也很少有日本人来英国，我想您应该乐于找到他。我得到的关于他的线索是：'Leadenhall街上东印度公司对面的文具店问Bango先生'。我不想就与他交谈的主题向您提出任何建议，对于有关日本的合适问题您比我更有发言权。我只有一个非常想问的问题，那就是在日本是否禁止进口黄金和白银。"①

洛克提供给斯隆一个从奥茨去到伦敦的"日本人"的线索，建议斯隆找到这个人并且代自己问一个关于日本是否禁止进口金银的问题，但斯隆回信说这个人其实是"中国人"（见下一封信）。

3. 第六卷　编号2224②

发信人：Dr. (later Sir) Hans Sloane

收信人：Locke

日期：18 March 1697

档案：B.L., MS. Locke c.18, ff.120-1.

主要内容：

这是斯隆给洛克的回信。斯隆感谢洛克寄来的可怕的指甲样本，称皇家学会

---

① 原文：There was lately in our neighbourhood a Japonese. I heard not of him till he was gon or else would have sought an opportunity to have spoke with him, for I am told he speaks English a little. We have soe little commerce with Japan and there are soe few of that country come into ours, that I thought it would not be unacceptable to you to know where he is to be found. The direction sent me was as followeth: "Enguire for Mr Bango at the Stationers over against the East India house in eadenhall street" I shall not say any thing to you concerning the heads to be talked on with him, you kow soe well better than I what questions are fit to be asked concerning that country. I would only be resolvd in this one whether the Importation of gold and silver be prohibited there. 见John Locke, E.S. De Beer (ed.), *The Correspondence of John Locke*, V6, Oxford: Clarendon Press, 1981, pp. 35-36。

② John Locke, E.S. De Beer (ed.), *The Correspondence of John Locke*, V6, Oxford: Clarendon Press, 1981, pp. 55-56。

对此非常感兴趣，并已将样本收藏在学会博物馆。斯隆通报了他那边的最新情况是Postellus①的书稿正在出售，但没有人愿意出超过10镑来购买。斯隆还向洛克借一本名为 *Beautes de la Perse* ②的书。接着斯隆说："我会找机会与您提到的中国人会谈，他来自Emoy③。我曾与他见过一面，但语言问题使我们基本无法交流。当时我去刚刚抵达伦敦的一艘船上找我的连襟，我就在那艘船上见到了他。"④

斯隆说洛克提到的"日本人"其实是来自厦门的中国人。

4. 第六卷 编号2483⑤

发信人：Locke

收信人：Nicolas Toinard

日期：15 August 1698

档案：The Historical Society of Pennsylvania, Philadelphia.

主要内容：

这是一封法文信。洛克在信中提到了几本新书，比如《论音乐作品》、Charles Henri Olerke的旅行报告、Drake的游记。洛克说："鉴于您对翻译西班牙文游记的喜爱，如果您愿翻译闵明我神父用基督之语（指西班牙文——译者）写

---

① Guillaume Postel, 1510—1581.

② A. Daulier-Deslandes: *Beautes de la Perse*, Paris, 1673.

③ 应为Amoy，即福建厦门。

④ 原文：I will take care to have some discourse with the Chinese you mention, he came from Emoy, I talk'd with him once but the language made us have little conversation, I saw him on board the ship when she first arrived when I went to inquire after a brother in law of mine who was supracargo of her and left behind and was the occasion of this man's coming. 见John Locke, E.S. De Beer (ed.), *The Correspondence of John Locke*, V6, Oxford: Clarendon Press, 1981, p. 56。

⑤ John Locke, E.S. De Beer (ed.), *The Correspondence of John Locke*, V6, Oxford: Clarendon Press, 1981, pp. 462-463.

的中国游记①，我会感到非常高兴。"②

5. 第六卷 编号2598③

发信人：Samuel Locke

收信人：Locke

日期：20 June 1699

档案：B.L., MS. Locke c.14, ff.199-200.

背景信息：

洛克时代有两家英国公司竞争与中国及远东的贸易，一个是老牌的东印度公司（British East India Company），1600年获英皇伊丽莎白一世授予的皇家特许状，1609年詹姆士一世给东印度公司颁发了一张不设期限的特许状。巨额利润很快引起其他利益集团对其垄断的不满，1694年威廉三世允许其他公司参与竞争。1698年，新东印度公司（English Company Trading to the East Indies）成立，在台湾建立贸易据点，频繁往来于福建厦门（Amoy）、浙江舟山（Chusan）之间，直到1700年清政府关闭除广州之外的其他港口。这封信的作者John Locke及其父Samuel Locke都为新东印度公司工作。1708年新、旧东印度公司合二为一。

这封信的作者Samuel Locke应该是洛克的远房堂兄弟或表兄弟，具体关系不可考。1697—1698年，Samuel Locke任英格兰银行主任；1698年新东印度公司即将成立时，他先被任命为资金托管人之一，继而出任这家新公司的主管；1715年去世。④Samuel Locke有四儿四女，其中长子约翰是新东印度公司的雇员，曾在印度苏拉特（Surat）工作过一段时间并曾到过中国；1705年升任波斯贸易主

---

① 指闵明我（Domingo Fernández Navarrete）的《中华帝国历史、政治、伦理及宗教概述》（*Tratados historicos, politicos, ethicosy religious de la monarchia de China*），马德里，1676年。

② 原文：Comme vous prenez plaisir de traduire les voyages et relations Espagniols je serois bien aise que vous voudriea bien traduire Navaretti de China en langue chrestienne。见John Locke, E.S. De Beer (ed.), *The Correspondence of John Locke*, V6, Oxford: Clarendon Press, 1981, p. 463。

③ John Locke, E.S. De Beer (ed.), *The Correspondence of John Locke*, V6, Oxford: Clarendon Press, 1981, pp. 645–646.

④ 参见Ibid., p. 645。

管；1717年被授予爵士头衔；1746年去世。①Samuel Locke及其长子是洛克关于与中国贸易情况的主要信息来源之一。

另外，重返英伦的洛克是其家族中最受尊敬的人物，因此作为与洛克同名的远房子侄，Samuel Locke的长子约翰在写给洛克的信中一律署名"John Lock"，以示尊重；后被封爵也称"Sir John Lock"；本书称之为"约翰"或"John Lock（later Sir John）"以示区别。而Samuel Locke与洛克是同辈，书信中署名不太统一，"Samuel Locke"和"Samuel Lock"都有，本书统一用"Samuel Locke"。特此说明。

主要内容：

Samuel Locke先是万分感激洛克对约翰的关照，接着说："约翰现在苏拉特，我们在两至三周内还要再派出三艘货船，一艘前往苏拉特，一艘前往科罗曼德尔海岸，还有一艘前往中国。上周一艘货船从中国回来，装载了价值22,000英镑的货物，保守估计销售价格在75,000到80,000英镑之间。随信寄去些酒②供您品尝。"③

6. 第六卷　编号2600.④

发信人：J.-B. Du Bos

收信人：Locke

日期：27 June/7 July [1699]

档案：B.L., MS. Locke c.7, ff. 230-1.

---

① 参见John Locke, E.S. De Beer (ed.), *The Correspondence of John Locke*, V6, Oxford: Clarendon Press, 1981, p. 499。

② 一夸脱装24瓶，一品脱装48瓶，6月16日送到Pawling's house，见B.L., MS. Locke c. 14, f.198。

③ 原文：... and that my son John may Returne to make you his personal acknowledgment for so great a favour. which in the meantyme I hope you will receive from him at Surratt at the Returne of the ships. of which wee intend to dispatch on away in 14 days or 3 weeks at furthest. and another for the Coast of Coromandel and a third for China. from whence one aryved Last weeke with the inclosed Cargo which Cost £22000 starling; and by the modestest Computation will yield at the sale £75. to £80000 starling. Sir as to the wine. being but a Taste. I shall be well paid for it if you will please but to accept of it. 见John Locke, E.S. De Beer (ed.), *The Correspondence of John Locke*, V6, Oxford: Clarendon Press, 1981, pp. 645-646。

④ John Locke, E.S. De Beer (ed.), *The Correspondence of John Locke*, V6, Oxford: Clarendon Press, 1981, pp. 647-648。

背景信息：

这封信的作者是Jean-Baptiste Du Bos（1670—1742），1691年毕业于索邦神学院。最重要的作品为*Réflexions critiques sur la poésie et sur la peinture* (1719)，该书受到伏尔泰的高度评价。1720年Du Bos当选法兰西学士院（Académie française）院士，1722年成为法兰西学士院永久秘书。

主要内容：

这是一封法文信。Du Bos讨论了几本书，特别提到："这座城市（指阿姆斯特丹）的一家出版社用拉丁语刊印了耶稣会士和其他在中国的传教士在罗马关于该国基督徒是否能行本国典礼礼仪的争论。这本书中关于中国人的信仰和宗教的讨论非常有趣。"①

这封信中提到的书就是《华人礼仪史》（*Historia Cultus Sinensium*），Du Bos向洛克推荐了这本新书，并且说该书是在阿姆斯特丹出版的，这说明该书注明的出版地——科隆很可能是为了逃避审查而伪托的。《华人礼仪史》是洛克"中国笔记"的直接知识来源，洛克最初知道这本书很可能就是因为这封信。

7. 第六卷　编号2637②

发信人：Samuel Locke

收信人：Locke

日期：30 November 1699

档案：B.L., MS. Locke c.14, ff. 202-3.

主要内容：

Samuel Locke在这封信中除了问候洛克的健康外，主要通报了新东印度公司与中国的贸易情况。他说："感谢您委托斯隆博士向我们推荐Cuninghame先生

---

① 原文：Un libraire de cette ville imprime en latin les pieces du procez pendant a Rome entre les Jesuites et les autres missionaires de la Chine sur les ceremonies nationales que lon peut permettre aux Chretiens. le livre sera curieux par la discussion des dogmes et de la religion de ces peuples. 见John Locke, E.S. De Beer (ed.), *The Correspondence of John Locke*, V6, Oxford: Clarendon Press, 1981, p. 647.

② John Locke, E.S. De Beer (ed.), *The Correspondence of John Locke*, V6, Oxford: Clarendon Press, 1981, pp. 737-738.

作为医生前往被感染的工厂。我们终于派出Eaton号搭载董事会和其他成员前往宁波（Liempo）和南京（Nanquien），以防前一艘船没有达成任务。Eaton号和另一艘船上装载着价值和数量巨大的羊毛，以及其他英格兰的产品，我们希望这些货物在寒冷的中国北部能够受到欢迎。两周内我们将派出第三艘船。"①

8. 第六卷 编号 2642②

发信人：Samuel Locke

收信人：Locke

日期：2 December 1699

档案：B.L., MS. Locke c.14, ff. 204-5

主要内容：

Samuel Locke向洛克通报了与中国联系的细节，他说："两周内我们将再派一艘船跟随Pounde医生去中国。如果您有口信要带给他，可以利用他与约翰在苏拉特的通信联系（约翰在信中提到了这一点）。我想告诉您，我们（将在中国建的）工厂将常常派船将产品运到苏拉特，因此Pounde医生和约翰都可以收到送到苏拉特的信。"

9. 第七卷 编号 2748③

发信人：J.-B. Du Bos

---

① 原文：Sir I had the honour by Dr Sloane to receive your Commands in recommending mr Cuninghame to goe Surgeon to the factory, which was Effected. And wee have fynnally dispatch the President Council and factors by the Eaton（船名）friggot to make the Settlement at Liempo（宁波）weer and at Nanquien（南京）in case the first doth not Succeede: wee have Imbark'd in this and another ship a great Treasure. [737] and very Considerable quantity of our Woollen. And other Eng: Manufacture, which wee hope will take a very good effect in those Cold northerne parts of China: which will be follow'd by a third ship in 14 days tyme. 见John Locke, E.S. De Beer (ed.), *The Correspondence of John Locke*, V6, Oxford: Clarendon Press, 1981, pp. 647-648。

② John Locke, E.S. De Beer (ed.), *The Correspondence of John Locke*, V6, Oxford: Clarendon Press, 1981, p. 748.

③ John Locke, E.S. De Beer (ed.), *The Correspondence of John Locke*, V7, Oxford: Clarendon Press, 1982, pp. 110-112.

收信人：Locke

日期：17/28 July [1700]

档案：B.L., MS. Locke c.7, ff. 236-7.

主要内容：

这是一封法文信。Du Bos向洛克通报了自己的近况，而后他说："耶稣会士和法国赴中国传教士关于孔子信仰和祖先崇拜的争论在这里特别激烈。每天，双方都有小作品出版，每一方都尽可能让对方显得可憎。他们都试图让公众相信，一方①对中国礼仪的宽容是出于对基督教的冷漠态度，而另一方②的坚持则完全是出于他们的嫉妒心理。索邦大学也参与到这场争论中，并将考察李明神父的信中的一个主张，即直到耶稣基督时代，中国人一直保存着真正的宗教。"

Du Bos向洛克介绍了正在罗马进行的"礼仪之争"的热烈程度，并且提到巴黎索邦大学对李明的审查③。

10. 第七卷 编号2784④

发信人：Samuel Locke

收信人：Locke

日期：27 September 1700

档案：B.L., MS. Locke c. 14, ff. 210-11.

主要内容：

Samuel Locke告诉洛克，约翰经过近10个月的危险路程最终安全抵达了苏拉特，并且向洛克通报了新、旧东印度公司与印度的贸易情况。关于中国他只说："我们整日盼望Nicholas爵士说已于去年四月出发的Norris号，以及从中国和婆罗洲来的另外一两艘船。"⑤

---

① 指遵守利玛窦适应政策的耶稣会士。
② 指反对利玛窦适应政策的传教士，如法国外方传教士。
③ 索邦大学的审查在1700年10月18日进行，结果将李明的著作列为禁书并且正式反对耶稣会士的立场。
④ John Locke, E.S. De Beer (ed.), *The Correspondence of John Locke*, V7, Oxford: Clarendon Press, 1982, pp. 154–155.
⑤ 原文：we Expect dayly the Norris from Surrat which Sir Nicholas writes will be dispatch in April Last. And on or two from China and Borneo。见John Locke, E.S. De Beer (ed.), *The Correspondence of John Locke*, V7, Oxford: Clarendon Press, 1982, p. 154。

11. 第七卷　编号 3046[①]

发信人：John Lock (later Sir John)

收信人：Locke

日期：23 November 1701[②]

档案：B.L., MS. Locke c.14, ff. 176-7.

主要内容：

这封信是约翰从福建厦门寄回英国的。约翰说："因为您屈尊给身在苏拉特的我写信，所以我非常荣幸地从远方写信给您，并将经常这样做。希望我从学校获得的知识和从商业贸易职业中获得的经验能够使我发现那些研究外国政策、宗教、政府和物产的专家所遗漏的细节[③]。然而，我无法到港口以外的中国其他地方，每天接触的都是与我一样进行贸易的人，并且我的绝大部分时间都用于卸货盘点、分析市场。但由于我是给您这样一位地位尊崇又待我如至亲的长辈写信，探讨人类如何获得对事物的理解，所以我还是尽量向您介绍我在日常工作中接触到的事实吧。"[④] 约翰主要从事中国与印度苏拉特之间的贸易，所以他向洛克描述了主要的货物，并声称与中国的贸易是利润最为丰厚的。[⑤]

---

① John Locke, E.S. De Beer (ed.), *The Correspondence of John Locke*, V7, Oxford: Clarendon Press, 1982, pp. 509–511.

② 这封信1702年9月30日由Samuel Locke转寄，洛克于同年10月6日收到。

③ 看起来这很可能是洛克对约翰的期许。

④ 原文：Since you were pleased to Honour mee with the Favour of a Letter to Surat, I esteem it a Priviledge given mee to write you from the remote Parts my fortune Leads mee to, and should make use of it much oftener if my education and Imployments, which has bin from the School, with Merchants and Merchandizing, were able to furnish mee with such discoveries as has escaped the notice of those who have made it their peculiar business to search into the Pollicy, Religion, Government, and the products of these Forreigne countries, which is difficult for mee to doe that goe noe deaper than a Sea Port, and am conversant constantly with people of my owne professions and the greatest part of my Time imploy'd in the disposeal of what I bring, and procureing effects proper for another market, but since I write to a person of soe great worth and soe well acquainted , how mankind coms to gather all their knowledge of these things, I shall not seek for further matter to troble you with then what I find in my dayly imployment。见John Locke, E.S. De Beer (ed.), *The Correspondence of John Locke*, V7, Oxford: Clarendon Press, 1982, p. 509。

⑤ 这封信发自厦门，并且是一封长信，信中对于与中国的贸易描述非常具体，但贸易毕竟不是本书的重点，因此我只将这封信的大意译出，同时将整封信放在本书附录2中，供有兴趣的读者查阅。

由这封信我们可以看出，当时洛克很可能正在为《人类理解论》搜集更多的证据，因此向约翰等在印度、中国等地工作的人详细询问这些国家的情况。从时间上看，洛克当时可能正在写或者正在准备写"中国笔记"。

12. 第七卷　编号3136①

发信人：John Lock (later Sir John)

收信人：Locke

日期：28 April 1702②

档案：B.L., MS. Locke c.14, ff. 178-9.

主要内容：

这是一封约翰从苏拉特写给洛克的回信。很显然洛克在之前的信中向约翰询问果阿的耶稣会学校的情况，但约翰说："我刚从中国回来，并且安排了几艘船返欧，还没有腾出时间来询问耶稣会学校的创立者是谁，以及它创立的时间。不过我猜测创立的时间应该是葡萄牙人进驻果阿③之后不久，而最初修建这所学校的人当中包括Jasper和Antony，他们在雨季离开。我会试着了解更多法国耶稣会士和方济各会士的构成情况。"④ 约翰在信的后半部分倒是非常详细地介绍了当时的皇帝Aureng Zeeb的情况。

---

① John Locke, E.S. De Beer (ed.), *The Correspondence of John Locke*, V7, Oxford: Clarendon Press, 1982, pp. 613-614.

② 1703年5月5日由Samuel Locke转寄给洛克。

③ 葡萄牙人于1510年占领果阿。

④ 原文：being Lately arrived from China and the Ships for Europeon their dispatch, I have not the Time to enquire who the Founder of the Jesuits Colledge was, or the time it was built but suppose not Long after the Portuguezes settled at Goa, those that first made these Stones which goe by the name of the place were Jasper and Antony, and the receipt Left the Colledge they Lived in, in the Rainy Season, I will endeavour to Learne of the French Jesuits and Capucin Padres what their composition is。见John Locke, E.S. De Beer (ed.), *The Correspondence of John Locke*, V7, Oxford: Clarendon Press, 1982, p. 613。

13. 第七卷　编号3152①

发信人：Edward Clarke

收信人：Locke

日期：20 June 1702

档案：B.L., MS.Locke c.27, f.207.

这封信的内容与中国无关，但洛克"中国笔记"关于"儒教"（Literati）的内容（B.L., MS.Locke c.27, f.207.）就写在这封信的背面（见图4-1和图4-2）。这封信是推断"中国笔记"写作时间的重要依据之一。

图4-1　B.L., MS.Locke c.27, f.207.

图4-2　B.L., MS.Locke c.27, f.207v.

14. 第七卷　编号3281②

发信人：Samuel Locke

收信人：Locke

日期：5 May 1703

档案：B.L., MS. Locke c. 14, ff. 221-2.

主要内容：

Samuel Locke随信转寄了约翰1702年4月28日从苏拉特寄给洛克的信（编号3136），并且说："约翰已经在苏拉特工作1年了，他积累了更多的处理印度

---

① John Locke, E.S. De Beer (ed.), *The Correspondence of John Locke*, V7, Oxford: Clarendon Press, 1982, pp. 637-638.

② Ibid., pp. 783-784.

以及中国、马六甲、南洋等地的贸易经验，并且得到了升职。"① 接着Samuel Locke通报了驻印度大使William Norris爵士在归国途中（刚过马六甲）去世的消息，并且通报了新东印度公司的贸易情况。最后，他说："我收到一封去年6月15日发自巴达维亚（Batavia）②的信。当时董事会主席Catchpoole先生和其他驻舟山的工作人员都在巴达维亚，现在他们都在返回舟山的途中，Pound医生也在其中。Pound医生一切都很好，还送给我一个纪念品。我希望不论是我本人还是我儿子能有机会为您提供更加有价值的信息。"③

15. 第八卷　编号3473④

发信人：Dr. (later Sir) Hans Sloane

收信人：Locke

日期：26 February 1704

档案：B.L., MS. Locke c.18, ff.128-9.

主要内容：

斯隆在信中提到："最近我们的注意力被从中国回来的耶稣会士洪若翰先

---

① 原文：Th'Inclosed came verry lately to my hand By the ship Scipio: from Suratt, where my son John was I thank God in good health this tyme 12 month: and hath much Improov'd in experience of the affairs in India, as also those of China, Mallacka and South Seas. to the generall satisfaction of the Court of Directors: who are now placeing him in a higher station。见John Locke, E.S. De Beer (ed.), *The Correspondence of John Locke*, V7, Oxford: Clarendon Press, 1982, p. 783。

② 印度尼西亚首都雅加达（Jakarta）的旧称。

③ 原文：Sir I have a letter from Batavia of the 15th June last where our President Mr Catchpoole was. and the Rest of the Chusan and among them Doctor Pound, who was verry well and sent mee a kind remembrance. I wish Sir that either my selfe or son Could Render you advyse of more Importance。见John Locke, E.S. De Beer (ed.), *The Correspondence of John Locke*, V7, Oxford: Clarendon Press, 1982, p. 784。

④ John Locke, E.S. De Beer (ed.), *The Correspondence of John Locke*, V8, Oxford: Clarendon Press, 1989, pp. 215-216.

生①和一个声称自己来自台湾岛的日本人②所吸引。下次见面的时候，我想您会很乐意听我为您讲述他们的见闻。"③

第三节　小结

按通信人划分，提到中国的洛克书信主题和内容如下表：

表 4-1　洛克书信中的中国

收/发信人	信件编号和日期	关于中国的主题	具体内容
Dr. Pieter Guenellon	第五卷　编号2028　6/16 March 1696	新书	威森用弗拉芒语写成的关于鞑靼的书已经印刷了，但要到夏天才会正式发行。Avril神父于1693年用法语写成的关于鞑靼的书对于理解威森的书很有帮助。

---

① 洪若翰（Jean de Fontaney, 1643—1710），法国耶稣会士。1685年法王路易十四派遣六名"国王数学家"前往中国，洪若翰是最终抵达中国的五人之一，并因向康熙帝奉献金鸡纳霜（奎宁）而治好康熙帝的疟疾而闻名。法国人樊国梁《燕京开教略》："康熙偶患疟疾，洪若翰、刘应进金鸡纳，皇上以未达药性，派四大臣亲验，先令患疟疾者服之，皆愈。四大臣自服少许，亦觉无害，遂请皇上进用，不日疟瘳。"
② 乔治·萨玛纳札（George Psalmanazar, 1679?—1763），骗子，出生于法国南部，本名不明。为了能在法国各地免费旅行，萨玛纳札一开始冒充要到罗马朝圣的爱尔兰僧侣，但是很快这个伪装就被识破，因为法国当地许多人对爱尔兰很熟悉。萨玛纳札于是决定采用一个更异国情调的伪装，他利用在耶稣会的神学校所得到有关远东的传教士报告，假扮成一位日本基督徒。在到罗马的计划失败后，萨玛纳札在1700至1702年开始在德意志各诸侯国间旅行，并在1702年出现在荷兰，担任临时雇佣兵及士兵。这时萨玛纳札的注意力已经从日本转移到更罕为人知的台湾岛。1702年末，萨玛纳札遇到苏格兰圣公会随营司铎William Innes，并在1703年从鹿特丹抵达伦敦。在抵达伦敦后，"有着奇异行为的外国人"的新闻在英国受到关注。之后25年，虽然不时有人提出质疑，但是萨玛纳札面对质疑却都能将不利的批评——反驳。之后坦白事实，于是被逐出学术界，而后革心返回基督教会，1763年在伦敦死去。
③ 原文：Wee have been here very much diverted by Mr. Fontaney a Jesuit from China and one who says he comes from Formosa and is a Japonese. I could make you very merry with what I have heard from them which I will leave till our next meeting in the mean time I am。见John Locke, E.S. De Beer (ed.), *The Correspondence of John Locke*, V8, Oxford: Clarendon Press, 1989, p. 216.

第四章　"中国笔记"的基础：洛克书信与中国　187

（续表）

收/发信人	信件编号和日期	关于中国的主题	具体内容
Dr. (later Sir) Hans Sloane	第六卷　编号2219 15 March 1697	"日本人"和贸易	洛克听说有一个"日本人"从奥茨到伦敦去了，托斯隆问他日本是否禁止进口金银。
Ibid	第六卷　编号2224 18 March 1697	"中国人"	斯隆说洛克提到的"日本人"其实是来自厦门的中国人。
Ibid	第八卷 编号3473 26 February 1704	从中国回来的传教士和自称来自台湾岛的日本人	法国耶稣会士洪若翰和欧洲骗子George Psalmanazar。
Nicolas Toinard	第六卷　编号2483 15 August 1698	翻译中国游记	洛克建议将闵明我的中国游记从西班牙文译为法文。
Samuel Locke	第六卷　编号2598 20 June 1699	贸易	派往中国的货船及货值
Ibid.	第六卷　编号2637 30 November 1699	同上	派往中国的医生，董事会前往宁波和南京，大批羊毛和其他产品运往中国北部。
Ibid.	第六卷　编号2642 2 December 1699	贸易和通信	中国将建厂，此后苏拉特和中国之间的通信会比较畅通。
Ibid.	第七卷　编号2784 27 September 1700	贸易	派往中国的货船
Ibid.	第七卷　编号3281 5 May 1703	贸易	约翰的近况以及与中国贸易的情况
John Lock (later Sir John)	第七卷　编号3046 23 November 1701	中国现状	约翰从厦门发信，表示无法回答洛克关于中国政策、宗教、政府和物产的问题，只能提供日常贸易中所接触到的事实。
Ibid.	第七卷 编号3136 28 April 1702	果阿的耶稣会学校	约翰从苏拉特回信，暂时无法回答洛克关于果阿的耶稣会学校的创立者和创立时间的问题。
J.-B. Du Bos	第六卷 编号2600 27 June/7 July ［1699］	新书	Du Bos告诉洛克《华人礼仪史》是"礼仪之争"的文献，在阿姆斯特丹出版。

（续表）

收/发信人	信件编号和日期	关于中国的主题	具体内容
Ibid.	第七卷 编号2748 17/28 July［1700］	"礼仪之争"	Du Bos向洛克介绍了正在罗马进行的"礼仪之争"的热烈程度，并且提到巴黎索邦大学对李明的审查。
Edward Clarke	第七卷 编号3152 20 June 1702	无	"中国笔记"第207页所用的信纸

如上表所示，洛克在与六位亲友[①]的通信中提到中国，他们分别是Dr. Pieter Guenellon（1封）、Dr. (later Sir) Hans Sloane（3封）、Nicolas Toinard（1封）、Samuel Locke（5封）、John Lock (later Sir John)（2封）、J.-B. Du Bos（2封）。其中Dr. Pieter Guenellon、Nicolas Toinard和J.-B. Du Bos主要是从巴黎或阿姆斯特丹向洛克通报最新出版的关于中国的书籍；Dr. (later Sir) Hans Sloane本人就是游历甚广的收藏家，因此洛克常常与他互相通报在伦敦出现中国人、"日本人"或来华传教士；John Lock (later Sir John)是东印度公司派驻印度和中国工作的职员，洛克显然对他抱有很大的希望，渴望从他那里了解关于中国政治和宗教等方面的最新、最真实的情况，但由于约翰只能在中国港口活动，接触的人范围非常有限，并且工作繁忙，因此常常不能圆满地回答洛克的询问；Samuel Locke是新东印度公司的董事，也是约翰的父亲，他常常向洛克转交约翰从中国和印度发回的信，另外向持有新东印度公司股票的洛克通报与中国贸易的最新情况。

由此可见，洛克大约从1696年开始密切关注中国，他积极向友人询问在欧洲出版的关于中国的最新书籍、在英国出现的东方人或返欧传教士、与中国的贸易情况，并且渴望获得有关中国政治和宗教的第一手资料。洛克非常重视这些有限的信息，并根据这些信息采取了相应的行动：他购买了威森的中国地图（见彩图12）并将之挂在书房的墙上；他建议丘吉尔兄弟将闵明我的巨著《中华帝国历史、政治、伦理及宗教概述》的英译本收入《游记与旅行丛书》（见附录1）；他购买了大量关于"礼仪之争"的书籍，其中包括李明的著作和《华人礼

[①] 与Edward Clarke的信中事实上并未提到中国，因此不算。

仪史》，后者成为"中国笔记"的直接知识来源。洛克书信为洛克"中国观"的形成提供了大量的线索，也是洛克"中国观"的重要组成部分，因此，我将洛克书信中的中国作为"中国笔记"的认识基础。

第五章 "中国笔记"的核心：洛克著作与中国

第一节 洛克早期未刊作品与中国

洛克早年在牛津时（1652—1667）曾写过两本关于自然法的论著，其一为《两篇政府短论》（*Two Tracts on Government*）（下文简称《短论》）①，其二为《自然法论文集》（*Essays on the Law of Nature*）（下文简称《论文集》）②。两本著作在洛克生前均未出版③，直至20世纪才被重新整理出版。在当时宗教战争和世俗战争的大背景下，洛克在这两部著作中主要关注的是国家应该赋予公民

---

① John Locke, *Two Tracts on Government*, ed. Philip Abrams, Cambridge: Cambridge University Press, 1967. 为区别于1689年出版的《政府论》（*Two Treatises of Government*），本书将洛克的这部早期作品译为《两篇政府短论》。

② John Locke, *Essays on the Law of Nature*, ed. W. von Leyden, Oxford: Clarendon Press, 1954.

③ Maurice Cranston在其所写的《洛克传》中提到《自然法论文集》写完后大约30年，詹姆斯·泰瑞尔敦促洛克将之整理出版，洛克依言做好了出版准备，但最终放弃出版。Maurice Cranston认为洛克这一决定丝毫不让人惊讶，因为当时洛克已经在《人类理解论》中更好地论述了经验论，并且《人类理解论》中的部分内容与《自然法论文集》相矛盾。详见Maurice Cranston, *John Locke: A Biography*, Oxford University Press, 1985, p. 66。

的宗教宽容的尺度。事实上，宗教宽容和人该如何生活一直是洛克政治哲学的两大中心论题。

《短论》由上下两篇组成，上篇用英文写成，约成篇于1660年秋，当时洛克即将获得牛津大学希腊语讲师教席；下篇用拉丁文写成，约写于1662年。洛克写作《短论》的时候刚刚步入而立之年，刚刚开始自己在基督学院的学术生涯。当时正值斯图亚特王朝复辟期间，清教徒希望继续享受克伦威尔统治时期所享有的宗教宽容。1660年，当时31岁、以叛逆著称的基督学院学生小白戈肖（Edward Bagshaw, junior）出版了一本小册子，名为《关于宗教崇拜中无关紧要事情的大问题》（*The Great Question Concerning Things Indifferent in Religious Worship*）①，洛克的《短论》就是对这本小册子的回应，要回答的核心问题是：行政长官是否有权干涉宗教活动中"无关紧要"（indifferent）的事。所谓"无关紧要的事"，是指在道德上无所谓好坏的事，而道德的善恶是自然法的范畴，因此"无关紧要的事"指的是自然法中没有规定的事。②

《论文集》写于1663年，由《短论》中讨论的问题生发而来，并与第二篇拉丁文的《短论》同在一本笔记中。《论文集》主要基于1660年初，洛克与朋友加布里埃尔·陶尔森（Gabriel Towerson）关于自然法的讨论。③ 1664年，洛克在担任牛津大学道德哲学学监期间还开过自然法课程。当时洛克的自然法观点基本是霍布斯主义的，（虽然洛克本人不愿意承认自己受到霍布斯的影响），之后的二十年，洛克没有再写过自然法论著，直到1689年的《政府论》（*Two Treatises of Government*），而这时洛克的政治思想已经发生了极大的转变。

在讨论《短论》和《论文集》中对中国的关注之前，我们有必要对其主题——"自然法"（the Law of Nature）以及洛克基本的"自然法"观点做简要

---

① 这本小册子发表时未署名，但包括洛克在内的大部分人都清楚其作者就是小白戈肖。洛克收藏的这本小册子见B. L. MSS. Locke, e. 5。
② 《两篇政府短论》详见John Locke, Philip Abrams (ed.), *Two Tracts on Government*, Cambridge: Cambridge University Press, 1967。或John Locke, Mark Goldie (ed.), *Political Essays*, Cambridge: Cambridge University Press, 1997。
③ 1660年11月5日，陶尔森写信给洛克提到两人之间关于自然法的讨论已经是长篇累牍，并建议洛克考虑两个关键问题，详见B. L. MSS. Locke, c.22, f.3。洛克对此的回应详见B. L. MSS. Locke, e.6; F.30; F.31。

的介绍。正如莫里斯·克兰斯顿在《洛克传》[1]中所说的那样：

> 20世纪我们很少使用"自然法"这个词，它极易与经验主义科学家所寻求的"自然法则"相混淆，同时这个词本身也是一个让人迷惑的概念。"自然法"是指"造物主明示给所有理性存在、并令其必须遵守的道德法"。这一观念最迟产生于斯多葛学派时期，从理论上说对罗马法意义重大，即便实践中不是那么回事。……文艺复兴以后，"自然法"又成了新兴的国家理论的宠儿，然而最根本的问题没有变："自然法"是否存在？所有理性存在都明白地了解"自然法"吗？"自然法"是强制遵守的吗？[2]

这些正是洛克试图回答的问题。洛克在《短论》中论证了"自然法"的存在，他说"既然上帝存在并定下宇宙运行的法则，那么上帝也必然定下关于人类行为的法则，这种法则就构成了'自然法'。"[3] 紧接着，洛克便开始讨论人类对"自然法"的理解是先验的（innate）、来源于传统的（traditional）还是来源于经验的（sensory）。洛克认为人类对"自然法"的理解不仅来源于经验（sensory or empirical），而且与数学一样是显而易见的（demonstrable）。最后洛克得出结论："自然法"是必须遵守的。

莫里斯·克兰斯顿认为："洛克正面回答了关于自然法的问题，但回答得并不好。"[4]他认为"洛克更多地是在论证知识来源于经验，而不是论证自然法的

---

[1] Maurice Cranston, *John Locke: A Biography*, Oxford University Press, 1985.

[2] 原文：The "Law of Nature" is an expression seldom used in the twentieth century. It is too easily conf-used with the laws of nature which empirical scientists seek, and in itself it is a bewildering concept. The Law of Nature is "the moral law which the Creator has made evident to and compelling upon every rational being". It is a notion at least as old as Stoic philosophy. It had an important place in the theory, if not in the practice of Roman jurisprudence. ... After the Renaissance the concept again figured prominently in the new theories of the state. But the crucial questions remained: Does the Law of Nature exists? Is it evident to every rational being? Is it compelling? 见Maurice Cranston, *John Locke: a biography*, Oxford University Press, 1985, pp. 64-65。

[3] 原文：If God exists and has made laws governing the working of the universe, God must also have made rules relating to men's conduct. Such rules constituted the Law of Nature。见Maurice Cranston, *John Locke: A Biography*, Oxford University Press, 1985, p. 65。

[4] Maurice Cranston, *John Locke: A Biography*, Oxford University Press, 1985, p. 65.

存在"①。他还援引《自然法论文集》的编者W. 冯·莱登的说法——"洛克对经验主义的兴趣实在远超于对自然法的兴趣"——来解释洛克相对混乱的自然法论点。

不论洛克的自然法论述是否成功,从《短论》和《论文集》中我们能够清楚地看到牛津时期的洛克就已经开始关注并积极引用游记文学了。正如安·泰尔博特所说,

> 显然洛克在牛津期间就开始阅读游记文学了,但游记文学让洛克印象深刻的并不是人类的基本理性,而是人类行为的多样性,人类信仰的任意性,以及人类为捍卫自己的信仰所付出的极大努力。游记文学使洛克相信习俗的力量能够强大到超越理性、甚至自我保护的本能。②

洛克在约成文于1662年底的拉丁文的《短论》(下篇)中提到了著名的"中国围城事件"。洛克援引中国人宁可死也不剪辫子这一极端事件来证明习俗和传统的力量有时能够超越人的理性。

> 最近我们获得来自中国东部一座城市的报道。这座城市被围多日,居民已经同意投降。城门向敌军打开,所有居民为征服者之命是从。他们将自己连同妻子、族人、自由、财产,简言之神圣的和世俗的一切,全都交到敌人手中。但当敌人命令他们剪掉头上的辫子的时候,他们再次拿起武器开始激烈反抗,直至全军覆没。这些中国人能够接受整个民族成为敌人的奴隶,却无法接受敌人对他们头发的一点儿干涉。头发本是最无足轻重的东西,身体的自然生长物而已,然而中国人的民族习俗将之神圣化了,于是人们为了捍

---

① Maurice Cranston, *John Locke: A Biography*, Oxford University Press, 1985, p. 65.

② 原文: It is clear that Locke was already reading travel literature while he was at Oxford, but his reading had not impressed him with the fundamental rationality of humanity. What struck him was the diversity of human behaviour, the arbitrary character of what they believed and the lengths to which they were prepared to go to defend those beliefs. His reading convinced him that social convention was so powerful it could over-ride reason and even the instinct for self-preservation。见Ann Talbot, *"The Great Ocean of Knowledge": The Influence of Travel Literature on the Work of John Locke*, Leiden: Brill, 2010, p. 105。

卫头发竟然宁愿放弃生命本身和自然的实利。①

洛克关于"中国围城事件"的信息来源很可能是卫匡国的《鞑靼战纪》（*De Bello Tartarico Historia*）。《鞑靼战纪》原文用拉丁文写成，在欧洲影响极大。1655年译为英文，附在曾德昭（Alvarez Semmedo）《大中国志》（*History of that Great and Renowned Monarchy of China*）之后在伦敦出版。我在洛克藏书目录中找到三本卫匡国的书，分别为：

（1）1925. Sinicæ historiæ decas prima … 4°, Monachii, 1658.
436. Lo: $\underline{58}$. p. $\overline{362}\dfrac{8}{9}$ L.

（2）1926. Sinicæ historiæ decas prima … 8°, Amstelædami, 1659.
436. Lo: 8°Am: $\underline{59}$. p. $\overline{413}\dfrac{7}{306}$ L.

（3）1927. Martinius, M. Regni Sinensis a Tartaris devastate Enarratio 12°Am: [16] 61.
P $\overline{120}\dfrac{6}{29}$.②

第一本为1658年首版于慕尼黑的《中国上古史》③，第二本为次年在阿姆斯特丹再版的《中国上古史》，第三本就是1661年在阿姆斯特丹再版的拉丁文

---

① 原文：We have recently heard reports of a city, situated in the East, among the Chinese, which after a prolonged siege was driven at last to surrender. The gates were thrown open to the enemy forces and all the inhabitants gave themselves up to the will of the triumphant victor.They had abandoned to their enemy's hands their own persons, their wives, families, liberty, wealth, and in short all things sacred and profane, but when they were ordered to cut off the plait of hair which, by national custom, they wore on their heads, they took up their arms again and fought fiercely until, to a man, all were killed. "These men, although they were ready to allow their whole civil existence to be reduced to slavery by their enemies, were so unable to allow them even the lest interference with their hair, worn according to an ancestral custom, that the slightest of things and one of no significance, a mere excretion of the body, but all but sacrosanct by general esteem and the custom of their race, was easily preferred to life itself and the solid benefits of nature。见John Locke, Philip Abrams (ed.), *Two Tracts on Government*, Cambridge: Cambridge University Press, 1967, p. 217。又见John Locke, Mark Goldie (ed.), *Locke: Political Essays*, Cambridge University Press, 1997, pp. 59–60。
② 见John Harrison & Peter Laslett, *The Library of John Locke*, Oxford University Press, 1965, p. 185。
③ 该书的全名为《中国历史初编十卷：从人类诞生到基督降世的远方亚洲或中华大帝国周邻记事》，记述了上自远古、下至公元前1年（即汉哀帝元寿二年）的中国历史。

本《鞑靼战纪》①。《鞑靼战纪》中记载鞑靼人在浙江顺利占领杭州和绍兴后，"他们本可以照样解决浙江省南部的城市，然而，当鞑靼人公告百姓剃发时，士兵和市民都拿起武器，为保护头发拼死战斗，胜过保御皇帝和国土，不仅把鞑靼人赶出城，还把他们赶到钱塘江边，甚至赶过江，杀死很多人。如果他们真追过江去，也许能够收复省城及其他城市，但他们没有乘胜追击，只满足于保住自己的头发，留在南岸对抗鞑靼人，在那里坚守。这样，鞑靼征服之旅被阻达一年之久"②。卫匡国并未说明"浙江省南部的城市"具体指哪一（几）座城市。根据中国的历史记载，卫匡国指的应该是1645年6月清廷下令江南人民剃发易服，因而引起的江南多地人民的反抗，其中江阴和嘉定两地最为激烈，后遭到清军的残酷镇压，史称"江阴八十一日""嘉定三屠"。洛克收藏的《鞑靼战纪》为1661年阿姆斯特丹再版的拉丁文本，而洛克的《短论》写于1662年底，书中说："最近我们获得来自中国东部一座城市的报道。"可见洛克关于"中国围城事件"的记述应该来自于卫匡国的《鞑靼战纪》。

《论文集》中也从游记文学中引用了很多不同风俗的例子，比如《第五篇：自然法能从人类的普遍同意中被认识吗？不能》（V. Can the Law of Nature be Known from the General Consent of Men? No）开篇就否定了"人民的呼声就是上帝的声音"（The voice of the people is the voice of God）这一格言。文中

---

① 《鞑靼战纪》的版本：1654年安特卫普初版，拉丁文原名为 *De Bello Tartarico Historia*；同年该拉丁文版在安特卫普的另两家出版社、科隆和维也纳四次再版；同年还被译成其他5种语言出版，分别为：（1）英文版（伦敦）：*Bellum Tartaricum, or the conquest of the great and most renowned Empire of China*, London, 1654；（2）法文版（巴黎）：*Histoire de la guerre des Tatares contre la Chine*, Paris, 1654；（3）荷兰文版（阿姆斯特丹）：*Historie van den Tartarschen oorloch*, Tot Delft, 1654；（4）意大利文版（米兰）：*Breve historia delle guerre seguite in questi ultimi anni tra Tartari e Cinesi*, Milano, 1654；（5）德文版（阿姆斯特丹）：*Histori von dem Tartarischen Kriege*, Amsterdam：Blaeu, 1654。此后，从1654—1706年间，此书转译成欧洲9种语言，先后再版25次，部分版本有一些插图版画，有的达10幅。其中，1661年阿姆斯特丹再版的《鞑靼战纪》，书名改为 *Regni Sinensis à Tartaris Tyrannicè evastati depopulatique concinna Enarratio*（《关于被鞑靼皇帝侵略并占领的中华帝国的传奇故事》），书首还有一幅"持刀背弓，身骑战马的鞑靼武士，另一只手提着一个中国人头战斗场景"。参见http://blog.sina.com.cn/s/blog_669e82e70101fk3y.html，访问时间：2015年3月10日。

② ［西］帕莱福、［比］鲁日满、［意］卫匡国著，何高济译，《鞑靼征服中国史·鞑靼中国史·鞑靼战纪》，北京：中华书局，2008年，第372页。

洛克引用了古埃及人、斯巴达人、罗马人、亚述人（Assyrians）、拉曼铁司人（Garamantes）、德布里斯人（Derbices）、印度人的各种与欧洲迥异的风俗来证明："人类没有关于道德上的正当的普遍同意。……当我们审视各种美德和罪恶时——并无人质疑它们即真正的自然法——就可轻而易举地发现，其中无一不是人类在公共权威和习俗的支持下形成的不同观点。"① 在引用了埃利亚努斯（Aelianus）②记述的撒丁岛子女棒杀年迈父母的习俗和德布里斯人（Derbices）杀死年逾七十的老人的习俗之后，洛克又举例说："还有些地方的人毫不犹豫地抛弃女婴，好像她们是私生儿和一种命运的捉弄，他们还从邻人处买得那些配偶以为繁衍后代之用。"③ 与上文引用的棒杀父母习俗不同的是，对于弃婴和买妻习俗，洛克既没有说明信息来源，也没有说明"有些地方的人"指的是哪国人。这很可能是由于当时的欧洲人比较轻易地就可以将这种习俗与"有些地方的人"对上号，联系17世纪游记文学中对中国风俗的描述，此处"有些地方的人"很可能是指中国人。例如，我在洛克的藏书目录中找到了金尼阁编译的《利玛窦中国札记》（Trigault, Nicolas, *De Christiana expeditione apud Sinas ex P. M. Riccius*, Augsburg, 1615），该书第一卷第九章题为"关于某些迷信的以及其他方面的礼节"，在该章的结尾处利玛窦补充了几种中国人"惊人的""愚昧无知"的做法，其中就包括"买妻"和"杀婴"的习俗，书中说："他们当中有很多人无法过没有女人在一起的生活，就把自己卖给有钱的主人家，以期在这家的女婢中找到一个妻子，而这样一来就把他们的子女永世变成奴隶。还有一些人则攒够了钱买一个妻子，等到孩子过多无法抚养时，就以大约一头猪或一匹便宜小驴的价格

---

① ［英］洛克著，李季璇译，《自然法论文集》，北京：商务印书馆，2014年，第39—40页。
② 埃利亚努斯（Claudius Aelianus, 170—235），生于普莱奈斯特（Praeneste），罗马作家和修辞学家。著有17卷《论动物的特性》（*De Natura Animalium*）、14卷《杂闻轶事》（*Various History*）和20篇《乡村书信集》（*Letters from a Farmer*）。其中《杂闻轶事》汇集了各种奇闻异事、简短的传记、精炼的格言、自然奇观、奇异的地方风俗等，着重讲述关于英雄、领袖、运动员和智者的道德故事，饮食报道，不同的服装和恋爱风格，各地不同的送礼、娱乐、宗教信仰和丧葬习俗等。其中介绍过飞蝇钓、漆器制作、蛇崇拜等奇闻异事。该书首版于1545年，后有两个英译本，分别为1576年Fleming的译本和1665年Stanley的译本。洛克关于撒丁岛和德布里斯人杀亲习俗的信息来源应该就是埃利亚努斯的《杂闻轶事》，虽然我在《洛克藏书》（John Harrison & Peter Laslett, *The Library of John Locke*, Oxford University Press, 1965）目录中未找到该书。
③ ［英］洛克著，李季璇译，《自然法论文集》，北京：商务印书馆，2014年，第42页。

把孩子卖做奴隶——价钱大约相当于一个克朗（crown）或一个半克朗。"①还说："中国有一种更为严重得多的罪恶是某些省份溺毙女婴的做法。这样做的原因据说是她们的父母无力养活她们。……由于他们相信灵魂转生或者轮回，这种野蛮行径就可能变得不那样恶劣了。……因此，这种屠杀无辜的事情不是偷偷干的，而是公开让大家都知道的情况下做的。"②

综上所述，早在1660—1663年间，洛克就在《短论》和《论文集》中关注和引用了游记中关于中国历史和风俗的记载。洛克对游记文学的钟爱在其学术生涯的开端就显露无疑，并且终生未变。然而牛津时期的洛克与大部分年轻人一样，更加关注游记文学中对各地奇异风俗的描述，在自己的作品中对游记文学的引用比较随意而零散。可以说年轻的洛克还不能理性、系统地使用游记文学的材料，对于各国的文化还没有准确、完整的认识，还没有形成自己的"中国观"。这与近40年后《人类理解论》（第四版）时洛克的精准老练形成了鲜明的对比。

第二节　《人类理解论》与中国

《人类理解论》是洛克在世时以真名公开发表的两部著作之一，也是洛克最重要的作品。相对于早期论文中对中国猎奇式的随意引用，《人类理解论》对中国信仰的论断集中而明确，是洛克中国观的核心，也是洛克"中国笔记"的总纲。

洛克在《人类理解论》（第四版）第一卷第四章第八节"上帝的观念不是天赋的"中写道：

> 此外，我们还见到有许多国家虽然已经文明大有进步，可是他们因为在这方面不曾适当地运用其思想的缘故，竟然没有上帝底观念和知识。安南人就是属于这一类的，我想人们亦正可以同我一样，不必惊异这一层。不过关于这一层，我们可参阅法王在安南近来所派代表给我们的记述。据

---

① ［意］利玛窦、［比］金尼阁著，何高济等译：《利玛窦中国札记》，北京：中华书局，1983年，第91页。
② 同上书，第92页。

这位代表底记述看来，中国亦正是一样情形。我们纵然不相信乐老波①（La Loubere）底话，可是驻华的传教士们，甚至于耶稣教派的人们，一面虽然十分赞美中国，一面亦异口同声地告我们说：中国底统治阶级——士大夫们——都固守中国的旧教，都是纯粹的无神论者。关于这种情形，我们可参阅纳屋雷德②（Navarette）"游记集"1卷同"中国仪礼史"③（Historia Cultus Sinensium）。④

从前人们普遍认为洛克在《人类理解论》中只是将中国作为无神论的例子以驳斥"上帝观念是天赋的"，换言之，中国在《人类理解论》中所起的作用与在洛克早期论文中的作用没有什么差别。然而，"中国笔记"手稿的发现使我们意识到，中国在《人类理解论》（第四版）中的出现绝不仅仅是信手拈来的例子这么简单，它不仅是洛克对斯蒂林弗利特攻击的回应，更是当时已经初步形成的洛克"中国观"的集中表达，后来的"中国笔记"则是其"中国观"的具体呈现。为了更加清楚地说明这一点，我们可以从《人类理解论》的版本、洛克—斯氏论争、《人类理解论》中关于中国论述的特点三个方面进行梳理。

一、《人类理解论》的版本

关于中国的论述并不是从一开始就出现在《人类理解论》当中的，那么，中

---

① 今译"拉·洛贝尔"。
② 中文名"闵明我"。
③ 今译《华人礼仪史》。
④ ［英］洛克：《人类理解论》（上册），关文运译，北京：商务印书馆，1959年，第50页。英文原文：But there are others to be found, who have enjoyed these in a very great measure, who yet, for want of a due application of their thoughts this way, want the idea, and knowledge of God. 'Twill I doubt not be a surprise to let them consult the King of France's late envoy thither, who gives no better account of the Chinese themselves. ‖ And if we will not believe La Loubere, the missionaries of China, even the Jesuits themselves, the great encomiasts of the Chinese, do all to a man agree and will convince us that the sect of the Litterati, or Learned, keeping to the old religion of China, and the ruling party there, are all of them atheist. Vid. Navarette in the Collection of Voyages, vol. the first, and Historia cultus Sinensium. John Locke, *An Essay of Human Understanding*, Book I Chapter IV §8. 需要指出的是，关文运先生将"Vid. Navarette in the Collection of Voyages, vol. the first"译为"纳屋雷德（Navarette）'游记集'1卷"是明显的误译，应改为"《游记与旅行丛书》（第一卷）收录的闵明我的著作"。

国是什么时候出现在该书里的呢？我们有必要先对《人类理解论》的版本进行简单的梳理。

1671年，初稿。在洛克手稿中，人们陆续发现了《人类理解论》出版前的多个版本①，其中最早的两个版本是：哈佛大学的Dr. Benjamin Rand在拉夫雷斯伯爵拥有的洛克手稿中发现《人类理解论》的原稿，并于1931年整理出版。② 而后是1935年1月R. I. Aaron和Jocelyn Gibb在拉夫雷斯档案的一本大摘录笔记（commonplace book）的开始部分发现的了一份更早的原稿，并于1936年整理出版。③ Aaron和Gibb所发现的手稿写作时间在前，称为"稿A"（Draft A）；Rand所发现的手稿写作时间在后，称为"稿B"（Draft B）。根据洛克在笔记中所做的注释判断，"稿A"写于1671年夏，很可能是六月末和七月；"稿B"写于同年秋或初冬。④ 尽管这两份初稿的写作时间只相差几个月，它们之间的差异相当明显。"稿A"比较粗糙，观点阐述不够完整，结构也比较仓促；"稿B"内容更加成熟、完整，大部分行文与《人类理解论》（第一版）完全一致。然而，"稿A"涉及《人类理解论》I—IV卷的全部内容，"稿B"则只涉及前三卷的内容。⑤

1689年底，第一版。1688年3月，当时在鹿特丹的洛克委托即将回伦敦的David Thomas代为询问《人类理解论》能否在伦敦全文出版。同年4月25日，David给洛克写信，汇报自己与出版商A. 丘吉尔的兄弟见面讨论，后者说对能印1000—1120册的好书，他们一般出价20—30镑。同年5月10日，David再次写信给洛克，说与丘吉尔本人进行了会面，后者说他们一般不为待出版的书籍付款，书籍在出版之前首先要由出版社和作者信任的人审阅，出版费用由出版社负担，作

---

① 详见John Locke, Peter Nidditch & G.A.J. Rogers (ed.), *Drafts for the 'Essay Concerning Human Understanding' and other Philosophical Writings*, Oxford: Clarendon Press, 1990。

② John Locke, Benjamin Rand (ed.), *An Essay concerning the Understanding, Knowledge, Opinion, and Assent*, Cambridge: Harvard University Press, 1931.

③ John Locke, R. I. Aaron and Jocelyn Gibb (ed.), *An Early Draft of Locke's Essay*, Oxford: Clarendon Press, 1936.

④ 详见John Locke, R. I. Aaron and Jocelyn Gibb (ed.), *An Early Draft of Locke's Essay*, Oxford: Clarendon Press, 1936, Introduction, p. xiii。

⑤ Ibid., pp. xi-xiii.

者将得到一半的净利润。① 1689年，洛克一回到伦敦就与丘吉尔会面，显然属意其出版《人类理解论》。然而最终丘吉尔并未出版《人类理解论》，而是将《政府论》和《论宽容》（*A Letter Concerning Toleration*）的英译本匿名出版，后两篇显然更加符合辉格党人A.丘吉尔的品味和需要。洛克为了保密，将与《政府论两篇》出版相关的所有通信和文件全部销毁了。最终《人类理解论》初版由当时出版界的新人Thomas Bassett出版，1689年5月24日在John Freke和Edward Clarke的见证下，洛克签署了出版协议。该协议详细规定了纸张质量、书籍大小、印刷速度等出版细节。根据协议，洛克应得稿酬29镑。② 1689年8月23日，丘吉尔获得《政府论》的出版许可，马上开始印刷，当年10月就开始出售了；《人类理解论》也于1689年12月上市，然而两者的出版时间却都定为1690年。按照当时的惯例，出版商尽量将出版时间推后，以便书籍可以在更长的时间里被称为"新书"。③

1694年5月，第二版。为回应马勒伯朗士的英国追随者约翰·诺里斯（John Norris）④的批评，1692年洛克写了《洛克答诺里斯先生的非议》的论文片段，1693年初又写了《评诺里斯先生的某些著作》和《对马勒伯朗士关于在上帝之中看到一切的意见的考察》，《人类理解论》第二版的很多新材料就来源于这些片段和论文。同时，第二版第2卷第9章第8节增加了对好友莫利纽克斯（Molyneux）所提问题的回答，这个问题是天生盲人在复明后单凭视觉能否辨别例如球体和立方体这些不同的形状。第二版最重要的改动是在第2卷增加了新的讨论人格同一性的第27章"同一性和差别性"，在第21章"能力"中则以大部分是新的长得多的关于意志和自由的讨论作为全章的中心内容。

1695年底，第三版，基本未改动。这段时间，洛克在辉格党的政治和改革活动中发挥了极大的影响力。1694年英格兰银行成立，洛克是最初的支持者和捐助者之一；洛克极力主张贸易自由和言论自由，他组织了一个名为"学院"的政治俱乐部对议会施加影响，最终于1695年废除"出版管理法"；针对当时非常严

---

① Maurice Cranston, *John Locke: a biography*, Oxford University Press, 1985, p. 298.
② 详见Maurice Cranston, *John Locke: a biography*, Oxford University Press, 1985, pp. 318-319。
③ 详见Maurice Cranston, *John Locke: a biography*, Oxford University Press, 1985, pp. 326-327。
④ 牛津圣灵学院研究员，贝梅顿修道院院长，《论理念或可知世界》的作者。

重的流通银币的磨损和盗削问题，洛克提出铸造成色十足的新币以取代旧币的建议，并于1695年发表了《再论降低利息和提高货币价值的后果》①，最终促成了按洛克的主张进行的货币改革。

1699年12月，第四版。1690年代，反对三位一体信条的英国索西尼主义者（Socinianism）②和正统派的争论达到高潮，洛克也被卷入了论战。先是加尔文教信徒约翰·爱德华兹（John Edwards）对洛克的《基督教合乎理性》一再攻击，洛克先后于1695年和1697年发表了《为受爱德华兹非难的基督教合乎理性等申辩》和《再申辩》两本小册子予以反驳，否认自己是索西尼主义者。接着伍斯特主教爱德华·斯蒂林弗利特（Edward Stillingfleet，下文简称"斯氏"）对《人类理解论》进行了激烈的攻击，认为洛克哲学不可避免的逻辑结论是消灭实体，而实体观念是基督教神学家用以解释最根本基督教信条——如圣餐（Eucharist）、化身（Incarnation）、三位一体（Trinity）——的基础，因此洛克哲学必然导致消灭三位一体的上帝从而动摇基督教的基础，并走向无神论。这样的指控对洛克来说是相当严重的，在当时只有国教徒才能担任政府职务，如果指控成立，洛克不仅公职不保，而且有被当作异教徒的危险。作为回应，洛克于

---

① 1668年起，洛克就开始写作关于货币改革的文章，并于1691年发表《论降低利息和提高货币价值的后果》，因此1695年的论文名为《再论》。
② 17世纪三四十年代兴起的"剑桥柏拉图派"强调宗教中的道德因素，不看重各教派对宗教礼仪和信条的争吵，提倡在国教的范围内实行宗教宽容；反对宗教狂热，弘扬理性，提出"理性神学"，认为真正的宗教应当和理性和谐；反对加尔文教的"预定论"，肯定人的意志自由；同时率先系统地批判无神论；哲学上反对天主教正统经院哲学和亚里士多德主义，倾向柏拉图学说和新柏拉图主义。他们被称为"自由主义派"（Latitudinarianism），由于主张的近似，又常常被人们（尤其是反对者）与"索西尼派"（Socinianism）和"唯一神教派"（Unitarianism）联系在一起。王朝复辟时代，很多国教的神学家都是"自由主义者"，其中就包括后来成为洛克论敌的斯氏。详见Maurice Cranston, *John Locke: A Biography*, Oxford University Press, 1985, pp. 124-128。

1697年和1698年写了三封信对自己的哲学基本观点和概念作了澄清和说明。① 洛克与斯氏论战的一些问题在1699年12月出版的《人类理解论》（第四版）中有所反映。第四版最明显的不同是增加了新的两章，即第2卷第33章"观念的联结"和第4卷第19章"狂热"。1697年开始动手但没有完成的《对理智的指引》本来也准备作为新增的一章，因篇幅过长改为独立的著作，洛克去世后两年在《遗著》中发表。

1706年，第五版。《人类理解论》（第四版）出版后，洛克再也没有发表著作，但他继续在笔记中记下对《人类理解论》的修改意见，直到生命的最后一刻。洛克去世后出版的第五版就是依据这些意见修改而成。②

综上，《人类理解论》的创作时间前后超过30年，自出版之日起就引起巨大反响，既享受赞誉也饱受攻击。洛克在回应朋友的询问和对手的论战的过程中，不断反思和修改《人类理解论》，在世时就先后出版了四版。仔细比较各个版本③，我们就会发现，《人类理解论》前三版中，洛克引用旅行家、传教士、水手和商人在南美和南非的亲身经历来证明全体不信上帝之社会的存在，并未提到

---

① 1696年，斯蒂林弗利特发表Discourse in Vindication of the Doctrine of the Trinity将洛克卷入公开论战的漩涡；作为回应，1697洛克发表第一封信A Letter to the Bishop of Worcester；同年，斯氏发表Answer to Mr Locke's [First] Letter；同年，洛克发表第二封信Mr Locke's Reply to the Bishop of Worcester；1698年，斯氏发表Answer to Mr Locke's Second Letter；1699年，洛克发表第三封信Mr Locke's Reply to the Bishop of Worcester's Answer to his Second Letter。尽管洛克在信中的口吻尽量保持对主教的尊敬，但很明显洛克对这场论争越来越不耐烦。如果不是1699年斯氏过早逝世，这场论争很可能还会持续下去。关于洛克与斯氏的论争详见Maurice Cranston, *John Locke: A Biography*, Oxford University Press, 1985, pp. 276-277, pp. 410-415和Edward Stillingfleet, G.A.J. Rogers (ed.), Origines Sacrae, *The Philosophy of Edward Stillingfleet, Including His Replies to John Locke*, Bristol: Thoemmes Press, 2000. 另外，Roger Woolhouse主编的《人类理解论》的附录将第五版脚注中洛克对斯氏的回应整理出版，也是很好的参考，参见John Locke, Roger Woolhouse (ed.), *An Essay Concerning Human Understanding*, Penguin Books, 1997 edition 2004 reprint, pp. 637-726.
② 除上述文献外，本书对《人类理解论》各版本的总结还参照了胡景钊、余丽嫦：《十七世纪英国哲学》，北京：商务印书馆，2006年，第290—293页。
③ 参见John Locke, *An Essay Concerning Human Understanding*, Peter H. Nidditch ed. Oxford: Clarendon Press, 1975. 本书是英国谢菲尔德大学哲学系主任尼迪奇（Peter H. Nidditch）历时十年编撰的《人类理解论》的校勘本，较为清晰地展示了《人类理解论》各版本的变化。2017年胡景钊先生的中文全译本出版，见［英］约翰·洛克著，胡景钊译：《论人类的认识》，上海：上海人民出版社，2017年。该书为中国学者了解洛克思想的发展提供了极大的便利。

中国。直到洛克去世前的最后一版——1699年12月的第四版——中国才第一次出现在《人类理解论》中。那么，洛克为什么在第四版中加入有关中国的内容呢？我认为最直接也是最重要的原因就是与斯氏的论争。

二、洛克——斯氏论争

在上文介绍《人类理解论》（第四版）的时候，我已经对洛克——斯氏论争进行了概述。当时，洛克与斯氏的论争人尽皆知，而斯氏在哲学史上的地位主要就来源于他与洛克的论争。尽管如此，无论是思想上还是政治上，两人的差异都不像想象的那么大。两人都是皇家学会的会员，都是波义耳的朋友，都与剑桥柏拉图主义者交往。① 洛克与斯氏的论争牵扯到17世纪的宗教改革、科学革命、新柏拉图主义传统等众多问题，比较复杂，本书只聚焦于该论争如何促使洛克在《人类理解论》中加入关于中国的内容。

如上文所述，洛克与斯氏的共同点不少，其中之一就是对游记文学的收藏。据约翰·哈里森和彼得·拉斯莱特统计，在洛克藏书的所有类别中，最受洛克钟爱的是游记地理类书籍（Geography and Exploration），共275种，其中游记类195种，地理类80种。② 虽然此类书籍只占总藏书量的7.6%，但考虑到当时该类书籍的总出版量，洛克几乎拥有了能够获得的所有该类书籍，并且在自己的著作中频繁引用，可见他对该类著作的偏爱。洛克所收藏的游记地理类书籍的数量在当时无人能及，斯氏是少数接近这一数字的收藏家之一。根据都柏林的《玛舍图书馆图书总目》（Catalogue of the Marsh Library, Dublin），斯氏拥有231部该类型的书籍，其中92部与洛克的藏书同名。正是由于斯氏本人收藏了大量的游记文学并且对洛克引用的游记文学内容非常熟悉，才使得斯氏有能力在洛克最为擅长的游

---

① 详见Ann Talbot, *"The Great Ocean of Knowledge", the Influence of Travel Literature on the Work of John Locke*, Leiden: Brill, 2010, Chapter Nine 'After the Essay: Travel Literature in the Stillingfleet Controversy', 尤其是第162—163页。

② John Harrison and Peter Laslett, *The Library of John Locke*, Oxford: Clarendon Press, 1965, p. 18.

记文学领域对洛克发起攻击。① 1702年,《宗教的起源》②出新版,书中汇集了斯氏生前对洛克指控,其中至少有39处引用游记文学,并讨论了多位洛克曾引用过的游记作家,对洛克所引用游记文学的来源和内容提出全面质疑。这里我们着重看看斯氏对《人类理解论》中"无神论社会"的攻击和洛克的回应,以便清晰地了解洛克为什么在第四版的第一卷第四章第八节的位置添加关于中国的内容。

斯氏受教于剑桥大学圣约翰学院,深受剑桥柏拉图主义的影响,对天赋观念论深信不疑,是英国国教的坚定捍卫者。斯氏坚持"逆向进化"(REVERSE EVOLUTION)的人类历史观,假设所有人类原本都拥有关于上帝的完整认识,然而从创世纪开始,人类逐步退化堕落,最终不同程度地遗忘了对上帝的认识。因此,社会越文明,就越能彰显对上帝的信仰;而没有宗教信仰的社会必然是最为堕落的社会。针对洛克在《人类理解论》第一卷第四章第八节中所引用的无神论社会,斯氏首先质疑洛克信息来源的可靠性,认为洛克"非常不恰当"地选择了材料,原因是洛克所引用的作者与他们所描述的人并不熟悉,而那些更加了解这些人的专家反对他们的论述。这等于是说洛克所引用的关于无神论社会的描述都是无稽之谈。针对斯氏的指控,洛克先就自己所引用材料的可靠性做了非常详细的说明。

> 既然您质疑我所引用作者的可信度,用您的话说,我"选得相当糟糕",那么我不得不说,关于萨尔达尼亚的何腾托人(the Hottentots of Soldania)③的记述来自于英格兰国王派往莫卧儿王朝(Great Mogul)的使

---

① 当然,也有可能斯氏是为了更好地攻击洛克而着意收集游记文学作品,例如,洛克在《人类理解论》中引用了耶稣会士Sagard在美洲的经历,而Jesuit Relations在当时的英国非常罕见,洛克是少数几个看过这本书的英国人之一。为了驳斥洛克,斯氏大费周章地找到这本书并引用Sagard关于加拿大的Huron人信仰唯一的造物主——上帝的结论来攻击洛克。
② 《宗教的起源》又名《对基督教信仰立场的理性描述:关于真理、〈圣经〉的神圣权威及其所包含的要点》(A Rational Account of the Grounds of Christian Faith, as to the Truth and Divine Authority of the Scriptures, and Matters Therein Contained),1666年首版。
③ 萨尔达尼亚湾是南非西南海岸的小海湾,为大西洋岸的内陆深水港,距开普敦105千米,以16世纪初葡萄牙航海家萨尔达尼亚(Antonio de Saldanha)的名字命名。1652年4月6日,荷兰船长赞·范里贝克(Jan van Riebeeck)率三艘船只抵达开普敦附近地区,受命建立一个专为远航亚洲的途经船只提供补给的中途站。当时的荷兰人称当地的游牧民族为何腾托人(Hottentots),称居于沿海地域以采贝为生的民族为史特兰洛帕人(Strandlopers),称以狩猎为生的人为布西曼人(Bushmen)。

臣①。东方游记的权威、享有盛誉的特维诺②先生专门将之译为法文并发表在自己的《行纪》中（阁下认为这是不明智的）。为了让您满意并略微认可托马斯·罗伊爵士的叙述，一个名叫库尔（Coore）的懂英文的当地人曾清楚地告诉特里（Terry）③先生：萨尔达尼亚人不信上帝。但如果这个当地人也不入您的眼，那么我希望您能够相信还健在的英国国教的圣徒的话，他也认同托马斯·罗伊爵士的叙述。这位让人尊敬的先生④在两年前刚刚发表的《苏拉特游记》中也提到萨尔达尼亚人，他说："他们堕落到偶像崇拜以下，既没有牧师也没有寺庙，除了月初和月中的一点庆祝活动外，他们没有任何宗教仪式。自然在现世为他们提供了丰富的便利，以至于他们全然不知

---

① 托马斯·罗伊爵士（Sir Thomas Roe），英王詹姆士一世派往印度莫卧儿皇帝扎亨吉朝廷上的大使，著有《托马斯·罗伊爵士使印度记（1615—1619）》（参见Thomas Roe, W. Forsten (ed.), *The Embassy Of Sir Thomas Roe to India 1615-19: As Narrated in His Journal and Correspondence*, New Delhi: Munshiram Manoharlal Publishers Pvt Ltd, 1990）。洛克在《人类理解论》第一卷第四章第八节中引用了他的报告中关于南非萨尔达尼亚湾的何腾托人的记述。
② 让·特维诺（Jean de Thevenot, 1633—1667），法国著名的东方旅行家，1665年出版《勒望特之旅》（*Relation d'un voyage fait au Levant*）记录他在埃及的行程，这本书后来成了他的游记集《行纪》（*Relations de diverses voyages curieux*, 1666—1672）的第一部分。《行纪》也收录了托马斯·罗伊印度行纪的法译本。特维诺《行纪》的英译本参见Jean de Thevenot, Archibald Lovell (trans.), *The travels of Monsieur de Thevenot into the Levant in three parts, viz. into I. Turkey, II. Persia, III. the East-Indies*, London: H. Clark, 1687。
③ 爱德华·特里（Edward Terry, 1590–1660），托马斯·罗伊爵士出使莫卧儿王朝时的随行牧师，著有《东印度行纪》（*A Voyages to East Indies*）（1655），参见Edward Terry, *A voyage to East-India wherein some things are taken notice of, in our passage thither, but many more in our abode there, within that rich and most spacious empire of the Great Mogul: mixt with some Parallel Observations and Inferences upon the Story, to profit as well as delight the Reader*. London: J. Martin, and J. Allestrye, at the Bell in St. Pauls Chutch-Yard, 1665。
④ 指约翰·奥文顿（John Ovington），著有《苏拉特游记》（*Voyage to Suratt*, 1696）。

上帝的存在，也不在意自己的来世。"①

接着，洛克反驳了斯氏对洛克所引用的无神论社会本身的质疑。

然而面对这些人是无神论者的清晰证据，阁下却说"关于这些人的记述说明他们根本不配称为人类的标准"。我认为这样的论点站不住脚，除非有一天人们发现一种"能作为人类标准的"人。我引用这些人的唯一目的就是证明世界上的确有人没有关于上帝的天赋观念。然而，为了继续争论（除此之外还有什么别的理由呢？），您简直是在说那些南非的卡非人（Caffres）根本不是人，不然您所说的这些话还能有什么意思呢？"根据对萨尔达尼亚的卡非人的记述，这个民族很奇怪，连常识都没有，很难被称为人类。"等等。②

---

① 原文：But because you question the credibility of those authors I have quoted, which you say *were very ill chosen*: I will crave leave to say, that he whom I relied on for his testimony concerning the Hottentots of Soldania, was no less a man, than an ambassador from the King of England to the Great Mogul. Of whose relation, Monsieur Thevenot, no ill judge in the case, had so great an esteem, that he was at the pains to translate it into French, and publish it in his (which is counted no unjudicious) collection of *Travels*. But to intercede with your Lordship, for a little more favourable allowance of credit to Sir Thomas Roe's relation; Coore, an inhabitant of the country who could speak English, assured Mr Terry, that they of Soldania had no God. But if he too have the ill luck to find no credit with you, I hope you will be a little more favourable to a divine of the Church of England now living, and admit of his testimony in confirmation of Sir Thomas Roe's. This worthy gentleman, in the relation of his his voyage to Surat, printed but two years since, speaking of the same people, has these words, 'they are sunk even below idolatry, are destitute of both priest and temple, and saving a little show of rejoicing, which is made at the full and new moon, have lost all kind of religious devotion. Nature has so richly provided for their convenience in this life, that they have drowned all sense of the God of it, and are grown quite careless of the next.' 见John Locke, Roger Woolhouse (ed.), *An Essay Concerning Human Understanding*, Penguin Books, 1997 edition 2004 reprint, pp. 647-648。

② 原文：But to provide against the clearest evidence of atheism in these people, you say 'that the account given of them, makes them not fit to be a standard for the sense of mankind'. This, I think, may pass for nothing, till somebody be found, 'that makes them to be a standard for the sense of mankind'. All the use I made of them was to show, that there were men in the world, that had no innate idea of a God. But to keep something like an argument going (for what will not that do?) you go near denying those caffres to be men, what else do these words signify? 'A people so strangely bereft of common sense, that they can hardly be reckoned among mankind, as appears by the best accounts of the caffres of Soldania,' *etc*. 见John Locke, Roger Woolhouse (ed.), *An Essay Concerning Human Understanding*, Penguin Books, 1997 edition 2004 reprint, p. 648。

从上述笔记来看，斯氏先是质疑洛克所引用的无神论社会的信息来源不可靠，接着又说，即便世界上有这样的无神论社会，这些连上帝都不知道的人根本就算不上是人。在今天看来，这简直是无理取闹了。面对斯氏种族主义的循环论证，洛克的驳斥显然是成功的。然而，洛克依然在《人类理解论》（第四版）中加入了中国作为无神论社会的例子，很显然这是对斯氏攻击的回应，换句话说，洛克很可能觉得面对中国这个例子，斯氏连无理取闹的余地也没有了。这是为什么呢？

首先，知识来源难以质疑。不论斯氏的攻击在今天看来多么不可理喻，在当时的历史文化语境中，我们必须承认斯氏不仅是主教，也是一位严肃的学者。如上文所述，斯氏的游记文学收藏量仅次于洛克，并且对游记文学中记述的异域文化非常熟悉。事实上，斯氏也常常在自己的作品中引用游记文学，甚至提到中国。在1697年版的《宗教的起源》中，斯氏就引用金尼阁编《利玛窦中国札记》（又名《基督教远征中国史》）（1615）说："中国人最初信仰上帝，并且儒家士大夫依然信仰这个上帝。"① 斯氏甚至引用1700年就被索邦神学院裁定为禁书的李明（Louis le Comte）的《中国近事报道》来论证中国人在未受基督教启示的情况下就曾经拥有关于真正上帝的认识。斯氏认为只有在一个民族中生活相当长时间并且会说该民族语言的人才有可能对宗教的存无作出准确的判断，很显然耶稣会士更加符合这一标准，因此与莱布尼茨一样，斯氏受耶稣会士的影响较大。因此，我们不难理解洛克在《人类理解论》（第四版）中说："我们纵然不相信拉·洛贝尔（La Loubère）的话，可是驻华的传教士们，甚至于耶稣教派的人们，一面虽然十分赞美中国，一面亦异口同声地告诉我们说：中国的统治阶级——士大夫们——都固守中国的旧教，都是纯粹的无神论者。"这简直是直接对斯氏说："你不相信别人没关系，连你最相信的耶稣会士也说中国人是无神论者。"这样就消除了斯氏质疑信息来源的可能性。

其次，描述对象难以质疑。与南非和南美的土著民族不同，在17世纪末的

---

① 爱德华·斯蒂林弗利特著，G. A. J. 罗杰斯主编，《宗教的起源：爱德华·斯蒂林弗利特的哲学，包括对约翰·洛克的回应》（卷一）（1702年版），布里斯托：托马斯出版社，2000年，第286页。
（Edward Stillingfleet, *Origines Sacrae, The Philosophy of Edward Stillingfleet, Including His Replies to John Locke*, G .A. J. Rogers ed., vol. 1, Bristol: Thoemmes Press, 2000, [1702 edition] p. 286.）

欧洲，中国的形象是一个遥远的强大的帝国，具有高度发展的文明，无论是文明程度还是生产力水平都不低于（甚至还高于）欧洲，这是当时欧洲人的共识。因此，斯氏很难将中国定义为"堕落的民族"，更别说质疑中国人"不配为人"了。洛克证明了"中国人是无神论者"，也就无可辩驳地证明了"世界上有无神论社会的存在"，也就有力地证明了"关于上帝的观念并不是天赋的"，最终驳斥了"天赋观念说"。

三、《人类理解论》中关于中国论述的系统性

洛克在《人类理解论》（第四、五版）第一卷第四章第8节"上帝的观念不是天赋的"中写道：

> 上帝底观念不是天赋的——如果我们可以想象有任何天赋的观念，则我们可以根据许多理由说，上帝底观念更可以说是天赋的。因为我们如果没有天赋的神明观念，则我们便不能设想有任何天赋的道德原则。因为没有立法者底观念，我们便不能有了法律底观念，便不能有遵守法律的义务。古人在史传上所贬斥的那些无神论者不用说了，即在近代，自航海以来，人们不是曾在色尔东尼（Soldania）海湾、以及巴西（Brazil）、布鸢岱（Boranday）、嘉里伯群岛（Carribee Islands）发现了整个的国家，没有上帝底观念，并且不知道宗教么？尼古拉（Nicolaus del Techo）关于开孤路（Caaiguarum）族底归化，曾经写到："我见这个种族，没有表示上帝和人类灵魂的字眼，他们没有神圣的教仪，亦没有偶像。"我们不但见有许多国家，蛮性未除，没有文字和教育底帮助，没有艺术和科学底进步。此外，我们还见到有许多国家虽然已经文明大有进步，可是他们因为在这方面不曾适当地运用其思想的缘故，竟然没有上帝底观念和知识。安南人就是属于这一类的，我想人们亦正可以同我一样，不必惊异这一层。不过关于这一层，我们可参阅法王在安南近来所派代表给我们的记述。据这位代表底记述看来，中国亦正是一样情形。我们纵然不相信乐老波（La Loubere）底话，可是驻华的传教士们，甚至于耶稣教派的人们，一面虽然十分赞美中国，一面亦异口同声地告诉我们说：中国底统治阶级——士大夫们——

都固守中国的旧教,都是纯粹的无神论者。关于这种情形,我们可参阅纳屋雷德(Navarette)"游记集"1卷同"中国仪礼史"(Historia Cultus Sinensium)。我们如果一注意邻近人民底生活和交际,我们亦很有理由来相信,即在文明国家中,许多人心中亦并没有强烈而明显的神明印象。从此我们亦就看到,讲坛上所以责怨人们底无神主义,亦并不是没理由的。现在虽然只有一些浪子无赖靦然自认无神,可是人们如果不是因为恐怕官吏底刀锋、邻人底责骂,结舌不敢出声,则我们一定更会听到无神底论调。因为他们如果到了不必恐怕刑罚或羞耻的时候,他们底口舌一定会公然宣布其无神主义,一如他们底行为一向所表示的那样。①

在这一节中,洛克引用了大量无神论的例子来证明"上帝的观念不是天赋的"。他将无神论者分为三类:(1)史书中记载的无神论者;(2)近代大航海以来,欧洲人在海外发现的无神论社会;(3)当时欧洲"文明国家"中的隐性无神论者。相较于第一类和第三类零散的无神论个体,第二类整个的无神论社会无疑更具冲击力。洛克将这些海外无神论社会又进一步分为两类:其一是"蛮性未除,没有文字和教育的帮助,没有艺术和科学的进步"的社会,如萨尔达尼亚湾、巴西、文莱、加勒比群岛的无神论社会,以及尼古拉(Nicolaus del Techo)记述的乌拉圭土著;其二是那些"虽然已经文明大有进步,可是他们因为在这方面不曾适当地运用其思想的缘故,竟然没有上帝的观念和知识"的国家,如安南和中国。因此,作为与非洲、南美和太平洋"蛮族"相对的"文明"的无神论社会,中国在关于"上帝的观念不是天赋的"论证中占有特殊重要的位置。

《人类理解论》对中国宗教信仰的结论肯定而明确:"中国的统治阶级——士大夫们——都是纯粹的无神论者。"信息来源清晰准确:首先是法王特使拉·洛贝尔出使暹罗的记述,其次是驻华传教士尤其是耶稣会士的报道,最后明确指出主要参考文献是丘吉尔兄弟《游记与旅行丛书》第一卷中收录的闵明我的著作和《华人礼仪史》。②

由此可见,在"礼仪之争"的大背景下,洛克对于"中国的统治阶级——士

---

① [英]洛克著,关文运译:《人类理解论》(上册),商务印书馆,1959年,第49—51页。
② 详见本书第六章第二节第二点"《人类理解论》引用的关于中国的书籍"。

大夫们——都是纯粹的无神论者"这一结论是非常谨慎的,是通过大量阅读和深入思考得出的慎重结论,绝不是道听途说、人云亦云的轻率之语。洛克在《人类理解论》中提到中国的目的是以中国为例,证明中国这样的具有高度发展的文明的国家也没有上帝的观念,因此上帝观念并不是天赋的,以此驳斥天赋观念说。虽然洛克在《人类理解论》中关于中国的论述只是聊聊数语,但洛克对中国的关注是深刻而持久的,最终在"中国笔记"手稿中对中国人的哲学和宗教进行了系统的梳理。

第三节　小结

虽然洛克很早就在各种游记文学中读到过中国,然而洛克对中国的系统了解和思考开始较晚。除了在《短论》中明确提到"中国围城事件"以外,洛克从未在其他作品中提到中国。同时考虑到我们上一章所梳理的洛克书信,洛克在书信中真正提到关于中国的信息开始于1696年3月,在此之前,洛克并未在书信中表达过对中国的兴趣。由此,我们可以推测,洛克在1696年左右开始真正关注与中国相关的消息,并注意搜集关于中国的最新书籍,1699年第四版的《人类理解论》是洛克"中国观"集中表述,而写于1702左右的"中国笔记"则是洛克"中国观"的具体呈现。然而,在整理洛克"中国笔记"手稿的时候,我强烈地感觉到"中国笔记"并不是洛克"中国观"的终点,洛克似乎在酝酿和准备更大的计划。我们知道,"洛克生命的最后10年里,他花越来越多的时间思索和写作有关宗教的东西"[①]。"中国笔记"讨论的就是中国人的宗教和哲学,并且在"拉夫雷斯档案"中,"中国笔记"与洛克晚年所归纳的基督教基本概念订在一起,洛克可能试图进行某种比较宗教学研究。另外,"洛克在他的文章中暗示,他计划写一部伦理学的系统著作"[②]。"中国笔记"也很有可能是为这部著作做准备。

---

① ［美］格瑞特・汤姆森著,袁银传、蔡红艳译,《洛克》,北京:中华书局,2014年,第90页。
② Richard I. Aaron, *John Locke*, Oxford: Oxford University Press, 1971, p. 256.

第六章 "中国笔记"的知识来源：洛克藏书与中国

第一节 洛克藏书概述

洛克不仅是17世纪著名的思想家，也是当时有名的图书收藏家。他的私人藏书在当时的欧洲虽然不是规模最大的，但无论从数量还是质量上说均属上乘。英国学者约翰·哈里森和彼得·拉斯莱特合著的《洛克藏书》[①]对洛克藏书进行了详尽的文献学研究，该书分为"洛克与他的书"和"洛克藏书目录"两大部分：第一部分结合洛克的生平和著作详细叙述了洛克藏书的过程、分类、编目和传承情况；第二部分则提供了洛克藏书的详细目录。该书内容翔实，叙述清楚，为搞清洛克藏书的总体脉络提供了绝佳指南。遗憾的是，这本书不仅没有中译本，英文原本也非常少见。本节主要基于该书，同时也参考了多种洛克传记中提供的信息，力图将洛克藏书的基本情况简略而完整地呈现出来。

---

① John Harrison & Peter Laslett, *The Library of John Locke*, Oxford University Press, 1965.

一、洛克藏书的阶段与目录

图书收藏需要的三个最基本条件：收藏者的兴趣、购买图书的资金和存放图书的地点，其中最容易出现问题就是第三个条件。洛克生活在一个风云变幻的年代，一生的大部分时间都居无定所，直到晚年定居奥茨。不难想象，在这样变动不居甚至神秘莫测①的生活状态中要携带或存放大量的图书是非常困难的。那么，洛克最终藏书目录中的3641种或4042册图书是怎样逐渐积累起来的呢？结合洛克的藏书情况，我以"流亡荷兰"为界将洛克的一生分为三个阶段，简要介绍各个阶段洛克的藏书的发展情况。

（一）牛津岁月

1647年15岁的洛克获得奖学金就读威斯敏斯特公学，进而于1652年获得牛津大学基督学院（Christ Church）的奖学金，1656年获学士学位，1658年获硕士学位，1660年获希腊语讲师教职，1663年获修辞学高级讲师教职，1664年获得道德哲学学监的教席，1665年作为外交使团的秘书赴勃兰登堡（Brandenburg），1667年成为后来的沙夫茨伯里（Shaftesbury）伯爵幕僚，1675年底到法国养病，1679年回国后继续充当幕僚，直至1682年沙夫茨伯里伯爵逃亡荷兰。

洛克在牛津读书时基本是靠奖学金生活，父亲也提供一部分生活费，洛克最大的开销就是购买自己感兴趣的书籍，比如笛卡尔的书，也购买一些时髦的小说。获得教职之后就有一定的收入，1661年父亲去世后又给洛克留了一笔不大的遗产，洛克可支配的钱变多了，大部分开销依然是书籍。我们在《洛克藏书》"附录一"中能够找到一份洛克在基督学院的藏书目录，主要依据是洛克写于1681年7月14日的名为《牛津藏书目录》（A catalogue of my books at Oxford）的

---

① 据洛克在牛津的同事回忆："他（指洛克）过着一种机巧的和让人难以捉摸的生活……没有人知道他去了哪里，什么时候走的，或者什么时候回来。""1685年蒙茅斯政变失败后，英国王室向荷兰政府要求引渡洛克回国，洛克一度以范·登·林登（van den Linden）医生的假名藏匿起来。"［美］格瑞特·汤姆森著，袁银传、蔡红艳译，《洛克》，北京：中华书局，2014年，第11页。

日记，当中记录的图书共计288种、305册。① 然而，洛克在牛津的藏书至少经过两次浩劫，第一次是1683年7月21日牛津大学下令烧书，洛克的部分藏书被烧，当时洛克在现场；第二次是1684年11月，洛克被基督学院开除学籍，洛克在牛津的住处被闯入，物品被强行搬出，场面混乱而狼狈。当时洛克已经流亡荷兰，并不在场，此后终其一生，洛克再未踏足牛津。

（二）流亡荷兰

沙夫茨伯里伯爵的逃亡并去世让洛克感到巨大的危险，于是1683年洛克流亡荷兰。流亡前，洛克将一部分他在伦敦的藏书搬到朋友詹姆斯·泰瑞尔②家中，另一部分留在伦敦的房东史密斯比太太（Mrs. Rabsby Smithsby）那里。1684年被基督学院开除学籍后，詹姆斯·泰瑞尔又保存了洛克留在牛津的藏书。

荷兰是当时欧洲出版业的中心，洛克在荷兰大量购书，以补充其在英国的藏书。虽然洛克偶尔会购买一些在英国已经收藏的书籍，但总的来说，他在荷兰购买的书籍大部分是在英国没有的，并且洛克从未想过要把自己在英国的藏书搬到荷兰，这说明洛克从来不认为自己会一直流亡海外。洛克主要从鹿特丹的书商亚伯拉罕·威斯特斯坦（Abraham Weststein）那里购书，最感兴趣的就是"关于遥远的、新近发现的国家的地理、自然和人的游记"。

1689年2月，洛克陪同玛丽皇后乘坐伊莎贝拉（Isabella）号回英国时带了16个大箱子，其中13箱装满了在荷兰买的书。据记载，洛克离开荷兰时还留下了68本书，可能是留给了鹿特丹住所的房东，也可能留给了书商。

（三）荣归英伦

1689年回到英国后，当年洛克就有三部作品③出版。他的名气变得很大，大

---

① 该目录详见《洛克藏书》"附录一"（John Harrison & Peter Laslett, *The Library of John Locke*, Oxford University Press, 1965, pp. 269-277）；关于牛津所藏书籍的版本和分类见John Harrison & Peter Laslett, *The Library of John Locke*, Oxford University Press, 1965, pp. 14-15。
② 詹姆斯·泰瑞尔是蒂莫西·泰瑞尔（Timothy Tyrrell）爵士的儿子和继承人，住在离牛津不远的奥克利（Oakley），与洛克的性格大相径庭，但是洛克的朋友。
③ 《人类理解论》《政府论》和《论宽容》，第一本是公开以洛克之名发表的，后两本都是匿名发表。有趣的是，洛克在为藏书编目时，将自己的匿名作品都归于不同的主题下，而不是归于自己名下。

量批判或支持其观点的文章相继出现，并且很多人慕名将自己的书献给洛克，这增加了洛克的藏书数量。

同时，作为"光荣革命"的功臣，洛克的仕途一片光明。1689年5月，洛克出任上诉委员（Commissioner for Appeals），年薪200镑；1696年5月，洛克在新成立的贸易委员会（Council for Trade and Plantations）任职，年薪1000镑。收入增加使得洛克有更多可支配的资金来购买书籍，又进一步增加了洛克的藏书量。

1691年开始，洛克定居奥茨，终于有了永久存放藏书的地点，于是洛克开始安排将自己存放在各处的藏书陆续运到奥茨来。除了留在伦敦住所的藏书之外[①]，从荷兰带回的书籍和詹姆斯·泰瑞尔保管的书籍在1692年春都抵达了奥茨，洛克藏书基本汇于一处。

据约翰·哈里森和彼得·拉斯莱特从洛克的日记、书信、图书目录等线索中统计出来的数据，1679年洛克从法国回来时，他的藏书约有500—600种，分别存放于伦敦和牛津；1681年他在牛津的藏书有288种；1683年流亡荷兰前，总藏书量大约1000种，（1684—1691年流亡期间，其中约700种存放在Oakley in Buckinghamshire，由詹姆斯·泰瑞尔保管）；1689年，洛克回到英国时，藏书量增加到1700种；定居奥茨前，洛克又增加了大约200种；定居奥茨后，洛克又将自己的藏书量增加了一倍，最终达到3641种。[②]

二、洛克藏书的分类

约翰·哈里森和彼得·拉斯莱特的《洛克藏书》将洛克藏书分别按照主题、语种和出版地进行了分类，其中与本书关系最密切的是主题分类，见下表。

[①] 虽然1691年初洛克就正式定居奥茨，但他依然保留了在伦敦的住所，并在那里度过每年最温暖的一百多天。洛克在伦敦的房东由史密斯比太太变为保林（Pawling）先生，后来保林先生的住所从Dorset Court in Channel Row搬到Little Lincoln's Inn Fields，洛克的东西包括藏书也跟着搬迁了。在伦敦住所共有100多本书，洛克去世的时候是148本，大都是作者不太在意的书，并没有纳入最终图书目录。

[②] John Harrison & Peter Laslett, *The Library of John Locke*, Oxford University Press, 1965, pp. 17-18.

表 6-1　洛克藏书的主题分类①

	主题	数量（种）	比例（%）
1	神学（其中圣经31；圣约书24；圣经词汇索引12；祈祷文等5）	870	23.9
2	医学（其中药剂学25）	402	11.0
3	政治与法律（其中法学59）	390	10.7
4	希腊文和拉丁文的古典文学	366	10.1
5	地理与探险（其中游记195；地理类80）	275	7.6
6	哲学	269	7.4
7	自然科学（其中物理69；自然史61；化学48；动物学29；植物学13；天文学9；矿物学13）	242	6.6
8	现代文学（其中法文96；英文73；意大利文28；西班牙文10；荷兰文4）	211	5.8
9	历史与传记	187	5.1
10	经济（其中农业4）	127	3.5
11	参考书与图书目录（其中字典65）	101	2.8
	其他	201	5.5
	总计	3641	100

关于洛克的藏书有两点需要说明：其一，洛克时代的知识分类与今天我们所熟悉的学科分类差异很大，例如，关于某一地区的动植物情况的书籍在今天应归于自然史或自然科学领域，而洛克很可能会将之归于医学类，与化学、矿物学甚至天文学书籍放在一处。再比如与本书关系最为密切的探险游记类书籍，洛克不仅大量收集甚至还亲自编辑过该类书籍，他从这些书籍中摘录了关于世界各民族的生活与风俗的大量信息，洛克将这些摘录簿命名为"Ethica"（伦理学）。按照今天的学科分类，这类书籍和摘录应归为"社会人类学"（Social Anthropology）或"比较人类学"（Comparative Anthropology），也有些国内外

---

① 参见John Harrison & Peter Laslett, *The Library of John Locke*, Oxford University Press, 1965, p. 18 Table 1。该书1971年的第二版中还添加了"附录V"，收录了更加具体的主题分类索引，参见*Ibid*, 2nd edition, 1971, pp. 292-308。

学者主张将其称为"人种历史学"（ethnohistory）[①]。因此，表6—1只是粗略地将洛克藏书归为几大主题，难以苛求完整和准确。其二，根据常识，洛克不可能收藏了所有曾经阅读或引用过的书籍，也不可能阅读过所有收藏的书籍，同时，一些洛克曾拥有的书籍也并未出现在其最终藏书目录中，因此，洛克藏书目录是洛克曾阅读和参考书籍一个非常重要的证据和线索，但绝不是唯一的线索，洛克著作、书信、日记、笔记中所提到和引用的书籍也应该被考虑在内。

三、洛克藏书的特点

其一，偏爱游记。在洛克所藏的各类书籍图书中，洛克最为钟爱的是游记地理类（Geography and Exploration）书籍。如表6-1所示，该类书籍共计275种，其中游记类195种，地理类80种。虽然此类书籍只占总藏书量的7.6%，但考虑到当时该类书籍的总出版量，洛克几乎拥有能够获得的所有该类书籍。不仅如此，洛克还依据这些书籍做了大量摘录，更在自己的著作中频繁引用，足见他对该类著作的偏爱。

其二，以使用为目的。洛克从不以展示为目的收藏那些"精美、稀有、奇特"的书籍。相反，他会按照自己的写作计划搜集相关书籍，并且在写作中大量引用。以《人类理解论》对游记地理类作品的引用为例，1690年的第一版中，洛克引用了9本该类专著；而1705年第五版中，这一数字增加到16本，其中15本是

[①] "ethnohistory"指研究非西方的人种和文化的历史，拉赫（Donald F. Lach）用这个词来指门多萨、金尼阁等人的作品。国内学者如张国刚、吴莉苇也借鉴了这种用法。

游记，另一本也可以归为比较人类学或比较宗教学的专著。①由此可见，洛克藏书与洛克思想发展的关系非常密切。通过考察洛克在不同时期收藏和引用相关书籍时的不同选择，我们能够看出洛克对相关历史事件的态度。

其三，正文不做标记。洛克没有做页边注的习惯，读书笔记一律以"摘录簿"的形式记录。据《中国藏书》统计，少数洛克藏书的封面内页有价格等小标记，30本藏书的封底内页有铅笔手写的页码表，但所有洛克藏书的正文都没有任何标记。这意味着即便找到洛克藏书的原本，我们也很难判断它们对洛克的重要性。因此，洛克的藏书、"摘录簿"和著作是一个整体，我们必须把它们放在一起来看。

---

① 根据约翰·哈里森和彼得·拉斯莱特统计，洛克在《人类理解论》中引用的游记作者有：Thévenot, Isaac Vossius, Peter Martyr, Garcilasso de la Vega, Léry, Baumgarten, Pietro della Valle, La Martinière, Terry, Ovington, Techo, La Loubère, Jacques de Bourges, Choisy and Navarette，还有 *Historia Cultus Sinensium* [688]。其中六种1670年代购于法国：Thévenot [2889], Garcilasso de la Vega [3058], Léry [1718], Pietro della Valle [3046], La Martinière [1928], Jacques de Bourges [407]。这六种书在洛克流亡荷兰之前分放在牛津和伦敦，洛克流亡荷兰后又买了一本La Martinière。洛克1681年为牛津藏书编目时买了Terry on East India [2857]，流亡荷兰期间，这本书存放在Oakley。Choisy的*Voyage de Siam*, 1687 [693] 刚一出版就被编入洛克在荷兰的藏书目录。而*La Loubère on Siam*, 1691 [1811], *Ovington on Suratt*, 1696 [2160], *Historia Cultus Sinensium*, 1700 [688]都出版于《人类理解论》第一版之后，所以在之后的修订本中陆续出现）。Peter Martyr [1930]购于荷兰。洛克定居奥茨后购买了Hakluyt [1374], Purchas [2409], Tasman's *Voyage mad towards the South Terra Incognita* [2833], Thomas's *Pensilvania and West New Jersey*, 1698 [2891]，其中后两本是一出版就买了。Isaac Vossius，Baumgarten和Techo均未出现于最终目录，然而这三本书都计划在丘吉尔兄弟编辑的《游记与旅行丛书》中出英文本，洛克在《人类理解论》中称Baumgarten为"不是每天都能遇到的好书"。……洛克定居奥茨后购买了Hakluyt [1374], Purchas [2409], Tasman's *Voyage mad towards the South Terra Incognita* [2833], Thomas's *Pensilvania and West New Jersey*, 1698 [2891]，其中后两本是一出版就买了。甚至有一本伪称为洛克身后作品的书就名为*A Catalogue and Character of most Books of Voyages and Travels*。详见John Harrison & Peter Laslett, *The Library of John Locke*, Oxford University Press, 1965, pp. 28-29。

第二节 洛克的中国藏书

一、洛克藏书中关于中国的书籍①

经过反复查找和筛选，笔者初步确定洛克藏书中至少有41种关于中国的书籍②，如下表：

表 6-2　洛克的中国藏书

序号	作者	书名	出版地	出版时间
1	**Alexandre**, Noël③	*Apologie des Dominicains missionaires de la Chine*④	Cologne	1699
2	*Ibid*	*Conformité des cérémonies Chinoises avec l'Idolâtrie Greque et Romaine*⑤	*Ibid*	1700

---

① 本部分的资料基础为John Harrison and Peter Laslett, *The Library of John Locke*, Oxford: Clarendon Press, 1971，另参见Ann Talbot,"The Great Ocean of Knowledge": *The Influence of Travel Literature on the Work of John Locke*, Leiden: Brill, 2010, pp. 315-316。

② 需要说明的是，洛克藏书目录不仅条目众多，而且语种多样，加上洛克时代的知识分类与今天我们熟悉的学科分类差异很大，有些书籍很难仅从类目和标题判断是否与中国相关，因此本书只梳理那些主题与中国直接相关的书籍。一些与中国并不直接相关的书籍，如航海游记集和全球史地类书籍，尤其是涉及中国周边地区如印度和暹罗的外交文献和游记，也可能涉及中国，但这些并非本书关注的重点。

③ 诺埃尔·亚历山大（Noël Alexandre，拉丁名Natalis Alexander，1639—1724），法国神学家、基督教历史学家。1654年加入道明我会，任雅各宾修道院（Couvent des Jacobins）哲学教授。1675年获索邦神学院神学博士，1706—1709年任道明我会会长。诺埃尔曾受聘于路易十四时代著名政治家柯尔贝尔（Jean-Baptiste Colbert，1619—1683）任其子的家庭教师，并曾享受路易十四授予的特殊津贴，是当时颇具影响力的宗教界人士。

④《为入华道明我会传教士辩护》，法文本，科隆，1699年。该书又名《驳泰利埃神父的〈论新基督徒〉》（*Réponse au livre du Père Le Tellier, jésuite, intitulé, Defense des Nouveaux Chretiens*）。1682年，《耶稣会士的礼仪》（*La Morale pratique des Jésuites*）在巴黎出版，严厉批评耶稣会士对待中国礼仪的态度和做法。1687年，耶稣会士泰利埃神父（Père le Tellier）出版《论新基督徒》（*Défense des Nouveaux Chrétiens*）进行回应，1694年5月23日，该书在罗马被禁。诺埃尔的《为入华道明我会传教士辩护》是对泰利埃神父的驳斥。

⑤《中国礼仪与希腊罗马偶像崇拜之比较》，法文本，科隆，1700年。在洛克藏书中，该书与C. Le Gobien: *Remarques d'un docteur en théologie sur la protestation des jésuites*, 1700. 合订为一册，参见John Harrison & Peter Laslett, *The Library of John Locke*, Oxford University Press, 1965, p. 106 Entry 690&691。

（续表）

序号	作者	书名	出版地	出版时间
3	Ibid	*Lettre d'une personne de Piété sur un Ecrit des Jésuites intitulé la censure réfuté touchant la religion et le culte des Chinois*①	Ibid	1701
4	Ibid	*Lettre d'un docteur de l'Ordre de Saint Dominique*②	Ibid	1700
5	Ibid	*Lettre d'un Dr de l'Ordre de St Dominique [i.e. N. Alexandre] sur les cérémonies de la Chine au R. P.*③	Ibid	1700
6	Ibid	*Lettre d'un Dr de l'ordre de St Dominique [i.e. N. Alexandre] au R. P. le Comte sur son Système de l'ancienne religion de la Chine*⑤	Ibid	1700
7	——	*Lettre de Mess: des Missions étrangères au Pape, sur les Idolâtries et superstitions Chinoises*⑤	Ibid	1700
8	**Alfaro**, Pedro de⑥	*Voyage into China*⑦	London	1588

---

① 《一位基督徒对耶稣会士关于中国宗教和礼仪论述的驳斥》，法文本，科隆，1701年。
② 《论中国礼仪——道明我会修士（诺埃尔）致李明神父的信》，法文本，科隆，1700年。
③ 《论中国礼仪——道明我会修士（诺埃尔）致Dez神父的信》，法文本，科隆，1700年。
④ 《论中国古代宗教体系——道明我会修士（诺埃尔）致李明神父的信》，法文本，科隆，1700年。
⑤ 《论中国人的偶像崇拜和迷信——巴黎外方传教士致教皇的信》，法文本，科隆，1700年。这封信的作者不明，但在洛克藏书中，该信与以上三封诺埃尔的信合订为一册，是"礼仪之争"中耶稣会反对者的一本书信集。
⑥ 佩德罗·德·阿尔法罗（Pedro de Alfaro），西班牙方济各会修士。1577年8月2日，佩德罗一行十八人抵达马尼拉。1579—1580年，佩德罗和另三名方济各会士游历广东省并著游记。该游记后被胡安·龚萨雷斯·德·门多萨（Fr. Juan Gonzàlez de Mendoza, 1545—1618）收入《中华大帝国史》（*História do Grande Reinad da China*）第二部分。
⑦ 《中国纪行》，英文本，伦敦，1588年。该书为佩德罗游记的英译本，收录于门多萨的《中华大帝国史》英译本中。

(续表)

序号	作者	书名	出版地	出版时间
9	**Barros**, João de①	*L'Asia de fatti de' Portoghesi nello scoprimento, & conquista de' mari, & terre di Oriente*②	Venetia	1561
10	**Bergeron**, Pierre③	*Relation des voyages en Tartarie*④	Paris	1634
11	**Bourges**, Jacques de⑤	*Relation du voyage de Mons l'Eveque de Beryte*⑥	Paris	1666
12	**Bouvet**, Joachim⑦	*Portrait historique de l'Empereur de la Chine*⑧	Paris	1697

---

① 若昂·德·巴罗斯（João de Barros，1496—1570），著名葡萄牙历史学家，著有《亚洲十年》（*Décadas da Ásia*，即Decades of Asia，又译《亚洲旬志》），记述葡萄牙人在印度及其他亚洲国家的历史，1552、1553、1563年分别出版了第一、二、三卷，巴罗斯去世后，1615年又出版了第四、五卷。

② 《亚洲：葡萄牙人经由海路及陆路发现及征服东方史》，葡文本，威尼斯，1561年。该藏本的封底内页有洛克亲笔手书的5项页码表。

③ 皮埃尔·贝哲隆（Pierre Bergeron，1580？—1637？），法国律师、作家及法国殖民史家，不仅将大量中世纪的游记文学编辑出版，还改写了很多当时前往东方的法国旅行家的游记使其成为畅销作品。贝哲隆通常不在自己改写和编辑的游记作品中署名，是17世纪早期较为著名的代笔作家。参见Grégoire Holtz. *L'ombre de l'auteur: Pierre Bergeron et l'e'criture du voyage au soir de la Renaissance*, Geneva: Librairie Droz, 2011。

④ 《鞑靼游记》，法文本，巴黎，1634年。

⑤ 贾可·德·布尔日（Jacques de Bourges，1634—1714），法国外方传教会会士，1679年起任西东京主教（Vicar Apostolic of Western Tonking，旧称Tonkino Occidentale）。1660年11月，布尔日与同伴从马赛起航，经过21个月的艰难航行，他们于1662年8月抵达了暹罗国的首府大城府（Ayuthia）。当时正值暹罗的那莱王（Somdet Phra Naraï，1629—1688，1657—1688在位）执政早期，布尔日一行成为法国与暹罗正式外交往来的开端。

⑥ 《贝鲁特主教行纪》，法文本，巴黎，1666年。全名*Relation du voyage de Monseigneur l'évêque de Beryte Vicaire apostolique du royaume de la Cochinchine, Par la Turquie, la Perse, les Indes, &c. jusqu'au Royaume de Siam & autres lieux. Par M. de Bourges, Prêtre, Missionnaire Apostolique*，是历史上第一本关于暹罗的法文书，1666年巴黎出版，1668、1683年再版。该书详细记录了贝鲁特主教一行在暹罗的经历，同时对暹罗进行了系统的介绍，为当时的欧洲提供了最早的关于暹罗及周边地区的第一手信息。

⑦ 白晋（Joachim Bouvet，1656—1730），字明远，耶稣会士，清康熙二十六年（1687年）来华，1688年2月7日入京并在钦天监供职。1693年奉康熙皇帝之命出使法国，1697年抵达巴黎并将康熙皇帝的礼物进献路易十四。1699年返京，深得康熙皇帝的赞许，被任命为皇太子的辅导老师。

⑧ 《康熙皇帝传》，法文本，巴黎，1697年。

第六章 "中国笔记"的知识来源：洛克藏书与中国　221

（续表）

序号	作者	书名	出版地	出版时间
13	**Brand**, Adam①	*A Journal of an Embassy from their Majesties John & Peter Alexowits Emperors of Muscovy into China 1693*②	London	1698
14	**Brune**, J de la③	*Confucius, La Morale de Confucius philosophe de la Chine*④	Amsterdam	1688
15	**Churchill**, A&J	*A Collection of Voyages and Travels in 4 volumes*⑤	London	1704

---

① 亚当·布兰德（Adam Brand，1692？—1746），德国商人、探险家，曾数次前往莫斯科经商。1692年，俄国沙皇彼得大帝任命巨商叶利扎里·伊兹勃兰特·伊台斯（又译雅布兰，Eberhard Isbrand Ides，1657—1708）为特使出使中国，亚当·布兰德担任伊台斯的秘书。该使团于1693年抵达北京，1694年返回。伊台斯从国库贷款六千卢布购置货物并在中国销售一空，这使得俄国政府相信与北京的贸易有利可图，成为俄国官方商队北京贸易的前奏。

② 《沙皇使节雅布兰1693至1695年使华旅行记》，英文本，伦敦，1698年。该书德文原名 *Beschreibung der chinesischen Reise, welche vermittelst einer Zaaris Gesandschaft durch dero Ambassadeur Herrn Isbrand Ao. 1693, 1694 und 1695, von Moscau uber Gross-Ustiga, Siberien, Dauren udn durch die Mongolische Tartatey verrichtet Worden*），1698年于汉堡出版，随即风靡欧洲。英译本同年出版、1707年再版，1699年法文本和荷文本出版。布兰德曾将该书手稿摘要寄给莱布尼茨，后者将其译为拉丁文并收入1697年出版的《中国近事》（*Novissima Sinica*）。

③ 让·德拉·布吕纳（又译布隆，？—1743？），新教神学家、历史学家。西方学界对于该书作者是否为布吕纳一直有争议，详见Edmund Leites：" *Confucianism in Eighteenth-Century England: Natural Morality and Social Reform*", *Philosophy East and West* 28(2) (1978), pp. 155—156.

④ 《中国哲学家孔子的道德箴言》，法文本，阿姆斯特丹，1688年。1688年，巴黎书商Daniel Horthemels将该书与《论中国哲学家孔子的道德学说》（*Lettre sur la morale de Confucius, philosophe de la Chine*, Paris 1688）合订出版，后者的作者为法国哲学家傅歇（Simon Foucher，1644—1696），他是马勒伯朗士和莱布尼茨哲学的坚定反对者。

⑤ 《游记与旅行丛书》（四卷本），英文本，伦敦，1704年。很多人认为洛克参与了该书的编写并为该书作序，这并未得到证实，但洛克的确提议并推动了该书的出版。

（续表）

序号	作者	书名	出版地	出版时间
16	**Comte**, Louis le①	*Nouveaux mémoires sur l'état présent de la Chine*②	Paris	1697
17	*Ibid*	*Lettre au Duc de Mayne sur les cérémonies de la Chine*③	Liege	1700
18	**Faure**, Jacques le④	*Lettre sur l'estat présent de la Chine*⑤	Paris	1662
19	**Gobien**, Charles de⑥	*Dissertatio apoloogetica [sic] de Sinensium ritibus politicis*⑦	Liege	1700
20	*Ibid* with le Comte⑧	*Les nouveaux mémoires sur l'état présent de Chine vol 3*⑨	Paris	1698
21	**Haithonus**, Armenus⑩	*De Tartaris Liber*⑪	Basel	1532

---

① 李明（Louis le Comte，1655—1728），法国耶稣会士。1687年，作为路易十四的"国王数学家"，与洪若翰（Jean de Fontaney）、白晋（Joachim Bouvet）、张诚（Jean-François Gerbillon）、刘应（Claude de Visdelou）和塔夏尔（Ta Xiaer）一起前往中国，次年抵达。后因卷入了与葡萄牙的保教权之争，1691年被迫返回法国。

② 《中国近事报道》，法文本，巴黎，1696年。该书以替耶稣会士的"适应政策"辩护为目的，是"礼仪之争"的重要文献，同时也是一本关于中国的百科全书，对伏尔泰、魁奈、莱布尼茨等启蒙思想家都产生过影响。1700年，该书被索邦神学院列为禁书。

③ 《论中国礼仪书》，法文本，列日，1700年。

④ 刘迪我（Jacques le Faure，1613—1675），法国耶稣会士，曾任耶稣会中华省副省长。1656年来华，1675年在上海去世。

⑤ 《中国现势报道》，法文本，巴黎，1662年。

⑥ 郭弼恩（Charles de Gobien，1653—1708），法国耶稣会士，法王的忏悔神甫勒特利（P. Le Tellier）的秘书，耶稣会在欧洲东方传教事务的负责人，专门负责入华耶稣会士们寄回法国的书简与著述等档案。1702年，郭弼恩在巴黎推出《耶稣会士书简集》首卷，并陆续出版至第8卷，后由杜赫德（Jean-Baptiste du Halde，1674—1743年）接手。

⑦ 《论中国的政治礼仪》，拉丁文本，列日，1700年。

⑧ 郭弼恩与李明合著。

⑨ 《中国近事报道》（第3卷），法文本，巴黎，1698年。

⑩ 中世纪土耳其历史学家。

⑪ 《鞑靼之书》，拉丁文本，巴塞尔，1532年。

（续表）

序号	作者	书名	出版地	出版时间
22	——①	*Historia Cultus Sinensium*②	Cologne	1700
23		*Contimuatio historiæ cultus Sinensium*③	Cologne	1700
24	**Herrada**, M[artín] de.④	*Voyage into China*⑤	London	1588
25	IGNACIO, M[artín] d.⑥	*Voyage round the world*⑦	London	1588
26	**Kircher**, Athanasius⑧	*China monumentis qua sacra qua profanis... illustrata*⑨	Amsterdam	1667

---

① 匿名。
② 《华人礼仪史》，拉丁文本，科隆，1700年。全名《华人礼仪史——关于华人礼仪的各种文献及法国宗座代牧、其他传教士与耶稣会士之间的论争》（*Historia cultus sinensium seu varia scripta de cultibus Sinarum, inter vicarios apostolos Gallos aliosque missionarios, et Patres Societatis Jesu controversis*），该藏本的封底内页有洛克亲笔手书的12行页码表。
③ 《华人礼仪史续篇》，拉丁文本，科隆，1700年。
④ 马丁·德·拉达（Martin de Lada，1533—1578），门多萨的《大中华帝国志》中将其称作Herrada，奥斯定会士。1565—1572年在菲律宾宿务（Cebu）传教，史称"宿务神使（the apostle of the Christian Faith in Cebu）"，后成为奥斯定会驻菲律宾的负责人。拉达在宿务开始学习汉语，1575年6月26日，拉达与教友Jeronimo Marin陪同菲律宾官员访华，同年7月5日抵达厦门并访问了福建的其他几个城市，1575年10月28日返回马尼拉。拉达著书记述福建之行，详细描述了中国人及其生活方式，后被收入门多萨的《中华大帝国史》。
⑤ 《中国行纪》，英文本，伦敦，1588年。该书为拉达神父福建游记的英译本，收录于罗伯特·帕克（Robert Parke，？—1689？）翻译的《中华大帝国史》英译本中。
⑥ 马丁·伊格纳西奥·罗耀拉（Martín Ignacio de Loyola，1550—1606），西班牙方济各会士，曾于1582—1584年和1585—1589年两次完成环球航行，并曾两次从欧洲前往南美洲，是17世纪以前旅行范围最广的欧洲人。1582年6月21日，罗耀拉从西班牙港口加的斯（Cadiz）出发，一路向西航行。途经中国时在福建登陆，罗耀拉一行被当地官员当做奸细押解至广州，羁押一年后被遣送至澳门释放。这次环球航行的游记于1586年在罗马出版，后被收入门多萨的《中华大帝国史》。
⑦ 《环球游记》，英文本，伦敦，1588年。该书为罗耀拉神父环球游记的英文版，收录于罗伯特·帕克（Robert Parke，？—1689？）翻译的《中华大帝国史》英译本中。
⑧ 阿塔纳修斯·基歇尔（Athanasius Kircher，1620—1680），百科全书式学者，耶稣会士。基歇尔与来华传教士关系密切：他是卫匡国（Martin Martini，1614—1661）的数学老师；白乃心（Johann Grueber，1623—1680）从欧洲来中国以前，曾和基歇尔商定，将随时把在东方旅途的见闻告诉他；曾德昭（Alvarus de Semedo，又名谢务禄，1585/1586—1658）、卫匡国、卜弥格（Michel Boym，1612—1659）从中国返欧时都曾和他见过面，提供给他关于中国和亚洲的第一手材料。
⑨ 《中国图说》，拉丁文本，阿姆斯特丹，1667年。全名《中国的宗教、世俗和各种自然、技术奇观及其有价值的实物材料汇编》（*China Monumentis qua Sacris qua profanes, Nec non variis Naturae &Artis Spectaculis, Aliarumque rerum memorablilium Argumentis illustrate*）。

（续表）

序号	作者	书名	出版地	出版时间
27	**Leibniz**, Gottfried Wilhelm von①	*Novissima Sinica*②	Hanover	1699
28	**Martini**, Martino③	*Sinicae historiae decas prima*④	Munich/Amsterdam	1658/1659
29	**Martinius**, M.	*Regni Sinensis a Tartaris devastati Enarratio*⑤	Amsterdam	1661
30	**Mendoza**, Juan González de⑥	*Historia della China*⑦	Rome	1586
31	*Ibid*	*The historie…of China… Transl. out of Spanish by R. Parke*⑧	London	1588

① 戈特弗里德·威廉·莱布尼茨（Gottfried Wilhelm Leibniz, 1646—1716），德国哲学家、数学家，一位百科全书式的伟大人物。

② 《中国近事》，拉丁文本，汉诺威，1699年。全名《中国近事：为了照亮我们这个时代的历史机遇，我们将在本书中展示给大家一份第一次带到欧洲的有关中国政府首次正式允许基督教在华传播的报告。此外，本书还提供很多迄今为止鲜为人知的情况：欧洲科学在中国的发展，中国人的风俗习惯与道德，特别是关于皇帝本人的高尚精神，以及关于中俄之间的战争及和平协议》。

③ 卫匡国（1614—1661），意大利耶稣会士，1648年来华，至少游历了中国内地15省（两京、13布政司）中的六七个省，因此非常熟悉中国的文化地理。1650年，卫匡国作为耶稣会代理人赴罗马教廷为中国礼仪辩护，途经德、法、英、比、挪威诸国，向欧洲宣传自己对中国文化的认识。1654年底，卫匡国在罗马教廷进行了关于中国礼仪的辩论并取得胜利，教廷随后颁布了有利于耶稣会的敕令。1657年，卫匡国再次赴华，1661年病逝于杭州。

④ 《中国上古史》，拉丁文本，慕尼黑，1658年初版；阿姆斯特丹，1659年再版。洛克收藏了1658和1659年两个版本，1659年版的封底内页有洛克亲笔手书的5项页码表。

⑤ 《鞑靼战纪》，英文本，阿姆斯特丹，1661年。

⑥ 胡安·冈萨雷斯·德·门多萨（Juan González de Mendoza, 1545—1618），西班牙奥古斯丁修会会士，1581年曾作为西班牙国王的使节赴华，但因局势所迫未能成行。后历任卡斯蒂利亚省教区奥古斯丁教士大会会长、西西里岛利巴利主教、恰巴斯省的主教等要职。

⑦ 《中华大帝国史》，原名《中华大帝国历史与现状》（*Historia de las cosas más notables, ritos y costumbres del gran reyno de la China*），西文本，罗马，1585年。该藏本的封底内页有洛克亲笔手书的4项页码表。

⑧ 《中华大帝国史》，英文本，伦敦，1588年。罗伯特·帕克（Robert Parke, ? —1689?）译，英译本全名《大中华帝国历史以及那里的形势：巨额财富、大城市、政治政府和珍稀的发明》（*The Historie of the great and mightie Kingdome of China, and the Situation therefore: Together with the great riches, huge cities, politike government, and rare inventions in same*）。

第六章 "中国笔记"的知识来源：洛克藏书与中国　225

（续表）

序号	作者	书名	出版地	出版时间
32	*Ibid*	*Rerum morumque in regno Chinensi maxime notabilium historia...*①	Antwerp	1655
33	**Navarrete**, Fernandez Domingo②	*Réponse à l'Apologie des Jésuites de la Chine composée par le P. Diego Moralez*③	Cologne	1701
34	*Ibid*	*Tratados historicos, politicos, ethicos y religiosos de la monarchia de China*④	Madrid	1676
35	**Nieuhoff**, Johan⑤	*L'ambassade de la Compagnie Orientale des Provinces Unies vers l'empereur de la Chine*⑥	Leyden	1665

---

① 《中华大帝国史》，拉丁文本，安特卫普，1655年版。
② 闵明我（Domingo Fernández Navarrete，1610—1689），西班牙道明我会修士。1657年来华，主要在福建传教，1673年代表道明我会前往罗马参与"礼仪之争"并深受教皇英诺森十一世的赏识，是当时欧洲"中国礼仪"问题的权威。
③ 《与Diego Moralez神父论在华耶稣会》，法文本，科隆，1701年。
④ 《中华帝国历史、政治、伦理及宗教概述》，西文本，马德里，1676年。
⑤ 约翰·纽霍夫（Johan Nieuhoff，1618—1672），荷兰画家、旅行家，1654年被荷兰东印度公司指派为Peter de Goyer和Jacob de Keyser率领的访华使团的管事。该使团1657年3月17日从广东乘船出发，同年7月18日抵达北京，9月24日受到顺治帝接见。纽霍夫用写实笔法记录了沿途所见的城市、乡村、宫殿、寺庙、河流等景物，1658年返回荷兰后，纽霍夫将这次中国之行的笔记和画稿交给弟弟Hendrik Nieuhoff，后者于1665年将其整理出版，名为《荷兰东印度公司谒见中国皇帝记》。
⑥ 《荷兰东印度公司谒见中国皇帝记》，法文本，莱顿，1665年。该书原名*Het Gezandtschap der Neêrlandtsche Oost-Indische Compagnie, aan den grooten Tartarischen Cham, den tegenwoordigen Keizer van China: Waarin de gedenkwaerdigste Geschiedenissen, die onder het reizen door de Sineesche landtschappen, Quantung, Kiangsi, Nanking, Xantung en Peking, en aan het Keizerlijke Hof te Peking, sedert den jaren 1655 tot 1657 zijn voorgevallen, op het bondigste verhandelt worden. Beneffens een Naukeurige Beschrijvinge der Sineesche Steden, Dorpen, Regeering, Weetenschappen, Hantwerken, Zeden, Godsdiensten, Gebouwen, Drachten, Schepen, Bergen, Gewassen, Dieren, et cetera en oorlogen tegen de Tartar : verçiert men over de 150 afbeeltsels, na't leven in Sina getekent*，一经出版即大受欢迎，并迅速被译为法文（1665年）、德文（1666年）、拉丁文（1668年）、英文（1669年）出版。书中纽霍夫所绘的约150幅插图成为18世纪流行于欧洲的中国风的主要素材。

（续表）

序号	作者	书名	出版地	出版时间
36	**Palafox y Mendoza**, Juan de①	*The History of the Tartars*②	London	1679
37	**Ramusio**, Giovanni Battista③	*Navigationi et Viaggi*④	Venice	1559-65
38	**Sousa**, Manuel de Faria y⑤	*Asia Portuguesa*⑥	Lisbon	1666
39	**Spizelius**, Theophilus⑦	*De re literaria Sinensium*⑧	Amsterdam	1660

---

① 帕莱福（Juan de Palafox y Mendoza，1600—1659），西班牙多明我会修士，曾任西班牙奥斯马主教，1639年赴墨西哥任普布拉等地主教，后由西班牙国王菲利普四世委任为新西班牙即墨西哥总督。

② 《鞑靼征服中国史》，英文本，伦敦，1679年。西文版原名 *Historia de la conquista de la China por el Tartaro*，1670年巴黎出版；法译本同年出版；英译本原名 *The History of the Conquest of China by the Tartars Together with an Account of Several Remarkable Things, Concerning the Religion, Manners, and Customs of Both Nation's, but Especially the Latter*，1676年伦敦出版。

③ 赖麦锡（Giovanni Battista Ramusio，1485—1557），意大利地理学家和游记作家。赖麦锡博学多才、精通多国语言，他热衷于搜集欧洲各国探险家发回的关于地理发现的报道，并将之翻译为意大利文整理出版。

④ 《航海与旅行》，意大利文本，威尼斯，1559—1565年。该书收录了包括马可·波罗（Marco Polo）、尼科洛·达·康提（Niccolò Da Conti）、麦哲伦（Ferdinand Magellan）在内的多位探险家的第一手报道，第一卷于1555年出版，次年出版第三卷，由于送印前手稿毁于火灾，第二卷1559年才出版。该书是欧洲第一本航海游记集，开创了后来风靡欧洲的同类作品的先河。

⑤ 曼努埃尔·德·法利亚·俄·索萨（Manuel de Faria y Sousa，1590—1649），葡萄牙历史学家、诗人，多用西班牙文写作。

⑥ 《葡萄牙的亚洲》，西文本，里斯本，1666年。本书为三卷本，1666—1675年在里斯本出版。J Stevens将其译为英文，名为《葡萄牙的亚洲：葡萄牙人发现并征服印度的历史》（*The Portuguese Asia: Or the History of the Discovery and Conquest of India by the Portuguese*），1695年在伦敦出版。

⑦ 斯比塞尔（Theophilus Spizelius，1639—1691），德国路德宗教士，奥格斯堡圣詹姆士教堂高级牧师。

⑧ 《中国文学》，拉丁文本，阿姆斯特丹，1660年。该书介绍了《易图》，并详述太极阴阳八卦学说，在已知文献中首次将《易图》称为"binarium"（二进制）。

（续表）

序号	作者	书名	出版地	出版时间
40	**Trigault**, Nicolas[①]	*De Christiana expeditione apud Sinas ex P. M. Riccius*[②]	Augsburg	1615
41	Ibid	*Histoire de l'expédition chrestienne au royaume de la Chine*[③]	Lyon	1616

二、《人类理解论》所引用的关于中国的书籍

在《人类理解论》（第四、五版）中，洛克明确列出的关于中国的参考书有：

（一）法王特使拉·洛贝尔（Simon de La Loubère）出使暹罗的记述，指的是《暹罗国纪》（*Du royaume du Siam*）。该书的法文本1691年在阿姆斯特丹出版，洛克还收藏了该书的英译本[④]。另外，仔细翻检洛克藏书总目，我们发现洛克在撰写《人类理解论》（第四版）时参考了数本法王特使撰写的暹罗行纪，除拉·洛贝尔的《暹罗国纪》外，还包括布尔什（Jacques de Bourges）的《贝鲁特主教行纪》（*Relation du Voyage de Mons L'Evêque de Beryte*，法文本，1666年巴黎出版）；施瓦兹（François Timoleon de Choisy）的《暹罗行纪》（*Journal du voyage de Siam*，法文本，1687年阿姆斯特丹出版），该藏本封底内页有洛克亲笔手写的一行页码表；塔夏尔（Guy Tachard）的《暹罗行纪》（*Voyage de Siam*，法文本，1687年阿姆斯特丹出版）。在洛克藏书中，后两本《暹罗行纪》合订为一册。此外，洛克还收藏了的塔夏尔《暹罗行纪2》（*Second voyage au*

[①] 金尼阁（Nicolas Trigault，1577—1629），法国耶稣会士，1610年来华，主要在南京传教。在华期间，金尼阁与李之藻、杨廷筠交往密切，并深受龙华民的赏识。1613年，他受龙华民特遣返罗马晋见教皇，向教廷请准以中文举行弥撒。返欧途中，他把利玛窦的回忆录手稿《基督教远征中国史》由意大利文翻译成拉丁文，并作了补充和润色，定名改为《利玛窦中国札记》。这本著作刊印后，在欧洲引起轰动，耶稣会内掀起了到中国传教的热潮。1615年6月，金尼阁获得教皇诏谕，允许中国教士用本国文字举行宗教仪式，准许当地人士任神职，并可用中文翻译《圣经》。

[②] 《基督教远征中国史》（《利玛窦中国札记》），拉丁文本，奥古斯堡，1615年。

[③] 《基督教远征中国史》，法文本，里昂，1616年。

[④] *A new historical relation of the Kingdom of Siam*, by A. P. Gen. R. S. S. 2 vols in 1, London, 1693.

Siam，法文本，1689年巴黎出版）。很明显，洛克经过阅读和比较，在撰写《人类理解论》（第四版）时在数本暹罗行纪中选择了最新出版的，同时也是最权威的一种——拉·洛贝尔的《暹罗国纪》。

（二）驻华传教士尤其是耶稣会士的报道。洛克认为他们"一面虽然十分赞美中国，一面亦异口同声地告诉我们说：中国底统治阶级——士大夫们——都固守中国的旧教，都是纯粹的无神论者"①。如上文所述，洛克收藏了大量来华传教士撰写的关于中国的书籍。通过大量阅读，洛克得出两个结论：其一，来华传教士对中国的基本态度是赞美的；其二，他们一致认为"中国的统治阶级都是无神论者"。

（三）闵明我的著作和《华人礼仪史》，洛克将它们视为关于中国最重要的参考文献。其中闵明我的著作指的是《中华帝国历史、政治、伦理及宗教概述》（*Tratados historicos, politicos, ethicosy religious de la monarchia de China*）②。该书是道明我会士闵明我从1645年到1670年代的传教笔记，叙述了闵明我从西班牙出发经美洲到马尼拉，再从澳门到中国传教12年，后又从澳门到达罗马，最后在马德里定居的历程。值得注意的是，闵明我在礼仪之争中支持龙华民（Niccolò Longobardi）的观点，自称是"伟大的龙华民的忠诚学生"③。清初历狱时，闵明我在广州从利安当（Antonio Caballero）手中获得龙华民的《孔子及其教理》一文的残稿。该文介绍了《中庸》《论语》《易经》《诗经》《礼记》等儒家经典的许多观点，特别是大量引用了明代儒家的重要著作《性理大全》④。闵明我将之从葡萄牙文译为西班牙文并收入《中华帝国历史、政治、伦理及宗教概述》

---

① ［英］洛克著，关文运译：《人类理解论》（上册），北京：商务印书馆，1959年，第50页。

② 1676年该书以西班牙文在马德里出版并在欧洲广泛传播，有英、法、意等文字的译本以及多种缩写本，被当时欧洲思想界当作撰写中国历史的史料来源。这部庞大的著作分为七个论题，其中第六部分是作者的个人行记，英国学者J. S. Cummins将这部分进行校订后单独出版，收入剑桥大学1962年出版的"哈克卢特学会丛书"，中文译本见闵明我著，何高济，吴翊楣译：《上帝许给的土地：闵明我行记和礼仪之争》，郑州：大象出版社，2009年。

③ J. S. Cummins, *A Question of Rites: Friar Domingo Navarrete and Jesuits in China*, Cambridge, 1993, p. 159.

④ 参见张西平著：《儒学西传欧洲研究导论：16—18世纪中学西传的轨迹与影响》，北京：北京大学出版社，2016年，第70—71页。

一书的第五章。洛克对闵明我的著作非常推崇，在他的建议下，1704年丘吉尔兄弟出版四卷本《游记与旅行丛书》（A Collection of Voyages and Travels），并将该书的英译本收入第一卷。《华人礼仪史》则收藏在"拉夫雷斯档案"中，洛克在该书的封面和封底内页都用铅笔做了详细的页码记录，并依据该书写下了"中国笔记"。①

三、洛克"中国笔记"中列出的关于中国的书籍

洛克"中国笔记"的第一部分（MS. Locke. c.27., f.178）是一张A3纸大小的书目，用"摘录簿"的典型方法列出39本关于中国的书籍。该页的上方依次列出"A—Z"23个大写字母（未使用"I、U、W"三个字母），所列书籍按照书名或作者名的首字母分列于各字母以下。②

178
China

[1] **Gobien**, Eclairissement③ Bernard④ 00 Mar⑤ p. 352

[2] Elucidatio Continuatio⑥ p. 58. 90. 107

[3] Apologetics dissertatio⑦ ib. p. 97

[4] Nouveaux memoires sur l'etat present de la Chine, tome 3⑧, 12°, pars 98⑨

[5] Continuatio de l'histoire de l'Empereur et Ecclairissement⑩

[6] Eclairissment donné à Monseigneur le Duc de Maine sur les honneurs des

---

① 详见本书第七章。
② 本部分是我根据"中国笔记"手稿第一部分所列书目转写整理而成，安·泰尔博特提供了拉丁文书名的翻译，见MS Locke c. 27, f.178。
③ Clarification.
④ It's the publisher.
⑤ March 1700.
⑥ Explaination continued.
⑦ Dessertation in defence.
⑧ VOLUME 3.
⑨ Paris 1698.
⑩ Continuation of the history of the emperor.

chinois rendent à Confucius et aux morts[①] Bernard Aout 00[②] p. 225

[7] **Comte**. Lettre au Duc de Mayne sur les cérémonies de la Chine, elle explique en détail les cérémonies et Civilitez des Chinois[③] Bernard 00 Aout p. 226

[8] Lettre écrit au Pape par M^{ss} des Mission Etrangères auz sujet des cérémonies chinoises Elle est fort estimée des personnes de bon gout[④] Bernard 00 Aout p. 230

[9] **Ghirardini**. Relation d'un Voyage fait à la Chine sur l'Amphitrite en l'année 1698 p le Sr G...i peintre Italien[⑤] 12°

[Locke's comment] Cette relation est écrite d'une manière assez cavalière et assez burlesque. On voit clairement que l'auteur est une homme de lettres qui sait contre fait et qui a voulu prendre le charactère d'un peintre. Il y a des endroits écrits assez finement et qui ne ressemblent en rien au reste du stile[⑥] Bernard 00 Aout p. 234

[10] Réponse à la lettre des Messieurs des Missions étrangères au Pape sur les cérémonies des Chinoises[⑦] Bernard 00. Nov. 590.

[11] Apologie des Dominicains[⑧] 12° 99

[12] Apologie des Dominicain second vol. Bernard Avril 00[⑨] p. 473

[13] Continuatio Historia Cultus S[⑩]

---

① Clarification given to my Lord the Duke de Maine on the honours which the Chinese pay to Confucius and the dead.

② August 1700.

③ Letter to the Duke de Maine on ceremonies on China is explained in detail the ceremonies and civilization of the Chinese.

④ Letter written to the pope by my lords of the mission to foreigner on the subject of the ceremonies of the Chinese which is highly esteemed by persons of good taste.

⑤ Account of a journey made to China on the Amphitrite (name of ship) in the year 1698 by Segnior (Mr. in Italian) Ghirardini an Italian painter.

⑥ [Locke's comment] This account is written in a manner quite funny and amusing. It's clear that the author is a man of letters who wants to present himself in the character of a painter. There are some passages which are quite finely written and do not resemble the rest in style.

⑦ A reply to the letter of Messieurs (Mr. in French) of the French mission to foreigners to the pope on the ceremonies of the Chinese.

⑧ Defense of the Dominican's position.

⑨ April 1700.

⑩ Continuation of Historia Cultus Sinensium.

[14] ~~Historia Cultus Sinensium vol. 1.2~~

[15] Préjugés légitimes en faveur du Décret d' Alexander. 7. De.[①] Bernard <u>00</u> Nov. 591

[16] De Sinensium ritibus Alexandri 7^{mi} papa decrete permissis de[②] Bernard 00 Nov. p 592

[17] Quatrième lettre d'un docteur en théologie de l'ordre St Dominique sur l'Idolâtries et les superstitions de la Chine[③] de: Bernard <u>00</u> Nov: 592

[18] Cinquième lettre[④] ib. 594

[19] Sixième lettre[⑤] ib.

[20] ~~Lettre de l'Abbe de Lionne~~[⑥]

[21] Lettre d'un D^r de la faculté de Paris à une autre D^r sur les propositions dénoncées en Sorbonnes[⑦] Bernard <u>00</u> 594

[22] Monseigneurs de la facultié de la Théologie de Paris contre le propositions extraites des Nouveaux mémoires sur l'estat présent de la Chine; de l'histoire de l'édit de l'Empereur de la Chine; et de la lettre sur les protestations des Jésuites contre censure[⑧] Bernard Jan 01 p. 111

---

① Pope Alexander's decree of the Chinese rites.

② Of the Chinese rites Pope Alexander's decree.

③ A false letter from a doctor of theology of the order of St. Dominic on the idolatries and superstitions of the Chinese.

④ Fifth letter.

⑤ Sixth letter.

⑥ Letter from the Abbe de Lionne (a missionary who spent a lot of time in China, a friend and correspondent of Malebranche and an opponent of the Jesuits). 巴黎外方传教会的阿尔蒂斯·德·利阿纳（中国名字叫梁宏仁）是马勒伯朗士的好友，在中国居住多年，参与了"礼仪之争"，并在康熙皇帝下令逮捕他们之前返回巴黎。他向马氏介绍了中国的官学，并多次恳求他写一本小册子来批驳中国哲学特别是"理"这一观念的无神论的错误，来帮助他们在中国的传教事业。应其要求，马氏写了《一个基督教哲学家和一个中国哲学家的对话——论上帝的存在和本性》，1708年出版。

⑦ Letter from a doctor of the faculty of Paris to another doctor on the propositions denouced by the Sorbonnes.

⑧ The gentlemen of the faculty of theology of Paris against propositions exacted from the Nouveaux memoires on the present state of China; and the history of the edict of the emperor of China; and of the letter of protestation from the Jesuits against censure.

[23] Réponse de la censure[①], ib. p. 112

[24] Remarques d'un Dr en Théologies sur la protestations des Jésuites, avec une réponse au nouveau libelle de ces pères contre la censure de Sorbonne[②] Bernard: Jan 01. p 114

[25] Notizie ritorno all'uso de voce Sinensi <u>Tien</u> Coelum et <u>Xangti</u> Alti dominus[③] Continuatio Hist. p. 66

[26] Notizie circa l'uso delle [.] elle celle parole Cinesi <u>Kingtien</u> coelum colito[④] continuatio. p. 66

[27] Ristretto delle notizie circa l'uso della voce Cinesi Xangti[⑤] continuatio p. 66

[28] **Tellier**, Defensio Novorum Christianorum[⑥] continuatio. p. 8. 9. 90

[29] Breve ristretto delle notitie gia dedotte circa delle tabelle[⑦] de: Continuatio. p. 66

[30] **Antonÿ a St. Maria**, relatio sectarum Sina[⑧]. Continuatio. p. 7. 84. 85. 89. 107. 110

[31] Responsum Memoriali Dr Charmot continuatio[⑨]. p. 73

[32] Observationes re [...] eales patrum Societatis[⑩]. Continuatio. p. 73

[33] Observationes in [...] reverendissi Di. Maigrot[⑪]. Continuatio 73

[34] Disputatio Telleriana defensiones novorum Christianorum[⑫]. Continuatio. p. 85

---

① Response to criticism.
② Remarks of a doctor of theology on the protestations of the Jesuits with a response to a new pamphlet from these fathers against the censure of the Sorbonne.
③ Notes on the use of the Chinese words *Tien* (Heaven) and *Xangti* (High Lord).
④ Notes about the use of these Chinese words *King Tien* (worship heaven).
⑤ Summary of notes about the use of the Chinese word *Xangti*.
⑥ Defense of the new Christians.
⑦ A brief summary of the previous notes about the tablets.
⑧ An account of the sects of China.
⑨ A document in response from Dr. Charmot.
⑩ Observations from the fathers of the Society.
⑪ Observations of very reverent Lord Maigrot.
⑫ Disputing Tellier's defense for new Christians.

[35] Sarpetrÿ epistola ad Sacrum Congregationem①. Continuatio. p. 107A

[36] Memoriale procuratoris Societatis②. Continuatio. p. 91

[37] ˣHist. Cultus Sinensium③ 8° Col: <u>00</u> ˣContinuatio. Hist④ de 00

[38] ˣ**Lionne**, Lettre de Mr l'abbe de Lionne⑤ <u>00</u>

[39] ˣLettre d'une personne de Piété sur une [...] Jésuites⑥ 12. <u>01</u>

[40] ˣ**Gabiani**, dissertatio apologetic de Sinensium ritibus politicus⑦ 8° Jul <u>00</u>

第三节　小结

在17世纪的欧洲，书籍是人们获取关于世界知识的最主要媒介。洛克对非欧洲经验的认识主要来自于他所阅读和收藏的游记地理类书籍，洛克关于中国的知识则主要来源于他所阅读和收藏的关于中国的书籍。纵观洛克的中国藏书，我们不难发现以下特点：

其一，出版时间相对集中。

洛克的中国藏书中出版于16世纪的有8本，占19.5%；出版于17世纪及18世纪初的有33本，占80.5%；其中出版于1697—1704年这8年的就有18本，占总数的43.9%（见表6-3）。

表 6-3　洛克中国藏书的出版时间

出版时间		数量	比例
16 世纪		8	19.5%
17 世纪及 18 世纪初	1697 年以前	15	36.6%
	1697—1704 年	18	43.9%
总计		41	100%

---

① Sarpetrÿ letter to the secred congregation.

② A document from the procurator of the Society.

③ Historia Cultus Sinensium.

④ Continuation to Historia Cultus Sinensium.

⑤ Letter from L'abbe de Lionne.

⑥ Letter from a person of piety on one [...] Jesuits.

⑦ Dissertation in defense of the Chinese political/civil rites.

从出版时间来看，洛克的中国藏书符合"礼仪之争"的进展和欧洲出版关于中国书籍的总体情况：1697年阎当训令导致教廷重议礼仪，1704年教皇克莱芒十一世颁布禁止基督徒行中国礼仪的敕谕。在敕谕并未公布的情况下，1705—1707年间教皇特使多罗访华并在中国掀起轩然大波，康熙皇帝也被卷入"礼仪之争"。因此，1697—1710年是"礼仪之争"的最高潮。随着"礼仪之争"的进展，从17世纪末开始欧洲掀起一场规模浩大的有关中国礼仪的文本运动。据统计，在"礼仪之争"的高潮期，有关文本无论刊与未刊的数量都处于峰值，以耶稣会士讨论中国礼仪的作品为例，1698—1707年刊布的作品有34部，其中1700年是这一巅峰阶段的最高点，这一年耶稣会士关于"礼仪之争"的文本有9部在欧洲出版。①

同时，洛克所藏中国书籍的出版时间与洛克开始密切关注中国的时间也是吻合的：洛克在1699年出版的《人类理解论》（第四版）中首次提到中国；根据笔者对洛克书信的梳理，中国从1696年开始频繁出现在洛克与亲友的私人书信中并一直持续到1704年洛克去世前夕；而根据笔者对洛克"中国笔记"手稿的研究，"中国笔记"的成稿时间大约在1702年左右。

由此可见，17—18世纪之交的十数年是"礼仪之争"的最高潮，是欧洲全面关注和认识中国的起点，也是洛克"中国观"最终形成的关键时期。

其二，种类和立场多样。

洛克的中国藏书可以分成地理游记类书籍和涉及"中国礼仪"的论争类文献两大类。前者为旅行家、外交人员、传教士、史学家等撰写的关于中国历史、地理、宗教和风土人情的介绍性书籍，无明显修会立场，共22本；后者是"礼仪之争"中对立的两个阵营（耶稣会士和反耶稣会的其他修会）之间的论争性文献，共18本。②从数量上看，地理游记类书籍略多于论争性文献。而在涉及"礼仪之

---

① 详见张国刚：《从中西初识到礼仪之争——明清传教士与中西文化交流》，北京：人民出版社，2003年，第505—507页，图7-1、表7-4和表7-5。
② 关于洛克藏书的修会立场，笔者只选择了那些立场鲜明的文献，比如卫匡国的《鞑靼战纪》和《中国上古史》虽然属于中国古代历史和地理类，但从立场到选材都贯彻着耶稣会适应政策，在礼仪之争中也是被攻击的重点，因此它们被列为代表耶稣会立场的文献。而卫匡国的数学老师——基歇尔的《中国图说》虽然影响极大，书中也大量使用了贯彻适应思想的传教士们的资料，但"书中占支配地位的思想是欧洲的赫尔墨斯思想，而不是耶稣会的适应思想"（见［美］孟德卫著，陈怡译：《奇异的国度：耶稣会适应政策及汉学的起源》，郑州：大象出版社，2010年，第131页），因此未被列为代表耶稣会立场的文献。

争"的论争性文献中，耶稣会士的作品10本，反耶稣会的作品8本，双方文献的数量基本持平（见表6-4）。可见，洛克关于中国宗教的结论并不是只基于一家之言的成见，而是综合了解关于中国文化的大量信息后得出的审慎结论。

表 6-4 洛克藏"礼仪之争"文献的修会立场

立场	作者	作品
耶稣会	白晋	《康熙皇帝传》，巴黎，1697 年
	李明	《中国近事报道》，巴黎，1697 年
		《论中国礼仪书》，列日，1700 年
	刘迪我	《中国现势报道》，巴黎，1662 年
	郭弼恩	《论中国的政治礼仪》，列日，1700 年
	郭弼恩，李明	《中国近事报道》（第三卷），巴黎，1698 年
	卫匡国	《中国上古史》，慕尼黑/阿姆斯特丹，1658/1659 年
		《鞑靼战纪》，阿姆斯特丹，1661 年
	金尼阁	《基督教远征中国史》（拉丁文本），奥格斯堡，1615 年
		《基督教远征中国史》（法文本），里昂，1616 年
反耶稣会	诺埃尔	《为入华道明我会传教士辩护》，科隆，1699 年
		《中国礼仪与希腊罗马偶像崇拜之比较》，科隆，1700 年
		《论中国礼仪——道明我会修士（诺埃尔）致李明神父的信》，科隆，1700 年
		《一位基督徒对耶稣会士关于中国宗教和礼仪论述的驳斥》，科隆，1701 年
	匿名	《华人礼仪史》，科隆，1700 年
		《华人礼仪史续篇》，科隆，1700 年
	闵明我	《与 Diego Moralez 神父论在华耶稣会》，科隆，1701 年
		《中华帝国历史、政治、伦理及宗教概述》，马德里，1676 年

第七章 "中国笔记"的直接知识来源:《华人礼仪史》①

第一节 洛克"中国笔记"直接知识来源的认定

作为一本典型的读书笔记,洛克"中国笔记"应该是洛克根据关于"中国人的宗教和哲学"这一主题的一本或几本专著所做的摘要。洛克"中国笔记"的第一部分列出了39本礼仪之争中出版的关于中国的专著,我们是如何确定《华人礼仪史》(Historia Cultus Sinensium,下文简称HCS)是"中国笔记"最直接的知识来源的呢?

首先,洛克在《人类理解论》关于中国的论述的最后说:"关于这种情形,我们可以参阅《游记与旅行丛书》(第一卷)收录的闵明我的著作和《华人仪礼史》。"② 这说明洛克在1699年出版的《人类理解论》(第四版)引用中国为无

---

① 洛克"中国笔记"索引中提到的《华人礼仪史》的相关章节的拉丁文原文见本书附录3,英文译稿见本书附录4。作为"礼仪之争"的重要文献,《华人礼仪史》只有拉丁文本,本书首次将相关章节译为英文,这是本书的重点之一。
② [英]洛克著,关文运译:《人类理解论》(上册),北京:商务印书馆,1959年,第50页,笔者对译文稍做修改。

神论社会时主要参考的就是上述两本书,这与"中国笔记"的写作时间非常接近,因此"中国笔记"的主要参考文献也非常有可能是这两本书。而闵明我的游记集以描述传教经历和见闻为主,与"中国笔记"偏理论性的内容不太一致,因而我猜测HCS更有可能是"中国笔记"的直接知识来源。

其次,"中国笔记"正文中(手稿第197页和第201页)两次明确提到参考HCS一书中的相关页码①,其中第197页(见彩图10)为"祭孔"主题的第8页也是最后一页,该页手稿上数第4段原文为"The account of Confucius & that worship paid him read in the words of Roberedo, the Jesuits, Hist Cult Sinensium, p. 453."(对于孔子的记述和祭孔仪式参见耶稣会士罗博雷托在《华人礼仪史》第453页的记述。)第201页(见彩图11)是"祭祖"主题的第2页,在该页手稿右侧的空白部分上方洛克专门做了一个注释:"Vid Hist Cultus Sinensium p. 460 how the ceremony was performed in a Temple wherein were six altars."(见《华人礼仪史》第460页,一座内设六个供桌的家庙所举行的祭祖仪式。)因此,我初步锁定HCS为"中国笔记"的直接知识来源。

再次,我在牛津大学博得礼图书馆亲自查阅了"拉夫雷斯档案"中洛克收藏的HCS,发现该书整体保存相当完好,但边角损坏比较严重,很显然是曾被大量翻阅过。按照洛克的习惯,除了特定的关于版本和价格的标记外,洛克极少在藏书中划线或做标记,本书也不例外。但洛克在该书封面后的空白衬页(见彩图8)上用铅笔写了一行字:"Celsus says the Seres (which I take to be Chineses) had noe god Origen contra Celsus tt 7° versus finem"[克理索②说赛里斯人③(我认为

---

① 事实上,"中国笔记"中还有一处提到HCS中的页码,即手稿第199页(B.L., MS. Locke. c.27., f.199)右上角小标题下方,注明"240",指的就是HCS的第240页。因为此处只是标注了对应页码,但未明确注明引用内容,因而本书未将其正式列入。

② 克理索(Celsus),2世纪后期希腊柏拉图主义哲学家,早期基督教的反对者,曾著《真话》(*The True Word*,约177年),为目前所知最早的全面攻击基督教的作品,但该书早已散佚,我们只能从俄利根所著的《驳克理索》一书的引用和驳斥中了解该书的大概内容。克里索似乎对古希腊宗教很感兴趣,并了解犹太人的逻各斯,因此《真话》很可能成书于反基督教时代的亚历山大里亚。克里索在书中攻击耶稣的神迹,说"耶稣靠巫术施了神迹"。

③ 赛里斯(Seres),希腊文,意为"丝国",古希腊对中国的称呼。这一称呼最早出现在公元前400年希腊作家克泰夏斯(Ctesias)的作品中,普林尼(Pline L'Ancie, 23—79)在《自然史》(*Historie Naturelle*)一书中也提到"赛里斯人"。详见张西平:《欧洲早期汉学史——中西文化交流与西方汉学的兴起》,北京:中华书局,2009年,第2—4页。

指中国人）不信神。——俄利根①《驳克理索》卷七近结尾处②]。而在该书封底内页（见彩图9），洛克用铅笔列出14行页码。因为在洛克的藏书中，洛克亲自做如此细致标记的书籍数量极少，这说明洛克极为重视该书，并且非常仔细阅读过该书，很可能做了摘抄或笔记。因而，我进一步锁定HCS为"中国笔记"的直接知识来源。

最后，"中国笔记"的"索引"中所列的关于各个主题的页码与HCS中各主题的页码一致。"中国笔记"手稿第212页正反面是"索引"部分，正面按照"中国笔记"正文顺序依次列出其中涉及的12个主题，编号为A—L；背面大致按照参考书的页码顺序列出各主题在该参考书中所涉及的页码，集中在该书的第3—244页。我逐一将"索引"中的页码与HCS相对照，发现除个别笔误外，两者能够很好地对应起来。至此，我基本确定HCS就是"中国笔记"的直接知识来源。

那么，HCS到底是一部什么样书呢？洛克又是为什么在大量关于中国的书籍中选中它作为"中国笔记"的直接知识来源呢？

第二节 《华人礼仪史》是一本什么样的书？

如前文所述，洛克终其一生都非常钟爱游记地理类书籍，并在自己的作品中大量引用世界各地尤其是大航海新发现的地区和民族的风俗。在相当长的时间里，中国只是众多遥远的、与欧洲迥异的文明之一，并没有引起洛克特别的关注。除了在牛津时代的两篇未刊论文中用到与中国相关的例子外，洛克再未提到过中国。在《人类理解论》的初稿和初版中列举了很多不同地区的风俗，其中也没有中国。1689年《人类理解论》的发表引发了旷日持久的论争，其中主要集中

---

① 俄利根（Origenes Adamantius，185—254），基督教著名的神学家和哲学家，生于亚历山大里亚，卒于该撒利亚。在神学上，他采用希腊哲学的概念，提出"永恒受生"的概念来解说圣父与圣子关系，对基督教影响至今。他的著作对基督教神学发展有很大的影响力，但是他的数项神学主张被在第二次君士坦丁堡公会议中被定为异端，因此天主教会与东正教会皆未将他列为圣人。他著有维护基督教的巨著《驳克理索》（*Contra Celsum*）等作品。

② 《驳克理索》原文为希腊文，洛克标注"tt"表示"翻译本"；"7°"表示"第七卷"；"versus finem"为拉丁文，意为"towards the end"，即"近结尾处"。

第七章 "中国笔记"的直接知识来源:《华人礼仪史》

于1696—1699年的与斯氏论战的焦点之一就是洛克所引用的无神论社会的例子是否恰当。斯氏攻击洛克引用的南美和南非的无神论社会的信息来源不可靠,进而提出如此野蛮的人不配称为人。这样的指控迫使洛克开始寻找更加有说服力的无神论社会的例证。

与此同时,在华耶稣会士与托钵修士之间的"礼仪之争"已经从罗马天主教廷内部扩展到知识界甚至整个欧洲社会,"出版社源源不断地流出各种支持或反对耶稣会士的书和小册子,欧洲一时间几乎被关于'礼仪之争'的论文、书籍和宣传册淹没。……仿佛礼仪问题对欧洲人比在中国的传教士更重要似的"①。中国迅速占领了欧洲主流思想家的视野,洛克与他的论敌们也不例外。如上文所述,斯氏在《宗教的起源》一书中就曾引用耶稣会士关于中国宗教的论点。

在这样的背景下,作为一个文明高度发展的强大的东方帝国,中国开始从众多异文化中凸显出来,真正引起洛克的兴趣。从1696年开始,洛克的书信中常常提到中国,他开始积极地透过各种渠道打听关于中国的消息,比如旅欧的中国人、英国与中国的贸易、欧洲最新出版的关于中国的书籍和地图集等。而当时关于中国的最新的也是最权威的信息来源就是"礼仪之争"中在华各修会发回欧洲的报告,洛克关于中国的藏书中近一半都是1697年以后出版的,"中国笔记"第一部分的书目中所列的也都是涉及"礼仪之争"的书籍,其中就包括HCS。

HSC的全名为《华人礼仪史——关于华人敬礼的各种文献,法国宗座代牧、其他传教士与耶稣会传教士之间的争论》(*The History of the Chinese Rites or various writings about the Chinese rites debated among the French apostolic vicars and other missionaries and the fathers of the Society of Jesus*)。《洛克藏书》中该书的条目为:"688. Historia Cultus Sinensium. 8°Col.〔17〕00 p. $\overline{676}$. $\frac{7}{10}$. Oak Spring. 12-line page list in pencil."②没有作者信息。事实上,HCS在《洛克藏书》和其他书籍中一直被认为是作者不详的文献。除了作者不详外,该书的出版地也很成问题。1700年7月7日,杜·波从阿姆斯特丹发给洛克的信中说:"*Un libraire de cette ville imprime en latin les pieces du procez pendant a Rome entre les*

---

① 张国刚:《从中西初识到礼仪之争——明清传教士与中西文化交流》,人民出版社,2003年,第519页。
② John Harrison & Peter Laslett, *The Library of John Locke*, Oxford University Press, 1965, p. 106.

Jesuites et les autres missionaires de la Chine sur les ceremonies nationales que lon peut permettre aux Chretiens. le livre sera curieux par la discussion des dogmes et de la religion de ces peuples."（这里的书商正在发行一些来自于罗马正在进行的论争的拉丁文文献，该论争是在耶稣会士和其他驻华传教士之间进行的，主要论辩哪些民族礼仪是基督徒可以接受的。这应该是本有意思的书，因为它谈到了这些人的信仰和宗教。）[1]德比尔《洛克书信集》的脚注中说："*Historia Cultus Sinensium seu Varia Scripta de Cultibus Sinarum, inter vicarious apostolicos Gallos aliosque missionarios, et patres Societatis Jesu controversis, oblate Innocentio XII...*, Cologne, 1700; a continuation, 1700. The publisher is Jean Louis de Lorme, c. 1666/70—c.1724/6; publishing in Amsterdam 1694—1711; later resident in Paris: van Eeghen, i. 15-20, etc.; vol. ii, nos. 57-58. L.L., nos. 688-689."[2]因此杜·波在信中提到的这本关于正在进行的法庭辩论的书就是HCS，那么该书的出版地应该是阿姆斯特丹，而不是科隆。在当时的欧洲，罗马教廷内部的文件是不允许外传的，虽然当时很多有关礼仪之争的文件透过各种渠道流入出版社，然而只能暗地进行。加上该书多处涉及唯物论，当时无论罗马教廷还是世俗当局都对此深恶痛绝，因此HCS在当时应该是一本非常有争议的作品，出版商很可能试图通过伪造出版地来躲避审查。当然，也有可能当时的阿姆斯特丹和科隆同时出版该书，那么就足见其畅销程度。

我们从现有图书目录文献中可以得出以下结论：HCS是一本关于当时正在罗马教廷进行的耶稣会士与其他传教士关于中国礼仪问题的法庭辩论的文献合集，作者不详，伪出版地为科隆，真实出版地为阿姆斯特丹，出版时间是1700年夏。

我手中有一本HCS，可能是Bibliotic Baudcloo图书馆的影印本，经过与"拉夫雷斯档案"所藏HCS对照，该影印本与洛克所用的是同一版本，这极大地方便了我们的研究。我们先来看看该书的两张标题页：

---

[1] E.S. De Beer (ed.), *The Correspondence of John Locke*, V6, Oxford: Clarendon Press, 1981, pp. 647-648, Letter 2600.

[2] Ibid., p. 647.

第七章 "中国笔记"的直接知识来源：《华人礼仪史》　241

图7-1　HCS出版标题页　　　　　图7-2　HCS正文标题页

出版标题页1除了包括该书的全名外，还提供了该书的写作目的："献给教皇英诺森十二世及所有宗教裁判所负责这个案子的主教们"，还补充说："本书的附录是耶稣会士在礼仪之争中的作品"，另外注明出版地点为"科隆"，出版时间为1700年。正文标题页则指明本书的内容是"论耶稣会士呈给宗教裁判所的关于阎当主教训令的观点"，并且明确地说该书的作者是夏尔莫（Nicolaum Charmot，即Nicolas Charmot）、阎当（Domini Maigrot，即Charles Maigrot）以及其他在华的巴黎外方传教会士，另外注明该书的发表日期是1698年7月29日。该书由三本独立的书合订而成，其中第1—278页是正文部分，由五个部分组成："第一部分　关于祭祖和祭孔""第二部分　关于祖先牌位""第三部分　关于'上帝''天'以及它们在中文里的意思""第四部分　阎当主教训令的第二点——关于'敬天'牌匾""第五部分　阎当主教训令的最后一点以及观察员（指耶稣会士代表）对其提出的各种侮辱性和不诚实的攻击"；第177—278页为1698年夏尔莫写的一本小册子，名为《论观察员和其他耶稣会士攻击阎当主教训令的主要论点》，共分三个部分；第279页开始是大量论文汇编，对耶稣会士提交给教皇的辩论材料所做的逐条攻击，其中大部分论文出自夏尔莫之手。后两本书可以被视为附录。因此，HCS是代表巴黎外方传教会观点与耶稣会在罗马进行宗教法庭辩论的文件合集，书中收录了很多外方传教会士和其他传教士的证词，也包括耶稣会士的证词，全书捍卫的是阎当训令，但最主要的作者和编者是夏尔莫。该书应该在法庭辩论期间流出，即1698年7月29日，但最终出版是在1700年。

依据这些线索，我们就比较容易在礼仪之争的历史文献中找到关于该书的更多信息了。例如，张国刚先生在《从中西初识到礼仪之争——明清传教士与中西文化交流》中提到："阎当1693年底派外方传教会会友夏尔莫（Nicolas Charmot）代表他去罗马递交训令，同时还有一封信，信又附带随函，都写于1693年11月10日。"① 该页注释6还说对于当时阎当派往罗马的使者到底是夏尔莫还是Louis Quemener有不同的记载，但不论有无其他代表随行，夏尔莫的确是阎当派往罗马教廷的特使。除了阎当的训令和信，"夏尔莫本人还另外带去一整套收集来的反对中国礼仪和耶稣会士适应方法的记录和著述"②。不仅如此，当夏尔莫抵达罗马时，圣职部的神学委员会无暇研究这份训令，于是夏尔莫返回巴黎，让巴黎主教Louis A. de Noilles关注此事，巴黎主教按惯例将训令交付索邦（Sorbonne）神学院审查，并直接导致了1700年李明的《中国现势新志》被禁。③ 而夏尔莫的"炒作"也成功地引起了罗马的关注，"1697年，圣职部在英诺森十二世的指示下开始调查阎当的声明"④。于是开始了旷日持久的论辩和调查，直到1704年11月20日圣职部颁发指令全面禁止基督徒执行祭祖祭孔礼仪。因此，张国刚先生说："礼仪之争在欧洲起先只是多明我会士黎玉范和耶稣会士卫匡国在罗马的神学讨论，继而发展为神学家阿尔诺（Antoine Arnauld）和耶稣会士勒泰利埃之间的学院背景下的讨论，而当夏尔莫将阎当的训令带到巴黎加以鼓动之后，礼仪问题则成为全体欧洲公众、特别是巴黎感兴趣的事件。"⑤ 基于上述信息，我们有理由相信HCS很可能就是当时夏尔莫"另外带去的一整套收集来反对中国礼仪和耶稣会士适应方法的记录和著述"中部分文件的合集。

---

① 张国刚：《从中西初识到礼仪之争——明清传教士与中西文化交流》，北京：人民出版社，2003年，第443页。
② 同上书，第444页。
③ 详见上书，第444—445页。
④ 同上书，第445页。
⑤ 同上书，第518页。

又如，张西平先生在《欧洲早期汉学史——中西文化交流与西方汉学的兴起》中提到1700年莱布尼茨给维利乌斯的信中说："虽然有几个朋友指责我赞同您的传教事业，我想是因为有人将您新发展的教徒斥为崇拜偶像者，但我还是很高兴看到在罗马成书、不久前在科隆印刷的论文集终于得以出版，该书的标题让人信赖，而且我仍然没有发现什么可以改变我观点的东西。"……"这里所说的书就是阎当和Giovanni Jacopo Fatinelli两人联合在1700年出版的《中国人的礼仪以及有关中国礼仪的各种著作史》。"①此处提供了两个重要信息，首先，莱布尼茨在1700年写给维利乌斯的信②中提到HCS，并说该书"在罗马成书、不久前在科隆印刷"，与上文杜·波1700年写给洛克的信相对照，HCS很可能是同时在科隆和阿姆斯特丹两地出版；其次，张先生认为HCS是"阎当和Giovanni Jacopo Fatinelli两人联合出版"的。关于第二点，我最初以为是张先生的笔误，然而世界最大的图书资源搜索网站所提供的关于HCS的标准图书信息为："Fatinelli, G. J., & Petit, M. J.-G. (1700). *Historia cultus Sinensium, seu varia scripta de cultibus Sinarum, inter vicarios apostolicos Gallos aliosque missionarios, & patres Societatis Jesu controversis, oblata Innocentio XII. pontifici maximo et Sacrae congregationi eminentissimorum cardinalium dirimendae huic causae praepositorum: adjuncta appendice scricptorum patrum Societatis Jesu de eadem controversia.*

---

① 张西平：《欧洲早期汉学史——中西文化交流与西方汉学的兴起》，北京：中华书局，2009年，第646页。

② 我在《中国近事：为了照亮我们这个时代的历史》书后所附的李文潮先生搜集整理的《编年表：莱布尼茨与中国》中并未找到关于这封信的信息，倒是有一封1700年1月18日莱布尼茨写给维利乌斯的信，信中"莱布尼茨强调应该对中国的习俗有个合乎理性的解释，并且寄去自己的短文《论尊孔》。在这篇文章中，莱布尼茨提到了龙华民和（多明我会的）闵明我。（全集I, 18, 第168封信；中国通信，110—115）"。参见［德］莱布尼茨著，［法］梅谦立、杨保筠译：《中国近事：为了照亮我们这个时代的历史》，郑州：大象出版社，2005年，第205页。张西平先生和李文潮先生所注明的在Rita Widmaier编的《中国通信》（*Leibniz korrespondiert mit China*, 1990）一书中的位置是相同的，因此指的应该是同一封信。1月1日应该是根据旧的儒略历（Julian calendar）定下的日期。莱布尼茨在这封信的空白处做了关于HCS的注释，后来又划去了。张西平先生也提到："根据Widmaier在整理这篇手稿时的发现，在手稿中写有阎当的《中国人的礼仪以及有关中国礼仪的各种著作史》一书的书名，显然他是看过这本书的，实际上可以说是对阎当和龙华民等人的一个小小的回击。"（张西平：《欧洲早期汉学史——中西文化交流与西方汉学的兴起》，北京：中华书局，2009年，第655页。）

Coloniae, M. DCC." 也将Giovanni Jacopo Fatinelli作为作者之一。关于G. J. Fatinelli我们只知道他是当时与巴黎外方传教士一起工作的意大利传教士，曾于1709年与Giuseppe Maria Tabaglio共同出版的意大利文的《关于中国诉讼案的反思：铎罗禁教敕令消息传至欧洲以来》（*Considerazioni sù la scrittura intitolata Riflessioni sopra la causa della Cina dopo venuto in Europa il decreto dell'Emo di Tournon*），目前没有任何证据表明他与HCS有关。至于M. J.-G. Petit，到目前为止，我们对他一无所知，也未发现他与HCS有关。不过，1700年同时在科隆出版的似乎还有HCS的续篇，名为*Continuatio Historiæ Cultus Sinensium, Seu Varia Scripta De Cultibus Sinarum, inter Vicarios Apostolicos Gallos aliosque Missionarios, & Patres Societatis Jesu controversis*，我到目前为止并未见过该书。另外，在李文潮编《编年表：莱布尼茨与中国》中还提到一封1700年6月28日莱布尼茨收到的信："庞松为莱布尼茨通报了礼仪之争中赞成与反对的有关文章与书信，提到N. Charmot的《中国礼仪史》（*Historia cultus Sinensium*, 1700）以及《中国礼仪之争文献》（*Documenta controversiam missionarium apostolicorum imperii Sinici... conspectantia*, 1699）。（全集 I，18，第321封信）"①这是迄今为止，我找的唯一一份将夏尔莫作为HCS作者的文献。不论如何，HCS在当时是一部非常畅销的关于正在进行的礼仪之争的拉丁文文献集，目前学界对其作者信息的了解是模糊的甚至是错误的，根据该书的内容来看，其作者应为夏尔莫无疑。

第三节 小结

据统计，考狄书目②中关于"礼仪之争"的著作有近300部③。而洛克中国藏书中的同类作品有35种，"中国笔记"第一部分列出的关于礼仪之争的作品有39

---

① ［德］莱布尼茨著，［法］梅谦立、杨保筠译：《中国近事：为了照亮我们这个时代的历史》，郑州：大象出版社，2005年，第207页。
② Henri Cordier, *Bibliotheca Sinica*, vol. I, Paris, 1904.
③ 张西平先生的统计是"近260部"（张西平：《欧洲早期汉学史——中西文化交流与西方汉学的兴起》，北京：中华书局，2009年，第358页），吴莉苇的统计是近300部（吴莉苇：《当诺亚方舟遭遇伏羲神农——启蒙时代欧洲的中国上古史论争》，北京：中国人民大学出版社，2005年，第79页）。

种（其中有2种后来被洛克划掉了，其中就包括HCS）。那么，是什么原因促使洛克在众多同类作品中选择了HCS作为"中国笔记"几乎唯一的知识来源呢？我认为主要有以下三方面原因：

首先，HCS的主题与观点符合洛克的需要。HCS的主题正是洛克最关注的中国宗教问题，而论点刚好符合洛克想要证明的"中国的统治阶级——士大夫们——都是纯粹的无神论者"的结论，这是洛克选择该书的最重要原因。

其次，作者与材料的权威性。本书的作者夏尔莫是南京宗座代牧阎当派往罗马的特使，刚刚从中国带回第一手的信息，非常具有权威性；另外，因为本书是宗教法庭辩论文件的合集，论辩双方提出任何观点都引用了若干证人的证词，而每次引用证人证词时均对其可靠性进行了相当具体的说明，这无疑增加了该书的权威性。

最后，该书巨大的公众影响力。如上文所述，夏尔莫不仅准备了充分的论辩材料，并且精于曲线施压、宣传造势等"炒作"手段，阎当选择他作为特使实为明智之举。该书很可能在科隆和阿姆斯特丹两地同时出版，并莱布尼茨、杜·波等都第一时间在信件中提到该书，这些都说明该书的出版在当时非常轰动，是一本极具影响力的畅销书，对礼仪之争起到了推波助澜的作用。正如张国刚先生所说，礼仪之争在欧洲起先只是神学讨论，"而当夏尔莫将阎当的训令带到巴黎加以鼓动之后，礼仪问题则成为全体欧洲公众、特别是巴黎感兴趣的事件"[①]。

基于上述三个原因，洛克选择HCS作为"中国笔记"的直接知识来源就是意料中事了。

此外，关于"中国笔记"与HCS之间的关系，有三点应该引起重视：

其一，HCS虽然是"中国笔记"的直接知识来源，但并不是唯一知识来源。仔细对比"中国笔记"和HCS的相关章节，我们就会发现"中国笔记"中关于中国宗教和礼仪的很多观点和细节并非源自HCS，这些内容显然来自于洛克阅读的其他关于中国的书籍，其中很可能包括耶稣会士的作品。

其二，洛克只选取了HCS中关于中国宗教和礼仪的事实性描述，对于该书的

---

① 张国刚：《从中西初识到礼仪之争——明清传教士与中西文化交流》，北京：人民出版社，2003年，第518页。

主体——耶稣会士与其反对者的论争——置之不理。

其三，HCS代表了以阎当为首的巴黎外方传教士在"礼仪之争"中的立场，其中关于中国宗教的结论有二：（1）中国人是无神论者；（2）中国人是偶像崇拜者。本书对这两个结论之间的内在矛盾性暂不做讨论，但非常明确的是洛克对这两个结论的态度是截然相反的。在"中国笔记"中，洛克并未像在《人类理解论》中那样明确的声称"中国的统治阶级——士大夫们——都是纯粹的无神论者"，而是强调中国哲学的根本基础是"万物同一体"、中国人不相信"纯粹精神"和灵魂不朽、中国人的"天"和"上帝"指"物质的天"、"理"和"太极"指物质第一性，这些论述的自然结论就是"中国人的哲学是无神论"。同时，"中国笔记"明确地将"儒教"与"佛教""道教"分开，说后两者进行偶像崇拜，很明显的是洛克并不认为儒教信徒是偶像崇拜者。

综上，洛克"中国笔记"选取了HCS中关于中国宗教和礼仪的事实描述作为直接知识来源，综合了其他关于中国的书籍对于中国宗教的介绍，最终自然得出了"中国的统治阶级——士大夫们——都是纯粹的无神论者"的结论。洛克对于天主教内部的"礼仪之争"本身明显表现出疏离和漠然。

结　论

　　正如我在前言中所说，由于材料的缺乏，长期以来国内外学界均认为洛克与中国没有关系，这使得洛克思想研究和17世纪中西文化交流史研究的链条中都缺失了重要的一环。首先，作为英国经验论的重镇，洛克如果忽视包括中国在内的其他国家和民族的经验，这是不符合逻辑的，对此"莱布尼茨与中国"的研究专家方岚生先生发出了这样的诘问："作为'经验论者'的洛克，怎么会对非欧洲世界的经验如此无动于衷？"① 其次，洛克生活的时代（17世纪后半叶至18世纪初）正值中西文化交流的"蜜月期"，耶稣会士向欧洲输入的中国知识在欧洲思想界引起巨大反响，"礼仪之争"更是将中国置于欧洲公众舆论的风口浪尖，整个欧洲迅速掀起了一股"中国热"。作为兴趣广泛的藏书家和享誉欧洲的思想家，洛克如果身处这样的"中国热"当中却对中国无动于衷，这显然有违常理。牛津大学博得礼图书馆所藏洛克"拉夫雷斯档案"中"中国笔记"的发现和公开使我们找回了这重要的一环。

　　本书遵循西方"语文学"传统和中国"文献学"传统，从洛克"中国笔记"的文献来源和档案现状入手，对"中国笔记"手稿进行辩读、转写、翻译、注

---

① ［美］方岚生著，曾小五译，王蓉蓉校：《互照：莱布尼茨与中国》，"前言"，北京：北京大学出版社，2013年，第5页。

释和整理，力图将这一全新材料的原貌清晰完整地呈现出来；接着，对"中国笔记"追本溯源，整理分析"中国笔记"产生的时代背景、认识基础和知识来源，力图在中西文化交流史的语境下，从具体的文本材料中梳理出洛克的"中国观"。基于现有材料，本书得出以下初步结论：

1. 洛克"中国观"的核心是对中国宗教的看法，一言以蔽之，洛克认为："中国的统治阶级——士大夫们——都是纯粹的无神论者"。洛克《人类理解论》（第四版）第一卷第四章第八节首次明确提出这一观点，并且在之后的"中国笔记"中进行了具体阐述。

2. 洛克对中国的兴趣产生得早，关注开始得晚。本书对洛克藏书、著作和书信的整理与分析表明，游记地理类作品是洛克的一生所爱，其中就包括介绍中国的书籍，并且早在17世纪60年代洛克就在其早期未刊作品中引用过中国的风俗。然而洛克对中国专门、系统的关注大概开始于1696年左右，从那时起，洛克来往的书信中频繁出现关于中国的各种信息，很显然洛克正在多方搜集关于中国的资料；紧接着洛克在1699年发表的《人类理解论》（第四版）中明确表明对中国人信仰的看法；1702年左右，洛克写下了"中国笔记"系统讨论中国宗教问题。

3. 洛克"中国观"的知识来源是关于中国的游记地理类作品，尤其是"礼仪之争"中介绍中国文化的文献。基于对洛克藏书的整理与分析，洛克搜集了"礼仪之争"双方（即耶稣会士与其反对者）的主要作品，但不同于同时代的马勒伯朗士、莱布尼茨等思想家在"礼仪之争"中立场明确、积极参与的状态，洛克对"礼仪之争"始终表现出一种疏离、漠然的态度，这与洛克作为英国国教徒的宗教立场是分不开的。

4. 洛克"中国笔记"的相当篇幅是基于《华人礼仪史》所做的读书摘要，因而《华人礼仪史》是"中国笔记"的直接知识来源，但绝不是唯一知识来源。洛克选择耶稣会士的反对者阎当和夏尔莫的作品作为"中国笔记"的直接知识来源绝不是因为洛克在"礼仪之争"中站在了巴黎外方传教士的一边，最根本的原因是《华人礼仪史》明确而具体地论证了"中国人都是无神论者"的观点。洛克在"中国笔记"中只是选取了该书中对中国哲学、宗教和礼仪的事实性描述，对于作为该书主体的神学结论和论争一概不予理会，这进一步表明洛克关注的重点在中国本身，而非"礼仪之争"本身。

5. 洛克对中国的论述虽然简略，但中国对洛克的重要性不容低估。洛克对中国的认识有一个不断加深的过程：在其早期未刊作品中，中国只是游记文学中证明人类信仰和风俗多样性的例证之一，可有可无；在《人类理解论》（第四版）中，中国作为具有高度发达文明的无神论社会，成为驳斥天赋观念论和回应伍斯特主教指责的最强有力例证，不可或缺；及至"中国笔记"，中国已经从例证变为洛克关于"物质能否思考"问题思考的重要部分，中国哲学为洛克提供了一元唯物论的一种全新可能。

需要说明的是，以上只是基于现有材料所作出的初步结论，而学术研究必然是循序渐进的过程。洛克"中国笔记"手稿是最近发现的全新材料，本书是聚焦洛克"中国笔记"、进而梳理洛克"中国观"的首次尝试，必然从文献收集整理工作做起，再逐步上升到分析阐释的层次，很难一蹴而就。本书的题目为：《洛克与中国：洛克"中国笔记"考辨》，因此本书要梳理的是洛克与中国之间的事实联系，这是从前没有人知道的。本书从洛克"中国笔记"手稿入手，通过转写、翻译和总结手稿内容，并追溯其知识来源，集中展现洛克对中国宗教的基本观点和研究过程；继而梳理洛克著作、藏书和书信中对中国的关注，系统展现洛克与中国之间的"事实联系"。至于洛克"中国观"与洛克哲学的内在联系，以及洛克"中国观"与17—18世纪欧洲思想家的"中国观"之间的联系，是下一步研究的内容。同时，本书整理了洛克藏书、书信和著作中明确提到中国的内容，还有大量思想和材料虽未明确提到中国，却与中国有所关联[①]，也有待进一步整理和深入分析。

---

① 例如《人类理解论》第三卷第十一章第二十五节中提到："Men, versed in physical Enquiries, and acquainted with the several sorts of natural Bodies, would set down those simple Ideas, wherein they observe the Individual of each sort constantly to agree."洛克提议创造一种插图书（pictorial dictionary），即在书的空白处印上图片，并说这尤其适用于来自遥远国度的东西，这种做法有助于区别同义词。这容易让人联想起莱布尼茨在寻找"原初语言"的过程中所提出的"象征性语言"（a symbolic language）的概念，两人似乎试图创建一种更加直观的交流媒介，这与中国文字有着内在的联系。

主要参考文献

一、中文著作

陈垣整理，李天纲校点：《康熙与罗马使节关系文书》，见［意］马国贤著，李天纲译：《清廷十三年：马国贤在华回忆录》"附录"，上海：上海古籍出版社，2004年。

陈受颐：《中欧文化交流史事论丛》，台北：台湾商务印书馆，1970年。

杜泽逊：《文献学概要》，北京：中华书局，2001年。

范存忠：《中国文化在启蒙时期的英国》，上海：上海外语教育出版社，1991年。

方豪：《中国天主教史人物传》，北京：宗教文化出版社，2007年。

方豪：《中西交通史》，上海：上海人民出版社，2008年。

葛桂录：《雾外的远音：英国作家与中国文化》，银川：宁夏人民出版社，2002年；福州：福建教育出版社，2015年。

韩琦：《中国科学技术的西传及其影响》，石家庄：河北人民出版社，1999年。

何兆武、柳卸林主编：《中国印象——外国名人论中国文化》，北京：中国人民大学出版社，2011年。

洪汉鼎：《诠释学——它的历史和当代发展》，北京：人民出版社，2001年。

胡景钊、余丽嫦：《十七世纪英国哲学》，北京：商务印书馆，2006年。

胡优静：《英国19世纪的汉学史研究》，北京：学苑出版社，2009年。

计翔翔：《十七世纪中期汉学著作研究——以曾德昭〈大中国志〉和安文思〈中国新志〉为中心》，上海：上海古籍出版社，2002年。

李季璇：《从权利到权力：洛克自然法思想研究》，南京：江苏人民出版社，2017年。

李天纲：《中国礼仪之争——历史·文献和意义》，上海：上海古籍出版社，1998年。

李天纲：《跨文化的诠释：经学与神学的相遇》，北京：新星出版社，2007年。

李文潮、波塞尔编，李文潮等译：《莱布尼茨与中国：〈中国近事〉发表300周年国际学术讨论会论文集》，北京：科学出版社，2002年。

刘小枫编，丰卫平译：《西方古典文献学发凡》，北京：华夏出版社，2014年。

吕大吉：《洛克物性理论研究》，北京：中国社会科学出版社，1982年。

孟华：《伏尔泰与孔子》，北京：新华出版社，1993年。

庞景仁著，冯俊译：《马勒伯朗士的"神"的观念和朱熹的"理"的观念》，北京：商务印书馆，2005年。

钱乘旦、许洁明：《英国通史》，上海：上海社会科学院出版社，2002年。

钱林森：《光自东方来：法国作家与中国文化》，银川：宁夏人民出版社，2004年。

钱锺书：《钱锺书英文文集》，北京：外语教学与研究出版社，2005年。

秦家懿、孔汉思著，吴华译：《中国宗教与基督教》，北京：生活·读书·新知三联书店，1990年。

秦家懿编译：《德国哲学家论中国》，北京：生活·读书·新知三联书店，1993年。

秦家懿：《秦家懿自选集》，济南：山东教育出版社，2005年。

苏杰编译：《西方校勘学论著选》，上海：上海人民出版社，2009年。

谈敏：《法国重农学派学说的中国渊源》，上海：上海人民出版社，1992年。

王楠：《劳动与财产：约翰·洛克思想研究》，上海：上海三联书店，2014年。

吴飞主编：《洛克与自由社会》，上海：上海三联书店，2012年。

吴旻、韩琦编校：《欧洲所藏雍正乾隆朝天主教文献汇编》，上海：上海人民出版社，2008年。

吴莉苇：《当诺亚方舟遭遇伏羲神农——启蒙时代欧洲的中国上古史论争》，北京：中国人民大学出版社，2005年。

吴莉苇：《中国礼仪之争：文明的张力与权力的较量》，上海：上海古籍出版社，2007年。

忻剑飞：《世界的中国观：近二千年来世界对中国的认识史纲》，上海：学林出版社，1991年。

忻剑飞：《醒客的中国观：近百多年世界思想大师的中国观感概述》，上海：学林出版社，2013年。

熊文华：《英国汉学史》，北京：学苑出版社，2007年。

许明龙：《孟德斯鸠与中国》，北京：国际文化出版公司，1989年。

许明龙：《黄嘉略与早期法国汉学》，北京：中华书局，2004年；北京：商务印书馆，2014年修订版。

许明龙：《欧洲十八世纪中国热》，北京：外语教学与研究出版社，2007年。

许明龙：《东传西渐：中西文化交流史散论》，北京：中国社会科学出版社，2015年。

严建强：《18世纪中国文化在西欧的传播及其反应》，杭州：中国美术学院出版社，2002年。

阎宗临：《传教士与法国早期汉学》，郑州：大象出版社，2003年。

阎宗临：《中西交通史》，桂林：广西师范大学出版社，2007年。

张大可、俞樟华：《中国文献学》，福州：福建人民出版社，2005年。

张国刚等：《明清传教士与欧洲汉学》，北京：中国社会科学出版社，2001年。

张国刚：《从中西初识到礼仪之争——明清传教士与中西文化交流》，北京：人民出版社，2003年。

张国刚、吴莉苇：《启蒙时代欧洲的中国观：一个历史的巡礼与反思》，上海：上海古籍出版社，2006年。

张弘：《中国文学在英国》，广州：花城出版社，1992年。

张隆溪：《阐释学与跨文化研究》，北京：生活·读书·新知三联书店，2014年。

张舜徽：《中国文献学》，上海：上海古籍出版社，2005年。
张西平：《中国与欧洲早期宗教和哲学交流史》，北京：东方出版社，2001年。
张西平：《传教士汉学研究》，郑州：大象出版社，2005年。
张西平：《欧洲早期汉学史——中西文化交流与西方汉学的兴起》，北京：中华书局，2009年。
张西平主编：《莱布尼茨思想中的中国元素》，郑州：大象出版社，2010年。
张西平：《儒学西传欧洲研究导论：16—18世纪中学西传的轨迹与影响》，北京：北京大学出版社，2016年。
张西平：《20世纪中国古代文化经典在域外的传播与影响研究导论》，郑州：大象出版社，2018年。
张星烺编注，朱杰勤校订：《中西交通史资料汇编》，北京：中华书局，2003年。
张允熠、陶武、张弛编著：《中国：欧洲的样板——启蒙时期儒学西传欧洲》，合肥：黄山书社，2010年。
周宁编：《世界之中国：域外中国形象研究》，南京：南京大学出版社，2007年。
朱谦之：《中国哲学对于欧洲的影响》，福州：福建人民出版社，1985年。
邹化政：《〈人类理解论〉研究——人类理智再探》，北京：人民出版社，1987年。

二、中文译著

［德］阿塔纳修斯·基歇尔著，张西平、杨慧玲、孟宪谟译：《中国图说》，郑州：大象出版社，2010年。
［法］艾田蒲著，许钧、钱林森译：《中国之欧洲》，郑州：河南人民出版社，1994年；桂林：广西师范大学出版社，2008年。
［法］安田朴著，耿昇译：《中国文化西传欧洲史》，北京：商务印书馆，2000年，2013年再版。
［葡］安文思著，何高济、李申译：《中国新史》，郑州：大象出版社，2016年。
［英］彼得·拉斯莱特著，冯克利译：《洛克〈政府论〉导论》，北京：生活·读书·新知三联书店，2007年。
［美］邓恩著，余三乐、石蓉译：《从利玛窦到汤若望：晚明的耶稣会传教

士》，上海：上海古籍出版社，2003年。

［法］杜赫德编，郑德弟、吕一民、沈坚译：《耶稣会士中国书简集：中国回忆录》，郑州：大象出版社，2001—2005年。

［美］方岚生著，曾小五译，王蓉蓉校：《互照：莱布尼茨与中国》，北京：北京大学出版社，2013年。

［英］G.F. 赫德逊著，王遵仲等译：《欧洲与中国》，北京：中华书局，1995年。

［比］高华士著，赵殿红译：《清初耶稣会士鲁日满常熟账本及灵修笔记研究》，郑州：大象出版社，2007年。

［法］戈岱司编，耿昇译：《希腊拉丁作家远东古文献辑录》，北京：中华书局，1987年。

［德］汉斯-格奥尔格·伽达默尔著，夏镇平、宋建平译：《哲学解释学》，上海：上海译文出版社，2016年。

［美］J.J. 克拉克著，于闽梅、曾祥波译：《东方启蒙：东西方思想的遭遇》，上海：上海人民出版社，2011年。

［德］柯兰霓著，李岩译：《耶稣会士白晋的生平与著作》，郑州：大象出版社，2009年。

［美］唐纳德·F.拉赫著，刘绯等译：《欧洲形成中的亚洲第二卷·奇迹的世纪》，北京：人民出版社，2013年。

［美］唐纳德·F.拉赫、［美］埃德温·J.范·克雷著，许玉军等译：《欧洲形成中的亚洲第三卷·发展的世纪》，北京：人民出版社，2013年。

［德］莱布尼茨著，［法］梅谦立、杨保筠译：《中国近事：为了照亮我们这个时代的历史》，郑州：大象出版社，2005年。

［法］蓝莉著，许明龙译：《请中国作证：杜赫德的〈中华帝国全志〉》，北京：商务印书馆，2015年。

［意］利玛窦、［比］金尼阁著，何高济、王遵仲、李申译，何兆武校：《利玛窦中国札记》，北京：中华书局，1983年。

［法］李明著，郭强、龙云、李伟译：《中国近事报道1687—1692》，郑州：大象出版社，2004年。

［德］利奇温著，朱杰勤译：《十八世纪中国与欧洲文化的接触》，北京：商务印书馆，1962年。

［美］列奥·施特劳斯著，彭刚译：《自然权利与历史》，北京：生活·读书·新知三联书店，2003年。

［英］洛克著，关文运译：《人类理解论》，北京：商务印书馆，1959年。

［英］洛克著，胡景钊译：《论人类的认识》，上海：上海人民出版社，2017年。

［英］洛克著，瞿菊农、叶启芳译：《政府论》，北京：商务印书馆，1982年。

［英］洛克著，李季璇译：《自然法论文集》，北京：商务印书馆，2014年。

［法］尼古拉·马勒伯朗士等著，陈乐民试译并序：《有关神的存在和性质的对话》，北京：生活·读书·新知三联书店，1998年。

［美］迈克尔·扎克特著，石碧球等译：《洛克政治哲学研究》，北京：人民出版社，2013年。

［西］门多萨著，何高济译：《中华大帝国史》，北京：中华书局，2013年。

［美］孟德卫著，张学智译：《莱布尼兹和儒学》，南京：江苏人民出版社，1998年。

［美］孟德卫著，江文君、姚霏译：《1500—1800：中西方的伟大相遇》，北京：新星出版社，2007年。

［美］孟德卫著，潘琳译：《灵与肉：山东的天主教，1650—1785》，郑州：大象出版社，2009年。

［美］孟德卫著，陈怡译：《奇异的国度：耶稣会适应政策及汉学的起源》，郑州：大象出版社，2010年。

［西］闵明我著，何高济、吴翊楣译：《上帝许给的土地：闵明我行记和礼仪之争》，郑州：大象出版社，2009年。

［美］理查德·E.帕尔默著，潘德荣译：《诠释学》，北京：商务印书馆，2012年。

［西］帕莱福、［比］鲁日满、［意］卫匡国著，何高济译：《鞑靼征服中国史·鞑靼中国史·鞑靼战纪》，北京：中华书局，2008年。

［法］皮埃尔-马克·德比亚齐著，汪秀华译：《文本发生学》，天津：天津人民出版社，2005年。

［美］史景迁讲演，廖世奇、彭小樵译：《文化类同与文化利用》，北京：北京大学出版社，1997年。

［英］斯图亚特·布朗主编，高新民等译：《英国哲学和启蒙时代》，北京：中国人民大学出版社，2009年。

［美］苏尔、诺尔编，沈保义、顾卫民、朱静译：《中国礼仪之争西文文献一百篇（1645—1941）》，上海：上海古籍出版社，2001年。

［英］索利著，段德智译：《英国哲学史》，济南：山东人民出版社，2007年。

王尔敏编：《中国文献西译书目》，台北：台湾商务印书馆，1975年。

［法］维吉尔·毕诺著，耿昇译：《中国对法国哲学思想形成的影响》，北京：商务印书馆，2000年。

［美］魏若望著，吴莉苇译：《耶稣会士傅圣泽神甫传：索隐派思想在中国及欧洲》，郑州：大象出版社，2006年。

［德］夏瑞春编，陈爱政等译：《德国思想家论中国》，南京：江苏人民出版社，1995年。

［法］谢和耐著，耿昇译：《中国与基督教：中西文化的首次撞击》，北京：商务印书馆，2013年。

［法］谢和耐、戴密微等著，耿昇译：《明清间耶稣会士入华与中西汇通》，北京：东方出版社，2011年。

［捷］严嘉乐著，丛林、李梅译：《中国来信》，郑州：大象出版社，2002年。

［葡］曾德昭著，何高济译：《大中国志》，上海：上海古籍出版社，1998年。

［英］詹姆斯·塔利著，梅雪琴、石楠、张炜等译：《语境中的洛克》，上海：华东师范大学出版社，2005年。

三、中文文章

［法］戴密微著，耿昇译：《中国与欧洲早期的哲学交流》，载《国际汉学》第7辑，2002年。

［法］傅飞岚著，徐克谦译：《西方学者道教研究现状综述》，载《国际汉学》第6辑，2000年。

黄一农：《明末清初天主教传华史研究的回顾和展望》，载《新史学》1996年第7卷第1期。

李东日：《近年来国外学者对利玛窦的研究评介》，载《国际汉学》第2辑，1998年。

［丹麦］K. 龙伯格著，耿昇译：《宋程理学在欧洲的传播》，载《国际汉学》第5辑，2000年。

［美］孟德卫著，吴莉苇译：《中国礼仪之争研究概述》，载《国际汉学》第5辑，2000年。

吴莉苇：《近代早期欧洲人的中国地理观，1500—1800》（博士后报告），历史学：北京大学，2005年。

武斌：《康熙时期中华文化在欧洲的传播——以莱布尼兹为例》，载《沈阳故宫博物院院刊》第1辑，2005年。

武斌：《中国思想对欧洲启蒙哲学的激励与开发》，载《沈阳故宫博物院院刊》第4辑，2007年。

徐海松：《耶稣会士与中西文化交流论著目录》，载黄时鉴主编：《东西交流论谭》（第二集），上海：上海文艺出版社，2001年。

张允熠：《关于16至18世纪之"中学西渐"的反思》，载《高校理论战线》2004年第9期。

四、西文著作

Aaron, Richard I., *John Locke*, (Oxford: Oxford University Press, 1971).

Allan, David, *Commonplace Books and Reading in Georgian England*, (New York: Cambridge University Press, 2010).

Anstey, Peter R. (ed.), *The Oxford Handbook of British Philosophy in the Seventeenth Century*, (Oxford: Oxford University Press, 2013).

Cranston, Maurice, *John Locke: A Biography*, (Oxford: Oxford University Press, 1985).

Dunn, John, *The Political Thought of John Locke*, (Cambridge University Press, 1969).

Goldie, Mark, *Locke: Political Essays*, (Cambridge: Cambridge University Press, 1997).

Hampson, Norman, *The Enlightenment: An evaluation of its assumptions, attitudes and values*, (London: Penguin Books, 1990).

Harrison, John and Laslett, Peter, *The Library of John Locke*, (Oxford: Oxford University Press, 1965).

King, Lord, *The Life of John Locke with extracts from his correspondence, journals, and common-place books*, (London: Henry Colburn and Richard Bentley, 1830).

Locke, John, *An Early Draft of Locke's Essays together with Excerpts from his Journals*, ed. R. I. Aaron and Jocelyn Gibb, (Oxford: Clarendon Press, 1936).

——, *An Essay Concerning Human Understanding*, edited with a foreword by Peter H. Nidditch. (Oxford: Clarendon Press; New York: Oxford University Press, 1979).

——, *The correspondence of John Locke*, ed. E.S. De Beer, 8 vols. (Oxford: Clarendon Press, 1976-1989).

——, *Essays on the Law of Nature*, ed. W. von Leyden, (Oxford: Clarendon Press, 1954).

Long, P., *A Summary Catalogue of the Lovelace Collection of the Papers of John Locke in the Bodleian Library*, (Oxford: Oxford University Press, 1959).

Mack, Eric. *John Locke*, (New York: Continuum, 2009).

Mackie, J. L., *Problems from Locke*, (Oxford: Clarendon Press, 1976).

Macpherson, C. B., *The Political Theory of Possessive Individualism: Hobbes to Locke*, (Oxford University Press, 1962).

Magee, Bryan, *The Story of Philosophy*, (London: Dorling Kindersley Limited, 2010).

Minamiki, George, *The Chinese Rites Controversy: From Its Beginning to Modern Times*, (Chicago: Loyola Press, 1985).

Mungello, D. E. (ed.), *The Chinese Rites Controversy: Its History and Meaning*, (Nettetal: Steyler Verlag, 1994).

Mungello, David E., *Drowning girls in China : female infanticide since 1650*, (Md.: Rowman & Littlefield Publishers, 2008).

Pfeiffer, Rudolf, *History of Classical Scholarship: From the Beginnings to the End of the Hellenistic Age*, (Oxford: Clarendon Press, 1968).

Rogers, G. A. J. (ed.), *Locke's Philosophy: Content and Context*, (Oxford: Oxford University Press, 1994).

Rogers, G. A. J., *Locke's Enlightenment: Aspects of the Origin, Nature, and Impact of His Philosophy*, (Hildesheim: Georg Olms AG, 1998).

Standaert, N. and Dudink, A. (eds.), *Oxford Bibliographies in Renaissance and Reformation "China and Europe, 1550—1800"*, (Oxford: Oxford University Press, 2012).

Talbot, Ann, *"The Great Ocean of Knowledge": the Influence of Travel Literature on the Work of John Locke*, (Leiden: Brill, 2010).

Tully, James, *A Discourse on Property: John Locke and His Adversaries*, (Cambridge: Cambridge University Press, 1980).

Woolhouse, Roger, *Locke: A Biography*, (Cambridge: Cambridge University Press, 2007).

Yolton, Jean S. and Yolton, John W., *John Locke: A Reference Guide*, (USA: G.K. Hall & Co., 1985).

Yolton, John W., *Thinking Matter: Materialism in Eighteenth-century Britain*, (Oxford: Basil Blackwell, 1984).

Yolton, John W. (ed.), *John Locke: Problems and Perspectives*, (London: Cambridge University Press, 1969).

附录1 《游记与旅行丛书》(Collection of Voyages and Travels)

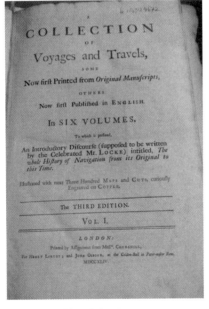

第一卷标题页

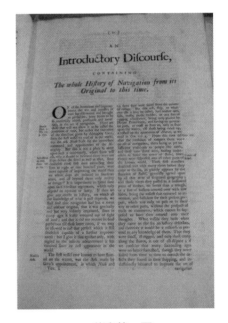

前言第一页

第一卷第一章：闵明我（Domingo Fernández Navarrete）的《中华帝国历史、政治、伦理及宗教概述》（Tratados historicos, politicos, ethicosy religious de la monarchia de China）的英译本

附录1 《游记与旅行丛书》(Collection of Voyages and Travels)

AN
ACCOUNT
OF THE
Empire of CHINA,
Hiſtorical, Political, Moral and Religious.

A

Short DESCRIPTION of that Empire, and Notable Examples of its Emperors and Miniſters.

ALSO

An ample Relation of many remarkable Paſſages, and things worth obſerving in other Kingdoms, and ſeveral Voyages.

There are added

The Decrees of Popes, and Propoſitions defined at *Rome* for the Miſſion of *China* ; and a Bull of our moſt Holy Father *Clement* X. in favour of the Miſſioners.

Written in *Spaniſh* by the R. F. F. *Dominick Fernandez Navarette*, Divinity Profeſſor in the College and Univerſity of St. *Thomas* at *Manila*, Apoſtolick Miſſioner in *China*, Superior of thoſe of his Miſſion, and Procurator General at the Court of *Madrid* for the Province of the Roſary in the *Philippine* Iſlands, of the Order of Preachers.

Printed for HENRY LINTOT ; and JOHN OSBORN, at the *Golden-Ball* in *Paternoſter Row*.

《中国帝国历史、政治、伦理及宗教概述》标题页

附录2　约翰发自厦门的信（全文）

Letter 3046[①]

John Lock (later Sir John) to Locke, 23 November 1701(2716, 3136)

B.L., MS. Locke c.14, ff. 176-7. Forwarded by Samuel Locke on 30 September 1702: p. 682; received by Locke on 6 October: Journal. I have failed to trace the voyage to Amoy or to identify Lock's ship. On this voyage he appears to have been a supercargo, i.e. the Company's representative on board for its trading venture, making all negotiations for the sale of the cargo and purchases of country goods; and dealing with customs officers, etc.; he would also be allowed make a private venture. For the supercargoes in the China trade see Morse, *East India Company trading to China*, i. 66-77; above, no. 2224.

Honourable Sir

Since you were pleased to Honour mee with the Favour of a Letter to Surat, I esteem it a Priviledge given mee to write you from the remote Parts my fortune Leads

---

[①] John Locke, E.S. De Beer (ed.), *The Correspondence of John Locke*, V7, Oxford: Clarendon Press, 1982, pp. 509-511. 其中注释为原文注释。

mee to, and should make use of it much oftener if my education and Imployments, which has bin from the School, with Merchants and Merchandizing, were able to furnish mee with such discoveries as has escaped the notice of those who have made it their peculiar business to search into the Pollicy, Religion, Government, and the products of these Forreigne countries, which is difficult for mee to doe that goe noe deaper than a Sea Port, and am conversant constantly with people of my owne professions and the greatest part of my Time imploy'd in the disposeal of what I bring, and procureing effects proper for another market, but since I write to a person of soe great worth and soe well acquainted , how mankind coms to gather all their knowledge of these things, I shall not seek for further matter to troble you with then what I find in my dayly imployment

I come from Surat in the Service of his Excellency Sir William Norris his Majesties Embassador to the the Great Mogull and Sir [509] Nicholas Wait his Consull at Surat, with a ship of the Natives burthen 400 Tons, sailed by an English Comander and Officers, and Laschars or blackfellows, their wages and hyre of the Ship for 12 months with the Bottomry of what mony was advanced for her outsett will amount to 25731 Rupees which is 64 Rppees per Ton, A Europe Ship of that Burthen for 12 months, at the usual Demorage [注释1.Demurrage; here the payment made in compensation for the detention of a vessel by the freighter beyond the time agreed upon: O.E.D.] the Companies pay is £9 Stg. per Ton at 27 Pence per Rupee, is Rupees 80 per Ton, soe that there is Lost by imploying a Europe Ship 16 Rupees or 36 Shillings in every Ton.

The Goods I brought from Surat were Putchuck, [注释2. A root used in medi-cine and for making joss-sticks（线香）: Ibid.] Olibanum, Mirh, Cominseed, Cotton, and Pearle, all which renders good Proffit, especially Cotton sold for above 100 per Cent. but being very bulky noe great value can bee brought of it, and Pearl gives 30 per Cent if brought well, for the most part $\frac{2}{3}$ of the Ships Stock is in Dollars [注释3. The Spanish dollar of silver, the medium of international exchange in China until 1857; intrinsic value 4s.2d; invoiced by the East India Company at 5s.: Morse, i.47n. For exports of silver to China see ibid. i.68.]or other Silver.

Comodities proper for Surat, are Copper as much as can bee procured, formerly Quicksilver Vermillion, but now not demaned, Sugar, Sugar Candy, Tutenegue, [注释 4. Tutenag, a whitish alloy of copper, zinc, and nickel, etc.: *O.E.D.*] Camphire, China Ware, and Gold, which last when it is at touch for touch, [注释5. Touch here is the process of testing the quality of gold or silver by rubbing it upon a touchstone: ibid., Touch, *sb.* 5; Morse, i.68-9.] and 100 waters, [注释6. This use of the word appears to be similar to that of the jewellers in regard to diamonds, etc. It may be Arabic in origin: *O.E.D.*, water, *sb.*20.] that is full fine, 1 Tale of Gold is worth just 10 Tale [注释7. Tael, the Chinese ounce: ibid. It was equated as $1\frac{1}{3}$OZ. Avoirdupois: Morse, vol.i, preliminaries.] of Dollar Silver, but usually there is allow'd 3 or 4 waters, according to the demand for it.

At our first arrival we agree with the Hoppo [注释8. The term here is applied loosely to the Chinese officer with whom the supercargoes discussed measurage dues: Morse, i. 80 n.] or Custom Master for the Ships Messuraege, [注释9. Measurage, the duty payable on the cargo of a ship: *O.E.D.*] which with Presents, houserent, and Linguister [注释10. Interpreter: ibid. See Morse, i. 67.] hyre, for the Ship I come in will come to 1500 Tale [注释11. Tale of currency, treated as the equivalent of 6s.8d.: Morse, vol.i, preliminaries.] or £500 Stg. and to purchase the foregoing Comodities, are obliged to trust the Merchants with most of our Mony and Goods and often are very dilatory in our dispatch, tho am now in hopes to Leave this Port in 3 or 4 days.

The Trade from Surat to China is at Present the most profitable, and by a modest Computation believe may cleer 55 per Cent. for my Imployers which will bee neer £7000 Stg. when am engaged in any other Voyage I shall take the freedom I doe now to give you a short Account of it, presuming what is Proffitable to private Merchants here is an increase of Riches to the Nation, which being so, you that are one of the Protectors of our Comerce, and Love to nourish the Least branches of it, will not bee displeased with what may bee offerd, from

Honourable Sir

your Most Obedient Servant

JOHN LOCK

Amoy in China 23th November 1701

Endorsed by Locke: J: Locke 23 Nov. 01 Answered 11 May. 03

附录3　"中国笔记"索引所列《华人礼仪史》相关章节拉丁文原文*

主题	页码	索引号
祖先（Progenitores）	3-6. 43. 11-115. 117-118. 219. 221. 229.	H
精神与人类灵魂（Spiritus & Anima humana）	87.	B
孔子（Confucius）	7-11. 152. 186. 190. 207.	F
地（Terra）	236. 238. 240.	G
星体（planeta）	237.	
山（montibus）	240.	
河（Fluminibus）	240.	
守护神（Genÿ）	182. 241.	G
精神和游魂（Spiritus et anima errantes）	220.	C
理（Li）与太极（Taikie）	85. 86. 87. 122. 126. 242.	A
上帝（Xanti, Rex Altus）	122. 123. 126. 127-144. 151. 242. 243.	D
天（Tien）	136. 138. 139. 141. 236. 238. 244.	E
佛教（Foe Idolotrae Bonzÿ）	131-134. 182.	J2
道教（Magi）	137.	K
儒教（Literati）		J1

* 参见本书第三章第二节"中国笔记"手稿第212页背面（Aqz030）。

SINENSIUM. 3

juris, non facti; ut si quis de aliquo contractu quærat utrum sit usurarius, multasque afferat rationes atque auctoritates ad probandum non esse usurarium, sive id ut certum, sive tantum ut probabile statuat, nemo unquam dixerit esse quæstionem facti, sed juris. Idque adhuc magis locum habet cum agitur de facto quod consistit in actibus externis, & publicis ceremoniis, quales sunt quæ in cultu Progenitorum & Confucii adhibentur. Tunc enim ad id probandum non auctoritates & rationes; sed inspectio, testes oculati & publica rei notitia requiritur.

ARTICULUS II.

Quinam & quales sint cultus Progenitorum & Confucii.

5. AT vero iisdem ego, quibus antea, vestigiis insistens, operæ pretium existimo factum ipsum circa ejusmodi cultus denuo explicare, atque Eminentissimorum Dominorum oculis subjicere.

De Cultu Progenitorum.

6. Sinæ præsertim Literariæ Sectæ, quæ est præcipua in toto Imperio, & cujus princeps est ipse Imperator, Parentes & Avos defunctos usque ad quartum gradum præcipuo cultu, tum publicè, tum privatim, venerantur. Ædes sacras seu capellas eis dedicatas ha-

4 HISTORIA CULTUS

habent, in quibus collocatæ funt tabellæ ex ligno caftaneo, certifque dimenfionibus confectæ, cubitalibus literis fic infcriptæ : *Thronus* feu *fedes animæ vel fpiritus* N. N. appofito cujufque nomine & dignitate. In medio autem ædis eft menfa feu altare cum aliis hinc inde minoribus menfis feu altaribus, ubi ejufmodi tabellæ reponuntur.

7. In his ædibus ter aut quater in anno, præfertim vere & autumno magno apparatu, *Ci*, hoc eft oblationem folemnem feu facrificium celebrant. Aliquot ante diebus Primogenitus feu Paterfamilias, & tres aut quatuor alii ex primoribus familiæ feliguntur, qui veluti Sacerdotes, Diaconi & Subdiaconi, Magiftri ceremoniarum, atque Acolytorum Minifterio fungantur. Hi diem futuræ oblationis fortitione eligunt ; tribus ante diebus jejunio vacant & à thoro conjugali abftinent; pridie vero ad vefperam victimas, porcum videlicet, capram aut alia animalia, infufo in auriculas calido vino probant. Si caput moverint, ut apta facrificio deligunt ; fi non moverint, ut inepta reprobant. Sic adoptatum animal in eorum confpectu ftatim mactatur. Ipfo die ante primum Galli cantum ad ædem feu capellam omnes confanguinei conveniunt. Singulis ordine difpofitis, accenfis fupra altare cereis cum thuris atque odorum fuffitu, Magifter ceremoniarum alta voce clamat : *Flectantur genua*, ftatimque omnes coram tabellis ter aut quater genuflectunt ; terram fronte percutientes, ac unus ex Miniftris certas quafdam precationum formulas recitat,

dein-

SINENSIUM.

deinde clamante Magistro ceremoniarum: *Levate*, sursum singuli in pedes se se erigunt. Postmodum præcipuus Minister qui officio veluti Sacerdotis fungitur, stans ad altare, vino plenum calicem in altum tollit, clamante Magistro ceremoniarum; *Offertur vinum*, cujus partem libat, partem vero super figuram hominis stramineam ibi positam fundit. Postea cæsorum animalium pilos detrahit, qui unà cum sanguine humi defodiuntur; capita autem & carnes in altum tollit, & coram tabellis offert, clamante interim Magistro cæremoniarum: *Offertur capra*, vel *porcus*. Simili modo offert flores, fructus, legumina; itemque sericos pannos & nummos papyraceos, quos in foco ante ædis portam accenso comburit, adhibitis ad singulos hos actus variis precationibus quæ ab uno ex Ministris recitantur. His ita peractis, Magister ceremoniarum denuntiat assistentibus debere eos ob exhibitum Proavis cultum prospera omnia expectare, salutem videlicet corporis, fructuum ubertatem, filiorum procreationem, honores longamque vitam.

8. Hæc probantur partim ex Ritualibus libris relatis apud Illustrissimum Navarrettam tom. 2. tract. 7. pag. 114. 115. & in tractatu manuscripto Patris Francisci Varo Dominicani Missionarii in Episcopum ac Vicarium Apostolicum electi, quem propria manu ex Autographo in Sina degens descripsi & penes me habeo, quod sub juramento affirmare paratus sum: & ex relatione similis sacrificii cujus oculati testes fuerunt Pater Joannes Bapt. Morales

6 HISTORIA CULTUS

rales Ordinis Prædic. & P. Antonius à Santa Maria Franciscanus, in quo præcipuus Minister, & unus ex Acolytis erant Christiani, aliisque testimoniis à me citatis in prioribus scriptis: denique ea ex tractatu Illustr. D. Gregorii Lopez Episcopi Basilitani ac Vicarii Apostolici Nankinensis quem ipsimet Jesuitæ producunt & plurimum laudant. Hunc si vidissem quando scriptum cui titulus: *Veritas facti*, composui, complura ex eo afferre potuissem ad probandam factorum veritatem, speciatim de jejuniis, continentia conjugali, & aliis prædictarum ceremoniarum circumstantiis.

9. Præter has solemnes oblationes quæ vere & autumno peraguntur, sæpe sæpius Sinæ ad easdem ædes se conferunt, præsertim in novilunio ac plenilunio singulorum mensium, ibique præfatas Progenitorum tabellas ter aut quater genuflexionibus profundisque usque ad terram totius corporis inclinationibus venerantur, cereos accendunt, thura & odores cremant, flores quoque fructus, legumina, aliosque cibos offerunt.

10. Qui vero tenuioris sunt fortunæ, nec ejus conditionis ut ædes seu capellas Progenitoribus defunctis dedicatas habeant, easdem oblationes & ceremonias ad eorum sepulchra extra Civitates posita, vel in privatis domibus, minori cum solemnitate & apparatu peragunt. Vix enim quemquam, etiam inter plebeios, reperias, qui domi non habeat locum aliquem ubi prædictas Avorum tabellas conservet, easque frequenter genuflexionibus, odorum suffitu,

SINENSIUM. 43

tere explicationes variorum locorum ex libris Sinensibus, quas affert ad probandum cultus Confucii & Defunctorum, juxta opinionem Jesuitarum, esse tantum quid civile & politicum. Adde plures ex iis locis quos adducit, evidenter contrarium probare; nec nisi obtorto collo ad confirmandam Jesuitarum sententiam trahi posse. Certe cultus illos esse sacros, ac proinde superstitiosos & idololatricos nemo negaverit, si constet in eis aliquid peti, aut sperari à defunctis, aut saltem eorum causa ac meritis obtinendum. Atqui Pater Gregorius Lopez adhuc Missionarius aliquando in Ecclesia Fokiensi coram Patre Varo Dominicano Patri de Govea è Societate dixit, certissimum esse Sinas à defunctis proavis sperare ac petere bona hujus vitæ. Id refert Pater Varo in tractatu Hispanico jam superiùs citato, quem in Sina exscripsi, & cujus exemplum penes me habeo: en ejus verba latinè reddita: *Pater Franciscus Lopez Sina cum in Ecclesia Fokiensi esset, coram me dixit Patri Antonio de Govea: si Patres Societatis opinionem suam ex eo confirmant, quod Sinenses à demortuis Parentibus bona non postulent, veritate non nituntur. Certe sum Sina & non nisi adultus baptismum suscepi; pro comperto autem habeo Sinas jam à pueritia, cum ejusmodi ceremoniis intersunt, bona & prospera petere ac sperare, idque tam certum est, ut nemo è Sinis, qui verum dicere velit, hoc unquam in dubium revocarit.* Unde etiam idem Illustrissimus Lopez in præfato tractatu cap. 2. §. 2. part. 2. Auctores idem disertè confirmantes profert, quos tamen ad alium

SINENSIUM.

etsi P. Joannes Bapt. Morales Sacræ Congregationi retulisset has vocari *Sedes animæ*.

186. Sacram Congregationem responsione sua permisisse istiusmodi tabellas pernego. Quæsierat Pater Joann. Bapt. Morales an liceret Christianis Sinensibus habere ejusmodi tabellas, quas dicunt esse *Sedes animæ Defuncti*, quæ collocatæ sunt in propriis altaribus cum rosis, candelis, lampadibus & odoramentis & ad quas existimant venire animas Defunctorum, atque in eis assistere, ad recipiendum sacrificia & oblationes. Respondit S. Congregatio omnino non licere habere illas tabellas in vero & proprio altari *Majoribus dicato, multo minus deprecationes & sacrificia eis offerre* : Quibus verbis S. Congregatio sat habuit propositæ quæstioni respondere, videlicet non licere habere istas tabellas in altari propriè dicto, multo minus eis sacrificia offerre, aut coram eis preces fundere: an vero easdem illas tabellas liceret habere in privatis domibus, coram eis genuflectere, cereos accendere, flores, legumina, aliaque edulia offerre, atque thura & odores cremare, cum de his interrogata non esset, nihil omnino respondit. Non solent Sacræ Congregationes, nisi ad ea de quibus consuluntur respondere, neque valet consequentia, ut si quid in casu proposito prohibendum definierint, in alio dissimili permisisse existimentur.

187. Idem fere dicendum de alia responsione quæ sequitur in eodem Decreto circa ceremonias exequiarum. Pro inviolabili more habent Sinæ, in domo Defuncti coram cadavere

HISTORIA CULTUS

vere mensam in modum altaris erigere, atque in ea imaginem Defuncti seu tabellam ejus, ut antea dictum est, nomine inscriptam collocare, cum ornatu florum; odorum & candelarum; ibique omnes qui ad condolendum veniunt, coram præparato altari & prædicta imagine Defuncti ter genuflectunt; capitibus usque ad terram demissis; aliquas candelas offerentes, & odoramenta ut in prædicto altari comburantur: quæsitum fuerat à Patre Joanne Morali, an licitum esset Christianis ista facere in exequiis Defunctorum. Respondit S. Congregatio *posito quod mensa parata sit quædam tabula, non autem verum & proprium altare, si cætera continentur intra limites obsequii civilis & politici, esse toleranda.*

188. Ubi advertendum responsionem esse tantum ex suppositione, & cum interposita conditione: *Posito*, inquit, *quod mensa sit quædam tabula, non autem verum & proprium altare*: ac deinde, *si cætera continentur intra limites obsequii civilis & politici*; quæ quidem conditio interposita, in medio relinquit illam quæstionem, an revera tabella sic inscripta: *Locus seu Sedes animæ Defuncti*, nihil habeat superstitionis atque idololatriæ; & an honores quibus colitur sint tantum civiles & politici; qua de re non libuit S. Congregationi judicium ferre. Unde patet nulla ratione inferri ab Observatore S. Congregationem hac sua responsione tabellas supradictas defunctorum permisisse aut approbasse.

289. Sane si verum est quod Joannes Morales in præcedenti quæsito exposuit, & fuse

SINENSIUM.

ántea à nobis probatum est, Sinas in eâ opinione esse, quod anima defuncti invitata oblationibus & precibus in eam tabellam adveniat, ibique assistat ut fruatur odoribus, aliisque eduliis sibi oblatis; fatendum omnino superstitiosum esse ejusmodi tabellarum usum, & Christianis minime permittendum, nisi sublatis his verbis: *Locus seu Sedes animæ defuncti*, aliisque adhibitis cautionibus quas præscribit Reverendissimus D. Maigrot, ut tabellæ illæ habeantur tantum velut imagines quæ Parentes in memoriam filiorum revocent. Quanquam adhuc melius videretur, illas omnino abolere, prout Reverendissimus D. Maigrot in sua Expositione docet, & prout anno 1669. censuerunt duo Sancti Officii Consultores à S. Congregatione delegati ad examinanda quæsita Patris Navarrettæ, videlicet Pater Laurentius Brancatus de Laurea Ordinis Sancti Francisci, & Pater Joannes Bona Ordinis S. Bernardi, ambo postea S. R. E. Cardinales dignissimi. Sic enim ad tertium quæsitum de ejusmodi tabellis responderunt: *Ad tertium de tabellis in quibus Gentiles existimant fieri præsentes animas defunctorum ad recipiendum oblationes &c. ut in dubio proposito, dicimus esse illicitum Christianis præfatas tabellas tenere, sive in templis, sive in privatis domibus; tam cum inscriptione illa,* Thronus seu Sedes animæ, *quam sine ea; & esse illicitum pariter eas cum Gentilibus aut seorsim venerari, vel oblationem aliquam eis exhibere, etiam seclusa falsa credulitate existentiæ animarum in illis.*

114 HISTORIA CULTUS

ARTICULUS II.

De eodem argumento.

190. Quantumvis obstrepat Observator, graviter accusandus est Martinius, quod hanc tabellarum inscriptionem: *Thronus seu Sedes animæ*, silentio præterierit, satque habuerit dicere in eis *defuncti nomen scriptum esse*. Hac reticentia & dissimulatione id suppressit, quo maxime probantur esse superstitiosæ & à Sinensibus haberi velut quoddam idolum, cum ad eas animam defuncti adventare, ibique requiescere ad fruendum dooribus aliisque ei oblatis existiment.

191. Id sensit * Observator, verbaque illa, *Thronus seu Sedes animæ*, peculiarem habere difficultatem non ignoravit. Unde Sinica vocabula *Xingoey*, vel *Xin Chu* vel *Xin Goey*, expendit, & quid proprie significent, longa oratione exquirit. Primum notat priscos Sinas dum Parentalia peragerent, habuisse in more puerum substituere, qui indutus vestibus demortui hominis, eum, ac si vivus esset, repræsentaret; postea vero huic defuncti vivæ figuræ substituisse tabellam supradictis vocibus inscriptam: deinde vero varias ex Libris Sinicis auctoritates affert ad probandum voces illas hoc unum significare, istiusmodi tabellis defunctos Majores, tanquam si præsen-

* *Ibid. Obs. 1. per totum.*

SINENSIUM.

sentes adessent, in memoriam filiorum revocandos.

192. Verum quid juvat auctoritates illas, totque sententias Sinicas in medium afferre? Compertum est Observatorem linguam Sinitam non callere, neminemque esse nunc Romæ qui illam calleat. Deinde quæcumque affert jam explicata & confutata sunt in responsionibus Illustrissimi Navarrettæ ad Apologias Patrum Fabri, & Brancati è Societate. Si sat esset in hac causa sententias & auctoritates Librorum Sinicorum proferre, possem S. Congregationi exhibere excerpta tractatûs à me jam sæpe citati, quem composuit Pater Varo Missionarius Dominicanus linguæ Sinicæ peritissimus; ubi allatis plurimis Scriptorum Sinensium auctoritatibus & testimoniis verba illa *Xingoey* & *Xin Chu* ita interpretanda demonstrat, ut significent Sinensibus persuasum esse animas defunctorum tempore oblationum tabellis insidere.

193. Neque audiendus *. Observator, dum hos ad primam tabellarum illarum originem revocat; monetque eas juveni illi qui Defuncti personam in Parentalibus sustinebat, successisse; ut inde inferat nihil in sua institutione superstitiosi habuisse, & si quid postea mali, privatorum ignorantia & superstitione, irrepserit, omitti posse, retento pristino usu tabellarum. Hac eadem arte oblationes Confucii & Progenitorum etiam solemnes, quantumvis superstitionis & idololatriæ plenas, defen-

* *Ibid.* §. Sciendum est.

SINENSIUM.

ARTICULUS III.

Quæstionis statum mutat Observator, ut multa in exequendo Reverendissimi D. Maigrot Edicto incommoda inveniat.

195. Quod quinto Edicti capite præscribitur, spectat solum ad tabellas Progenitorum, quas Sinæ apud se domi retinent, eas quotidie iteratis vicibus prono corpore salutantes, cereis accensis, cum thuris odore, & florum, leguminum, aliorumque eduliorum oblationibus. Quid ad hæc * Observator, ut quod præscribit Reverendissimus D. Maigrot magnas habere difficultates, variisque obnoxium esse incommodis ostendat? Ad ea quæ in obsequiis mortuorum usurpantur orationem convertit. In iis quippe etiam ejusmodi tabellæ adhibentur, ut supra notavimus. Itaque contendit fore ut Neophyti in magnas & inexplicabiles difficultates incurrant, si tunc velint, ex præscripto Edicti, voces illas: *Thronus seu Sedes animæ*, è tabellis expungere. At vana est & inutilis hæc objectio, cum hic tantum agatur de ejusmodi tabellis in privatis domibus non retinendis, neque adhibendis erga eas honoribus, de quibus modo dictum est. Reverendissimus D. Maigrot nihil de exequiis in Edicto suo statuit, neque etiam oblationes minus solemnes quæ singulis mensibus in

ædibus

* *Ibid. Obs. 2. per totum.*

118 HISTORIA CULTUS

ædibus Sacris Defunctorum celebrantur expresse prohibuit, ob rationes jam supra allatas, tametsi neutram ex illis ceremoniis superstitione vacare putaverit.

196. At, inquit * Observator, solemnes oblationes quæ Vere & Autumno Progenitoribus fiunt, idcirco prohibuit Dominus Maigrot, *quod ante ejusmodi tabellam peragantur, in qua præsens esse credatur Mortui spiritus. Absque hoc foret*, pergit ille, *in his oblationibus nihil superstitionis cerneret, nihil quod sacrificium redoleat, vel civilis cultus modum excedat.*

197. Sic illi libuit Edictum Reverendissimi Domini Maigrot interpretari. At hanc esse mentem ac sententiam Reverendissimi D. Maigrot pernego. Tametsi ab ædibus Sacris defunctorum abessent ejusmodi tabellæ, oblationes illæ non desinerent esse superstitionis & idololatriæ plenæ. Num, amabo, à superstitione vacant jejunia, & continentia conjugalis quæ præmittuntur; victimarum, injecto in auriculas vino calido, sortitio; earum, præsente Patrefamilias, cædes, vinum in ipsa ceremonia libatum, caput capræ, aut porci oblatum, panni serici & nummi papyracei igne cremati, cæteraque à nobis relata, quæ verum exhibent sacrificium? Nihilne in tot ceremoniis, quod civilis cultus modum excedat, quodque viventibus Mandarinis atque aliis non offeratur? Qui hoc dixerit, aut multum fallitur, aut alios vult fallere.

198. Neque etiam sequitur permissas fuisse à

* *Ibid. Obs.* 2. §. Neque vero.

SINENSIUM.

in tractatu quem ex autentico exemplo manu propria in Sina exscripsi. Idem etiam probat tractatus Illustrissimi Lopez, quem ipsimet Jesuitæ producunt Cap. 3. §. De oblatione *Ci* de novo addito, ubi plures auctoritates ex libris Ritualibus & antiquis commentariis afferuntur, quæ diserte ejusmodi deprecationes defunctis Imperatoribus & proavis fieri docent. Primus locus est ex Rituali Sinico dicto *Ly chy*, ubi Auctor loquens originaliter de oblationibus seu Sacrificiis *Ci* quales sunt oblationes solemnes quæ bis in anno Proavis mortuis offeruntur, sic habet. ,, In oblatione ,, seu sacrificio *Ci* habentur preces, habentur ,, gratiarum actiones, habetur etiam inde sequens morborum, calamitatum, peccato-,, rum infortuniorumque omnium cessatio, vel ,, potius fuga & extinctio. Secundus locus est Commentatoris in hunc textum *Ly ky*, qui ad explicandum quibus precibus in dicta oblatione *Ci* utendum sit, ex alio libro rituali hæc verba refert. ,, Primo petantur felicita-,, tes, petatur perpetuitas optimi gubernii ... ,, In vere ac æstate petenda sunt frumenta, o-,, riza & alia hujusmodi. Tertius locus est ex commentario in eundem librum *Ly ky* ubi hæc leguntur. ,, Oratori primario ,, seu ceremoniarum Magistro in hujusmodi ,, oblationibus seu sacrificiis adhibenda cura ,, est de sex generibus orationum seu precum. ,, Ad Coadjutorem vero seu secundarium O-,, ratorem spectat petere bona, felicitates &c. Quartus locus est ex Commentatore alterius Ritualis, ubi dicitur, ,, Statutis temporibus ,, sa-

SINENSIUM.

denti avaritia laborantium adverterit, vix unquam sibi persuadebit eos tot sumptus facturos, tantumque operæ ac studii in celebrandis Progenitorum cultibus posituros, nisi hoc pacto aliqua se bona hujus vitæ consecuturos sperarent. Certè complures apud eos reperias, quod expertus testari possum, qui cum Parentes adhuc vivos malè habuerint, eos post mortem iisdem illis ritibus diligentissimè colunt. Quis autem credat hoc eos ob solam erga defunctos Parentes pietatem ac reverentiam facere, quos vivos neglexerunt, aut etiam malè tractarunt, & non potius communi illa opinione ductos, quod qui proavos solemni illo ritu prosequuntur, felicitatem hujus vitæ, hoc est divitias, honores, bonam valetudinem & longam vitam sperare debeant? Quod si ejusmodi bona sperent, quis dubitet quin etiam ad illa consequenda in tanto ceremoniarum apparatu preces & vota adhibeant?

Observatio.

92. * Quod autem de Patre Adamo Schaal, hoc est plusquam ridiculum. Nempe, iste Pater, quo nemo alius communi sententiæ firmius adhæsit, scribens ad Dominicanum alterius opinionis ironicè sic loquutus est &c.

Responsio.

93. Perridiculum Observatoris effugium. P. Adamus Schaal Mathematices in Aula Pekinensi Mandarinus & componendo quotannis Kalendario, in quo dies fausti & infausti notantur, Præfectus, etsi in aliis Societatis utilitati

* **5.** Quod autem.

SINENSIUM.

grot pugnantia dicere, & Patres Dominicanos ac Franciscanos ab eodem Reverendissimo pessime tractari.

110. Cum autem Patrum Societatis Neophyti & Christiani in Sina longe aliorum omnium Missionariorum neophytos & Christianos superent, hinc etiam patet Reverendissimum Dominum Maigrot vero & optimo sensu dixisse, *dubitari merito posse an qui sunt in China Christiani iidem fere omnes non sint & idololatræ*. Nam præterquam quod Christiani omnes à Patribus Societatis baptisati aut instructi latè per diversas Sinæ Provincias diffusi cultus Progenitorum & Confucii frequentant, quibus accedunt complures alii quos, ut supra dictum est aliorum Ordinum Missionarii ex indulgentia ejusmodi cultibus immisceri permittunt; pluribus adhuc aliis modis Christiani tum Patrum Societatis, tum aliorum Missionariorum hac in parte peccant, sive tabellas Proavorum cum hac inscriptione: *Sedes seu locus animæ* domi retinentes, variisque salutationibus, ac odorum suffitu, nec non florum, leguminum, aliorumque eduliorum oblationibus venerantes; sive in exequiis mortuorum, coram hujusmodi tabellis, eadem modo dicta peragentes, multaque alia vana & superstitiosa usurpantes; unde Reverendissimus Dominus Maigrot, ut tantam religionis labem & confusionem tollendam ostenderet, rectè Summo Pontifici potuit dicere, dubitari merito posse an qui sunt in China Christiani, iidem fere omnes non sint & idololatræ.

P 3   111.

SINENSIUM.

VII.

149. Huc revocandum puto quamdam objectionem, quam non parum urget Observator. Pugnantia, * inquit, loquitur Reverendissimus D. Maigrot, dum Confucii & Progenitorum cultum idololatricum esse contendit, & nihilominus Literatos tanquam Atheos, qui neque spiritus, neque animam immortalem esse credunt, traducit. Qui enim, inquit, fieri potest, ut Sinæ Confucii & Progenitorum spiritus invocent ad tabellas, tanquam ad locum & sedem ubi requiescant; invitent, & ab eis bona sperent aut postulent, si nullam spiritualem substantiam agnoscunt, si animam hominis immortalem esse negant. Quam sint istæ contradictiones Sorbonico Doctore indignæ, nullus est, inquit, tyro qui non apprehendat.

150. Respondeo hæc tam confidenter tamque arroganter in Reverendissimum D. Maigrot dici non posse, nisi ab eo qui vere in rebus Sinicis tyro sit, vel qui earum minus peritos decipere velit. Sinæ juxta Literariæ Sectæ principia, veros spiritus atque adeo immortales hominum animas non agnoscunt, neque tamen has corpore solutas, penitus extingui aut evanescere existimant. Siquidem animo sibi fingunt, eas esse partem subtilissimæ illius materiæ, quam *Li* seu *Taikie* appel-

* 2. *Part. Obs. in* 3. *Cap. Mand. S. Ro.* 4. *Reverendissimum.*

F 4

SINENSIUM.

situ, & fructuum ac ciborum oblationibus veneretur.

De Cultu Confucii.

11. Confucius Philosophus in singulis Civitatibus ædem sacram seu capellam habet, quæ juxta Gymnasium seu ludum Literarium constructa est; in ea collocata est ejus tabella cum hac inscriptione aureis literis exarata: *Thronus seu sedes animæ Sanctissimi & Superexcellentissimi Protomagistri Confucii.*

12. Ad has ædes bis in anno, æquinoctio videlicet veris & autumni, omnes Literati conveniunt, ut Confucium tanquam communem Magistrum ac Sinicæ Philosophiæ Parentem, oblatione solemni venerentur. Præcipuus Mandarinus seu Urbis Gubernator Sacerdotis officio fungitur, adjunctis aliis Literatis qui Diaconi, Subdiaconi, Magistri ceremoniarum, atque Acolytorum partes obeunt, ut modo de oblationibus Progenitorum dictum est. Hi, præmisso, ut supra, aliquot dierum jejunio, & abstinentia à thoro conjugali, pridie æquinoctii, orizam aliaque legumina & fructus terræ Confucio offerenda in aula præparant: in area vero templi Confuciani Mandarinus qui Sacerdotem agit, supra mensam cereis accensis, impositis prunis thus aliosque odores cremat; deinde porcum & capram, aliave animalia postridie immolanda probat, injecto, ut jam dictum est, in aures vino calido. Idem porcum sic electum, antequam mactetur prono corpore salutat, ac deinde à Laniis coram eo mactatum simili modo iterum veneratur. Postea

A 4   pili

8   HISTORIA CULTUS

pili raduntur & cum intestinis & sanguine in sequentem diem servantur.

13. Postridie ante Galli cantum, Mandarinus cum aliis Ministris, cæterique Literati magno cum apparatu adsunt in æde Confucii: cereis accensis, supra mensam seu altare thus aliosque odores adolent: signum dante Magistro ceremoniarum Musici cantant; deinde Mandarinus tanquam Sacerdos, Magistro ceremoniarum clamante; *offerantur pili & sanguis victimarum*, eosdem pilos in catino positos unâ cum sanguine in altum tollit, & coram tabella Confucii offert; postmodum jubente Magistro ceremoniarum, omnes instructo ordine extra ad aream templi procedunt, ubi pilos ac sanguinem terræ infodiunt. Postea singuli ad sua loca redeunt, & carnes animalium asservantur: tunc Magister ceremoniarum alta voce clamat; *descendit spiritus Confucii*, quo dicto Sacerdos seu Mandarinus plenum vino calicem sumit, eumque in imaginem hominis è paleis contextam fundit; tum Confucii tabellam è loculo sumptam, super altare collocat, precationem summas Confucii laudes continentem recitando.

14. His peractis, incipit secunda pars sacrificii; clamante Magistro ceremoniarum; *Flectamus genua*, quo audito omnes genuflectunt, ac postmodum dicit, *Levate*, quo omnes statim surgunt: tum Mandarinus sive Sacerdos manus lavat, & oblatum sibi ab uno è Ministris pannum sericum, ab alio verò vas plenum vino suscipit. Clamat Magister ceremoniarum, *Sacrificus accedat ad Thronum Confucii.* Hic

Musicis

SINENSIUM.

Muſicis canentibus pannum ſericum, ac deinde vas vino plenum in altum tollit & Confucio offert. Magiſter ceremoniarum quater repetit, *Flectamus genua & levate*, & omnes quater genuflectunt toto corpore proſtrati, ac ſe ſe in pedes erigunt; tum pannus ſericus ignitis carbonibus comburitur, addita collecta ſeu precatione in honorem Confucii. Similiter poſt varias genuflexiones & reverentias, vinum offert cum precatione in qua ſpiritum Confucii tanquam præſentem alloquitur. Quinetiam Illuſtriſſimus Gregorius Lopez in tractatu supra citato cap. 5. quandam in honorem Confucii orationem refert ab uno ex Imperatoribus Sinenſibus compoſitam, quæ in ejuſmodi oblationibus ſeu ſacrificiis recitatur.

15. Ad tertiam deinde partem ſacrificii proceditur. Magiſter ceremoniarum clamat; *bibite vinum proſperitatis ac Felicitatis*, tum repetit ut ſupra; *Flectamus genua*, & alloquendo Sacrificum ait, *bibe vinum Felicitatis*; ſtatim autem Sacrificus illud exhaurit. Poſtea clamante Magiſtro ceremoniarum; *ſume carnem Sacrificii*, idem Sacrificus a Miniſtro carnes victimarum ſuſcipit, atque ambabus manibus ſublatas in altum offert, adjunctis duabus collectis quarum ultima ſic concluditur: *quodcumque tibi obtulimus purum eſt atque odoriferum: perfectis bis ceremoniis nos mortales in pace conquieſcimus, ſpiritus verò jucundatur. Ex bis ſacrificiis fiet ut bona & felicitates conſequamur.*

16. Poſtremo ſpiritum Confucii, quem adveniſſe ac tabellæ inſediſſe putant vel animo fingunt, ad ſuum locum abeuntem comitantur,

10   HISTORIA CULTUS

tur, & adjuncta folemni precatione deducunt: denique carnes facrificii inter affiftentes diftribuuntur, quas qui ederint, fe per Confucium beneficia & felicitates adepturos confidunt

17. Præter has folemnes oblationes, quæ bis in anno videlicet æquinoctio veris & autumni fiunt, aliæ funt minus folemnes quæ à Literatis toto anno frequentantur. Nam 1°. Doctores, Licentiati & Baccalaurei, ftatim atque in Gymnafio gradus adepti funt, ad contiguam Confucii ædem procedunt, ibique coram ejus tabella, accenfis fupra altare cereis, cum thuris & odorum fufitu, quater genuflectentes & toto corpore proftrati eum tanquam communem Magiftrum ac Parentem venerantur. 2. Mandarini, feu Urbium Gubernatores ac Magiftratus antequam dignitatem ineant, ad eandem Confucii ædem fe conferentes eum modo dictis ceremoniis venerantur. Tertio cujufque Urbis Mandarinus feu primarius Magiftratus bis fingulis menfibus, nempe novilunio & plenilunio, antequam ad audientiam pergat, comitantibus cæteris Officialibus & Literatis ad eandem ædem procedit, & accenfis pariter cereis, cum odorum fuffitu coram tabella Confucii iteratis vicibus genuflectit, & ad terram ufque fe profternit.

18. Porro obfervandum has fingulas in honorem Confucii oblationes feu ceremonias Imperatorum Sinenfium legibus publicoque Regni ufu ita ftabilitas effe, ut nemini liceat eas omittere, ftatutis, fi fecus fiat, graviffimis pœnis, videlicet amiffionis Mandarinatûs, vel

SINENSIUM.   18

vel dignitatis graduum, imo etiam vitæ, ut refert Illustrissimus Gregorius Lopez in Prologo tractatus de quo suprà. Vide etiam tractatus Reverendi P. *Varo* Dominicani cap. 5. art. 2.

19. Hæc sunt quæ circa cultus Progenitorum & Confucii, quod ad factum spectat, exponenda habui. Notandum autem illa ex Ritualibus & classicis libris, publicèque Sinarum usu ita certa & nota esse, ut ne ipsi quidem Jesuitæ ea negare aut in dubium revocare ausi fuerint, ut patet ex scriptis in hac controversia editis; & eorum Apologiis à Didaco Morales, Jacobo Fabro, Francisco Brancato, Bartholomæo Roboredo, & P. Tellier ejusdem Societatis compositis; imo & ex hisce observationibus id ipsum confirmatur. Quantumvis enim eorum interesset factum ipsum negare, vel saltem diminuere, si potuissent, id fere nusquam tentant: quin etiam Roboredus post relata ea, quæ de præfatis sacrificiis exposui, expressè fatetur ea sic se habere, prout illi objecta erant. Tota eorum disputatio eò tendit, ut hos ipsos cultus intra civilis & politici cultus terminos contineri, adeoque Christianis permitti posse doceant, quod non ad quæstionem facti, sed ad quæstionem juris pertinet.

AR-

152　HISTORIA CULTUS

Historia proferemus indubium etiam revocandi.

256. Quinetiam verendum est, ne si sæpius audiant, Majores suos per tria fere annorum millia verum Deum agnovisse & coluisse, Confucium verò, nostro quoque judicio, insignem virum fuisse omnique virtutum genere ornatissimum, atque iis etiam virtutibus, quæ Christianæ legis maxime propriæ sunt, quales sunt humilitas, modestia, paupertatis amor, offensarum condonatio, excelluisse; verendum, inquam, ne paulatim eis in mentem veniat, non ita necessariam esse Christianam legem ad perfectam justitiam & salutem æternam consequendam, adeoque posse eos ut Deistas rectè vivere, non susceptā Christi religione.

257. Christus Dominus, ejusque exemplo Apostoli Evangelicam legem, nullo ad Philosophorum Sectas, quæ tunc vigebant, habito respectu, publicarunt. Quid unaquæque veri haberet inter tot errores quibus scatebant, sibi examinandum minime putaverunt. Paulus quidem Athenis degens cum Epicureis & Stoicis disputavit, ut legitur Act. 17. v. 18. Sed solum eorum objectiones solvit erroresque confutavit. Sin verò in Areopago concionem habens, hac inscriptione, ignoto Deo, quam in quopiam eorum idolo legerat, in rem suam abusus est, & nonnulla Græcorum Poëtarum de immensitate Divini Numinis verba citavit; nequaquam tamen præclara illa ac vera dogmata, quæ Plato totaque ejus schola de Deo & plerisque humanæ vitæ officiis docet, in medium attulit, quò eos ad susci-

186 HISTORIA CULTUS

occultam aliorum idololatriam. Hæc enim inficit quidem cultum eorum externum, qui speciem sumit ab interno, sed extendi ad me non potest, nec ad vitiandas licitas per se mihi ceremonias, quibus Avos vel Magistrum Imperii colo.

Responsio.

15. An cultus Avorum & Confucii apud Sinas in sua prima institutione licitus ac mere politicus fuerit, non disputo. Illicitum esse ob introductam saltem jam à quadringentis aut quingentis annis, ut ipsimet Jesuitæ fatentur, superstitionem & idololatriam contendo. Neque vero illicitus est solum ob internam & occultam idololatriam, ut falsò sibi sumit Observator, sed ob externam & patentem. Num occultum quid & internum victimas sortitò eligere, jejunia & continentiam conjugalem præmittere, ipso die solemnitatis in ædibus ad hoc dedicatis, cereis accensis super Altare, thus & odoramenta coram tabellis Avorum & Confucii cremare; Caput porci aut capræ offerre, vinum libare, pannos sericos & nummos papyraceos, postquam oblati sunt, igne consumere, & alia rite ac solemniter peragere, quæ in Notis prioribus retuli? Hæ ceremoniæ simul sumptæ non speciem sumunt ab interno, ut asserit Observator, sed cultum constituunt per se superstitiosum & idololatricum, ac proinde Christianis omnino illicitum.

Observatio.

16. * Status ergo quæstionis ille est: an ob

* §. *Status ergo.*

HISTORIA CULTUS

rim, antequam Romam proficisceretur; cum tamen, inita subductaque temporum ratione, non amplius quam octo anni cum dimidio reperiantur. Si absolute decem annos dixissem, aliquem me reprehensioni locum dedisse non abnuerem; quanquam ad experientiam cultuum Sinensium de qua agitur, perinde est si quis octo tantum, aut decem annos in Sina degerit. Sed cum particulam *circiter* addiderim, nodum in scirpo quærit, qui id coram Eminentissimis Dominis reprehendendum ducit.

Observatio.

26. * Duo Patres interfuerunt Sacrificiis, hoc est viderunt ritus externos profundas inclinationes, odores incensos, oblatas carnes & alia ejusmodi quæ in Sina continuò fiunt amicis, hospitibus, Mandarinis adventantibus.

Responsio.

27. Falsissimum est, quod bona pace Observatoris dixerim, amicis, hospitibus, Mandarinis adventantibus ea fieri, quæ Pater Antonius à Sancta Maria & Pater Joannes Baptista Morales in eo sacrificio Progenitorum, cujus oculati testes fuêre, viderunt. Num solemnes ad Altare genuflectiones, & orationes per aliquod tempus hospitibus etiam Mandarinis adventantibus fiunt? Num calix vini ambabus manibus super caput tollitur & offertur, ac deinde ab offerente bibitur? Num simili modo caput capræ floribus intextum una cum

pilis

* *Ibid.*

SINENSIUM.   207

Responsio.

62. Quidquid de Confucii spiritu seu anima sentiant Sinæ Literati, tabella quæ sic inscribitur: *Sedes* seu *Locus animæ Sanctissimi & superexcellentissimi Protomagistri Confucii*, ubi spiritum ejus tempore oblationum, insistere ac requiescere putant, superstitione & idololatria non vacat; neque coram illa genuflectere, thus & odores cremare Christianis licitum est; multo minus vinum libare, capræ aut porci caput offerre, & reliqua obire quæ in solemni ejus cultu bis per annum fieri solent.

Observatio.

63. * Colunt (,Literati) & inferiori cultu tutelares, de quibus ante, spiritus.

Responsio.

64. His verbis Observator licitum declarat cultum genii tutelaris cujusque urbis, quem *Chin hoan* appellant. Atqui jamdiu omnes conveniunt illicitum esse & idololatricum hujusmodi cultum; eumque absolute prohibuit Decretum anni 1645: neque contra hanc prohibitionem quidquam mussitare ausus est Martinius.

Observatio.

65. † Ita Pater Semedo Christi Confessor, ut supradictum est, & 46. annorum Missionarius. Numquid mirum quod à Navarretta Dominoque Charmot hic citetur pro tuendis suis de Sina erroribus?

Responsio:

66. Quæ hic de Patre Alvaro Semedo habet

* § *Quod Spectat.*   † S. *Ita Pater.*

236 HISTORIA CULTUS

Primum factum

De voce Xangti, & de voce Tien.

Observatio.
126. * Resp. 1. primum istud factum sive antecedens esse falsissimum in eo sensu in quo verum illud esse oporteret, ut consequentiæ valerent. Ut autem id clare constet.

Responsio.
127. Hic replicat Observator quæ de hoc argumento in Observationibus ad Mandatum Reverendissimi Domini Maigrot habentur, & quæ à me confutata sunt in Notis ad easdem Observationes Sect. 3. Art. 1. 2. 3. 4. 5.

Observatio.
128. † Agitur de auctoritate Patris Semedo. Hic autem non modo non favet opinioni Domini Charmot, quod Sinæ omnes Literati non alium *Xangti* sive Deum agnoscant, quam cœlum materiale; sed est illi plane contrarius.

Responsio.
129. De facto à Patre Semedo relato agitur, non de ejus auctoritate in explicanda Sectæ Literariæ doctrina. Refert autem ille Reginæ Matris funus describens, *die octavo Lunæ oblata esse sacrificia Cœlo, Terræ, planetis, montibus, & fluminibus magna cum solemni-*

* §. Resp. 1.
† §. P. Semedo.

438　HISTORIA CULTUS

cultu apud eos coli ait Semedo. Deinde prætermisit etiam quæ apud Semedum proximè sequuntur his verbis : „ Ma come che non „ conobbero distintamente il vero Dio, ven-„ nero ad adorare tre cose le più celebri e „ poderose e utili del mondo, le quali chia-„ mano San Cai; cioe Cielo, Terra & Huo-„ mo. Quæ quidem verba totum Systema Observatoris evertunt. Si enim Literati eodem prorsus modo à multis jam sæculis cœlum, terram & homines colunt & adorant; patet ex sententia Semedi cultum illum; tum erga cœlum & terram, tum erga homines; puta Confucium & Progenitores mortuos, ut postmodum ipsemet Semedo explicat, esse cultum non mere civilem & politicum, sed sacrum ac religiosum, proindeque superstitiosum & idololatricum.

134. Hoc vere magnum piaculum haberi debet, in citando aliquo Auctore, ea quæ eodem loco leguntur, supprimere; ne Eminentissimi Judices in causa tam gravi quid verum ac justum sit deprehendant.

135. Pater Gabriel Magaillans celebris è Societate Missionarius in nova sua Relatione rerum Sinensium eodem modo, ac Pater Semedo de cultu Cœli, Solis, Lunæ ac Progenitorum loquitur cap. 13. pag. 20. ubi agens de Tribunali rituum, ait ejus esse cognoscere *de templis & de Sacrificiis quæ ab Imperatore offeruntur Cœlo, Terræ, Soli, Lunæ, ac suis Progenitoribus*; & eodem cap. pag. 209. agens de alio quodam Tribunali, ait *ejus curæ esse sartâ tectâ tenere templa in quibus Sinas Progenito-*

140 HISTORIA CULTUS

Responsio.

139. Egregia verò ratio non explicandi verba Auctorum, sed ad sensum nostrum detorquendi. De templo cœli cum aliqua probabilitate dici potest esse templum Cœlorum Domini. At per templum terræ significari templum Domini Terræ, absurdum videtur, præsertim si quis attendat Sinicæ Philosophiæ doctrinam de spiritibus tutelaribus terræ, fluminum, montium, civitatum, quacumque ratione Sinæ ejusmodi spiritus sibi animo fingant. Unde per templum terræ ad summum intelligi potest templum spiritus terræ. Porrò ex ejusdem Sectæ Literariæ principiis, quæ nullos agnoscit veros spiritus, sed hoc nomine appellat subtilissimam quamdam materiam, quæ maximè in cœlo, in terra, & in hominibus viget, rectè infert Reverendissimus D. Maigrot Sinas Literatos æque terram pro idolo ac cœlum materiale habere: imo & in colendis Progenitorum & Confucii spiritibus idololatriæ quoque scelus admittere, uti modo ex Patre Semedo audivimus.

Observatio.

140. * Hæc Secta, inquit Riccius, idola non colit, sed nec habet: unum numen veneratur, ideo quod ab eo conservari gubernarique hæc inferiora omnia arbitretur: Spiritus etiam, sed inferiore cultu, & contractiore dominio colit.

Responsio.

141. Secta Literaria non habet idola multi

* §. 20. Hæc Secta.

SINENSIUM.

lemnitate; unde recte intuli per cœlum hic intelligendum cœlum visibile & materiale, quemadmodum per terram; planetas, montes, & flumina; ibidem intelliguntur partes visibiles & corporeæ universi.

130. At, inquit Observator, Pater Semedo non existimat Sinas Literatos per *Xangti* intelligere cœlum materiale.

131. Respond. primò in loco Semedi à me allato non agi de voce *Xangti*, *Rex altus*, sed de voce *Tien*, *Cœlum*.

132. Secundò, locus Semedi à me allatus sumptus est ex cap. 17. pag. 105. Quæ autem citantur ab Observatore ut ostendat ex sententia Semedi, Sinas Literatos per *Xangti* rem aliam intelligere, quam cœlum materiale habentur cap. 18. pag. 110. Num verò mihi legendus fuit totus Liber, ut scirem an loco à me citato, aliquid alibi contrarium occurreret?

133. Tertiò eo ipso loco quem mihi objicit Observator, aliqua verba omittit, quæ ipsius falsam interpretationem arguunt. Nam postquam ait ex Patre Semedo, Literatos agnoscere Supremum Dominum & Imperatorem qui potest punire & compensare, appositis punctis supprimit sequentia verba: ,, Non ,, hanno però chiese nelle quali l'adorino, ,, ne officii che li facciano, ne orationi da ,, recitare, ne Sacerdoti ò Ministri, che li ,, prestino culto ,,: ex quibus verbis sequitur cœlum de quo supradictum est quòd ei Sinæ sacrificant, non esse Supremum illum Dominum & Imperatorem, quem nullo peculiari cultu

182 HISTORIA CULTUS

inde ab initio Societatis in Sina Missionarii conculcari idola à Neophytis, frangi, comburi: conculcarunt ipsi sæpissime, fregerunt, combusserunt.

Responsio.

7. Duplex est idololatriæ genus apud Sinas. Una est crassior & turpior, quam sequitur Secta Bonziorum seu Idololatrarum propriè dictorum, qui plurima ac turpissima in suis Pagodis seu fanis simulachra colunt. Alia est propria Sectæ Literatorum, quæ est præcipua Secta ac in toto Imperio regnans, cujus Caput ac Princeps est ipsemet Imperator. Hi juxta vulgata eorum Philosophiæ principia non cœlo tantum & terræ, sed & spiritibus montium, fluminum, atque idolo *Chin hoam*, hoc est tutelari cujusque Urbis genio sacrificant, ac præterea Progenitorum & Confucii Magistri tabellis idololatricos ac superstitione plenos cultus adhibent. De priori illa Bonziorum idololatria, nulla unquam fuit inter PP. Societatis & reliquos Missionarios disputatio. Omnes enim conveniunt esse rejiciendam; & hoc sensu verum est quod jam inde ab initio Societatis Missionarii jusserunt à Neophytis idola conculcari, frangi, comburi, & quod ipsimet sæpissime ea conculcarunt, fregerunt, combusserunt.

8. At propriè lis est circa cultus Progenitorum & Confucii, quales illos in Notis meis descripsi, quos jam ab initio Missionarii Ordinum Sancti Dominici & Sancti Francisci, corumque postea exemplo Reverendissimus Dominus Maigrot cæterique Vicarii & Missionarii

SINENSIUM. 241

ta & monstrosa, ut duæ aliæ Sectæ, quæ vocantur Magorum & idololatrarum: sed coelum, astra, ut veteres Persæ, aliasque præcipuas mundi partes colit. De hoc utroque idololatrarum genere quid censeat Sapiens videsis Sap. 13. v. 6. & v. 10. Notandum quoque his verbis Riccii spirituum cultum apud Sinas Literatos approbantis, declarari licitum cultum *Chin boan*, hoc est tutelaris spiritus seu genii cujusque civitatis, quem tamen cultum tanquam idololatricum, post Decretum anni 1645. ipsimet Jesuitæ rejiciunt.

Observatio.

142. * Nulla prorsus est in hac materia auctoritas Patris Kirkeri, nisi in quantum nititur auctoritate Patris Riccii.

Responsio.

143. Sic placet Observatori eorum auctoritatem, quos sibi contrarios offendit, elidere. In aliis rebus, quas etiam præsens non vidit, non leve pondus habebit Pater Kirkerus à Sotuelo ob singularem eruditionem ac Literaturam in Bibliotheca Scriptorum Societatis valde laudatus: de rebus Sinensibus nequidem audiendus erit, quod ex Europa nunquam egressus, hæc per se videre aut discere non potuit; quantumvis magna diligentia & indefesso labore insigne de hac materia opus composuerit, quod non sine laude in præfata Bibliotheca Scriptorum Societatis commemoratur, ac pleraque in eodem Libro ex Trigautio

* §. Nulla prorsus.

Q

220 HISTORIA CULTUS

„ sacrificandum esse animabus seu spiritibus,
„ quos *Ly Kuey* ac *Yeu huen* vocat, hoc est
„ spiritus & animas errantes, fixumque seu
„ determinatum locum non habentes (dicun-
„ tur autem esse animae illorum qui sine hae-
„ redibus decesserunt) eisque comestibilia ad
„ usum offerenda praescribit, ad hoc ut illi
„ spiritus vel animae hominibus non noceant,
„ infirmitates pellant, aliaque bona conce-
„ dant. Has auctoritates de precibus, quae
in oblationibus Progenitorum adhibentur,
ipsemet Illustrissimus Lopez adducit, quas
quidem postea explicare atque eludere conatur, adductis etiam aliis auctoritatibus quae
supra allatis contrariae videntur. Denique P.
Alvarus Semedo ab Observatore multum laudatus in sua rerum Sinicarum Relatione Part.
1. Cap. 18. post relatos honores & cultus Confucio & Progenitoribus exhiberi solitos; haec
addit: „ pro anima sua in altera vita nihil ex-
„ pectant aut petunt. At pro vita praesente
„ adjutorium postulant, bonam videlicet sor-
„ tem atque eorum gesta, & facta posse imi-
„ tari „. De quo videsis priores meas Notas
Sect. 1. Art. 3. numero 38. itemque Art. 7.
numero 81. An in prima ejusmodi rituum
institutione secus res se habuerit, nolim disputare. De prima illa institutione videtur in-
telligendus locus Libri Ritualis *Ly ky* citatus
ab Observatore. Patris Riccii ad defenden-
dos ritus Sinenses propensioris auctoritatem
non moramur.

91. Postremo qui naturam & mores Sinensium sua ubique commoda sectantium & ar-
denti

SINENSIUM. 85

&i fuerant Israelitæ; posteriore Chaldæi unde oriundi erant iidem Israelitæ, quos sic alloquitur Josue: *trans fluvium habitaverunt Patres vestri, ab initio Thare Pater Abraham & Nachor; servieruntque Diis alienis.* Jos. 24. v. 2.

VI.

146. Anceps etiam atque ambigua in hac materia est significatio vocis *Atheus.* Unde Observator † sensu apud Europæos vulgari eam accipiens, passim Reverendissimum D. Maigrot criminatur & in invidiam vocat, quod eo nomine Sinas Literatos atque etiam hodiernum Imperatorem appellet. Atqui proprie apud Sinas Athei dicuntur Literati, ut distinguantur à duabus aliis Sectis, Magorum videlicet atque Bonziorum, qui tot inter crassissimos errores in eo tamen recte sentiunt quod animas esse immortales, & post hanc vitam, pro meritis, vel proemio affici, vel poenas subire credunt. Literati vero coelum putant rerum omnium esse principium, sive coeli nomine intelligant subtilissimam materiam quam *Li* seu *Taikie* appellant, in varias rerum formas divisam ac figuratam, quæ est sententia antiquorum classicorum librorum & commentariorum Sectæ Literariæ; atque etiamnum inter omnes pene Literatos recepta:

† 2. *Part. Obs.* 4. *in* 1. *Cap. Mand.* §. Itaque Decretum. *Obs.* 3. *in* 2. *Cap. Mand.* §. 5. Eo ipso *Ibid.* §. 5. Falsissimum *Obs. in* 3. *Cap. Mand.* §. Jam vero.

F 3

86 HISTORIA CULTUS

pta: five eodem cœli nomine aliud quid excellentius intelligant, hoc est principium aliquod activum seu naturam intelligentem rerum omnium Creatricem & Gubernatricem, quam sententiam Observator post Patrem Matthæum Riccium veteribus Sinis ac primis Literariæ Sectæ Auctoribus tribuit, & quam vult etiam esse Imperatoris qui hodie regnat, & plurium in ejus Aula Literatorum.

147. Quapropter Athei nomen non eadem significatione apud Sinas accipiendum est, atque in Europa & apud Christianos. Apud hos enim significat eum qui impietatem profitetur, & tum intus in animo, tum etiam voce Deum esse negat, quod omnes detestantur: apud Sinas autem idem pene significat ac Literatum, seu Literariæ Sectæ discipulum; seposita quæstione, an Literati Deum & Providentiam negent, quomadmodum olim Epicurei; an vero Deum aliquatenus, modo scilicet valde imperfecto, agnoscant.

148. Frustra itaque Observator hujus verbi ambiguo Reverendissimum D. Maigrot criminatur atque Eminentissimos Dominos terret, quasi quis Imperatorem ac plerosque ejus Aulæ proceres Atheos sine magna eorum offensione dicere non possit. Hæc homines incautos ac rerum Sinicarum ignaros decipere possunt; at multum erravit Observator, si ejusmodi terriculis & captionibus Eminentissimos Patres commoveri, atque in fraudem deduci posse existimavit.

VII.

SINENSIUM. 87

VII.

149. Hac revocandum puto quamdam objectionem, quam non parum urget Observator. Pugnantia, * inquit, loquitur Reverendissimus D. Maigrot, dum Confucii & Progenitorum cultum idololatricum esse contendit, & nihilominus Literatos tanquam Atheos, qui neque spiritus, neque animam immortalem esse credunt, traducit. Qui enim, inquit, fieri potest, ut Sinæ Confucii & Progenitorum spiritus invocent ad tabellas, tanquam ad locum & sedem ubi requiescant, invitent, & ab eis bona sperent aut postulent, si nullam spiritualem substantiam agnoscunt, si animam hominis immortalem esse negant. Quam sint istæ contradictiones Sorbonico Doctore indignæ, nullus est, inquit, tyro qui non apprehendat.

150. Respondeo hæc tam confidenter tamque arroganter in Reverendissimum D. Maigrot dici non posse, nisi ab eo qui vere in rebus Sinicis tyro sit, vel qui earum minus peritos decipere velit. Sinæ juxta Literariæ Sectæ principia, veros spiritus atque adeo immortales hominum animas non agnoscunt, neque tamen has corpore solutas, penitus extingui aut evanescere existimant. Siquidem animo sibi fingunt, eas esse partem subtilissimæ illius materiæ, quam *Li* seu *Taikie* appel-

* 2. Part. Obs. in 3. Cap. Mand. S. Ro. 4. *Reverendissimum*.

F 4

122 HISTORIA CULTUS

Mattheo Riccio & Successore ejus Patre Nicolao Longobardo. Riccius qui anno 1581, in Sinam penetravit, postquam non sine diuturno & improbo labore Sinicam linguam didicisset, ex lectione veterum ejusdem gentis Philosophorum, priscos Sinas verum Deum agnovisse, & sub nomine *Xangti* adorasse, persuasum habuit, qua in opinione per longos annos usque ad mortem perseveravit, eamque sua auctoritate cæteris è Societate Missionariis, qui ei in excolenda hac Domini vinea primi adjutores fuerunt, persuasit. Longobardus anno 1596, Sinam ingressus in addiscenda lingua Sinica multum laboravit, & in legendis Sinensium libris diu versatus est: qua ex lectione deprehendit sententiam Patris Riccii parum esse certam, multoque verius videri priscos Sinas ac Philosophos, sicut & eorum discipulos, successu temporis usque ad hanc nostram ætatem, per *Xangti* nihil aliud intellexisse præter cœlum materiale seu subtilissimam materiam & quandam quasi quintam essentiam, quam *Li* sive *Tai Kie* appellabant, quæ per universas mundi partes diffunderetur, & in præstantioribus ejus naturis cùm cœlestibus, tum terrenis maxime vigeret. Unde consequens est, nunquam eos veros spiritus à materia separatos agnovisse, supposito tanquam fundatissimo suæ Philosophiæ principio, *omnia unum esse*; quæ fuit etiam sententia Democriti & Epicureorum, quam nostra hac ætate impius Spinosa in monstruosis suis operibus iterum in lucem revocavit.

204.

126 HISTORIA CULTUS

210. Infirmum prorsus ac debile est quod pro commendando nomine *Xangti* affert Observator; videlicet Fundatores Nationis Sinicæ primosque Sectæ Literariæ Auctores verum ac vivum Deum agnovisse, atque eum nomine *Xangti* appellasse; hanc veri Dei cognitionem per duo & tria annorum millia perseverasse apud Sinas, nec nisi longo post tempore apud plerosque Literatos obliteratam fuisse, qui per vocem *Xangti* nihil amplius intellexerunt, quam cœlum materiale, unde in Atheismi barathrum prolapsi sunt.

211. Hæc nituntur sola auctoritate Patris Riccii & sequacium ejus; qui hoc modo antiquorum Sinensium libros vulgo dictos classicos interpretantur, in quibus aliqua occurrunt quæ in hunc sensum torqueri possunt. Verum cum ejusmodi libri sint obscuri & in multis ænigmati similes, ratio & æquitas postulare videntur, ut eorum explicatio & intelligentia petatur ex commentariis quos Sinæ Literati, tum primis illis temporibus, tum postea tot sæculorum spatio ediderunt, quorum videlicet commentariorum tanta est auctoritas, ut nonnulli eorum veteribus illis classicis libris æquiparentur. Atqui omnium illorum commentariorum communis est doctrina, per *Xangti* intelligendum cœlum materiale, seu efficientem quamdam ejus virtutem, quam diximus *Li* vel *Tai Kie* appellari; & de veris spiritibus atque animarum immortalitate altum apud illos silentium.

212. Et quidem ea est adhuc hocce tempore

242　HISTORIA CULTUS

tió aliifque Societatis Scriptoribus vel monumentis retulerit.

Obfervatio.

144. * Quia primò Kirkerus expreſsè docet Part. 3. Cap. 1. Sinas Literatos idola juxta Confucii dictamina non colere, fed unum numen quod vocant Regem Cœlorum.

Refponfio.

145. Nihil clarius, nihil expreſſius quam, juxta Kirkerum, Sinas Literatos credere rerum omnium principium eſſe figuratum, & talis corpulentiæ, ut Sinenſibus comprehendi queat, quòd cœlo materiali feu efficienti ejus virtuti, quam *Li* feu *Tai kie*, vel etiam *Xangti*, id eſt Regem altum appellant, optime congruit. An alibi idem Kirkerus in longo ſuo Opere aliquid contrarium docuerit, vel ex aliis ut Riccio, Trigautio retulerit, non meum erat exquirere. Id oneris non ſumpſi, quando ab Eminentiſſimis Patribus juſſus ſum facti veritatem, ex Scriptoribus Societatis quantum fieri poſſet, probare: neque hac unquam ratione probabit Obfervator me falsò vel Semedum, vel Kirkerum produxiſſe.

146. Deinde loco quem opponit Obfervator, Kirkerus ita docet Sinas Literatos unum numen colere, quod vocant Regem cœlorum, ut ſtatim addat ex Trigautio, „ Regi Cœlo„ rum ſacrificandi ejuſque colendi munus ſo„ lum ad Regem ſpectare: in hunc finem Re„ gem duo habere templa ſane magnifica in „ utraque Regia Nankinenſi & Pekinenſi;
„ cœlo

* §. Quia primò.

SINENSIUM.

204. Longobardus, cùm Riccio in Missionariorum Societatis præfectura anno 1610. successisset, magis magisque in opinione concepta animum obfirmavit, atque etiam eruditissimum de ea tractatum composuit, quem Illustrissimus Navaretta 1. Tomo Operum suorum typis evulgavit. Hanc Longobardi sententiam apud Societatis Missionarios invaluisse ex eorum conventu anno 1628. in Civitate *Kiating* celebrato, patet. * In primo quippe articulo statuunt Regem alti sive *Xangti* quem secta Literaria prædicat, non esse verum Spiritum. *Siquidem*, inquiunt, *Sinæ veros spiritus non agnoscunt, sed solum vim operativam seu influxum Cœli ad producendum res universas, quas Cœlo seu Taikie ortum ducere existimant.*

205. Anno 1629, proximè sequenti Pater Palmeirus Sinensium Missionum Visitator, Missionarios Societatis de significatione vocabuli *Xangti* dissidentes reperiens, ut eos inter se conciliaret, prohibuit ne quis in posterum ea voce ad significandum Dei nomen uteretur. Verum postea Jesuitæ sententiam Riccii propagationi fidei magis commodam arbitrati, usum vocabuli *Xangti* revocarunt, spreto ac rejecto Longobardi tractatu, cujus lectione cum plurimi commoverentur, dicitur Pater Franciscus Hurtado Viceprovincialis anno 1645. cum flammis condemnasse, ut narrat Reverendiss. D. Maigrot in Expositione versus finem §. 3. *Observatione dignum.*

AR-

* *Navarretta tom.* 2. p. 110.

SINENSIUM.

pore omnium Literatorum sententia, si paucos excipias Christianos qui Patri Riccio assentientes, spretis commentariis, veteres libros classicos sensu ad Christianam veritatem accommodato benigne interpretantur. De hodierno Sinarum Imperatore, & quibusdam aliis inter Mandarinos Literatis, an verum & vivum Deum sub nomine *Xangti* agnoscant, sequenti articulo expendemus.

213. Prudentes autem & æqui Lectores considerent an verisimile sit, Patri Riccio paucisque aliis in Sinam ex Europa advenis veterum librorum Sinensium atque ipsius Confucii sensum & doctrinam melius perspectam fuisse, quam innumeris commentariorum Scriptoribus ac Literatis Sinensibus, qui immenso tot annorum spatio hanc Philosophiam excoluerunt, & Confucium pro communi Magistro habentes, ejus libros assidue & magna cum diligentia evolverunt.

214. Præterea ex hoc Riccii atque Observatoris Systemate sequeretur, antiquos Sinas per duo & amplius annorum millia verum ac vivum Deum agnovisse & adorasse, propemodum sicut eum agnoverunt & adoraverunt Abraham, Isaac, Jacob, Melchisedech: id quod nullatenus cum Sacra Bibliorum Historia congruit, quæ docet idololatriam jam tempore Abrahami valde communem fuisse, etiam in Provinciis vicinioribus locorum ubi Noë ejusque filii ac nepotes sedes suas fixerant; ætate vero Moysis non solum totam Ægyptum, sed omnes latè regiones inundasse; si Abrahami & Lothi posteros, nempe

128 HISTORIA CULTUS

pe Madianitas, Moabitas, Ammonitas excipias, apud quos utcumque veri Dei cultus perseveravit. Dixi utcumque; nam de Moabitarum & Ammonitarum idololatria mentio jam sub primis Judicibus habetur, Jud. 10. v. 6. id est de idolo Chamos proprio Moabitarum, & de Idolo Moloch proprio Ammonitarum, prout nominantur 3. Reg. 11. v. 5. & 7.

215. Nihil obstat quin veteres Sinæ Persarum, qui solem & ignem adorabant, similes fuerint. Utrique proprie non erant Athei, sed idololatræ, cum Supremi Entis ideam rebus corporalibus, quas præstantissimas agnoscebant, affigerent. Neque vero apparet quonam privilegio tota Sinensium natio ad duo vel tria annorum millia, veri numinis notitiam retinuisset, dum omni scientiarum genere cultissimæ doctissimæque Nationes, ut Chaldæi, Ægyptii, Græci ac Romani offusis idololatriæ tenebris, à cognitione & cultu Dei aberrabant.

216. Ultra adhuc progrediuntur recentiores Societatis Scriptores. Si enim eis fides adhibeatur, plures ex antiquis Imperatoribus Sinensibus virtutes omnes morales & politicas cum veri numinis notitia & cultu conjunxerunt. Confucium in primis Philosophum tanquam virum omni virtutum genere ornatissimum nobis exhibent, ac fere ut beatum in cœlo collocant. Atqui in ejus libris nuper editis nihil penitus occurrit, ex quo conjicias eum futuri Messiæ aliquam notitiam habuisse, cum tamen post Adami lapsum, ne-

SINENSIUM. 119

mo sine fide Redemptoris æternam salutem obtinere potuerit.

ARTICULUS III.

An hodie multi sint Literati Sinenses qui veri numinis notitiam habeant.

217. * Observator Patris *Bouvet* & Patris *Le Comte* Jesuitarum auctoritate ac testimonio nixus, supponit multos hodie esse Literatos Sinenses, qui verum Deum agnoscunt, & qui relictis commentariis à quingentis aut sexcentis annis in lucem editis, antiquos Libros classicos & Confucii scripta, eodem, ac Pater Riccius, sensu explicant: affirmat nominatim Imperatorem *Cambi* Tartarum hodie regnantem nequaquam esse Atheum; per *Kangti* Deum vivum & verum intelligere, eique singulis annis *pro suo munere Pontificis religionis totius Imperii*, sacrificare; ipsum denique molestissime laturum; si sensus Atheismo faventes sibi tribui resciret.

218. Quæ hanc in rem à Jesuitis afferuntur, parum firma aut probabilia videntur. Sanè constat hunc ipsum Imperatorem tanquam Sectæ Literariæ Principem nonnullos de Sinica Philosophia libros composuisse, in quibus de cœlo & subtilissima ejus parte, quam *Li seu Taikie* vocant, eodem prorsus modo disputat, ac Scriptores qui à quadringentis aut quingentis annis commentarios ediderunt; cæterique hujusce

* 2. *Part. Obs.* 3. §. Quare tertio.

I

130 HISTORIA CULTU

jusce temporis Literati ; ita ut non minus quam illi Atheus esse videatur, id est alienus ab agnoscenda substantia aliqua spirituali, cujuscumque materiæ aut corporis experte. Hanc rationem urget Reverendissimus D. Maigrot in sua Expositione circa medium §. 3. *Imperator* & §. *Verbum quod*, & eam quoque probat Pater Augustinus à Sancto Pascale Missionarius Ordinis Sancti Francisci in scripto cujus exemplum autenticum habeo.

219. Præterea idem Imperator singulis annis publicè cœlo sacrificat pro suo munere Pontificis religionis totius Imperii, ut loquitur Pater Bouvet in sua ad Observatorem epistola, iisdem prorsus ceremoniis, eodemque ritu, atque alii Imperatores Sinenses ejus prædecessores, præteritis sæculis, sacrificarunt. Deinde illud sacrificium offert tanquam Literariæ Sectæ Princeps, atque adeo non alia mente, non alio religionis sensu, quam cæteri Literati & Mandarini Regii Comitatus, qui illum in ea functione affectantur, ita ut cœli nomine non aliud, quam cœlum materiale seu efficientem ejus virtutem, intelligere censendus sit.

220. Si quando itaque idem Imperator, & nonnulli ex ejus Ministris vel aulicis in familiari cum Patre Bouvet aliisque Jesuitis congressu, significarunt se iis de existentia & natura Dei assentiri, credibile est id eos fecisse, ut Philosophiam suam commendarent, ad quam Patres Societatis se se in multis accommodare libenter vident.

AR-

SINENSIUM.

ARTICULUS IV.

De eodem argumento.

221. Etsi Observatori concederem, tum antiquos Sinenses, tum aliquos etiamnum ex Literatis per *Xangti* verum ac vivum Deum intelligere; non inde sequeretur idem illud vocabulum nunc à Christianis eadem significatione usurpandum, quod sequentibus rationibus patebit.

222. Primo quam longissime spatium illud temporis, quo antiqui Sinæ verum Deum agnovisse & coluisse dicuntur, extendas, vix ultra primum æræ Christianæ sæculum producitur, quo tempore Secta idololatrarum dicta *Foe*, ex Indiis orta in Sinam ingressa est, anno ut creditur, Christi sexagesimo quinto: ab illo enim tempore ut ait Illustrissimus Lopez in Prologo sui Tractatus, & Pater Intorcetta in vita Confucii, Literati, ut hujus Sectæ, quæ alteri Magorum dictæ *Tao*, conjuncta multum invalescebat, progressum impedirent, à pristina doctrina de Deo, & animæ immortalitate recesserunt, ac paulatim in impietatem & Atheismum devenerunt. Itaque juxta hanc computationem, fere à mille & quingentis annis vocabulum *Xangti* apud Literatos Sinenses verum Deum non significat: quod si admittatur, concedendum etiam non expedire ut Christiani Sinenses ejusmodi vocabulum, diversa plane significatione, ab

HISTORIA CULTUS

ea quam per tam longum temporis spatium obtinuit, adhibeant. Neque juvat objicere non à tanto tempore, sed à quadringentis, aut ut multum, quingentis annis Literatos Sinenses à Majorum suorum doctrinâ degenerasse & in Atheismum delapsos esse. Id enim ad quæstionem de qua agitur nihil refert, cum æque certum sit usurpari non debere vocem *Xangti* ad significandum Deum, sive plura, sive pauca sæcula numerentur, ex quo defiit in Sina hanc habere significationem.

223. Secundò tametsi cum Jesuitis supponeretur aliquot nunc esse Literatos Sinenses qui verum Deum agnoscant & nomine *Xangti* designent, negari non potest, quin reliqui hoc est totum Literatorum corpus, imo & universa Sinensium Natio hoc nomine intelligant cœlum materiale, seu efficientem ejus virtutem, quam significationem jam à quadringentis, ut minimum, annis obtinet. Jam vero quis dubitat, quin verba vim ac significationem suam ex publico ac præsenti usu accipiant, non vero ex quorumdam privatorum acceptione aut ex vetustissimo usu, cujus vix memoria superfit?

224. Tertio non juvat si dicas cum Observatore constare apud Sinas per hanc vocem *Xangti* non intelligi cœlum materiale à Christianis, sed Deum Opt. Max. id est substantiam spiritualem cujuscumque materiæ expertem omniumque Creatricem & Gubernatricem. Nam 1. apud plebeios Sinenses, imo & plerosque Literatos, non ita notum ac pervulgatum est, quid fides Christiana de divi-

næ

SINENSIUM. 133.

næ essentiæ spiritualitate doceat, quin facile in eo errare possint, existimantes vocem *Xangti* non aliud apud Christianos, quam apud se significare. 2. Cum valdè in suo sensu abundent, peculiarique hujus nationis vitio eà sint arrogantiâ, ut vix quicquam ab exteris discere velint, facile contingeret, ut vocem *Xangti* ex ore Christianorum & Divini Verbi Ministrorum audientes, sibi in animum inducerent, nos non aliter atque ipsi solent, Deum intelligere, & cogitatione comprehendere; præsertim cum experientia constet quàm difficile sit mentem à corporalibus rebus abstrahere, & substantiam mere spiritualem animo percipere. Non potest itaque sine maximo incommodo vox ista usurpari à Christianis, diversâ prorsus significatione, ab illâ quæ ad apud Sinenses communis est. Hac verborum communicatione accedendo ad Literatos, non lucrum, sed damnum facerent Christiani. Non enim id agitur, ut relictis erroribus, facilius illi ad nos transeant, sed potius ut nos falsas eorum de Deo opiniones probare videamur. Uno verbo scandali & confusionis erit occasio, si ad significandum Deum eam vocem usurpemus, qua ipsi ad sui Atheismi professionem utuntur.

I 3 AR-

134 HISTORIA CULTUS

ARTICULUS V.

Objectiones contra suppressionem vocis Xangti *expenduntur.*

225. Objicit * Observator, si vox *Xangti* excludi debet ex eo quod Literati cœlum materiale per hanc vocem significent, debere excludi quoque vocem *Tien Chu*, cùm sint multi apud Sinas idololatræ qui sub illa voce plurima venerantur.

226. Facilis est responsio. Si quid ambigui sit in voce *Tien Chu* ob variam significationem quam habet apud idololatras seu Bonziorum Sectam, nullum inde periculum est nullaque difficultas Christianis, quibuscum Bonzii & idololatræ nihil pene habent commune. Eamdem quidem vocem aliquando adhibent Literati ad significandum cœlum materiale, tanquam omnium corporum præstantissimum. Verum id rarius contingit : fere semper ea significatione vocem *Xangti* usurpant. Cum itaque, prout inter omnes convenit, ad significandum Deum adhibenda sit vox Sinica, rejectis Europæis nominibus, ob rationes supra allatas, omnino opportunum atque expediens videtur ut vox *Tien Chu*, jam à principio à Christianis adoptata, & apud eos communi usu recepta, retineatur, spreta illa ejusdem vocis ambiguitate, quæ nullius est momenti.

227.

* 2. *Part. Obs.* 3. §. Quia secundo.

SINENSIUM.

227. Alia objectio * Obfervatoris eſt, quod in libris permultis, jam à principio Miſſionis editis Deus Opt. Max. ſæpe fuerit vocatus *Xangti*, qui quidem libri per omnes Sinenſis Imperii Provincias ab omnibus paſſim leguntur, tam Chriſtianis, quam infidelibus: unde ejuſmodi libros ſupprimere fruſtra quis conaretur; eorum autem lectionem Chriſtianis interdicere, nimis durum atque incommodum eſſet.

228. Reſpondeo duo eſſe genera librorum, in quibus vox *Xangti* ad ſignificandum Deum occurrit. Alii deditâ operâ compoſiti ſunt ad probandum id quod voce *Xangti* apud Literatos ſignificatur, eſſe Deum Opt. Max. quem adoramus, adeoque vocem illam eadem ſignificatione apud Chriſtianos retinendam: alii ſunt in quibus de ea quæſtione ſiletur, ſed ſimpliciter ea vox ad ſignificandum Deum aliquando uſurpatur. Quod ad priores libros ſpectat, qui non ita magno numero ſunt, nihil incommodi timendum videtur, ſi eorum lectio Chriſtianis interdicatur, quæ non niſi damno & fraudi eis eſſe poteſt, poſito quod per vocem *Xangti* Sinæ tantum cœlum materiale ſeu vim ejus efficientem intelligant.

229. De aliis verò libris ubi ſimpliciter vox *Xangti* ad ſignificandum Deum uſurpatur, non videtur quod ſupprimendi ſint, aut eorum lectio Chriſtianis ſit interdicenda, modo moneantur retinendam eſſe ſolam vocem *Tien Chu*, neque licitum fore impoſterum in libris ad eorum uſum publicandis aliam adhibere.

230. Quin & illud notandum in Sina typographi-

---

* *Part. 2. Obſ. 2. §. Quarta ratio.*

136　**HISTORIA CULTUS**

graphorum formas, editis libris, non rumpi, sed integras ad sequentes editiones conservari; unde non ita difficile esset, mutatis locis ubi vox *Xangti* occurrit, novas procurare editiones librorum saltem magis necessariorum, quales sunt Catechismi, Horæ divini officii, precationum Libelli, & similes, si qui tamen ejusmodi adhuc cum voce *Xangti* reperiantur; idque eo facilius fieret, quod librorum editio apud Sinas parvo sumptu constet.

ARTICULUS VI.

De Vocabulo Tien (*Cœlum.*)

231. Postquam Reverendissimi Domini Maigrot Edictum circa vocabulum *Xangti* contra Observatorem defendi, inutile ac supervacaneum esset de vocabulo *Tien*, fusius disputare. Nam si vox *Xangti* (*Imperator Supremus seu Rex Altus*), qua quidquid est in Astris aliisque corporibus cœlestibus subtilius nobiliusque indicatur, ad significandum Deum, ob rationes supra allatas, adhiberi non debet; multo minus adhibenda est vox *Tien*, quæ cœlum in genere, id est omnes globos cœlestes, omniaque astra significat, cum dumtaxat nobilissimam excellentissimamque visibilis hujus mundi partem designet, quam idcirco veteres Persæ, sicut & Sinenses, divinis honoribus dignam esse putaverunt.

232. Neque hic velim omittere cultum illum

SINENSIUM.

lum cœli apud Sinas rem esse adeo certam & publicam, ut inter notissimas hujus Nationis consuetudines numeretur in libro Italico recens edito. Is liber, qui dum hæc scriberem, in manus meas incidit, inscribitur: *Notizie parie dell' Imperio della China in Firenze 1697.* adjunctæ sunt aliquæ epistolæ Patris Joannis Grueber Missionarii è Societate, qui è Sina anno 1662. rediit, ubi inter alia loquens de Tartaris qui Sinam occuparunt pag. 88. hæc habet: *Tartari sunt ejusdem religionis cum Sinensibus, adorantque omnia idola Sinensium ac maxime cursum cœli & planetarum, cui multum adscribunt.* Ex quo patet Patrem Grueber pro certo habere, Sinenses esse idololatras, ac cœli astrorumque cursui magnam virtutem, adeoque & divinitatem tribuere: id quod sine dubio de Literatis Sinensibus intelligendum, cum Tartarus Imperator qui hodie regnat, cæterique Tartari ejus Ministri Sectam Literariam sequantur, nihilque cum duabus aliis Sectis, idololatrarum videlicet & Magorum, commune habeant.

SECTIO

HISTORIA CULTUS

SECTIO QUARTA.

De Secundo Capite Edicti Reverendiſſimi D. Maigrot circa tabellas inſcriptas KING TIEN, id eſt, cœlum colito.

ARTICULUS I.

Jure merito interdictum à Reverendiſſimo D. Maigrot ne in Eccleſiis & ſuper altare collocentur tabellæ cum hac inſcriptione: cœlum colito.

233. Quæ præcedenti Sectione de vocibus *Xangti* & *Tien*, & de Literatorum Sinenſium Atheiſmo ſeu Idololatria dicta ſunt, ſufficere poſſent ad defendendum ſecundum Caput Edicti Reverendiſſimi Domini Maigrot, quo Chriſtianis uſum tabellarum prædictarum interdicit, ac nominatim prohibet ne in Eccleſiis appendantur, aut ſupra Altare collocentur.

234. Si enim conſtet Literatos Sinenſes à quadringentis ſaltem aut quingentis annis per vocem *Tien* cœlum materiale intelligere, cui tanquam rerum omnium viſibilium excellentiſſimæ maximum honorem ſeu cultum deferendum putant; ſi hodiernus Imperator tanquam

SINENSIUM.

quam Literariæ Sectæ Princeps, & totius Nationis primarius Pontifex eidem cœlo, non alio ritu, aliisve ceremoniis, quam prædecessores ejus Imperatores, publice sacrificat; necessario sequitur idololatricas esse ejusmodi tabellas, neque ab ea labe purgari posse, quod alio sensu à Christianis intelligantur; quasi verò vocis *Tien* significatio mutata sit, quod Imperator & aliqui alii Mandarini Literati Jesuitis in familiari congressu dixerint, se per istud vocabulum Dominum Cœli & Terræ, seu Deum Opt. Max. quem Christiani prædicant, intelligere.

285. Quando Imperator unam ex ejusmodi tabellis in qua propria manu scripserat *King Tien*, *Cælum colito*, Jesuitis Pekinensibus dono dedit, non quo sensu se verba illa intelligere dixit, sed quo à Literatorum Secta totaque natione accipiantur, attendere oportebat. Quapropter consultius fecissent Patres Societatis, si donum istud apud se retinuissent, ut benevolentiæ & amoris pignus, quo eos Imperator tanquam Mandarinos Mathematicos, & in aula sua conficiendo quotannis Kalendario præfectos honorare voluit. At hoc honore non contenti, adinstar illius tabellæ plures alias effingi curarunt, easque aliis Jesuitis in Provincias miserunt, ut in eorum Ecclesiis & super altare collocatæ publico cultui exponerentur; qua in re verendum est ne studio obsequendi Imperatori, ejusque gratiam magis ac magis promerendi, non satis quid Christianæ Religioni congruerat, attenderint.

286.

HISTORIA CULTUS

286. Observator * retinendam esse vocem *Tien* ad significandum Deum hac ratione probare conatur; videlicet quod sit satis frequens in nostris etiam scripturis hæc figura, qua ad exprimendum Deum continens ponitur pro contento, sive Cœlum pro Deo Cœli, quam in rem varios locos ex Scriptura Sacra adducit. Sed hæc in casu præsenti nihil omnino probant, cùm significatio vocis *Tien* ex publico usu & doctrina communi Literatorum Sinensium certam significationem habeat, quam nequidem per translationem verbi mutare licet ob periculum ambiguitatis in materia adeo gravi. Ejusmodi figura qua continens pro contento ponitur valet ad explicandum Sacræ Scripturæ locos, aut etiam has vulgares Christianorum locutiones, è Cœlo expectandum esse adjutorium, Cœlum tantam injuriam inultam non dimissurum, pluresque alias similes; sed frustra adhibetur ad explicandam vocem quæ apud universam nationem Sinensium & Literariam Sectam, significat ipsum Cœlum materiale tanquam omnium corporum præstantissimum, præter quod nullam aliam excellentiorem substantiam agnoscunt.

237. Hinc etiam patet falsam esse ratiocinationem † Observatoris, dum vocem *Tien* cum voce Latina *Deus* comparat, quam Apostoli non repudiarunt ad significandum supremum numen, tametsi ea Gentiles abute-

---

* *Part. 2. Obs. 4. §. Ratio secunda.* † *Part. 2. Obs. 2. in 2. Cap. Editti §. Sicut ergo.*

SINENSIUM. 141

ferentur ad significandum Jovem aliosque falsos Deos. Non enim eadem est ratio vocis *Tien*, nisi manifesta petitione principii supponas hac voce Deum significari tum apud omnes antiquos Sinenses; tum etiam hocce tempore apud plerosque Literatos. At res contrario plane modo se habet. Vox *Tien* à longissimo jam tempore, ut de antiquis Sinensibus hîc sileam, apud Literariam Sectam & in tota Sina non est appellativum supremi numinis nomen ut apud Latinos *Deus*, sed dumtaxat materiale Cœlum tanquam mundi præstantissimum corpus summo ac peculiari honore dignum, significat; unde idoli loco eis est, haud secus ac Græcis & Latinis Gentilibus Jupiter fuit. Quapropter haud abs re Reverendiss. D. Maigrot in sua Expositione hæc verba *Cœlum colito*, his verbis *Jovem colito*, confert, præsertim cum Jupiter, secundum etymologiam idem sit ac juvans Pater, quo nomine credibile est veteres Latinos Cœlum intellexisse, quod influxu suo inferiora corpora juvet ac foveat.

238. Denique quantumvis in Scriptura Sacra & in vulgati Christianorum sermone receptum sit Cœli nomine Deum intelligere, attamen si quis tabellam construeret his verbis inscriptam: *Cœlum colito*, eamque in altari collocaret, ut ab omnibus videretur & coleretur, nemo est qui illam, tanquam Religioni contrariam non respueret. Eam Episcopi aut alii Superiores Ecclesiastici juberent amoveri, & si quid tale Romæ contingeret, S. Congregatio S. Officii adversus hujus no-

vi-

142 HISTORIA CULTUS

vitatis reos inquireret, eosque debita pœna afficeret. Quid igitur censendum de iisdem tabellis in Sina, ubi Literatorum Sectæ solemne est hæc ipsa verba, *Cælum colito*, ad significandum cultum suum idololatricum adhibere? Nonne qui ejusmodi tabellas in Ecclesiis super altare collocant, veritatem cum errore, lucem cum tenebris, Christum cum Belial conjungunt? Nonne Religio Christiana infidelium sannis & irrisioni objicitur, ubi viderint ab Evangelii Ministris & Prædicatoribus adoptari & publico usu consecrari ea ipsa verba, quibus ipsi idololatriam suam seu Atheismum exprimere solent?

ARTICULUS II.

Expenduntur utilitates quas ejusmodi tabellæ dicuntur habere ad fidem Christianam inter Sinas confirmandam & propagandam.

239. Longè aliter ac Reverendiss. D. Maigrot, de hisce tabellis censet * Observator. Si hunc audiamus, non solum nihil Christianæ fidei contrarium continent, sed aptissimæ sunt ad destruendam in Sinis idololatriam, & ad propagandam Evangelii prædicationem.

240. Rem ita se habere valde optandum esset. Omnes illas tabellas laudarent, & Jesuitarum zelum ac prudentiam in eis admittendis

* 2. *Part. Observat.* 3. *in* 2. *Cap. Mand.* §. *Primo & seqq.*

SINENSIUM,

tendis & super Altare collocandis prædicarent. At dolendum quod tot præclaras tabellarum utilitates non alia ratione probet Observator, quam quod existimet antiquos Sinas per tria circiter annorum millia verum Deum sub nomine *Xangti* agnovisse & coluisse, multosque asserat adhuc esse inter Literatos qui eundem verum Deum cognoscant, neque inter Atheos, neque inter idololatras numerandi; atque ex iis esse hodiernum Imperatorem multosque ejus Ministros ac Mandarinos. At hæc omnia valde esse incerta, vel potius omnino vana & falsa supra demonstratum est.

241. Universa Literatorum Natio, fatentibus Jesuitis ipsoque Observatore, à quadringentis vel quingentis annis in Atheismum delapsa est, non aliud rerum omnium principium agnoscens, præter Cœlum materiale, atque ab eo tempore omnes eorum Scriptores in suis commentariis eodem hoc sensu libros Classicos, & Confucii, quem tanquam communem Magistrum venerantur, doctrinam, nullo contradicente, interpretati sunt.

242. Quæ de hodierno Imperatore & nonnullis ejus Mandarinis dicuntur, solo Patrum *Bouvet* & *le Comte* testimonio nituntur, ut jam observatum est. Aiunt se ex colloquiis cum hoc Imperatore sæpè habitis, certos esse, eum minime esse Atheum, sed nomine *Xangti* verum Deum, quem Christiani prædicant, agnoscere. Luditur in ambiguo vocis Athei: Imperator *Cambi* non est Atheus, quo sensu hoc nomen sumitur apud Europeos & Christianos,

144 HISTORIA CULTUS

stianos, ut significet eum qui nullum numen aut primum rerum omnium principium agnoscit. At alio sensu Atheus dicendus est; quod utramque idololatrarum & Magorum Sectam, quæ varia numina agnoscit, abhorreat; & juxta Sectæ Literariæ principia, non aliam rerum omnium causam agnoscat præter Cœlum aut efficientem Cœli virtutem; cui proinde, more aliorum Imperatorum prædecessorum suorum, sacrificat; unde merito simul & Atheus & Idololatra dicendus est.

243. Quidquid sit de privata Imperatoris & quorumdam ex ejus Ministris de Divinitate sententia, quam palam non profitentur, ut patet ex gestis inter eundem Imperatorem & Patrem Verbiest Jesuitam Mandarinum; prout ab Observatore referuntur; constat totum corpus Sectæ Literariæ adeoque & ipsius Nationis in eadem semper sententia & doctrina perseverare; quæ simul dici potest & Atheistica & Idololatrica, quod satis est, ut tabellæ, de quibus agitur, à Christianis rejiciantur.

244. Ad experientiam provocat Observator: affirmat postquam admissæ sunt tabellæ illæ in Ecclesias Jesuitarum, insertam esse populorum animis majorem de veritate ac sanctitate legis Divinæ persuasionem: Mandarinos ac Regulos frequentius ad eos accessisse; denique longe majores Divinæ gloriæ fructus animarumque proventus Missionarios Societatis retulisse, quam multorum annorum Olimpiadibus sine illis tabellis habuissent.

245. Ad hæc probanda * citat Annales nescio quos: neque enim quinam sint Annales isti

* Ibid. §. Et vero, ex-

HISTORIA CULTUS

cujus textum hic refert Dominus Charmot, quo solo jugulatur ejus opinio.

Responsio.

150. Mihi propositum fuit probare Literatorum Sectam hocce tempore, & à multis retro sæculis per hæc vocabula *Tien* & *Xangti* nihil aliud intelligere, quam cœlum materiale. Hoc autem evidenter sequitur ex interrogatione Patris Magaillanensis, & ex responso Literati ad ejus quæsitum. Hic enim ad interrogata respondens agnoscit homines, utpote hebetes & corporeis rebus addictos, supremi numinis oblitos, nihil aliud præter cœlum materiale cogitare, quod de Literatis intelligendum ipsa verborum series satis ostendit. An verò veteres Sinæ aliud per *Tien*, *Cœlum*, intellexerint, & etiamnum aliqui inter Literatos eo nomine cœlum immateriale; seu substantiam intelligentem rerum omnium fontem & originem significent, nequaquam mihi examinandum proposui. Sufficit saltem à quadringentis aut quingentis annis priorem illam de cœlo materiali significationem communem esse inter omnes pene Literatos totamque Sinensem Nationem; ut inde inferam admittenda non esse inter Christianos vocabula illa ad significandum Deum Opt. Max. ut late ostendi in Notis meis. Sect. 3. Art. 1. 2. 3.

151. At, inquit Observator, sequuntur eodem loco apud Patrem Magaillanensem verba, quæ de industria & mala fide omisi. Siquidem. Literatus ille continuò adjungit, ,, Quod tamen in templis Cœli, Terræ, So-
,, lis;

SINENSIUM.

ARTICULUS IV.

De eodem argumento.

221. Etsi Observatori concederem, tum antiquos Sinenses, tum aliquos etiamnum ex Literatis per *Xangti* verum ac vivum Deum intelligere; non inde sequeretur idem illud vocabulum nunc à Christianis eadem significatione usurpandum, quod sequentibus rationibus patebit.

222. Primo quam longissime spatium illud temporis, quo antiqui Sinæ verum Deum agnovisse & coluisse dicuntur, extendas, vix ultra primum æræ Christianæ sæculum producitur, quo tempore Secta idololatrarum dicta *Foe*, ex Indiis orta in Sinam ingressa est, anno ut creditur, Christi sexagesimo quinto: ab illo enim tempore ut ait Illustrissimus Lopez in Prologo sui Tractatus, & Pater Intorcetta in vita Confucii, Literati, ut hujus Sectæ, quæ alteri Magorum dictæ *Tao*, conjuncta multum invalescebat, progressum impedirent, à pristina doctrina de Deo, & animæ immortalitate recesserunt, ac paulatim in impietatem & Atheismum devenerunt. Itaque juxta hanc computationem, fere à mille & quingentis annis vocabulum *Xangti* apud Literatos Sinenses verum Deum non significat: quod si admittatur, concedendum etiam non expedire ut Christiani Sinenses ejusmodi vocabulum, diversa plane significatione, ab

HISTORIA CULTUS

ea quam per tam longum temporis spatium obtinuit, adhibeant. Neque juvat objicere non à tanto tempore, sed à quadringentis, aut ut multum, quingentis annis Literatos Sinenses à Majorum suorum doctrinâ degenerasse & in Atheismum delapsos esse. Id enim ad quæstionem de qua agitur nihil refert, cum æque certum sit usurpari non debere vocem *Xangti* ad significandum Deum, sive plura, sive pauca sæcula numerentur, ex quo desiit in Sina hanc habere significationem.

223. Secundo tametsi cum Jesuitis supponeretur aliquot nunc esse Literatos Sinenses qui verum Deum agnoscant & nomine *Xangti* designent, negari non potest, quin reliqui hoc est totum Literatorum corpus, imo & universa Sinensium Natio hoc nomine intelligant cœlum materiale, seu efficientem ejus virtutem, quam significationem jam à quadringentis, ut minimum, annis obtinet. Jam vero quis dubitat, quin verba vim ac significationem suam ex publico ac præsenti usu accipiant, non vero ex quorumdam privatorum acceptione aut ex vetustissimo usu, cujus vix memoria superfit?

224. Tertio non juvat si dicas cum Observatore constare apud Sinas per hanc vocem *Xangti* non intelligi cœlum materiale à Christianis, sed Deum Opt. Max. id est substantiam spiritualem cujuscumque materiæ expertem omniumque Creatricem & Gubernatricem. Nam 1. apud plebeios Sinenses, imo & plerosque Literatos, non ita notum ac pervulgatum est, quid fides Christiana de divi-

næ

134   HISTORIA CULTUS

ARTICULUS V.

Objectiones contra suppressionem vocis Xangti *expenduntur.*

225. Objicit * Obſervator, ſi vox *Xangti* excludi debet ex eo quod Literati cœlum materiale per hanc vocem ſignificent, debere excludi quoque vocem *Tien Chu*, cùm ſint multi apud Sinas idololatræ qui ſub illa voce plurima venerantur.

226. Facilis eſt reſponſio. Si quid ambigui ſit in voce *Tien Chu* ob variam ſignificationem quam habet apud idololatras ſeu Bonziorum Sectam, nullum inde periculum eſt nullaque difficultas Chriſtianis, quibuſcum Bonzii & idololatræ nihil pene habent commune. Eamdem quidem vocem aliquando adhibent Literati ad ſignificandum cœlum materiale, tanquam omnium corporum præſtantiſſimum. Verum id rarius contingit: fere ſemper ea ſignificatione vocem *Xangti* uſurpant. Cum itaque, prout inter omnes convenit, ad ſignificandum Deum adhibenda ſit vox Sinica, rejectis Europæis nominibus, ob rationes ſupra allatas, omnino opportunum atque expediens videtur ut vox *Tien Chu*, jam à principio à Chriſtianis adoptata, & apud eos communi uſu recepta, retineatur, ſpreta illa ejuſdem vocis ambiguitate, quæ nullius eſt momenti.

227.

* 2. *Part. Obſ.* 3. §. Quia ſecundo.

182　HISTORIA CULTUS

inde ab initio Societatis in Sina Missionarii conculcari idola à Neophytis, frangi, comburi: conculcarunt ipsi sæpissime, fregerunt, combusserunt.

Responsio.

7. Duplex est idololatriæ genus apud Sinas. Una est crassior & turpior, quam sequitur Secta Bonziorum seu Idololatrarum propriè dictorum, qui plurima ac turpissima in suis Pagodis seu fanis simulachra colunt. Alia est propria Sectæ Literatorum, quæ est præcipua Secta ac in toto Imperio regnans, cujus Caput ac Princeps est ipsemet Imperator. Hi juxta vulgata eorum Philosophiæ principia non cœlo tantum & terræ, sed & spiritibus montium, fluminum, atque idolo *Chin hoam*, hoc est tutelari cujusque Urbis genio sacrificant, ac præterea Progenitorum & Confucii Magistri tabellis idololatricos ac superstitione plenos cultus adhibent. De priori illa Bonziorum idololatria, nulla unquam fuit inter PP. Societatis & reliquos Missionarios disputatio. Omnes enim conveniunt esse rejiciendam; & hoc sensu verum est quod jam inde ab initio Societatis Missionarii jusserunt à Neophytis idola conculcari, frangi, comburi, & quod ipsimet sæpissime ea conculcarunt, fregerunt, combusserunt.

8. At proprie lis est circa cultus Progenitorum & Confucii, quales illos in Notis meis descripsi, quos jam ab initio Missionarii Ordinum Sancti Dominici & Sancti Francisci, corumque postea exemplo Reverendissimus Dominus Maigrot cæterique Vicarii & Missionarii

SINENSIUM,

lum cœli apud Sinas rem esse adeo certam & publicam, ut inter notissimas hujus Nationis consuetudines numeretur in libro Italico recens edito. Is liber, qui dum hæc scriberem, in manus meas incidit, inscribitur: *Notizie parie dell' Imperio della China in Firenze 1697.* adjunctæ sunt aliquæ epistolæ Patris Joannis Grueber Missionarii è Societate, qui è Sina anno 1662. rediit, ubi inter alia loquens de Tartaris qui Sinam occuparunt pag. 88. hæc habet: *Tartari sunt ejusdem religionis cum Sinensibus, adorantque omnia idola Sinensium ac maxime cursum cœli & planetarum, cui multum adscribunt.* Ex quo patet Patrem Grueber pro certo habere, Sinenses esse idololatras, ac cœli astrorumque cursui magnam virtutem, adeoque & divinitatem tribuere: id quod sine dubio de Literatis Sinensibus intelligendum, cum Tartarus Imperator qui hodie regnat, cæterique Tartari ejus Ministri Sectam Literariam sequantur, nihilque cum duabus aliis Sectis, idololatrarum videlicet & Magorum, commune habeant.

I 5 SECTIO

附录4 "中国笔记"索引所列《华人礼仪史》相关章节的英文译稿[①]

Historia Cultus Sinensium **(HCS)**

Translation of pages cited by Locke in MS. Locke. c.27.

[HCS pages 1-11]

First Section

Of the Cult of the Ancestors and Confucius

Article I

What questions should be asked about this kind of cult?

1. The Fathers of the Society[②] have declared and claimed throughout their above

---

① "中国笔记"索引所列《华人礼仪史》相关章节拉丁文原文参见本书附录3。本英文译稿为安·泰尔博特女士由拉丁文译为英文,韩凌校注。为尽量保证材料的连续性和完整性,我们对"中国笔记"索引所列页码进行了排序,将相邻或相近的页码组合在一起连贯译出。另外,基于所译内容与"中国笔记"的相关性,我们尽量将索引所列页码前后的内容也一并译出,以利阅读。

② It refers to The Society of Jesus better known as the Jesuits.

writings that the questions relating to the cult of the ancestors and Confucius are settled questions. On the contrary, I contend that these settled questions are in dispute; therefore that these same questions should be looked at again. The cult of the tablets of Confucius and the ancestors consists in burning odours, offering wine, the heads of goats or pigs and other similar things; the question is whether this is a religious and idolatrous ceremony or is only civil and political and whether therefore it is licit or illicit for Christians.

2. The Sacred Congregation① approved this and several other distinct questions when they ordered me to draw out from the Mandate of the Very Reverend D. Maigrot② facts which could be proved from the writings of the Society, which in the writing entitled *The Truth* are abundantly proved by me. When the facts were ambiguous, omitted, or denied they were discovered by me from proof, evidence and statements. I have brought together the generally agreed facts so that we can go forward to the question of law which the Sacred Congregation should judge and let it be known whether this cult is lawful (licit) or unlawful (illicit) for Christians.

3. But that is what the author of the Observations studiously guards against, scarcely ever touching on the facts and where it cannot be avoided immediately hurrying past them. Nowhere does he explain the things that are going on in the cults of Confucius and the ancestors but it is wrapped up in so many words that if the Eminent Fathers and Judges do not pay attention, the truth in this case will escape them.

4. There is little agreement even among themselves. All their works go against

---

① The Sacred Congregation of Rites was a congregation of the Roman Curia, erected on January 22, 1588 by Pope Sixtus V and its functions reassigned by Pope Paul VI on May 8, 1969. The Congregation was charged with the supervision of the liturgy and other sacraments, and with the process of canonization of saints. With the reforms of Paul VI, it was divided into the Congregation for the Causes of Saints and the Congregation for Divine Worship. The secretary, or second-highest official, of the Congregation once served as the personal sacristan to the Pope.

② 阎当（Charles Maigrot，1652—1730），巴黎外方传教会会士。1680年来华，1687年起任福建宗座代牧。1693年，在福建长乐发布禁止中国天主教徒祭祖祭孔的禁令，并于次年派人至罗马上呈该令，掀起"礼仪之争"的高潮。

judgement and reason. Indeed the opinions of the Fathers of the Society are entirely contrary to what is the probable and safer, and perhaps the only safe, option. Their reasoning has its place in questions of law, not of fact. Just as if someone were to ask whether a contract were legal and the experts put forward reasons to prove that it was not legal, or that it was certain, or only probable. No one says that is a question of fact, it is a question of law. What is relevant here is that this case consists of external actions and public ceremonies such as those that take place in the worship of the ancestors and Confucius. In this case proof, not opinions and arguments, but investigation, eye witnesses and public knowledge are required.

Article II

What is the character of the cults of the ancestors and Confucius?

5. And truthfully I will set these previous comments aside and undertake the important work of explaining the existing facts about these cults afresh and subject them to the eyes of the Lord Almighty.

About the Cult of the Ancestors

6. The Literati are the chief sect in China, the sect is the most eminent in the whole Empire and its leader is the Emperor himself. Parents and dead ancestors up to the fourth degree are chiefly venerated by the cult whether in public or in private. They have sacred temples or chapels in which are gathered tablets made of chestnut wood and made to a definite size, inscribed in letters going downwards: "The throne of seat of the soul of N. N." setting out his name and titles. And in the middle of the temple is a table or altar with other smaller tables or altars round about the place where the same kind of tablets are placed.

7. In these temples there is great preparation three or four times a year especially in the spring and autumn. This is the solemn oblation or sacrifice they celebrate. Several days before the ceremony the first born or head of the family and three or four others from the leading families are selected who act as priest, deacons, sub-deacons, Masters

of Ceremonies and also acolytes of the ministry[①] are chosen. The day for the oblation is picked out by casting lots[②]. They fast for three days before the oblation and abstain from their wives. The evening before, they test the sacrificial animals by pouring warm wine into their ears. If the head shakes, it is regarded as an appropriate sacrifice; if it does not, the animal is rejected as unsuitable. The chosen animal is immediately slaughtered in their sight. On the day itself before cock crow, the whole family meet in the temple or chapel. They are placed in a regular order, candles and tapers are lighted on the altar and perfumes burned. The Master of Ceremonies exclaims in a loud voice, "Bend your Knees." Immediately everyone present makes three or four genuflections and touches the ground with their foreheads. One of the ministers recites a prayer. Then the Master of Ceremonies cries, "Arise." As one they stand on their feet. After this, the one chosen as chief minister who officiates as priest stands at the altar and lifts up a cup full of wine. The Master of Ceremonies cries, "The wine is offered." He pours some as an offering on the figure of a man made of straw. After this the hairs of the cut up animal are plucked off and mixed with the blood. The head and meat are also raised up and offered to the tablets. Meanwhile the Master of Ceremonies cries, "The goat is offered, or pig." In a similar way, flowers, fruits, legumes and other things such as silk cloth and paper money are offered. They are burned in the fire in front of the temple. Accompanying these actions are various prayers which one of the minister recites. These things thus completed, the Master of Ceremonies announces that those who have assisted in the ceremony for the cult of the ancestors can expect prosperity, good harvest, bodily health, sons, honours and long life.

  8. This account of the rituals is from the famous Navarrete volume 2, section 7, pages 114 & 115 and in the manuscript of Father Franciscus Varo, Dominican missionary and Apostolic Vicar who wrote it in his own hand while he was in China. It was affirmed under oath and from a similar account of sacrifices eye witnessed

---

① It is referred to as "Assistants" in Locke's notes.
② The word used is "sortitione" which can mean casting lots or divination by throwing stones or bones.

by Father Johannes Baptista Moralez Order of Preachers and Father Antonio Maria Franciscanus in which the chief minister and one of the acolytes were Christians. Other testimonies were given to me in previous writings and subsequently from a tract of the illustrious D. Gregorio Lopez[①], Bishop of Basilitani and Vicar Apostolic of Nanking whom the Jesuits brought out and greatly praised. I brought together this writing under the title *The Truth*. More than one of the things asserted can be proved especially the fasting and the marital abstinence and other particular of the ceremonies.

9. Besides these solemn ceremonies in spring and autumn the Chinese often go to the temples chiefly in the new moon and the full moon of each month when they perform three or four deep genuflections to the tablets of their ancestors, inclining their whole body to the ground. Candles are lighted, tapers and perfumes burned, flowers and fruit, legumes and other food offered.

10. Those with slender fortunes who do not have temples or chapels dedicated to their ancestors make the same oblations and ceremonies at their tombs which are outside the towns, or in private houses, where they are performed with less solemnity and pomp. The common people who do not have another place keep their ancestors' tablets at home and make frequent genuflections, offer perfumes, fruits and food in their honour.

The Cult of Confucius

11. Each city has a temple or chapel dedicated to the philosopher Confucius, which is built next to the school or university of the Literati and in it are gathered his tablets with this inscription engraved in golden letters: "The throne or seat of the soul of the most holy and most excellent first master Confucius."

12. In this temple twice a year that is at the spring and autumn equinox all the literati gather so that they can venerate with solemn oblations Confucius who is the

---

① 罗文藻（Lo Wen-tsao，拉丁名Gregorio Lopez，1616—1691），福建人，1633年由意大利方济各会士利安当领洗入教，后成为第一个中国籍主教。

common master and father of all the Chinese philosophers. The leading mandarin or governor of the city performs the office of priest, assisted by the other literati who play the part of deacons, sub-deacons, master of ceremonies, and also acolytes, in the same way that oblations to the ancestors are performed. Before they fast for several days, as explained above, and abstain from conjugal relations. The day before the equinox, rice and other pulses and fruits of the earth are prepared in the hall for offering to Confucius. In the courtyard of the temple of Confucius, the Mandarin who acts as priest lights candles on the table in front of the tablet and burns other odours on the coals[①], then a pig or goat or other animal chosen for sacrifice the day before by pouring warm wine into its ears, as said before, brought and is saluted with a bow after that it is slaughtered in the same way. Afterwards the hairs are plucked and mixed with the intestines and kept for the following day.

13. The next day before cock crow, the mandarin and all the other literati make great preparations at the temple of Confucius: candles are lighted; tapers and other odours are burned, at a sign from the master of ceremonies the musicians play. Then the mandarin or priest raises the hair mixed together with the blood. The master of ceremonies cries, "The hair and blood of the victim are offered." and in front of the tablets of Confucius they are offered. Presently the master of ceremonies gives the order and they all go out in a line to temple courtyard where the hair and the blood are buried. After that, each returns to his place and the meat of the animals is guarded carefully. Then the master of ceremonies exclaims loudly, "The spirit of Confucius descends." This said, the priest or mandarin raises a full cup of wine and pours it on the image of a man made of straw. Then reciting prayers containing high praises of Confucius he picks up Confucius' tablet from its place on the altar.

14. This done, the second part of the sacrifice begins; the master of ceremonies exclaims "Kneel." and hearing which all kneel. After that he says "Rise." and they all stand up. Then the mandarin or priest washes his hands and a piece of silk cloth

---

① The Latin word for "coal" is "pruna" which means "charcoal".

is offered to him by one of the ministers; from another he takes a full jug of wine. The master of ceremonies calls, "The sacrifice approaches the throne of Confucius." The musicians play. The silk cloth and then the wine are lifted up high and offered to Confucius. The master of ceremonies repeats four times, "Kneel." and "Rise." and everyone kneels and prostrates their whole body four times. Then the silk cloth is burned on the coals and prayers or collects are recited to Confucius. In the same way, after various genuflections and reverences the wine is offered with prayers addressed to the spirit of Confucius. This is from the illustrious Gregorio Lopez in chapter 5 of the writing cited above. Once one of the Chinese emperors composed a prayer in honour of Confucius which is recited in these oblations or sacrifices.

15. The sacrifice then proceeds to the third part. The master of ceremonies cries "Drink the wine of prosperity and happiness." Then he repeats as above "Kneel." and saluting the sacrifice says, "The wine of happiness is drunk." Immediately that sacrifice is poured out. Afterwards the master of ceremonies cries out "Eat the meat of sacrifice." A minister takes hold of the meat in both hands and offers it on high. Next, two prayers conclude the sacrifice, "So to you we have offered that which is pure and sweet smelling. We mortals are at peace and the spirit rejoices. And from these sacrifices good and happiness will follow."

16. Finally they believe that the spirit of Confucius comes to the tablets and rests there or the soul comes to this place and after they have said solemn prayers, the meat of the sacrifice is distributed among the assistants and those who eat it believe they will obtain benefits and happiness.

17. Besides these solemn sacrifices which take place at the spring and autumn equinoxes, there are other less solemn ones which all the literati frequent. Doctors, graduates and bachelors proceed to the temple of Confucius where they light candles on the altar and burn tapers and perfumes immediately they have obtained their degrees in the school. Firstly, they venerate their common master and parent with four genuflections and by prostrating their whole body. Secondly, mandarins, both governors of cities and magistrates, go to the same temple of Confucius and venerate him in the

manner described before they take up their office. Thirdly, the mandarins and leading magistrates of the city go to the temple at each new moon and full moon and before hearing legal cases, taking with them other officials and literati, and light candles and burn perfumes in front of the tablet of Confucius, kneeling and prostrating themselves on the ground.

18. The emperors of China have established these oblations or ceremonies in honour of Confucius by law so that no one may omit them, except on pain of the most severe penalties, such as the loss of their office, or their degree, or even their life. The illustrious Gregorio Lopez says this in the prologue to the writing mentioned above. It can be seen also in chapter 5, article 2 of the writings of the Reverend P Varo, Dominican.

19. I have explained the observed facts relating to the cult of the ancestors and Confucius. It should be noted however that the Jesuits neither deny nor call these facts from the rituals, classic books, and public customs of the Chinese into doubt. So it is demonstrated from the published writings in this controversy and from the apologies of Didaco Morales, Jacobo Fabro, Francisco Brancate, Batholomeo Roboredo[1], and P Tellier who are members of the Society. It can be confirmed from their observations. However much it is in their interests to attempt to deny or diminish by way of exception, they can never do it. For also Roboredo after he describes the sacrifices which I have previously explained acknowledges that it is just as I have set out. All of them dispute the interpretation so that these cults are confined to the limits of civil and political cults so much so that they teach that Christians can be permitted to take part in them because this is not a question of fact but of law.[2]

---

[1] Bartolomeo Roboredo was president of the Macao Jesuit college and had written a reply to Morales' criticisms of Jesuit accommodationism. See J.S. Cummins, *The Travels and Controversies of Friar Domingo Navarrete 1618-1686*, London: Hakluyt Society, p. lxiii.

[2] It means the fact isn't in dispute, while the interpretation is. We know the facts of the Chinese rites. The question is whether it's legal or not. There is a Latin saying which goes like "ignorania facti excusat ignorantia juris non excusat," which means ignorance of the facts is an excuse, ignorance of the law is not an excuse.

[HSC page 43]

Article VII

How credible are the external authorities on which the Jesuits base their opinions?①

Now I have already noted that the Jesuit neophytes are not permitted to take part in the cults of Confucius and the ancestors and that opinion and practice has persisted since year '40②, it has been so since the year 1581 when Father Matteo Ricci entered China until the year 1628 when the Missionary Society meeting was held in Canton....③

Many adduce from these places evidence to prove the contrary and twist themselves into knots trying to prove the Jesuits' opinions. Indeed no one denies these cults are sacred and sometimes superstitious and idolatrous, because they consist in seeking and hoping to win merit from the dead and pleading their case with them. And when Father Gregorio Lopez was in the church of Fokien④ in front of Father Varo the Dominican Father of Govea and the Society, he said that it is most certain that the Chinese hope for and seek benefits in this life from their dead ancestors. It is cited by Father Varo in the Spanish writings I have mentioned above, which were written when he was in China and an example of which I have in my possession. In Latin it reads, "Father Francisco Lopez when he was in the church of Fokien in front of me said to Father Antonio de Govea: If the Fathers of the Society uphold their opinion that the Chinese do not seek benefits from their dead ancestors, it would not be true. I am certain that the Chinese, even baptised adults do so, they are accustomed to it from childhood, and perform these ceremonies in the hope of obtaining benefits and

---

① It starts from page 38. The first paragraph of Article VII is translated underneath.
② It refers to 1640.
③ This is the beginning part of Article VII "How credible are the external authorities on which the Jesuits base their opinions?" on page 38. Page 43 starts from the following paragraph.
④ 福建

prosperity and no one in China who speaks the truth can ever call this into doubt." This also comes from the illustrious Lopez in the preface to his writing chapter 2 paragraph 2 part 2. The same author offers confirmation of these and other misrepresentations that the Jesuits maintain and which are contrary to the evidence.

[HSC pages 85—87]

VI

146. The meaning of the word "atheist" is ambiguous in two respects in this subject matter. The Observer taking the meaning commonly understood among the Europeans accuses the Most Reverend Father D. Maigrot of ill will because it is the name used by the Chinese literati and current emperor. But anyhow among the Chinese, the literati are called atheists to distinguish them from the other two sects, that is the Magi and the Bonzÿs, who both, alongside the grossest errors, also hold that souls are immortal and will be rewarded or punished in the afterlife on the basis of merit . The literati believe the heavens to be the principal of all things. Whether by the name of heaven they understand a subtle matter which they call *Li*① or *Taikie*②, which is divided into different forms and shapes, which is the ancient opinion of the classical books and commentaries of the sect of the literati; and almost all the literati accept this. Or by the name of heaven they understand another most excellent thing, this they understand as an active or natural principle which creates and governs all things. This was the opinion that Father Matteo Ricci attributed to the ancient Chinese and the early authors of the sect of the literati and which is the opinion of the reigning emperor today and many of the literati at his court.

147. The name atheist does not have the same meaning among the Chinese as it does in Europe and among the Christians. For in Europe it signifies something that

---

① 理
② 太极

is generally known to be impious and denies the intuition of the soul and the voice of God, and is therefore hated by everyone. Among the Chinese however the same word signifies to the sect of the literati, or those of that teaching, a different question. The literati deny God and Providence in the same way that Epicurus used to do, but actually they recognise God to some degree in an imperfect way.

148. And thus in error the Observer whose ambiguous words the Most Reverend D. Maigrot challenged cannot say without great offence that the emperor and many of the leading members of his court are atheists. The Jesuits use intimidation to frighten and intimidate the Judges who are unaware of Chinese matters and can be deceived.

149. At this point the Observer urges that previous objections should be removed and withdrawn because they are not sufficient. The disagreement remains, says the Most Reverend D. Maigrot if it is argued that the cults of Confucius and the ancestors are idolatrous and nevertheless the literati are the same as atheists who neither believe in spirits nor immortal souls. For who, he says, could, as the Chinese do, call the spirits of Confucius and the ancestors to the tablets, as to the place and seat where they rest, if they did not recognize substantial spirits or denied the immortality of the souls of men. These are the contradiction which the doctors of the Sorbonne pointed out. No one, it is said, is a beginner who has not made a start.

150. My response is that as the Most Reverend D. Maigrot has said it is not possible to decide which of these two positions is true or false or to choose the lesser evil unless we can establish how matters stand in China. The Literati are the principal sect among the Chinese, they do not recognize true spirits or the immortality of the souls of men nor however the soul is entirely extinguished or does it disappear when it leaves the body. The soul persists and becomes part of the subtle matter which they call *Li* or *Taikie*.[①]

---

① The following paragraphs in HSC are about Chinese medicine, two forces, i.e. *Yin*（阴）and *Yang*（阳）, etc.

[HSC pages 111—115]

Second Section
The tablets of the dead ancestors
Article I
An examination of the witness's objections to the five points of the Reverend D. Maigrot's Edict about the deceased

186. I[①] deny altogether that the Sacred Congregation gave its permission to these tablets. Father Juan Bautista Moralez inquired whether it was permitted for Christians to have these tablets which were said to be the seats of the souls of the dead ancestors and are gathered together on their altars with candles, lamps and perfumes, and to which it is thought the souls of the dead ancestors come and are present to receive sacrifices and oblations. The Sacred Congregation responded it was completely impermissible to have the tablets and their altars. "They are more or less offering sacrifices and earnest prayers to the ancestors." These words of the Sacred Congregation were in response to the question asked, so it can be seen that in these very words it is not permitted to have these tablets and their altars, more or less to offer sacrifices to them and to pray in front of them; however it is permitted to have the same tablets in private houses, to kneel in front of them, to burn candles, to offer flowers, pulses and other edible things, and burn incense and other perfumes, nothing at all was said about this, it is not abolished. The Sacred Congregation is not accustomed to giving way in this manner on a proposition which it has prohibited after serious consideration and having assessed the consequences, and having given permission in a different situation.

187. The same can be said about the other response following the decree about the funeral ceremonies. For it is an inviolable custom of the Chinese, that in the house of the dead person, in front of the dead body to set up a table in the manner of an altar and on it to put an image or the dead person or a tablet with their name inscribed, as

---

① Referring to Nicolas Charmot.

was said above, decorated with flowers, perfumes and candles. Those who pay their condolences come to it and kneel in front of the altar, lowering their head to the ground, offering other candles and perfumes which are burned on the altar as described before. Father Juan Moralez asked whether this was permissible for Christians to take part in these ceremonies for the dead. The Sacred Congregation: "provided that the table and the tablet are not an altar it could be allowed within the limits of a civil and political funeral ceremony."

188. Turning to the reply, there are conditions and restrictions imposed: "Given that the table is not a true altar," and then "if the proceedings are contained within the limits of a civil and political funeral ceremony." These conditions accepted there still remains the central question of the tablet inscribed thus: "The place or seat of the soul of the deceased." According to the judgement of the Sacred Congregation this thing is not acceptable if it has anything idolatrous or superstitious and if the honours paid to it are more than civil and political. From which it can be seen that there is no reason to infer that the Sacred Congregation has erased its reply and permitted and approved the tablets to the dead.

189. From the question that Juan Moralez earnestly asked, and as was proved by us, the Chinese are of the opinion that the soul of the departed is invited with oblations and prayers to come to the tablet where it derives enjoyment from the perfumes and other foods offered to it, the use of the tablets is entirely superstitious and Christians should be only minimally be permitted if these words are written: "The place or seat of the soul of the deceased" and other guarded phrases added which the Reverend D. Maigrot prescribed so that the tablet takes on the character of an image which reminds the children of the parent. Although it is better as can be seen to abolish them as the Reverend D. Maigrot teaches in his exposition. In the year 1669, two consultants from the Sacred Office were selected to examine the inquiry of Father Navarrete that is Father Laurence Brancata de Laurea of the Order of St Francis and Father Juan Bona of the Order of St Bernard, both of whom were later raised to the dignity of cardinal. They responded in the following way to the question of the tablets: "On the third question of

the tablets on which the gentiles believe the souls of the dead are present and receive oblations, we say, it is not allowed for Christians, as mentioned, to venerate tablets whether in temples or in private houses with the inscription "Throne or seat of the soul". Finally it is not permitted for them to take part in venerations with the gentiles or other oblations, also the false beliefs about the existence of the soul must be removed.

Article II

The same arguments

190. However much the Observer roars against it, Martini[①] is seriously called to account because of these tablets of inscription. He silently passed over the words "Throne," or "Seat of the soul," and said "The name of the deceased is written". This reticence and dissimulation suppresses the proof that the Chinese are superstitious, and that they have what amount to idols to which the souls of their deceased ancestors come and there rest and enjoy the fruits and odours and other oblations offered to them.

191. The Observer is aware of it and these words: "Throne or seat of the soul" he has exceptional difficulty in ignoring. What the Chinese words *Xin Goey*[②] or *Xin Chu*[③] mean and what they signify correctly requires a long investigation. First it should be noted that when their parents passed away the early Chinese substituted a boy who was dressed in the clothes of the deceased to represent the dead. Afterwards the living figure was replaced with the inscribed tablets: then indeed various classic Chinese books assert as proof that the boy signified the same as the tablets of the dead ancestors and those present recalled the memory of the dead.

192. Are these classic authors and all the established opinion of the Chinese to be ignored? Surely no one now in Rome would do that. For these things are set out, explained and refuted in the replies of the illustrious Navarrete to the Apologies of Fathers Fabri and Brancati of the Society. I can now show the Sacred Congregation

---

① 卫匡国

② It may refer to "神归".

③ It may refer to "神出".

how it is set out in extracts from the opinions of the classic Chinese authors which were brought together most skilfully by Father Varo of the Dominican mission in the Chinese language. He interprets the words *Xin Goey* and *Xin Chu* to mean that the Chinese believe that the soul of the dead rests on the tablets at the time of the oblation.

193. We have recalled the origin of those early tablets, and those youths who represented the person of the deceased but the Observer infers that nothing was originally superstitious in this institution but that later ignorance and superstition crept in and that if these can be removed, the custom of the tablets can be retained untouched. The same solemn oblations are made to Confucius and the ancestors and cannot be defended.

[HSC pages 117—118]

Article III

The Observer changes the questions so that many things become inappropriate in the Very Reverend D. Maigrot's Edict.

195. Coming to the five points of the Very Reverend D Maigrot's Edict, let us look at the tablets which the Chinese keep in their houses and which they salute every day by prostrating themselves, lighting candles and scented tapers, offering flowers, pulses, and other edible things. The Observer raises great objections and various difficulties to show that the things prescribed by the Very Reverend D. Maigrot are unworkable. He makes use of the funeral ceremonies of the dead to turn the question around in his speech. In these, certainly, also the same tablets are used, as we have noted above. And thus he argues that the new converts to Christianity will run into great and insurmountable difficulties if they follow the orders of the Edict and the words "Throne or seat of the soul" are removed from the tablet and that it is useless to say this wording should not be retained and displayed when the same tablets are so much used in private houses. The Very Reverend D. Maigrot says nothing about the funeral ceremonies in the Edict, nor about the less solemn oblations. Only ceremonies

in temples that are dedicated to the dead are expressly prohibited. The reason was explained already. These ceremonies are not believed to be empty of superstition.

196. But, says the Observer, solemn sacrifices are made to the ancestors in spring and autumn on that account Lord Maigrot prohibits "What was done in front of the same tablets in which the spirits of the dead were believed to be present, up to now nothing superstitious was seen in these ceremonies, nothing was detected in this sacrifice except a civil ritual."

197. Thus he interprets the Edict of the Very Reverend Lord Maigrot. But this is the mind and opinion of the Very Reverend D. Maigrot. Even when these tablets are removed from the temples sacred to the dead, the ceremonies associated with them do not cease to be entirely superstitious and idolatrous. What can be empty of superstition in the fasting, the conjugal abstinence, which have been described, the pouring of warm wine into the ears of the sacrificial victims, the presence of the head of the family, the slaughter, the wine pouring of wine at the ceremony, the offering of the head of a goat or pig, burning silk cloth and paper money, and the other things which have been related to us? If it be so that nothing in the whole ceremony goes beyond a civil ritual, why do the living mandarins and others make such offerings? Whoever said this was deceived or wished to deceive.

[HSC pages 122—123]

Ricci who entered China in the year 1581, after long and arduous labours in the difficult Chinese language, was convinced by reading the ancient philosophers that the early Chinese believed in God and worshipped him under the name *Xangti*[①] in which opinion he continued for many years until his death. It was his authority that persuaded the rest of the missionaries of the Society who diligently continued his work. Longobardi entered China in 1596, laboured hard to learn the language and in time

---

① 上帝

turned to reading Chinese books it seemed to him that the opinion of Father Ricci was not entirely certain. He saw many truths in the early Chinese philosophers. Equally they and their disciples for many ages until our own time meant nothing by *Xangti* but the material heaven, nothing intelligent unless it was an extremely subtle matter or at one time a kind of essence which they call *Li* or *Taikie* which is dispersed through all parts of the universe, and animates those things in nature, in heaven and earth, which are the most excellent. It follows from this that they never have believed in true spirits separate from matter. The fundamental principle of their philosophy is that everything is one, which was also the belief of Democritus and Epicurus, and in our own time the impious Spinoza in whose monstrous works the idea was revived.

204. Longobardi succeeded Ricci as the leader of the missionaries of the Society in 1610. He was more and more convinced of his opinion about the concept of the soul, and he composed an extremely learned thesis which the illustrious Navarrete published in volume 1 of his works. Longobardi's opinion was put forward when the missionaries held their meeting in the city of Canton. At the beginning the article stated that what the literati call the High King or *Xangti* was not a true spirit. *"For indeed,"* he said, *"the Chinese do not recognise true spirits, but only the operative strength or influence of heaven to produce the things of the universe just as they value the movement of the heavens or Taikie."*

205. In the year 1629, following the official visit of Father Palmeirus to the Chinese mission, the missionaries of the Society became cautious about the meaning of the word *Xangti* and they agreed between them to prohibit the use of this word from then on to signify the name of God. However afterwards the Jesuits returned to the opinion of Ricci about the method of spreading the faith. They scorned and rejected Father Longobardi's writings, with which many agreed. It is said that Father Hurtado, the Viceprovincial leader, condemned Longobardi's thesis to the flames in the year 1645. So writes the Very Reverend D. Maigrot in his Exposition toward the end of paragraph 3. It is worthy of note.

[HSC pages 126—144]

210. The Observer's argument for the use of the name *Xangti* is absolutely weak and lame. It is that the founders of the Chinese nation and the earliest authors of the sect of the literati recognised the true and living God by that name and that this understanding persisted for two or three thousand years, after that time most of the literati understood by the name *Xangti* nothing but the material heavens and fell into the abyss of atheism.

211. This rests only upon the authority of Father Ricci and his followers who interpret the ancient Chinese books in this manner, and present these things in such a way that they are able to twist the meaning. Truly, these books are obscure and enigmatic in their images, argument, and balance is desired so that seeking understanding and explanation from the commentaries of the Chinese literati whether those produced in the earliest times or in later centuries. These commentaries are compared to the authority of some of the oldest classic books. And in all of those commentaries the common doctrine is: that by *Xangti* is understood the material heaven or an efficient power which as we have said is called *Li* or *Taikie* and they are silent about true spirits or immortal souls.

212. And to the present time, this is the opinion of all of the literati with few exceptions. The Christians who assisted Father Ricci remove the meaning from the commentaries and ancient classic books, accommodating them benignly with the Christian truth. The present Chinese emperor and others among the mandarins and literati understand the true and living God by the name *Xangti*, we will set this out in the following article.

213. However, it is considered to be true by careful and balanced readers, who have studied the ancient Chinese books and Confucius and the many writings which come out all the time from the Chinese literati who have studied this philosopher for many years and hold Confucius as their common master and have better perception and doctrine than Father Ricci and the few others who came to China from Europe.

214. Previously it followed from this for Ricci and the Observer that the ancient Chinese believed in and worshipped the true and living God for two thousand years or more. Thus they knew and honoured Abraham, Isaac, Jacob and Melchisedech①, that is to say they knew the history of the Holy Bible which taught against idolatry from the time of Abraham. They were settled in the provinces neighbouring those settled by Noah, his sons and nephews. In the age of Moses, not only Egypt but broad regions were flooded. So Abraham and Lot②, among whom the worship of the true God persisted, and the Midianites and Moabites and Ammonites③ descended from them. However it is said that the Moabites and Ammonites practised idolatry under the early judges④ Judges 10. V. 6. and that the idol Charnos belonged to the Moabites and the idol Moloch to the Ammonites 3. Kings. II. V. 8 & 7.

215. Nothing stood in the way of the ancient Chinese being like the Persians who worshipped fire. Other peoples were not atheists but had the idea of a supreme being who was corporeal. This was what was mainly believed. Nothing, indeed, distinguished the whole Chinese nation for two or three thousand years allowing them to retain the knowledge of true spirits, when other nations such as the Chaldeans, the Egyptians, the Greeks and the Romans wandered from the worship and knowledge of God into confusion, idolatry and darkness.

216. Recent writers of the Society have gone beyond this. For they claim that many of the Chinese emperors combine all virtues, moral and political, with the knowledge of true spirits and worship. Confucius in his first philosophy exhibited all kinds of virtues together with heavenly blessedness. And in the books most recently edited, knowledge of the future Messiah is combined with being able to attain eternal salvation after the fall of Adam without the Redeemer.⑤

---

① They are followers of the Jewish God Jehovah in the *Old Testament*.

② Lot is one of the sons of Noah.

③ They are some peoples mentioned in the *Bible* in the Middle East. Some of them became idolaters according to the *Bible*.

④ They refer to the early rulers of the Jewish.

⑤ According to Bouvet and Le Comte, the Confucian scholars prefigured Jesus.

Article III

217. The Observer relies upon the testimony of the Jesuits Father Bouvet and Father Le Comte, who have published the commentaries of many literati covering a period of 500 to 600 years, ancient classic books, and the writings of Confucius, and claim that they believed in the true God. But it was Father Ricci who explained the meaning (of these books). He insisted that the reigning emperor today, Camhi[①], is by no means an atheist, for *Xangti* meant the living and true God. He would take him only a single year, he said, "to present the Pope with the whole of China." If the meaning of atheism which he attributed to it is accepted, he (Ricci) bears an extremely heavy burden (of responsibility).

218. The things which are asserted by the Jesuits hardly seem probable. They do not correspond to what this same emperor who is the leader of the sect of the literati and has composed several books about Chinese philosophy in which the heavens and that subtle part of them which is called *Li* or *Taikie* he describes in the same straightforward manner as do the writers who have published commentaries for four or five hundred years and others of the literati. Thus he seems to be by no means an atheist. It is another matter whether he believes this substance is spiritual, some kind of matter or devoid of body. The Very Reverend D. Maigrot urges this argument in the middle of paragraph 3 "Emperor" and the one that begins "Words which" and is also discussed by Father Augustine of the Missionary Order of St Francis in writings of which I have an authentic example.

219. Above all the emperor sacrifices to heaven every year as the high priest of the religion of the whole empire. And Father Bouvet says in his letter to the Observer that this very same ceremony and ritual was performed by all the previous emperors of China who were his predecessors. He offers this sacrifice as leader of the sect of the literati and up to now no one, except certain of the literati and leading mandarins, has ever suggested that the ceremony was directed towards anything other than the material

---

① 康熙

heaven or its efficient power.

220. So when thus the same emperor and some of his ministers or members of the court met with Father Bouvet and some other Jesuits, they expressed their assent to the existence and nature of God. It is credible to make their philosophy compatible and the Fathers of the Society seem to like to do that.

Article IV

About the same arguments

221. And so the Observer conceded that while the ancient Chinese and some of the literati understand *Xangti* to be the true and living God, it does not therefore follow that this word can be adopted by the Christians, as the following argument shows.

222. First, it is a long time since the ancient Chinese worshipped the true God. It goes back before the beginning of the Christian era. Since that time the sect of idolaters called *Foe*① came into China 65 years after the birth of Christ. The illustrious Lopez says this in the prologue to his writings and Father Intorcetta in his life of Confucius. They together with the other sect of the Magi, called *Tao*②, grew strong. They impeded progress and the pristine doctrine of the God and the immortal soul receded, gradually becoming impiety and atheism. Thus after the space of about one and half thousand years, the word *Xangti* did not mean the true God among the Chinese literati. The Chinese Christians are not bound to this word. The significance is clearly different from that which obtained for a long space of time. Nor does it help to object that it was not such a long time ago. For four or five hundred years③, the ancestral doctrine of the Chinese literati degenerated and lapsed into atheism. We should certainly not use this word, whether we care talking about many centuries or a few, the word has lost the meaning that it used to have in China.

223. Second, we cannot deny as the Jesuits claim that now some of the literati

---

① 佛
② 道
③ To the Song Dynasty which the Jesuits dated the near-Confucianism.

recognise the true God by the name *Xangti*. But the remainder of the entire body of the literati and indeed the whole Chinese nation understand by this word the material heaven or its efficient power. This meaning has persisted for four hundred years at least. Now indeed, who doubts that this is significance and meaning of the word as it is understood and presented publicly and not among a few people privately, or in ancient memory the meaning of which scarcely survives?

224. Third, no one would think, with the Observer, that among the Chinese this word did not mean the material heaven to Christians, but God Almighty, that is a substantial spirit which is separate from matter and is creator and ruler of all. Point 1. Among the common Chinese and even some of the literati, it is not widely known that the Christian faith teaches a divine, spiritual essence. They will easily misunderstand this, if the word *Xangti* is used among the Christians. Point 2. The Chinese people are proud and do not want to learn from outsiders. Coming from the mouths of Christians and the divine words of ministers of religion, the word *Xangti* would induce in the soul of the listeners not what it means to us but the widespread and accustomed meaning of the word. It is consistent with experience that the difficulty in understanding and comprehending the concept of God is to abstract the mind from corporeal things and to understand a purely spiritual substance. Thus it cannot be without great inconvenience for the Christians to use this word with a fundamentally different meaning from that which it commonly had among the Chinese. Communicating the word to the literati will not bring benefits to Christianity. It will condemn it, for it will not be effective and will give them a false impression of God. One confusing and scandalous word will do this, if it replaces the meaning of God, and will give rise to atheism.

Article V

Objections against the use of the word *Xangti* explained

225. The Observer objects that if the word *Xangti* ought to be excluded because the literati mean by it the material heaven, the word *Tien Chu*[①] should also be excluded

---

① 天主

because many Chinese idolaters use it.

226. The reply is simple. If the word *Tien Chu* is ambiguous and has a different meaning among the idolaters or the sect of the Bonzÿs, there is no danger from that and no problem for the Christians because they have nothing in common with the Bonzÿs and the idolaters. The same word which the literati use to signify the material heaven or, as it were, what is most excellent in it, is always made use of to mean that. And so accordingly it is agreed by everyone that a Chinese word be put forward to mean God, the European names have been rejected for the reasons set out above, it seems both a great opportunity and convenient that the word *Tien Chu* now begin to be adopted by Christians and received among them as common usage and retained, spurning the ambiguous word which is of no weight.

227. Other objections. Because in many books edited since the beginning of the mission, God Almighty was always called *Xangti* and these books have been read in the provinces of the Chinese empire everywhere, whether by Christians or infidels, to try to suppress these books would be an error, or to ban Christians from reading them would be too difficult and hard.

228. I reply, there are two kinds of books in which the word *Xangti* is used to mean God. Some books have been written to prove that this word *Xangti* has the same significance among the literati as Almighty God does among the Christians. In other books the question of meaning is not mentioned, but the word is simply used to mean God. Looking at the first type of book, which are not numerous, there seems to be no risk of difficulty if Christians are banned from reading books which can be nothing but harmful and misleading because the word *Xangti* means nothing but the material heaven or its effective power in Chinese.

229. The other books where the word *Xangti* is simply used to mean God, there does not seem to be any reason to ban. Or Christians could be banned from reading them unless there was a warning that the word the *Tien Chu* was the correct one. And nor should its use be allowed when other books are written.

230. Why not keep the forms of Chinese typography in the published books but

change them in subsequent editions which should not be so difficult. Changing the places where the word *Xangti* occurs is necessary in new editions of books such as the Catechism, the Hours of Divine Office, small prayer books and so on. So the word *Xangti* can be changed, which is easy because few books have been published in China.

Article VI

    About the word *Tien*[①] (heaven)

231. After the Very Reverend D. Maigrot's Edict opposes the Observer's defence of the word *Xangti*, it is more than useless and vain to dispute the word *Tien*. For if the word *Xangti* (supreme emperor or high king) means whatever in the stars and other heavenly bodies is most noble, should be forbidden from being used to signify God for the reasons given above, the word *Tien* should similarly be forbidden, because it means the heavens in general, that is the heavenly orbs and all the stars, and all that is most excellent and noble in the visible world. As with the ancient Persians so it is with the Chinese, they believe them to be worthy of divine honours.

232. Nor should it be omitted that this worship of the heavens among the Chinese is public so that it is well known to the entire nation who are accustomed to it, as is discussed in books recently published in Italy. In these books which I have in my hands *News from the Empire of China* (Florence, 1697), there are some letters from Father Johann Grueber, missionary of the Society, who returned from China in the year 1662. Among other things about the Tartars who occupy China he has this on page 88: "These Tartars are of the same religion as the Chinese, they worship all the idols of the Chinese and the great course of the heavens and planets, on which many write." From this, Father Grueber shows that the Chinese are idolaters who attribute great virtue and divinity to the heavens and the great course of the stars to which they ascribe many things. It is without doubt that the Chinese literati know this, with the Tartar emperor who reigns today, and other Tartars in his government who follow the literati and they

---

① 天

have nothing in common with the two other sects that is the idolaters and the Magi.

Section Four

On the point in the Edict of the Most Reverend D. Maigrot about the tablets inscribed *KING TIEN*①, that is, worship heaven.

Article I

It should be forbidden by law according to the Most Reverend Maigrot to place tablets in churches and on altars with this inscription: worship heaven.

233. As in the previous sections where the words *Xangti* and *Tien* and the atheism or idolatry of the literati are discussed, a defence of the second point of the Edict of the Most Reverend D. Maigrot which bans the use of the aforementioned tablets by Christians in churches or placed above altars can be added.

234. For if it be agreed that the literati have meant the material heaven by the word *Tien* for the last four or five hundred years, worshipping that which is most excellent in the visible heavens, or the emperor today who is also the leader of the sect of the literati, and the chief priest of the whole nation, makes public sacrifice to this same heaven with no other rite than the previous emperors before him, it follows that these tablets are idolatrous, nor can it be purged of the stain because a different meaning is understood by the Christians. How can the meaning of the word *Tien* be changed to God Almighty for the Christians when it is commonly understood by the emperor and the literati in the way before mentioned.

285. *[sic]*②When an emperor gave as a gift one of the tablets in which he had written in his own hand "*King tien*" (worship heaven), to the Peking Jesuits, he said he did not understand the meaning of these words, but it is accepted to mean what the sect of the literati put forward. Why therefore did the fathers of the Society hold a meeting to decide if they should keep the gift, unless they were conscious of doing

---

① 敬天

② It should be 235.

wrong superintending the calendar of his court for so many years and they wished to pledge kindness and love to the emperor? But they were not happy about this honour and sent it to the other Jesuits in the provinces so that it was publicly displayed in their churches and their altars and worshipped, which is no less than zealously worshipping the emperor, and it took up more and more favour, it was not enough that the Christian religion was stretched to accommodate it.

286. *[sic]*① The Observer tries to prove the reason for retaining the meaning of God for the word *Tien*, claiming that this imagery is often used in our scriptures, because the expression meaning God is often written as Heaven or God of Heaven in several places in sacred scriptures. But the examples presented prove nothing because the word *Tien* has a definite and established meaning in the public usage and common doctrine of the literati which not in the translation of the word permits it to be changed without incurring great danger of misunderstanding. This same imagery of the Heaven which is used in Holy Scripture or in the speech of common Christians, who expect help from Heaven, cannot be used without serious consequences, but communicating and explaining the word which among the whole Chinese nation and the sect of the literati means the material heaven itself and when they worship some most excellent body than which nothing is more excellent would incur more problems.

237. For this shows the reasoning of the Observer to be false when he compares the word *Tien* to the Latin word *Deus*. For the Apostles② did not abandon the meaning of the supreme spirit to use the name Jove③ or of other false gods of the gentiles. For the argument in favour of *Tien* is nothing less than arguing that the word Jove should have been used by the early Christians unless it could be shown that not only did the word mean God among the ancient Chinese but that it still does among most of the literati. But this is not the case. The word *Tien*, now and for the longest time since antiquity, has not meant the supreme spirit among the sect of the literati and the

---

① It should be 236.

② The first followers of Jesus who spread Christianity in the Roman Empire.

③ Jupiter.

whole Chinese nation, as *Deus* does in Latin, but as far as this matter is concerned has signified the material heaven and the most outstanding corporeal things in the world which are deemed worthy of exceptional honour as was the origin of the Greek and Roman idol Jupiter. Wherefore the Very Reverend D. Maigrot compared the words "Worship heaven" to "Worship Jove" because the etymology of the word Jupiter is "helping father", by which name it is thought the Romans understood the heavens whose rains helped and fed their bodies.

238. The word heaven is accepted in sacred scripture and is used by common Christians to mean God, but if these words are inscribed on a tablet: "Worship heaven" and that tablet is placed on an altar, so that everyone can see it and worship it, no one will know enough about religion to reject it. If bishops and senior churchmen everywhere and the Sacred Office in Rome agree that the tablets should be removed, that should exert a powerful influence. What is the estimation of these tablets in China where the sect of the literati use these words: "Worship heaven" in their idolatrous worship? Is not the placing of these tablets on the altars of churches truly to make the error of replacing light with darkness, Christ with the Belial (the devil)? Is not the Christian religion mocked and derided when missionaries and priests adopt and make public use of the usual expression of idolaters or atheists?

Article II

The usefulness that these tablets have in spreading and establishing the Christian faith among the Chinese is examined.

239. The Observer has lengthily criticised the Very Reverend D. Maigrot about the tablets. And this is what we have heard: not only do they contain nothing that is contrary to the Christian faith, but they are useful in destroying idolatry in China and furthering the spread of Christianity.

240. Thus the business is the best possible. The tablets themselves and the zeal and wisdom of the Jesuits in admitting them to churches and placing them on the altar are all praised. But unfortunately the observer offers no other reason to demonstrate

the excellence and usefulness of the tablets than that they existed for about 3,000 years among the ancient Chinese who recognised and worshipped the true God by the name of *Xangti* and insists that many among the literati know the true God and count them neither as atheists nor idolaters, by which he means the present emperor and some of his ministers. But the validity of this uncertain or is totally false and empty as was demonstrated above.

241. It is acknowledged by the Jesuits and by the Observer that all the literati have lapsed into atheism for the past 400—500 years. They recognise no other principle but the material heaven in all the writings in their commentaries and their classic books, and the writings of Confucius, whom they venerate as their common master, are interpreted in that way.

242. We only have the observations of Fathers Bouvet and Le Comte as regards the current emperor and some of his mandarins. They have said on the basis of conversations with the emperor that they are sure he is scarcely an atheist but understands by the name *Xangti* the true God of the Christians. It is make believe to doubt that the emperor is not an atheist, who understands by this name the European and Christian concept of God. But there are other senses in which we can speak of atheism. Both the sects of the idolaters and the Magi which acknowledge various spirits are idolaters. The sect of the literati shrinks from the beliefs of the Magi and idolaters. They believe that the cause of all things is heaven or its effective power. It is the custom of this emperor and his predecessors to make sacrifice to heaven. That should also be called atheism or idolatry.

243. Whatever is the private opinion of the emperor and his minister of religion is plainly of no profit as is shown by the actions of the emperor and the Jesuit Father Verbiest[①] to which the Observer referred. It accords with the consistent opinion and doctrine of the entire sect of the literati and the nation which can be similarly called atheism and idolatry. That is enough to reject the tablets for use by Christians.

---

① 南怀仁（Ferdinand Verbiest, 1623—1688），比利时耶稣会会士。

244. The Observer challenges from experience, claiming that after these tablets were admitted to the churches of the Jesuits, the souls of more people were persuaded of the truth and sanctity of divine law. Mandarins and leading men approached them and moreover the missionaries of the Society won the fruits of divine glories and a greater harvest of souls than they had done before they had the tablets.

245. To prove this he cites the Annales, I do not know why for this is not explained in the Annales.

[HCS pages 151—152]

It is acknowledged that the Chinese excel in politics and many other arts and sciences and are far from uncultured. But it must be understood that their particular vice is their exceptional pride and arrogance, so that they reject the ideas of other peoples and do not think they can learn from them. So that God, who rejects pride, although he can be everywhere, has permitted them to walk in ignorance and without knowledge of his great divine spirit. Not however on that account should they be described as actual atheism but rather they are idolaters and resemble the Persians who worshipped the heavens and the course of the stars.

255. It is not a little troublesome for missionary work among the Chinese that it is uncertain that the Chinese had knowledge of the true and living God. For all the literati during the space of 400—500 years have thought differently. The books and the histories persuade themselves that Confucius believed above all in nothing other than that the material heaven is the first principle of all things. It is laughable for missionaries to try to get round these facts, opinions and assertions, seizing hold of this handle of obstinate error will give rise to heresy as we can have no doubt from the history of the Hebrew people.

256. Why, if their ancestors acknowledged the true God for 3,000 years, did the virtues appropriate to Christian law which are humility, modesty, poverty, forgiveness and reverence never come even slightly into the mind of Confucius, who was, in our

judgement, a remarkable man possessed of all kinds of virtues. It is not necessary to be a Christian to be just and recognise eternal consequences. For that matter a deist can live well without accepting the Christian religion.

257. We can learn about Christ our Lord from the example of the Apostles, not the philosophy of the sects which then flourished. Whatever truths flow from them are drowned among many errors. Examining them will set little in order. Paul argued with the Athenians about Epicurus and the Stoics as is written in Acts. 17. V. 18. But only to refute their errors and objections. Without doubt they assembled in the Areopagus where in many places the inscription "the unknown god" could be read but it was misused in their affairs. Some Greek poets cited the immensity of the Divine Spirit, and that pre-knowledge, Plato's true teaching and all the learning of God and the experience of many human lives prepared them to accept the teaching of the evangelists with greater promptness and docility.

*[HCS page 182]*①

7. There are two kinds of idolatry among the Chinese. One is grosser and more wicked, which is that followed by the Bonzÿs, or idolaters as they are properly called, who worship many evil images in their pagodas. The other is that of the sect of the literati, which is the principal sect in the whole kingdom of China, whose head and leader is the emperor himself. They not only worship the principle of the heavens, as is well known, but also sacrifice to the spirits of mountains, rivers, and the idol *chin hoan*②, which is the tutelary deity of the city, and above all they conducts ceremonies that are full of superstition to the tablets of the ancestors and Master Confucius. Firstly, the fathers of the Society and the other missionaries have no argument

---

① This page comes from Nicolas Charmot's Brief Notes on the remaining observations of the Society of Jesus against the Mandate of the Very Reverend D. Charles Maigrot. First Part. "From the response of the Observer to the first statement submitted to the Sacred Congregation" (p. 179).

② 城隍

about the idolatry of the Bonzÿs. For all agree in rejecting it. From the beginning the missionaries of the Society have ordered their new converts to tread these idols underfoot, to break them and burn them.

8. But the same charge can be made against the cult of Confucius and the ancestors, according to what has been described to me, and from the beginning the missionaries of the order of St. Dominic and St. Francis judged them to be superstitious in the same way that the Very Reverend Lord Maigrot and the other French Apostolic Vicars judge them to be, while the fathers of the Society permit new converts to Christianity to perform these rituals claiming that they are civil and political.

[HCS pages 186—190]

Response

15. It is not disputed that the cult of Confucius and the ancestors is their main political institution. I argue however that it was superstitious and idolatrous until 400-500 years ago, as the Jesuits themselves admit. Nor is it only illicit because of private and inward idolatry, as the Observer falsely argues, but because of patent and overt idolatry. While the choice of sacrificial victims by lot is hidden and secret, fasting and conjugal continence are openly admitted, the same is true of the solemnities that take place in the temple the next day, candles are burnt on the altar, incense and perfumes are burnt in front of the tablets of the ancestors and Confucius, the head of a pig or goat is offered, wine is poured in libation, silk cloth and paper money is offered, as set out previously in the notes. What can be denied about this? These are not some kind of civil ceremony as the Observer argues, but a superstitious and idolatrous rite and are completely impermissible for Christians.

Observation

16. The situation in regard to this question is that these rituals and ceremonies have been examined with diligence and energy by the greatest and most experienced

experts in the Chinese language among the missionaries and have been found to be purely political and civil. They provide an easy door to salvation and the faith for countless Chinese who need the help of the rituals.

Response

17. Does this not make a mockery of the Apostolic Seat (the Pope) and the Most Eminent Fathers (the cardinals)? Nowhere does the Observer explain clearly that many missionaries, theologians and several other authors of the Society have proposed for a long time that it should be the task of Rome to pronounce whether it was permissible for Christians to take part in something which appears to be entirely superstitious and idolatrous. By these means, the skill of the Most Eminent Fathers is denied and the judgement of their office is dismissed so that the errors inherent in this question are never brought to light.

Observation

18. Thus 23 Chinese missionaries judged when they were imprisoned for the faith in Canton in 1668, and in fact three were Dominicans and one of them a Franciscan.

Response

19. The Franciscan was Father Antonio Sancta Maria, an outstandingly holy and zealous friar, who until his death, he died in Canton, insisted that the cult of the ancestors and of Confucius was not permitted for Christians. Of the three Dominicans Father Navarrete, was the leader of the order's missionaries in China and was afterwards archbishop of Santa Domingo in South America and he never agreed with the ideas and opinions of the Society as he writes in volume 2 of his works, which can be seen in the notes section 1, article 9.

Observation

20. Firstly I say we have members of the Dominican Order who are extremely

strong in Chinese matters who oppose the Very Reverend Navarrete.

Response

21. The Observer cites these Dominican experts falsely. They are Father Sarpetrius, the famous Father Lopez, and Father de Paz. We have seen how they speak in the previous notes Section 1, articles 7 & 8. Not only have these three opposed the Jesuits and not only Father Navarrete, but also Father Juan Batista Moralez, Johannes de Polanco, Timotheo de Sancta Antonio, Dominico Coronado, Francisco Varo, missionaries of the celebrated Order of Preachers[①] who spread the Gospel in China and Tunquin[②] for 60 years or more.

Observation

22. The Jesuits in China also praised this Navarrete and censured him greatly. Two years before his death the Society praised him. This was when he was made Archbishop in America in letters to the governor of San Domingo, which were sent to King of Spain, and the Jesuits were holding back from attacking him because they wanted to found a college in his city.

Response

23. These attacks on the honour and reputation of Navarrete were summarised and opposed in the first section of my notes, article 9, where I hope they are refuted. And other things are added in letters written two years before his death in which the Jesuits praise his zeal and piety better than the Observer admits. This shows that the Very Reverend Archbishop was neither hostile nor violent when he attacked the Jesuits over the Chinese rites and that, when praises they heaped upon him, they were holding back because their work in his city was in need of rejuvenation.

---

① Order of Preachers (OP) refers to the Dominicons.
② Tonkin, also spelled Tongkin, Tonquin or Tongking, is the northernmost part of Vietnam, south of China's Yunnan and Guangxi Provinces, east of northern Laos, and west of the Gulf of Tonkin.

Observation

24. Nothing from this Charmot① is worthy of belief.

Response

25. It is beyond measure to reproach my credibility because Father Juan Baptista Moralez who lived in China for about ten years spoke to me before he made his way to Rome. He understood the situation in no more than eight and a half years. We do not deny that others have stayed in China even longer than ten years. Although to have experience of the Chinese rites, eight years in China is just as good. But he is trying to tie the question up in knots when he brings it before the Eminent Lords.

Observation

26. Two fathers took part in sacrifices out of friendship because the Mandarins always offer this to their guests and it was seen to be an external ritual of bowing low, burning incense, offering meat and other things.

Response

27. This is false. The Observer says it was to maintain good relations because the Mandarins do this out of hospitality to their guests. But Father Antonio a Sancta Maria and Father Johannes Baptista Moralez saw this sacrifice to the ancestors with their own eyes. What about the kneeling and praying in front of the altar? What about raising a cup of wine above their heads and offering it with two hands? What about the offering of a goat's head in a similar manner decorated with flowers and with the hair and horns?

---

① 夏尔莫（Nicolas Charmot，1655—1714），巴黎外方传教会士。1685—1686年之交来华，旋于1686年底返欧。1689年，奉派返华担任巴黎外方传教会在华修院的长上，传教地区包含广东的广州、韶州以及福建的兴化、长乐、福州等地。更奉阁当之命于1694年1月自澳门出发回罗马递交训令，从而掀起"礼仪之争"的高潮。参见《〈两头蛇：明末清初的第一代天主教徒〉繁体第一版修订表》，https://www.docin.com/p-18515350.html，访问时间：2019年8月18日。

[HCS page 207]

Observation

61. But Lord Charmot argues that to the Chinese, Confucius has a spirit.

Response

62. Whatever the Chinese literati think about the soul or spirit of Confucius, the tablets are inscribed thus: "The seat or place of the soul of the Most Excellent First Master Confucius". They believe that the spirit stands and rests on it at the time of the oblation. It is not without superstition and idolatry. Nor is kneeling in front of it, and burning tapers and perfumes permissible for a Christian. No more nor less should the pouring of wine, the offering pig's or goat's head be allowed for Christians. And besides they are accustomed to come to perform this ritual twice a year.

Observation

63. The literati worship lesser cults of tutelary spirits.

Response

64. The Observer declares with these words that the cult of the tutelary genÿ of the cities, which are called *chin hoan,* is allowed. But this idolatrous cult is absolutely prohibited by the decree of the year 1645. Notwithstanding Martini dared to be silent about this prohibition.

Observation

65. Thus agreed Father Semedo the Confessor, as is said above and the missionaries in the year 1646. How can Navarrete and Lord Charmot cite this as an example of the errors of China?

Response

66. What Father Alvaro Semedo said is better and more thoroughly than the observer, number 128 & 129.

[HCS pages 219—221]

[This is part of a Response.]

It is also shown in chapter 3 of the writing of the illustrious Lopez which the Jesuits put forward that many authors from the book of rituals and ancient commentaries clearly teach that earnest prayers should be made to dead emperors and ancestors. The first place is in the Rituals of China called *Ly chy*[①] where the authors speaks of the origin of the offerings or sacrifices thus: these are solemn oblations which are offered twice a year to dead ancestors, and writes, "In oblations or sacrifices, there are prayers, there are actions of gratitude, these also take place following death, disasters, errors, and misfortunes, or in whatever possible terror or extremity." The second place is in the commentaries in this text *Ly Ky*[②] which explains the prayers said in the ceremony thus taking the words from other books, "First seek happiness, seek the best perpetual government... In spring and summer seek food and other things." The third place is from the commentary in the same book, *Ly Ky* where it is written, "The first speaker or master of ceremonies in these oblations or sacrifices should pray to six generations. The assistant or secondary speaker should seek benefits and happiness etc. The fourth place is the other commentary on rituals where it says "The mode and time of sacrifice to the souls or spirits which are called *Ly Kuey*[③] or *Yeu hoen*[④], that is the spirits or wandering souls which do not have a fixed or determined place (that is to say those souls which are without heirs) these must be offered food, so that these

---

① It may refer to《礼记》.
② It may also refer to《礼记》.
③ 离魂
④ 游魂

spirits or souls will not harm people and will drive out illness and give other benefits." These authors set out the prayers that should be used in the oblations for ancestors; the same illustrious Lopez says this and afterwards explains and elucidates these prayers citing other authors which seem contradictory. Then Father Alvaro Semedo[①], who is much praised by the Observer, describes in his Relation of China part 1, chapter 18 describes the honour and rituals customarily shown to Confucius and the ancestors. He says this，"They seek and expect nothing for the soul in another life. But they ask for help in this present life, such as good fortune and success in their affairs and to imitate them in their actions." You will see this in my Notes section 1, article 3, number 38 and also article 7, number 81. No one disputed the nature of these rites at first. From the outset, these institutions seemed understandable from the Book of Rituals *Ly Ky* cited by the Observer. Influenced by these authors Father Ricci did not hesitate to defend the Chinese rites.

91. Later the nature and customs of the Chinese made it possible to accommodate to the sects and avoid hard work. They made a great effort to persuade themselves that diligently studying the status of the rites for the ancestors would confirm that descendants hoped for benefits for themselves in this life. Indeed, in many cases, as the experts can testify, those who treated their parents badly while they were alive still diligently perform the rites for them after their death. Who would not believe in demonstrating piety and reverence for dead parents when everyone thinks that if the living neglect these duties evil will befall them, and because they hope to gain happiness in this life, that is wealth, honours, good fortune, health and long life by carrying out the solemn rituals for their ancestors?

Observation

92. What about Father Adam Schaal[②]. This is more than ridiculous. To say that,

---

① 曾德昭（Alvare de Semedo, 1585—1658），葡萄牙耶稣会士。
② 汤若望（Jean Adam Schall von Bell, 1591—1666），德国耶稣会士。

this same father who firmly stuck to the common opinion, wrote other opinions to the Dominicans would be ironic.

Response

93. The Observer's evasion is laughable. Father Adam Schaal was a mathematician at the court in Peking and a mandarin who composed calendars in which auspicious and inauspicious days were noted. He was the Director. It served the glory and advantage of others in the Society not a little. He was less convinced of the wisdom of tolerating the cult of ancestors and wrote to the Dominican missionaries revealing this. However he wrote ironically and that irony can be interpreted as a reason to doubt what he wrote.

[HCS page 229]

[This is part of a Response.]

110. However Christians and neophytes of other missionaries have long overtaken the numbers of neophytes and Christians of the Fathers of the Society, indeed, the Very Reverend D. Maigrot shows this, saying, "the merit of Christians in China can be doubted if they are not without idolatry." Particularly those Christians baptised by the Society or instructed by them frequent the cults of the ancestors and Confucius across many different provinces of China. It is so common that many other orders of missionaries permit the mixing of worship. The Society and other orders have committed the fault of allowing tablets of the ancestors inscribed with these words: "Seat or place of the soul" to be retained in the home. There they venerate them by burning perfumes, offering flowers, pulses and other foods. The same tablets are used in the funeral ceremonies for the dead. The Very Reverend Lord Maigrot spoke directly to the Pope about accepting such deviations and confusion of religion and questioned the merit of allowing Chinese Christians to follow idolatrous practices.

[HCS pages 236—238]

First Fact

The word *Xangti* and the word *Tien*.

Observation

126. The factual basis and the presuppositions of the first reply are totally false and indeed should be opposed lest consequences prevail. It is clear.

Response

127. The Observer replies in this way to the arguments of Maigrot's Mandate. I refuted his arguments in my Notes on the Observations Section 3, Articles 1, 2, 3, 4, 5.

Observation

128. Father Semedo did not agree with the opinion of Lord Charmot that all the Chinese literati understand nothing by *Xangti* except the material heaven because it is evidently not so.

Response

129. In fact in the case of Father Semedo he is not an authority on the teachings of the literati. He, however, describes the funeral of the queen mother[①], "On the eighth day of the moon, there are sacrifices to the heavens, earth and planets, mountains and rivers with solemnity, from where indeed it can be seen that they understand by heaven the visible material heaven and in the same way by the earth, the planets, the mountains and rivers, they also mean the visible and corporeal part of the universe." *[It is not clear where the quote ends because there are no closing quotation marks.]*

130. But, says the Observer, Father Semedo did not mean that the Chinese literati understood the material heaven by *Xangti*.

---

① It refers to the emperor's mother.

131. I reply that, first, it is not only the word *Xangti* or *Rex altus* but the words *Tien* or *Coelum*①.

132. Second, the places I have noted in Semedo as the most useful are from Chapter 17, page 105 which, however, is cited by the Observer to prove that in the opinion of Semedo the Chinese literati mean another thing than the material heaven by the term *Xangti* Chapter 18, page 110. How can I, who have read the whole book to find the place, be contradicted by others?

133. Third, in the same place that the Observer objects to me, he omits other words which reveal the falseness of his interpretation. For afterwards Father Semedo says, "The literati believe in the Supreme Lord and Emperor who can punish and reward." The Observer suppresses the following words, "They do not however have churches, in which they worship, nor officers who perform it, nor prayers to recite, nor priests and ministers who devote themselves to the worship." *[This is in Italian]* From these words it follows, as was said above, that the Chinese sacrifice to heaven not a Supreme Lord and Emperor of which Semedo does not speak of any special cult among the Chinese. Then Semedo also says these words, "But as they do not know the true God clearly, they have come to worship three things which are most outstanding and useful in the world which they call *Cai*② or heaven, earth and men." *[This is in Italian]* The whole system of the Observer avoids these words. Also if the literati have worshipped heaven and earth and man in this way for many centuries now, that worship, in the way that Father Semedo explains it, whether it is of heaven and earth or of men such as Confucius and the dead ancestors, is not a political and civil cult but is sacred and religious. Above all it is superstitious and idolatrous.

134. I have assumed the onerous task of reading and citing these authors so that the Eminent Judges will not be misled about the truth in undertaking a case so grave.

135. Father Gabriel Magaillans, celebrated missionary of the Society, in his

---

① It's Latin for heaven.

② 才、三才

new account of Chinese matters speaks in the same way as Father Semedo about the worship of the heaven, the earth, the moon and the ancestors chapter 13, page 20 where, discussing the Ministry of Rites[①], he speaks "of temples, and of sacrifices which are offered by the emperor to heaven, earth, sun and moon, and to the ancestors". In the same chapter page 209 discussing the same Ministry he says "it has in its care a temple at which the ancestors of the Chinese, the heavens, the earth, the sun and moon are worshipped."

[HCS pages 240—244]

Response

139. It is remarkable that he does not explain the words of the authors, but distorts them. Instead of the temple of heaven he speaks of the temple of the Lord of Heaven. But for the temple of the earth to mean the temple of the Lord of the Earth is obviously absurd. Above all whoever pays attention to the teachings of Chinese philosophy about the tutelary spirits of the rivers, mountains, and the cities, will see that the Chinese think all of these have their own spirits. From which it can be seen that the temple of the earth means the temple of spirit of the earth. What is more the principles of the sect of the literati do not acknowledge true spirits, but call by this name a subtle kind of matter, which is whatever is of most esteem in heaven, in earth and in men. Indeed, the Very Reverend D. Maigrot concluded that the Chinese literati are equally idolaters of heaven and earth and in the same way as we heard from Father Semedo in relation to worshipping the spirits of Confucius and the ancestors.

Observation

140. This sect, says Ricci, do not worship idols and do not have them. One spirit is venerated which is believed to guard and guide the lesser spirits which have lesser

---

① 礼部

cults and all come under its rule.

Response

141. The sect of the literati does not have many monstrous idols like the two other sects, which are called Magi and idolaters. They venerate heaven and the stars as in Persia and they worship the outstanding parts of the earth. From this it can be seen that they are like other kinds of idolaters which are listed in Sapientia (The Wisdom of Solomon)[①] see 13. v. 6 and v. 10. Ricci's words approving of the cult of the spirit among the Chinese literati should be noted. He permitted the cult of *chin hoan* that is the tutelary spirit or genius of the city. But after the decree of 1645 even the Jesuits rejected as idolatrous.

Observation

142. There is absolutely nothing in the work of Father Kirkerus[②] that does not demonstrate the authority of Father Ricci.

Response

143. The Observer leaves out whatever does not agree with his authors. This can be seen in other matters. It is significant that Father Kirkerus is praised for his exceptional erudition by Sotuelo in the collection of writings of the Society. But on questions relating to China no one will listen to him. They think they have nothing to learn. Yet the work he composed is distinguished by great diligence and incessant labour. It is praised in the preface to the Bibliotheca Scriptorum Societas (Library of

---

① The *Book of Wisdom* or *Wisdom of Solomon*, sometimes referred to simply as *Wisdom* or the *Book of the Wisdom of Solomon*, is one of the books of the *Bible* that is considered deuterocanonical by some churches such as the Roman Catholic Church and Eastern Orthodox Church, and non-canonical or apocryphal by others such as the Protestant Churches. It is one of the seven Sapiential or wisdom books included with the Septuagint, along with Job, Psalms, Proverbs, Ecclesiastes, Song of Solomon (Song of Songs), and Sirach.

② 基歇尔（Athanasius Kircher, 1602—1680），德国耶稣会士。

Writings of the Society). Many in that book including Trigault and other writers of the Society are contained in it.

Observation

144. Kirkerus taught that the Chinese literati did not worship idols alongside Confucius, but one spirit which they called the King of Heaven. Part 3, chapter 1.

Response

145. Nothing is clear. It means nothing. The Chinese literati believe the principle of all things to be a kind of matter. The Chinese mean by that the material heaven or it has come to mean its effective power which they call *Li* or *Tai Kie* or also *Xangti* or the high king. Elsewhere the same Kirkerus teaches contradictory things in his book. I have not been able to discover whether he gets these things from others, such as Ricci or Trigault. I have not taken the problem for granted because the Eminent Fathers ordered me to find out the facts. Many things can be demonstrated from the writings of the Society but neither Semedo nor Kirkerus proves what the Observer has said against me.

146. In one place the Observer opposes Kirkerus who teaches that the Chinese literati worship one spirit which they call the King of Heaven and immediately adds from Trigault, "Sacrificing to heaven is the role solely of the emperor and the emperor has two magnificent temples for that purpose both in Nanking and Peking. One is dedicated to heaven and the other to the earth. If ever the emperor himself is detained by business the most senior official of the place takes on his role. Large numbers of cattle and sheep are slaughtered and many other rites are performed to heaven and earth. (This is not Osiris and Isis① as with the Egyptians.)" Would anyone who read these words not believe that the worship of heaven among Chinese, as described by Kirkerus and Trigault was superstitious and idolatrous?

---

① They are Egyptian gods of heaven and earth.

Observation

147. I humbly ask the Most Eminent Fathers to dignify this evidence from Lord Charmot against the Jesuits with their attention and to incline towards the triumph of the Jesuits.

Response

148. I hope your Eminences will not dignify anything with their attention except truth and solid evidence and other proofs, such as Semedo and Kirkerus provide. They should also note the style of the Observer which is hardly modest so that not only is he angry and insulting, he heedlessly and inconsiderately accuses me everywhere of falsehood and bad faith. As for the triumph of the Jesuits it is a remote possibility. I wish for the triumph of only one thing in this case, which for me is the primary thing, and should be for the Jesuits, that is the triumph of truth, that is Christ.

Observation

149. This text of Charmot's refers to Father Semedo and after that to Father Kirkerus and they are followed by Father Magaillan of Portugal. Charmot only cuts his own throat with conjectures.

Response

150. As far as I am concerned, the proposition that the literati today and for many centuries past understood nothing by these terms *Tien* and *Xangti* but the material heaven has been proved. This follows from the evidence that Father Magaillan gathered in response to questions he asked the literati in his inquiry. The men he asked responded to his questions bluntly. They spoke to him of corporeal things. They mentioned no supreme spirit. They recognised nothing beyond the material heavens. That is all the literati understand by these words. Indeed, the ancient Chinese understood something else by *Tien* or heaven and also some among the literati now apply that name to the immaterial heaven, or an intelligent substance which is the source and origin of all

things. I do not propose to examine this. For the past four or five hundred years these words have meant the material heaven to almost all the literati and the whole Chinese nation. The Christians, therefore, cannot accept it as the word for God Almighty. I have set this out in my Notes section 3, articles 1, 2, 3.

151. The Observer continues to use Father Magaillan's words with omissions and bad faith. Indeed he continues to insist "However in the temples of heaven, earth, sun and moon."

*[HSC page 460]*①

VII. Father Martin Alexander explains the fourth and last question which pertains to the worship of dead ancestors in China, saying, the Chinese place no hope in the dead, nor do they offer prayers to them. "They seek and hope for nothing from them," he says. Father Martin narrated it to the Pope which seemed contrary to and rejected what was seen by Fathers Juan Baptista Moralez of the Order of St. Dominic and Antonio Sancta Maria of the Order of St Francis who had took a different view of these ceremonies. Father Antonio de Sancta Maria described them in his writings number 17, and the Illustrious Navarrete agrees with his testimony is his writing volume 2, page 168. In the ceremonies for the ancestors and for Confucius there is much that is superstitious and evil. **I.** In that place or temple were six altars, three ministers performed the sacrifice, one of which was the priest and the other two acted as deacons. Two young men also performed the office of acolytes. The one who took the role of priest was a Christian. The two deacons were non-Christians and one of the acolytes was a Christian. **II.** They approached the fifth altar and poured wine into cups and knelt. Afterwards they came to the sixth altar in the middle of the temple and made three deep bows. Kneeling and rising to their feet, they recited prayers, the master of

---

① 本页并未在"中国笔记"的索引中出现，但"中国笔记"正文第201页提到此页："Vid. Hist Cultus Sinensium p. 460 how the ceremony was performed in a Temple wherein were six altars.（参见《华人礼仪史》第460页，在一座内设六个供桌的家庙举行的祭祖仪式。）"，因此一并将本页译出。

ceremonies kneeling with them and presently getting up when the ceremony was done. **III.** The three leading ministers elevated the cups full of wine. Then in a loud voice the master of ceremonies said "The wine is offered." The priest drank the wine. **IV.** In the same way the head of a goat, with its skin, head and horns decorated with flowers was raised in a basin. The master of ceremonies cried out, "The goat is offered." **V.** And then paper was burnt on the fire and the master of ceremonies cried out in a loud voice, "Your ancestors will thank you on account of the honour you have paid them. And you will certainly have in consequence happiness, prosperity, abundant food, plentiful harvests, health and long life." It is a joke for the eminent priest to say that the Chinese do not seek or hope for anything from their ancestors.

It should be noted that there are two kinds of sacrifice offered to the ancestors: one is public and carried out in the temples twice a year; the other is less solemn and performed at domestic altars. The Speaker was an eye-witness to one of these domestic sacrifices which take place all over China.

All this is confirmed in the words of the Reverend Father Roboredo. These are his words *[what follows is in Spanish]* "We reply it is true that all of these temples, altars, images, sacrifices, ministers, adorations and ceremonies which the Chinese non-Christians have in honour of the dead ancestors are idolatrous and superstitious but not the civil ceremonies which they perform. Also it is true as many say that the tablets, those of the non-Christians, are placed and they make genuflections and offerings in front of the corpse. It is true that some of the Christians go to the temples and tombs and pay respect to their ancestors to avoid grief and a bad reputation. They keep images of their dead ancestors and they pay their respect to them in private as in public in the temples although with less solemnity. They pay respect to the dead, however the ceremonies are not idolatrous whether they take place in the temples, the tombs or the houses, and nor are those of the non-Christians which are performed in the same places. Certainly & etc."

[A Latin translation of the Spanish follows]

"We reply that all that is said about the temples, the altars, the images, the sacrifices and of their ministers, and other ceremonies of worship which the Chinese non-Christians practice in the worship of their dead ancestors, and whatever on their part these non-Christians believe, is idolatrous and superstitious, but such is not the case with ceremonies of civil honours which they perform. Equally it is true that after placing the tablets, the non-Christians also kneel before and make oblations to the corpse. Similarly, the Christians join the non-Christians and go to the aforementioned temples and tombs and pay the same respects to the dead ancestors to avoid grief and shame which others would cause them if they should neglect to perform these rituals. They also have images and tablets of their dead ancestors, as was said before, in their homes. They pay them the same honours as in the public temples but with less solemnity. They perform the same rituals for the dead bodies of the deceased. But these honours are not idolatrous for Chinese Christians whether they are performed in temples, tombs or private houses just as the same rituals are not idolatrous when they are performed for the dead by the non-Christians. Certainly & etc."

The Reverend Father Roboredo states that the worship of the ancestors and Confucius as practised by the non-Christians is idolatrous and so is everything to do with the temples, the tablets and the altars and does not see any reason why it should be permitted for Christians to take part in these ceremonies and sacrifices.

[End of Locke's references]

后　记

20世纪80年代以来，"明末清初中西文化交流史"研究在中国学界呈现蓬勃发展的态势，涌现出大量有价值的研究成果。然而，在这些研究成果中却似乎存在着几个问题，比如：研究"西学东渐"的多，研究"中学西传"的少；从事译介研究的多，从事影响研究的少；研究法、德人物的多，研究其他国家的少。而且迫于各种原因，许多研究是在二手资料的基础上进行的，容易导致重复研究。有幸得到洛克"中国笔记"这一一手文献，使我产生了由此窥探洛克对于中国认识的想法，此即为本书写作的第一动因，也是我在海外汉学领域的研究起点。接下来期望与更多同好者一起踏踏实实地进行原始文献的搜集整理和具体的个案研究，为"中西文化交流史"的进一步发展出一份力。

本书的出版得益于众多前辈、同仁的帮助，在此向他们表示诚挚感谢。

首先感谢我的恩师——张西平教授。在学术研究中，张老师秉承"学术为天下之公器"的精神，胸怀坦荡，不遗余力地提携年轻学者；在教书育人时，张老师贯彻"有教无类、言传身教"的原则，一视同仁，设身处地为学生谋划考虑；在日常生活里，张老师保持着一颗"赤子之心"，胸有大爱，心怀家国天下。蒙张老师不弃，将我收于门下并悉心指导，实乃吾之大幸。然天意弄人，入门不久，我即罹患重症，甚至一度徘徊于生死边缘。张老师那颗悲悯而柔软的心在第一时间感受到了我的执着和渴望，对我不离不弃，一路守护扶持。张老师将最新发现的洛克"中国笔记"手稿交给我做博士论文，帮我联系英国的访学导师，在论文写作的过程中手把手地指导把关，还先后几次将国外专家请到北京来协助我完成研究。张老师用最真挚的爱与包容"化腐朽为神奇"，使我这个资质不佳又命运多舛的学生也能走上学术之路。没有张老师就没有本书，也没有今天的我。

特别感谢英国学者安·泰尔博特（Ann Talbot）女士。作为洛克"中国笔记"手稿的发现者，安为我提供了大量宝贵的研究线索，并在我赴英访学期间多次陪我前往牛津大学博得礼图书馆和大英图书馆查找洛克手稿和藏书的第一手资料，同时与我一起逐字辨认和转写手稿，数易其稿，前后持续一年半的时间。我访学回国后，安·泰尔博特先后于2014年11—12月和2015年4—6月到北京协助我进行研究，"中国笔记"的直接知识来源《华人礼仪史》拉丁文本的英译稿就出自她手。与一个完美主义者合作并不是一件特别让人愉快的事，安忍受了我事无巨细的关注和无休无止的问题，有时过于密集的长篇邮件也使她不胜其扰，但她始终在我的身边。本书有一半是她的功劳。

感谢梁燕、顾钧、任大援、王美秀、孙立新、罗晓东、张健、陶家俊、韩大伟（David Honey）诸位前辈和专家给予的充分肯定和宝贵建议。感谢伦敦大学亚非学院的傅熊（Bernhard Fuehrer）教授在我赴英访学期间的耐心指导。感谢杨慧玲、刘美华、李慧、胡文婷、林霄霄诸位同门给予我的帮助和鼓励。感谢肖倪、胡启镔、卢志鸿、金梅、王保令、张人云、李楠诸位同事对我的关心和照顾。感谢张奉春、赵金霞、董振华、宣磊诸位医学专家以仁心仁术挽救了我的生命。感谢严悦编辑以耐心细致包容我的拖沓，保证本书的顺利出版。

最后感谢我最爱的家人：感谢母亲在我生病后一直陪伴在我的身边，照顾我和孩子的起居饮食；感谢父亲在我刚刚病倒的时候陪我治疗复健，后又返聘上岗，资助我的学费和治疗费用；感谢公婆几次伸出援手，帮我照顾孩子；感谢我的爱人虽并不理解我的选择，仍容忍我的一意孤行，在我最落魄的时候也未曾离我而去；感谢我的儿子从未埋怨过我这个不称职的妈妈，反而在我头发掉光、焦头烂额的时候以童真的话语与温柔的眷恋给予我巨大的力量。感谢家人为实现我的梦想而付出的巨大牺牲，愿我于有生之年能常伴你们左右，愿来生还做一家人。

韩 凌

2019年8月15日于北京